Phonographic Encounters

This cross-disciplinary volume illuminates the history of early phonography from a transnational perspective, recovering the myriad sites, knowledge practices, identities and discourses which dynamically shaped early recording cultures. With case studies from China, Australia, the United States, Latin America, Russia, Sweden, Germany, Spain, Portugal, France and Italy, *Phonographic Encounters* explores moments of interaction and encounter, as well as tensions, between local and global understandings of recording technologies.

Drawing on an array of archival sources often previously unavailable in English, it moves beyond Western-centric narratives of early phonography and beyond the strict confines of the recording industry. Contributions from media history, musicology, popular music studies, cultural studies, area studies and the history of science and technology make this book a key and innovative resource for understanding early phonography against the backdrop of colonial and global power relations.

Elodie A. Roy is a media and material culture theorist. She is the author of *Media, Materiality and Memory: Grounding the Groove* (Routledge) and is currently preparing a second monograph entitled *Shellac in Visual and Sonic Culture: Unsettled Matter.*

Eva Moreda Rodríguez is Senior Lecturer in Musicology at the University of Glasgow and the author of two books on music and politics in Francoist Spain. Her research into early recordings in Spain has received funding from the AHRC and the British Academy.

Phonographic Encounters

Mapping Transnational Cultures of
Sound, 1890–1945

Edited by
Elodie A. Roy and
Eva Moreda Rodríguez

Routledge
Taylor & Francis Group
LONDON AND NEW YORK

First published 2022
by Routledge
2 Park Square, Milton Park, Abingdon, Oxon OX14 4RN

and by Routledge
605 Third Avenue, New York, NY 10158

Routledge is an imprint of the Taylor & Francis Group, an informa business

British Library Cataloguing-in-Publication Data
A catalogue record for this book is available from the British Library

Library of Congress Cataloging-in-Publication Data
A catalog record has been requested for this book

ISBN: 978-0-367-43921-7 (hbk)
ISBN: 978-1-032-05711-8 (pbk)
ISBN: 978-1-003-00649-7 (ebk)

DOI: 10.4324/9781003006497

Typeset in Times New Roman
by codeMantra

Contents

Figures

Contributors

Siel Agugliaro is a PhD candidate in music history at the University of Pennsylvania. Siel's research considers the role of music in processes of identity formation and in the production of historical narratives. His current dissertation project, which has received support from the American Musicological Society and the Society for American Music, examines how Italian immigrants in the US used Italian opera for purposes of identity construction and social uplift at the turn of the twentieth century. Siel's first monograph *Teatro alla Scala e promozione culturale nel lungo Sessantotto Milanese* (Milan, 2015) considers the cultural policy promoted by La Scala in the politically challenged years between 1968 and the late 1970s. His article on the reception of George Gershwin's opera *Porgy and Bess* in Cold War Italy is forthcoming in *Music & Letters*. Siel has also contributed to scholarly publications in Europe and the US, including *Grove Music Online, Music & Letters, Notes, Rivista Italiana di Musicologia, Musica/Realtà* and *JSTOR Daily*.

Thomas Henry is an independent researcher and a 78 rpm record collector who runs the blog *Ceints de bakélite*. With a background in history and sociology of music from Paris École des Hautes Études en Sciences Sociales, his focus is on global music from the 78 rpm era. He has also carried out extensive research on the history of the phonograph and sound recording trade in Paris through the interactive mapping project *Disquaires de Paris*. A member of Paris Phono Museum, he is the former Vice-Chair of the International Association of Sound and Audiovisual Archives' (IASA) discography committee. After working for Gallica, the digital library of the National Library of France, he has been appointed Head of collections at Radio France in 2020.

Britta Lange is a lecturer at the Institute of History and Theory of Culture at Humboldt Universität zu Berlin. She received her PhD from Humboldt-Universität zu Berlin in 2005, where she also completed her Habilitation at the Institute of History and Theory of Culture in 2012. She was post-doctoral research fellow at the Max Planck Institute for the History of Science in Berlin (2005–2007) and a Lise Meitner research fellow at the

Institute of Social Anthropology at the Austrian Academy of Sciences in Vienna (2008–2010). Her research focus is on cultural history and cultural techniques, colonialism and postcolonial approaches, early photo, film and sound documents.

Eva Moreda Rodríguez is a Senior Lecturer in Musicology at the University of Glasgow. A specialist in Spanish music of the twentieth century, she is the author of the monographs *Music and Exile in Francoist Spain* (Ashgate, 2015), *Music criticism and music critics in early Francois Spain* and *Inventing the recording: The phonograph and national culture in Spain, 1877–1914*. The latter monograph was completed with the support of an Arts and Humanities Council Leadership Fellowship, and she has also received grants from the British Academy, the Leverhulme Trust and the Carnegie Trust for the Universities of Scotland.

Sergio Ospina Romero is Assistant Professor of Musicology at the Jacobs School of Music at Indiana University in Bloomington. His research activities deal primarily with sound reproduction technologies, jazz, and Latin American music in the early twentieth century. He is the author of two books: *Dolor que canta* (ICANH, 2017) and *Fonógrafos Ambulantes* (forthcoming) and of various articles and book chapters that have appeared in journals and books across the Americas. He has taught at the Universidad Nacional de Colombia, Cornell University, the Pontificia Universidad Javeriana and the Universidad de los Andes. Awards include Cornell University's Donald J. Grout Memorial Prize, the Klaus P. Wachsmann Prize of the Society for Ethnomusicology and honorary mentions at the Otto Mayer Serra Award and the Premio de Musicología de Casa de las Américas. Sergio is the director and pianist of Palonegro, an ensemble of Latin American music and Latin jazz.

Henry Reese is a historian based at the University of Melbourne, Australia. His PhD thesis, 'Colonial Soundscapes: A Cultural History of Sound Recording in Australia, 1880–1930' (2019), is the first cultural history of early sound recording in Australia. His research combines an interest in histories of sound and the senses with the history of settler colonial cultures. His research interests also include the history of photography, business and economic history, and the history of race and anthropology. His work has appeared in several journals, including *Labour History* and *Australian Historical Studies*, and in the 2017 Routledge collection *A Cultural History of Sound, Memory and the Senses*, which marks an emerging interdisciplinary interest in the history of the senses in Australia. Henry is also passionate about podcasting and audio storytelling as a mode of conveying historical content.

Elodie A. Roy is a sound and material culture theorist. Her research engages principally with the socio-material and environmental history of phonography; sound and intermedia studies; media objects in memory and heritage practices. She is the author of *Media, Materiality and Memory: Grounding the Groove* (Routledge 2015) and is currently preparing a second monograph entitled *Shellac in Visual and Sonic Culture: Unsettled Matter*, with support from the Association for Recorded Sound Collections (US). Roy notably held research and lecturing positions at the Glasgow School of Art, the University of Glasgow, Humboldt University of Berlin, and Newcastle University. She is currently the research fellow for the Leverhulme project 'Anonymous Creativity: Library Music and Screen Cultures in the 1960s and 1970s' at Northumbria University.

João Silva received his PhD in Musicology from Newcastle University in 2012. He studied at the Universidade Nova de Lisboa and lectures in specialist music schools in Portugal. Silva published the monograph *Entertaining Lisbon: Music, Theater, and Modern Life in the Late 19th Century* and regularly contributes to specialized publications and colloquia with his work on popular entertainment and its complex relationships with modernity, nationalism, historiography, technology and everyday life. He is program annotator for Portuguese cultural promoters, such as the Fundação Calouste Gulbenkian and Casa da Música, and works in music appreciation programmes.

Andreas Steen is Professor of Modern Chinese History and Culture at Aarhus University, Denmark. He studied Sinology, English Philology and Modern Chinese Literature at the Free University of Berlin and Fudan University, Shanghai. His fields of research concentrate on modern Chinese history and popular culture, in particular popular music, the cultural industries, sound and memory studies. These topics are addressed in a great number of articles, special mention needs his book *Between Revolution and Entertainment: Gramophones, Music Records and the Beginning of China's Music Industry in Shanghai, 1878–1937* (German: 2006, Chinese: 2015). Currently he is working on the book *Records and Revolutionaries*, exploring record production during the Maoist era.

J. Martin Vest is a lecturer in the Department of History, University of Michigan and holds a master's degree in history from Virginia Commonwealth University and a doctorate in history from the University of Michigan. His current research focuses on the intersections of sound, hearing, technology and American thought and culture, though his past work has touched on a variety of historical subjects, from the intellectual history of anarchism to tropes of insanity in twentieth-century popular culture. His dissertation, "Vox Machinae: Phonographs and the Birth of Sonic Modernity, 1877–1930," detailed the first half-century of the American recording industry, paying particular attention to the complex interrelationships the industry spawned between machines, money and ways of hearing. He is currently at work on a book based on his dissertation.

Ulrik Volgsten is professor of Musicology at Örebro University, Sweden. His research is concerned with the conceptual history of music aesthetics (composer, work, listener), and how factors such as copyright law and recording and playback technology has influenced the Western concept of music. Volgsten has also published articles on affect attunement and resonance.

Benedetta Zucconi teaches at the Department of Musicology and Sound Studies at the University of Bonn. Previously she graduated in musicology at the University of Pavia and obtained her PhD at the University of Bern. She is author of the book *Coscienza fonografica* (Arthur Rubinstein Award 2019, Gran Teatro La Fenice, Venice). She co-edited the edition of Bruno Maderna's writings and interviews, together with Angela Ida De Benedictis and Michele Chiappini (*Amore e Curiosità*, 2020). She held research fellowship from the Paul Sacher Stiftung Basel, the Istituto Svizzero in Rome, the Walter Benjamin Kolleg in Bern and the Leibniz Institute of European History in Mainz. Her research topics include history of music media, twentieth-century Italian avant-garde music and music theatre, as well as the entanglements between music, politics and economics. She is currently investigating the politics of branding and self-representation of record labels after the Second World War.

Karina Zybina spent one year at the University of Zurich working on the research project 'The church music of W.A. Mozart' (funded by the Swiss Federal Government Scholarship) after completing her Master's degree at the Moscow State Tchaikovsky Conservatory,. From 2012, she was working on her PhD thesis 'The litanies of Mozart and the Salzburg tradition at the University Mozarteum Salzburg' (completed in 2017). From 2012 to 2020, she participated in various research projects, among others, Music Printing in German Speaking Lands: From the 1470s to the mid-16th century at the University Paris Lodron Salzburg (principal investigator: Prof. Andrea Lindmayr-Brandl); from 2014 to 2017, she also worked as a research assistant at the Eliette and Herbert von Karajan Institute Salzburg. She is currently working on her postdoctoral project on reception, perception and performance histories of W.A. Mozart's unfinished compositions from the beginning the nineteenth century to the present day.

Acknowledgements

We are grateful to all the contributors for their enthusiasm, passionate scholarship and commitment to the project. We wish to thank Manuela Gerlof at De Gruyter for kindly allowing us to reprint Britta Lange's chapter, and to Reed McConnell for her agile translation of it from German. Our gratitude also goes to Genevieve Aoki at Routledge for commissioning the book, and to the two anonymous reviewers who provided helpful comments and guidance in the early phases of the project.

Introduction

Entangled phonographies

Elodie A. Roy

In its first and narrow understanding, the term 'phonography' – etymologically the writing or etching of sound – refers to sound recording as a scientific practice of inscription which 'cannot easily be disentangled from ideas about writing in general' (Feaster 2015, p. 140). We may add that such ideas about writing (and, indeed, such a writing technology as the phonograph), also stemmed from a predominantly occidental tradition of thought. As Jun'ichirō Tanizaki proposed in his 1933 bittersweet chronicle of the emergence of modern Japan *In Praise of Shadows*, the phonograph appeared to be 'well suited to the Western arts' but incapable of 'reproduc[ing] the special character of [Japanese] voices and […] music' (2001, p. 17). Tanizaki's melancholy reflection on the relationship between occidental writing technologies and the material development of Japanese arts and cultures invites us to reconsider the implicit Western-centric logic of phonography (and its associated discourses). In alignment with Edison's (1878) and Berliner's (1888) early celebrations of the phonograph and the gramophone as writing devices, Western conceptual approaches stemming from the fields of media and music studies, and developing in the wake of Marshall McLuhan's media materialist theory, have largely pursued the idea of phonography as a form of sonic writing (Gitelman 1999; Kittler 1999; Magnusson 2019). In Western culture, another related and prevalent way of envisioning audio recording technologies has been as mnemonic machines – simultaneously storing and producing audio traces, durably influencing the shaping of modern memory and heritage practices (Nora 1989; Sterne 2003; Müske 2010).

If the phonograph represented from the outset an occidental writing technology, the ways of writing about it have also often been Western-centric. The meticulous studies produced by early phonograph historians, discographers and curators[1] – flourishing across the 1950s–1980s period – tended to be geographically restrictive, frequently focusing on the history of the phonograph in the US and Europe, and ritually exposing the achievements of its early champions (including scientists, inventors and entrepreneurs). These early, now-classic cultural histories of recorded sound provide us with invaluable historical and technical information, though they implicitly contributed to establishing a normative 'canned narrative' of phonography.

DOI: 10.4324/9781003006497-1

In so doing, they partially enforced what Andrea F. Bohlman and Peter McMurray (2017) termed a monolithic 'phonographic regime' (characterised by tropes such as primacy, inscriptibility and linear technical perfectibility).

While the authors of *Phonographic Encounters: Mapping Transnational Cultures of Sound, 1890–1945* remain indebted to the existing canonical technocultural histories of the phonograph and recognise the productive (yet Western-centric) vitality of the concept of inscription, the present collection does not constitute a normative or standard narrative of sound recording, nor does it propose a novel philosophical or speculative inquiry into the realm of sound writing. Rather, this book makes an alternative and complementary argument by broadening (and decentring) the understanding of phonography beyond the notion of inscription. It frames phonography as a dynamic and multivalent socio-material practice of recording, collecting, retrieving and passing on sound – involving a vast variety of intermediaries, materials, machines and localities. In this understanding, phonography may be compared to what sociologist of texts Donald F. McKenzie (1999) influentially termed the collective and embodied practice of 'bibliography', simultaneously woven by and weaving together 'collectors, editors, librarians, historians, makers, and readers of books' (1999, p. 16). Against the rigid tropes of the 'phonographic regime', authors pay attention to what music sociologist Maisonneuve (2002) calls the mobile 'materialities' and 'socialibities' of phonographic practices, surveying emergent moments of synchronicities as well as dissonances across disparate territories. Accordingly, *Phonographic Encounters* introduces – and seeks to produce – new knowledge about the development of the technology of sound recording in the 1890–1945 period from a transversal, transnational and non-linear perspective.

Transnational phonography

As Andrew F. Jones noted in his study of the implementation of the gramophone in China, the record industry was 'from its very inception – transnational in character' (Jones 2001, p. 54; see also Tournès 2002): major record companies, including the Edison Phonograph Company (US, 1887), the Gramophone Company (England, 1897), the Victor Talking Machine Company (US, 1901), Pathé Frères (France, 1896) and Beka Record GmbH (Germany, 1904), were consolidated at the turn of the twentieth century, soon 'fann[ing] out in search of new markets and new material' and 'profoundly altering the nature of musical life around the globe' (Jones 2001, p. 54). Christina Lubinski and Andreas Steen, surveying the establishment of gramophone markets in China and India, further highlighted how the early record business 'travelled in the footsteps of imperialist expansion and colonial politics' (2017, p. 277). One of the earliest contributions to the field of global phonography was offered by Pekka Gronow and Ilpo Saunio in their *International History of the Recording Industry* (1998), which sought to '[tell] the history of the gramophone record in a global perspective' (Gronow and Saunio 1998, p. viii).[2] Gronow and Saunio's research – the first publication of its kind in English – has been an invaluable companion for many musicologists and cultural historians of recorded sound, though it often deliberately flattened country-specific differences in order to showcase an alleged global 'plot' underpinning technological development and record production. Since its publication in the late 1990s, it has been complemented by a number of country-specific articles and book-length studies documenting the emergence of phonographic practices beyond the anglophone realm, with individual studies dedicated to China (Jones 2001), India (Parthasarathi 2007), Malta (Alamango 2011/12), Portugal (Silva 2016), North Africa (Silver 2017) and Spain (Moreda Rodríguez 2021), to cite but a few of them. A small number of comparative studies were also conducted, for instance across the Baltic region (Gronow 2010) or between India and China (Lubinski and Steen 2017). While many of our authors remain attentive to the corporate history of recordings, *Phonographic Encounters* emphasises a range of more discrete para-commercial – and on some cases, infra-commercial – practices, critically recovering some of the entangled identities, discourses, epistemes and materialities underpinning the constitution of phonograph cultures across the globe.

In recent years, a number of valuable alternative approaches to early phonography have begun developing (see for instance Morat 2014). A number of these seek to explicitly uncover the ideological imperialistic framework underpinning the practices of recording, listening and consuming sound. Among these recent publications, Michael Denning's *Noise Uprising* (2015) surveys the recording, circulation and consumption of vernacular music in global ports after 1925, arguing for the transformative, decolonising potentials of phonograph practices – a study enacting Jones's proposal that 'studying the historical diffusion of gramophone culture and its imbrications with colonial modernity can help us place recent theoretical debates on the nature of transnational culture on firmer historical ground' (Jones 2001, p. 57).[3] Kyle Devine (2019; Devine and Boudreault-Fournier 2021), in his political ecology of recorded sound, offers us a provocative prompt to unpack the complex infrastructures, supply chains and histories of labour contained within the production of musical commodities from the turn of the twentieth century to the present day.

Taking its cue from these recent critical reframings of phonographic cultures, *Phonographic Encounters* approaches the history of recorded sound from a more diverse and global perspective, making visible and audible places, people, practices and source materials, which remain largely unknown or marginalised in the English-speaking literature on early recorded sound. As such, the collection notably operates as a gateway or work of translation, giving anglophone readers access to a range of hitherto inaccessible sources (with materials notably translated from Spanish, Portuguese, French, Italian, German, Russian, Chinese), whilst destabilising its familiar urban, metropolitan centres (including New York and London). Indeed, the cultural practice of translation is more than a straightforward or neutral process of 'passing on': it also entails its own logic of transformation, and therefore constitutes a political and 'iterative process of revision that moves back and forth in geographic circulation and discursive mobility, each time motivated by what is "untranslateable"' (Bhabha 2018, p. 7).

With its intersectional approach and enlarged geographical scope, the present book analyses how different spaces (understood both as material and as discursive formations) coexisted and occasionally conflicted with each other. Throughout the book, we understand the notion of transnational phonography beyond 'a vertical flow from more powerful nations to less powerful ones, or as a center-periphery model with music moving from dominant cultures to marginal cultures, from developed countries – particularly the United States – to the rest of the world' (Garofalo 1993, p. 17). To map transnational cultures of sound, therefore, means to recognise – and embrace – the irreducible unevenness of terrains and practices under study as well as the continuously mobile forces which shape them. In Homi K. Bhabha's words:

> Mobile inquiries do not simply pit themselves against larger settled geographies of nation, area, or region or set themselves up in opposition to them. Itineraries and networks are part of an ambulant mode of critical analysis that cuts across, or runs athwart, precincts of disciplinary priority and discursive permanence.
>
> (Bhabha 2018, p. 8)

Encounters, negotiations and embodied knowledge practices

This book illuminates and presents a collection of discrete moments and encounters with recorded sound in a transnational, multilingual context where:

> the practices or making sounds and listening to them are embedded in a wider cultural, social, and political framework, and that they are themselves being shaped by this framework at the same time as they are helping to shape it.
>
> (Morat 2014, p. 3)

It asks a number of interrelated questions regarding the circulation and heterogeneous constitution and embodiment of auditory knowledge, expertise and identities in the 1890–1945 period, a vast era which was traversed with diverse social, cultural and technological currents, was profoundly scarred by two World Wars, and witnessed the progressive dismantlement of global colonial powers (particularly of the British Empire). As Sterne forcefully argues, 'the history of sound contains multiple temporalities and a variety of intersecting chronologies' (Sterne 2003, p. 341). Taken together, the contributions do not seek to achieve a totalising effect, nor do they propose a petrified unity of space and time. Rather, the range of case studies demonstrates how practical and epistemic disparities, tensions and ruptures as well as convergences constituted 'gramophone culture' (to reuse Jones's [2001] deceptively homogenising term) in selected regional and local contexts. We navigate through a series of distinct spatio-temporal sites and textures – travelling from the makeshift recording studios set up by recording scouts in Latin America (Ospina Romero), to private and public phonograph recitals in Australia and Russia (Reese, Zybina), the experimental setting up of an early record club in Barcelona (Moreda Rodríguez), through to the invention of the record shop in Paris (Henry) or the intermedial circulation of fado in the turn-of-the-century Lisbon (Silva), to name only a few of the narratives unearthed in the book. As we continue our journey, new figures, cultural intermediaries and identities appear: the record seller or 'disquaire' (Agugliaro, Henry), the window dresser specialising in record shops (Vest) or yet again the record critic (Volgsten, Moreda Rodríguez, Zucconi). These portrayals in time and space constitute unique and valuable vignettes per se. Beyond their illustrative value, however, they also demonstrate how notions of technological modernity were negotiated, constituted and challenged through particular and local interpretations at different paces and across a wide range of public and private spaces (including the street, the studio, the shop, the lecture hall and the house). The book therefore makes its argument in a cumulative and polyphonic manner. A number of symmetries, synchronicities and patterns progressively emerge, though not everything neatly converges or 'fits' together.

Rather than constituting a totalising whole, *Phonographic Encounters* operates as a mobile constellation of discrete case studies. The authors in this book use case studies as a heuristic form, bearing in mind Diana Sorensen's words that:

> the knowledge produced by a case study operates within the analogical intelligibility of the example: a case study is not a generalizable, scientific model, but even as it exhibits its singularity in its story, it makes intelligible other, analogous examples or ensembles.
>
> (Sorensen 2018, p. 151)

Another important heuristic thread throughout the book has been the notion of 'encounter', borrowed from social anthropology (Raj 2007, p. 8). By recovering the processes underpinning intercultural interactions, authors develop a more nuanced work of conceptualisation, in which theoretical developments are concretely grounded in socio-material phenomena. For instance, in his book mapping the circulation and construction of scientific knowledge in South Asia and Europe in 'the globalized space of early modernity' (Raj 2007, p. 10), historian of science Kapil Raj surveyed the role of a wide range of mediators – or go-betweens – in engendering specialised scientific knowledge. Through extensive archival research, he studied the heterogeneous contact zones between 'knowledge communities with widely different specializations and, indeed, coming from diverse social spaces' (Raj 2007, pp. 232–233). The complementary notions of phonographic encounters and phonographic knowledge similarly alert us to the highly relational – and as such, always provisional – nature of auditory practices. Accordingly, the book delineates the different – sometimes overlapping and always intricate – socio-material trajectories and terrains of sound recording, people and technologies across the globe.

Sources and methodology

Most of the chapters in this book draw from an extended corpus of archival materials besides sound recordings, including magazine illustrations, record sleeves, posters, postcards, maps, photographs, trade journals, genealogical records and recording ledgers. Authors have meticulously and slowly set out to identify and follow entangled threads, unpicking the cultural, social, racial, economic and legal histories of recorded sound, amongst others – where and when these threads were accessible. As evidenced throughout the chapters, the notion of encounter constitutes a central modality of archival research, so that the latter could be tentatively termed 'a methodology of the encounter'. Historians such as Arlette Farge (1989) or Carolyn Steedman (2001) have mused upon the productive potentials and phenomenology of the archive, while ethnomusicologist Peter McMurray (2015) recently insisted that the sound archive both contain and anticipate multisensory and 'sensational histories beyond the audiovisual' (McMurray 2015). In addition to working within state or corporate archives, individual authors gleaned much of their source materials from non-traditional, informal archival spaces (such as the second-hand record shop, the flea market or the antique shop), thus allowing in turn to build another type of archive (Silver 2017, p. 23), and – crucially – to ask a wider and perhaps more provocative range of research questions. For instance, how was phonographic knowledge formed in everyday settings or politically instrumentalised? How were different groups of people and individuals listening or excluded from listening? How were identities constituted through socio-material processes of producing, exchanging and consuming musical commodities? And how can these different histories, geographies and trajectories of listening challenge our understanding of early phonography?

A key assumption of the book is that the local, national and transnational ramifications of early recording technologies can only be fully disentangled if and when recording technologies are understood in the broadest possible sense, as 'social artifacts all the way down' (Sterne 2003, p. 338). Accordingly, the authors in this collection come from a variety of disciplinary backgrounds, and the book benefits from the expertise and cross-disciplinary cooperation of musicologists, cultural historians, media historians and archivists. When we began developing this project, with a study day entitled 'Early Recording Technologies: Transnational Practices, History and Heritage' held at the University of Glasgow in June 2018, sound artists were also invited to join the conversation.[4] We realised early in the process that creative practitioners, collectors and curators played a crucial part in both reframing and re-presencing early recording technologies, but also in making explicit the often tacit knowledge practices involved in using and manipulating such technologies.[5] The shape of the book, with its distinct material and discursive boundaries, means that artistic contributions cannot be represented here. We hope however that the motifs introduced in the collection may continue to unfold across different terrains and formats, including the space of the art gallery, the museum or the digital exhibition – in order to inspire different ways of showcasing and narrating recording technologies in museum contexts.

Structure and chapter overview

It is outside the scope and intent of the book to provide full, chronological coverage of the history of recording technologies in all countries and areas. Rather, chapters have been selected and commissioned with a view to unveiling the complexities that surrounded different understandings of place and space in the early development of recording technologies, by providing a range of relevant, interconnected and contrasted studies covering all major areas of the world. The book is organised around four interrelated sections, addressing core issues of cross-cultural mediation and translation (Part I: 'Negotiating geographical and cultural boundaries: intermediaries, traders and operators'), listening identities in motion (Part II: 'Repertoires, auditory practices and the shaping of new listening identities'), phonographic knowledge and ideology (Part III: 'Phonography as ideology: the reordering of knowledge and sensibilities') and nascent sites of auditory consumption (Part IV: 'The social geographies of record-shopping') at transnational, intra-national and international levels.

Part I examines phonographic encounters, materialities and mobilities in South America, China and Australasia, analysing how the trajectories – in time and space – of artefacts, individuals, practices and ideas were profoundly shaped by understandings of place derived from nationalism, internationalism and colonialism. It attends to the crucial role of intermediaries, traders and operators – or 'cultural brokers' (Rempe and Torp 2017) – in the constitution of early phonographic cultures and soundscapes. In his chapter, Sergio Ospina-Romero examines the transnational expeditions carried out by recording scouts in Latin America for the Victor Talking Machine Company, bringing our attention to the precarious and often improvisatory nature of recording, and illuminating the polyvalent agency of the scout as a translator between terrains, epistemes and cultures. In doing so, he deconstructs the monolithic image of music corporations such as Victor and Columbia, arguing that 'by paying attention to the specific actions of specific individuals, in different positions throughout the corporate ladder, we can appreciate more clearly the extemporaneous – and often cluttered and anarchic – interplay that shaped the configuration of modern media empires' (p. 35). Specific cultural brokers and translators, such as entrepreneurs, recording scouts and intellectuals, also form the core of Andreas Steen's chapter on the rise of gramophone culture in China. The latter is measured and questioned in relation to a changing sociopolitical background, from the fall of the Qing Dynasty to the Founding of the Republic of China (1912) and up to the First World War. Steen is notably concerned with the interplay between new recording and listening technologies and traditional realms of music consumption, in particular the Peking Opera – exploring notions of modernization, Westernization and intercultural exchanges. Concluding the first part, Henry Reese gives us further insights into the mediation and instrumentalisation of phonographic knowledge in the Australian settler colonial context. His chapter describes the relationships between itinerant phonograph demonstrators, recordists and British settler audiences. Reese pays attention to the role of phonograph recitals in assembling a dispersed community as well as the role of recording experts in articulating 'a distinctive soundscape of settler colonial order and modernity' (p. 60). He asks how recorded sound (particularly recordings of bells) both contributed to building a normative colonial soundscape whilst displacing and in many instances silencing Indigenous soundscapes – urging us to 'listen more deeply for voices that were marginalised by the clangour of the settler state' (p. 74).

In Part II, authors focus on the entwined notions of auditory knowledge, musical consumption and listening identities. They examine how the circulation of imported phonographic commodities challenged or altered auditory and performance practices in selected regional and national contexts, but also in new spaces (such as the domestic or intimate environments of the house and the private listening club) and countries which have generally been marginalised (Portugal, Spain and Sweden). In addition to meticulously surveying the progressive hybridisation of listening identities, authors reflect on the changing understandings of national repertoires and of the nature of music as a polyvalent commodity. The section begins with João Silva's proposal for an intermedial approach to mechanical music in Portugal, in order to fully understand the co-constitution and continuous rearticulation of different spaces and media. In particular, he surveys the blurred boundaries 'between the stage, the street, the café, and the home' (p. 81) following the itineraries of musical goods in and beyond Portuguese urban contexts. The heuristic value of the intermedial approach is demonstrated with a case study of *Fado do 31*, a song which notably circulated in multimedia forms (sheet music, piano rolls, recordings, dance moves) and came to cross frontiers several times, each time acquiring a novel layer of meaning. In her chapter, Eva Moreda Rodríguez offers us rare insights into the life and operations of the short-lived *Discòfils* record listening club in 1930s Barcelona. The administrative documentation left by the club reveals much about the organisation, repertoires and personalities – from 'Barcelona's artistic, scientific and financial elite' (p. 108) – animating the record club. In particular, the regional, 'minimalist' approach is never dissociated from a wider reflection on historical processes: the microcosm of the record club continually dialogues with the larger national context, and individual histories of listeners are punctuated and eventually interrupted by broader political events, most dramatically the advent of the Spanish Civil War. In his chapter highlighting the joint 'mediatization of music' and 'musicalization of everyday life', Ulrik Volgsten maps out the emergence of novel listening practices in the contrasting context of interwar Sweden. In particular, great importance is placed upon the shift from 'playing' the gramophone to actively 'listening' to it in the post-1920 period. Volgsten maps out the distinctive spatial, critical and social environments associated with gramophone listening, closely attending to notions of privatization and intimacy, and retracing the role of the classical and popular music press (as well as of improved technologies) in privatising listening experiences.

Part III analyses the rise and development of aesthetic and ideological discourses around recording technologies in three distinct national contexts in Italy, Russia and Germany. In doing so, authors make manifest the inherent tension between the allegedly mobile, disembodied and uprooted nature of recorded sound, and the sometimes very place-specific discourses and ideologies that shaped understandings of early phonography. Drawing from a corpus of rare written and visual sources, Karina Zybina discusses the reception of the phonograph in pre-revolutionary Russia, bringing to light the cosmopolitan individuals and small intellectual circles who first welcomed this 'amusing toy' under the impulse of Czar Alexander III, subsequently using it to produce private, non-commercial test recordings. She moves on to document a shift from private phonographic practices to more informal public demonstrations coinciding with the introduction of the gramophone and commercial pre-recorded discs, retracing European influences – notably that of the multinational Pathé – on the framing of Russian repertoires at the dawn of the Revolution. In her chapter, Benedetta Zucconi produces a comparative study of how recorded sound was received in 1930s Italy in two highly distinct environments, namely the juridical realm and the aesthetic-philosophical circles influenced by the thought of Benedetto Croce. Taking as a point of departure the notion of 'phonographic awareness', her contribution provides an original counterpoint to other chapters in this collection, highlighting how the epistemological and ontological nature of recorded sound in Italy came to be negotiated and ultimately defined by markedly different types of public discourses. This notably allows her to relate the nascence of international copyright laws to the Italian juridical debates. The last chapter in this section concerns the relationships between acoustic knowledge and national sovereignty and nationalism in the context of the Nazi state. Britta Lange examines the recordings of German dialects made in repatriate camps outside Germany and gathered by the Berlin *Lautarchiv* (literally, Archive of Voices). Not only does she survey the archive as a mnemonic device for storing recordings in German dialects, she also investigates the political and ideological uses of the sound archive, highlighting in particular its role in building German identity beyond political and geographical frontiers.

Part IV shows how the modern concept of the 'record shop' was progressively constituted in three very different national and urban contexts and amongst different communities in the US and France. The chapters explore how physical recording shops contributed to shaping nascent consumption of recordings as well as ideologies of recording by integrating themselves within urban geographies while at the same time generating differential social spaces within the city. The section begins with a chapter investigating the visual culture of early record retailing spaces. Jacques Martin Vest surveys how records and phonograph became visual as well as visible commodities on the US high street before the First World War. In particular, he draws attention to the influential yet little known figure of window dresser Ellis Hansen, who designed innovative displays for the centralised Ready-Made Windows Program at the Victor Talking Machine Company (inaugurated in 1909). Vest resituates Victor's marketing programme within the history of advertising and consumer culture, whilst exposing how modern auditory identities were equally informed by practices of listening and looking. In his chapter, Siel Agugliaro vibrantly recovers the network of record dealers of Italian descent in South Philadelphia, revisiting the city where Berliner had first demonstrated his gramophone in 1888. The chapter presents the early record shop as a porous, liminal space where Italo-American identities were circulated, fashioned and performed, demonstrating how 'immigrant communities used the phonograph and recorded music both to negotiate their cultural connections with their respective motherlands and to define their own place in American culture and society' (p. 222). Particular attention is paid to Neapolitan record dealers who nurtured durable cultural transatlantic ties with Italy, whilst also cementing Italian communities in the US. Like Agugliaro, Thomas Henry makes extensive use of genealogical records, business directories, record sleeves and photographs, amongst other paraphernalia, to generate new research routes and insights into the record shop as a potent site of sociocultural mediation. Part IX concludes with his vivid archival reconstruction of the landscape of Paris's record retailers, from the prehistory of the record shop up to the comfortable listening salons of the 1930s. His investigation, originating from a digital mapping project, developed into a full geohistory (to reuse Fernand Braudel's term) and genealogy of the Paris 'disquaire', showing at the same time how regional and 'foreign' voices were represented in the capital city and ceaselessly rearticulated through musical commodities.

*

Rather than limiting ourselves to commercial recordings or to the already well-documented corporate histories of transnational record companies such as The Gramophone Company and Pathé Records (Martland 1997; Tournès 2002), this book turns to the para-commercial, experimental and largely undocumented histories and practices underpinning interconnected phonograph cultures. It is bound to remain a partial and situated contribution to the history of early phonography and should be read as an invitation to further develop case-sensitive research in the field of early technologically mediated auditory cultures, beyond and against the flattening ideological tropes often permeating accounts of the phonograph (Bohlman and Mc-Murray 2017, p. 7). Not everything which happened can be recaptured or even 'rediscovered': we remain acutely aware that many of the lives and histories of early phonography went, as it were, unrecorded. For instance, the heavy material contribution of women in this history, notably their central role in Western record-pressing plants, has largely been undocumented. Our role may precisely be to draw further attention to these archival gaps, obliterations and silences, in the hope of generating further engagement with what remains a productively polemical and frequently slippery object of study.

Notes

1 Among these texts, we could cite Leroy Hughbanks's *Talking Wax* (1945), one of the earliest histories of the phonograph, which was compiled as the technology was becoming obsolete. Subsequent canonical texts on early phonography would certainly include Roland Gelatt's *The Fabulous Phonograph, 1877–1977* (1955), Victor K. Chew's *Talking Machines* (first published in 1967), Oliver Read and Walter Welch's *From Tinfoil to Stereo: The Acoustic Years of the Recording Industry, 1877–1929* (1955) and its updated 1976 version. In the francophone realm, one of the key publications dedicated to the development of recorded sound was Daniel Marty's archive-driven *Histoire Illustrée du Phonographe* (1979), while the scrupulous cataloguing work of discographers such as Rainer E. Lotz and Walter Roller contributed to make legible the dense phonographic repertoire of the shellac era in Germany. Another crucial and exceptional book published in the German language was Curt Riess's *Knaurs Weltgeschichte der Schallplatte* (1966), which offered a rare world coverage of the history of recorded sound but was never translated into English.

2 The book stemmed from their previous *Äänilevytieto* (*The Record Book*) published in Finland in 1970.

3 See also Radano and Olaniyan (2016), Steingo and Sykes (2019).

4 These artists were Marie Guérin and Naomi Kashiwagi.

5 For a reflection on live curating and the reactivating of audio technologies from the past, see, for instance, Price (2013).

References

Alamango, A. (2011/12) Malta's Lost Voices: The Early Recording of Maltese Folk and Popular Music, 1931–32. *Journal of Maltese History*. 2(2), pp. 54–8.

Berliner, E. (1888) The Gramophone: Etching the Human Voice. *Journal of the Franklin Institute*. CXXV(6), pp. 425–47.

Bhabha, H. K. (2018) Introduction: On Disciplines and Destinations. In: Sorensen, D. (ed.) *Territories and Trajectories. Cultures in Circulation*. Durham and London: Duke University Press, pp. 1–12.

Bohlman, A. F. and P. McMurray (2017) Tape: Or, Rewinding the Phonographic Regime. *Twentieth-Century Music*. 14(1), pp. 3–24.

Denning, M. (2015) *Noise Uprising. The Audiopolitics of a World Musical Revolution*. London and New York: Verso.

Devine, K. (2019) *Decomposed: The Political Ecology of Music*. Cambridge: MIT Press.

Devine, K. and A. Boudreault-Fournier (eds.) (2021) *Audible Infrastructures. Music, Sound, Media*. New York and Oxford: Oxford University Press.

Edison, T. A. (1878) The Phonograph and Its Futures. *North American Review*. 126, pp. 527–536.

Farge, A. (1989) *Le goût de l'archive*. Paris: Editions du Seuil.

Feaster, P. (2015) Phonography. In: Novak, D. and M. Sakakeeny (eds.) *Keywords in Sound*. Durham and London: Duke University Press, pp. 139–150.

Garofalo, R. (1993) Whose World, What Beat: The Transnational Music Industry, Identity, and Cultural Imperialism. *The World of Music*. 35(2), pp. 16–32.

Gelatt, R. (1977) *The Fabulous Phonograph, 1877–1977. Second revised edition*. New York: Cassell & Company Limited.

Gitelman, L. (1999) *Scripts, Grooves, and Writing Machines. Representing Technology in the Edison Era*. Stanford: Stanford University Press.

Gronow, P. (2010) The Emergence of a National Record Industry in the Baltic Region. Paper presented at The 2010 Baltic Audiovisual Archival Council Conference, Riga.

Gronow, P. and I. Saunio (1998) *An International History of the Recording Industry*. London and New York: Cassell.

Hughbanks, L. (1945) *Talking Wax or the Story of the Phonograph*. New York: The Hobson Book Press.

Jones, A. F. (2001) *Yellow Music. Media Culture and Colonial Modernity in the Chinese Jazz Age*. Durham and London: Duke University Press.

Kittler, F. A. (1999) *Gramophone, Film, Typewriter*, trans. Geoffrey Winthrop-Young and Michael Wutz. Stanford: Stanford University Press.

Lubinski, C. and A. Steen (2017) Traveling Entrepreneurs, Traveling Sounds: The Early Gramophone Business in India and China. *Itinerario*. 41(2), pp. 275–303.

Magnusson, T. (2019) *Sonic Writing. Technologies of Material, Symbolic, and Signal Inscriptions*. New York and London: Bloomsbury.

Maisonneuve, S. (2002) La constitution d'une culture et d'une écoute musicale nouvelles: Le disque et ses sociabilités comme agents de changement culturel dans les années 1920 et 1930 en Grande-Bretagne. *Revue de Musicologie*. 88(1), pp. 43–66.

Martland, P. (1997) *Since Records Began. EMI: The First 100 Years*. London: B. T. Batsford.

Marty, D. (1979) *Histoire Illustrée du Phonographe*. Lausanne: Edita.

McKenzie, D.F. (1999) *Bibliography and the Sociology of Texts.* Cambridge: Cambridge University Press.

McMurray, P. (2015) Archival Excess: Sensational Histories beyond the Audiovisual. *Fontes Artis Musicae.* 62(3), pp. 262–275.

Morat, D. (2014) *Sounds of Modern History. Auditory Cultures in 19th and 20th-century Europe.* New York and Oxford: Berghahn.

Moreda Rodríguez, E. (2021) *Inventing the Recording: The Phonograph and National Culture in Spain, 1877–1914.* New York and Oxford: Oxford University Press.

Müske, J. (2010) Constructing Sonic Heritage: The Accumulation of Knowledge in the Context of Sound Archives. *Journal of Ethnology and Folkloristics.* 4(1), pp. 37–47.

Nora, P. (1989) Between Memory and History: Les Lieux de Mémoire. *Representations.* 26, pp. 7–24.

Parthasarathi, V. (2007) *Not Just Mad Englishmen and a Dog: The Colonial Tuning of 'Music on Record,' 1900–1908.* Working Paper no.2/2008. New Delhi: Jamia Millia Islamia.

Price, K. (2013) Artifacts in Performance. In: Weium, F. and T. Boon (eds.) *Material Culture and Electronic Sound.* Washington, DC: Smithsonian Institution Scholarly Press, pp. 43–65.

Radano, R. and Olaniyan, T. (2016) *Audible Empire: Music, Global Politics, Critique.* Durham: Duke University Press.

Raj, K. (2007) *Relocating Modern Science: Circulation and the Construction of Knowledge in South Asia and Europe, 1650–1900.* London: Palgrave Macmillan.

Read, O. and W. L. Welch (1976) *From Tinfoil to Stereo: Evolution of the Phonograph.* Indianapolis: Howard W. Sams & Co.

Rempe, M. and C. Torp (2017) Cultural Brokers and the Making of Glocal Soundscapes, 1880s to 1930s. *Itinerario.* 41(2), pp. 223–233.

Riess, C. (1966) *Knaurs Weltgeschichte der Schallplatte.* Zürich: Droemer Knaur.

Silva J. (2016) *Entertaining Lisbon: Music, Theater, and Modern Life in the Late 19th Century.* New York and Oxford: Oxford University Press.

Silver, C. B. (2017) *Jews, Music-Making, and the Twentieth Century Maghrib.* Doctoral dissertation, University of California, Los Angeles.

Sorensen, D. (2018) Mobility and Material Culture: A Case Study. In: Sorensen, D. (ed.) *Territories and Trajectories. Cultures in Circulation.* Durham and London: Duke University Press, pp. 151–160.

Steedman, D. (2001) *Dust.* Manchester and New York: Manchester University Press.

Steingo, G. and J. Sykes (2019) *Remapping Sound Studies.* Durham and London: Duke University Press.

Sterne, J. (2003) *The Audible Past. Cultural Origins of Sound Reproduction.* Durham and London: Duke University Press.

Tanizaki, J. (2001) *In Praise of Shadows.* Transl. by Thomas J. Harper and Edward G. Seidensticker. London: Vintage.

Tournès, L. (2002) Jalons pour une histoire internationale de l'industrie du disque: expansion, déclin et absorption de la branche phonographique de Pathé (1898–1936). In: Marseille, J. and P. Eveno (eds.) *Histoire des industries culturelles en France, XIXe-XXe siècles.* Paris: ADHE éditions, pp. 465–477.

Part I

Negotiating geographical and cultural boundaries

Intermediaries, traders and operators

1 Recording studios on tour

Traveling ventures at the dawn of the music industry

Sergio Ospina Romero

In 1917, George Cheney and Charles Althouse, recording experts of the Victor Talking Machine Company, spent almost the whole year on a transnational recording tour. They went first to Puerto Rico and Venezuela, and, after a few days in the United States, embarked on an expedition through Argentina, Chile, Bolivia, Peru, and Ecuador with blank and recorded masters going back and forth between Victor's headquarters in New Jersey and different stations in South America. While on tour, Cheney and Althouse kept a meticulous register in a ledger book of the various performers and numbers they recorded in each place. Sometimes, these ledgers turned almost into a travelogue as the technicians accounted for multiple episodes and included various details about their experiences overseas as well as facts, vocabulary, or information that seemed to be relevant for their mission. Having technical expertise about the recording process was not enough. In some pages of the ledgers, for example, they wrote various things in Spanish that they would need to remember on a regular basis, such as instructions for the performers while in front of the recording horn, multiple rows with conjugations of common verbs, and repetitions of a single phrase like, quite tellingly, "Lo siento mucho" ("I am sorry").[1] Indeed, in a trip like this, many things could go wrong—and actually did—just as many other things were simply out of control, so that apologizing could be almost intrinsic to the act of recording.

Notwithstanding the material challenges of traveling with the recording equipment, recording ventures of various kinds were a common endeavor during the acoustic era, that is, between 1877 and 1925. Considering the vulnerability of the technology and the various provisions needed to set the gear optimally, it was apparent that the acoustic paraphernalia was not supposed to be portable. Nevertheless, the recording industry engaged in traveling adventures almost from its inception. Edison's original business model included itinerant shows in the late 1880s—with echoes in various parts of the world before the turn of the century; anthropologists began taking phonographs with them for their ethnographic fieldwork as early as 1890; in the early 1900s the demand for original musical contents was being supplied by recruiting international performers; and by 1910 various companies

DOI: 10.4324/9781003006497-3

had already set recording expeditions to multiple parts of the world (Brady 1999; Feaster 2007; Suisman 2009; Hochman 2014; Pérez González 2018; Moreda Rodríguez 2019). Recording companies in the United States seized the opportunity whenever they could to bring foreign performers to their state-of-the-art studios in New York and New Jersey, either by taking advantage of the increasing immigrant population or by mobilizing musicians from remote lands. Still, this practice did not prevent them from engaging in international ventures with a bulk of equipment transported in numerous trunks on transoceanic steamships. In light of their design and operability, neither phonographs nor recording studios were meant to go on tour. Yet they did. The expansive dynamics of the business in the early days of the music industry did not have room for second thoughts. Untapped markets created the demand for troops of resourceful recording experts to whom, in light of their multifaceted labor while being abroad, I call recording scouts (Ospina Romero forthcoming).

By 1906 Victor had already established itself as one of the leading recording companies in the United States. By means of its corporate agreement with the British Gramophone Company and the Deutsche Grammophon in Germany as well as the appeal of its flat discs and the unparalleled success of some of its "exclusive stars"—such as Enrico Caruso and John Philip Sousa's band—Victor consolidated a stable and profitable business in North America, represented by millions of sales in records and talking machines (Suisman 2009; Liebersohn 2019). Yet the rest of the planet offered an appealing and unexploited area of business, and Victor expanded internationally very soon and very rapidly. And so did Edison, Columbia, Odeon, Pathé, the Gramophone Co., and a few other companies from the United States and Europe at the dawn of the twentieth century. Although almost every major company in the business at the time engaged in one way or another with foreign or ethnic repertoires, Victor, the Gramophone Co., and Odeon proved to be the most visible players in the game of sending recording technicians around the world. Since 1902, by virtue of the corporate agreement between Victor and the Gramophone Co., not only the records produced by each company could be commercialized (or reissued) by its transatlantic partner, but the two companies divided their areas of operations worldwide. While Victor was given the prerogative over the Americas, China, and Japan, the rest of the world—primarily Europe, Africa, and the other part of Asia—was for the Gramophone Company. Victor and Gramophone had the right and responsibility of representing each other's interests and artists in their respective territories. Furthermore, the same scheme of world areas under their purview determined the specific destinations of their recording expeditions. Thus, while Gramophone's travels focused on central and southern Europe, Russia, and Southeast Asia, Victor sent recording convoys throughout Latin America and, on one occasion, to East Asia. Still, although the relationship between both companies was reciprocal in multiple levels—including their mutual cooperation in terms of equipment and personnel—it was not necessarily a leveled field of power dynamics, as Victor eventually owned over 50% of the Gramophone Co. (Gronow 1982; Barnum 1991; Martland, 2013). As a matter of fact, while sharing with the readers of its trade journal the great appreciation for its talking machines in the royal circles of England, Spain, Italy, Egypt, and Persia, Victor made it clear that "Gramophone is the name under which the Victor is known in Europe" ("Royal Appreciation of the Gramophone," *The Voice of the Victor*, Vol. IV, No. 1, January 1909, p. 5).

Michael Denning has recently depicted the recording business as something marginal during the acoustic era (Denning 2015, pp. 67–8 and 86–7). Nevertheless, such assessment is rather inaccurate, to say the least. It was certainly a blossoming industry of increasing proportions, and it was precisely the intensity of its global outreach before 1925 what made possible the post-1925 recording revolution Denning focuses on. Let's consider briefly some numbers from the data available. To begin with, as Pekka Gronow has shown, while nearly 3 million records were sold in 1900, close to 140 million—equivalent to $106 million dollars—were sold in 1921. As early as in 1907, India imported 600,000 records, and a little later, when a local factory was established, the annual capacity increased to 1 million. Argentina imported 880,000 records in 1909, 1,750,000 in 1910, and 2,690,000 in 1913, while most European countries imported between 100,000 and 200,000 records annually on average through the 1910s—notwithstanding local production. In Russia alone, record sales reached 20 million copies in 1915. Whereas the Gramophone Co. issued 200,000 titles between 1898 and 1921, current reconstructions of Victor discographies during the acoustic period have long gone past the 120,000 recordings (Gronow 1983, 1998; *Discography of American Historical Recordings*). In 1908, Columbia set its first record's factory in Japan, and by 1913 at least three local companies had emerged—as it would be also the case in Brazil and Argentina in 1913 and 1919, respectively (Johnson 2002, pp. 36–7; Cañardo 2017, pp. 14–19; Pérez González 2018).

In terms of the production of phonographs and other talking machines, the numbers went from 345,000 in 1909 to 514,000 in 1914 and to 2,230,000 in 1919 (Gronow 1983). Between 1905 and 1914, at least 449,603 packages with phonographic merchandise (representing a total value of more than $11 million dollars) left the port of New York, aiming to multiple destinations around the planet; more than 30% of those packages went to Latin America and the Caribbean (Liebersohn 2019, pp. 181–6). Likewise, between 1914 and 1919—despite WWI—the manufacture value of phonographic products in the United States grew from $27 to almost $160 million—an increase of over 500% (*Talking Machine World* 17, 15 June 1921, p. 105). Through most of the 1920s, in spite of the competition with radio and some financial setbacks, the industry kept growing. US companies sold about 100 million records annually, with record sales in most countries of the world ranging between 100,000 and 1 million per year (Gronow 1983). Early in the decade, one label alone in Australia was importing nearly 100,000 records per month, and by 1925, when the acoustic era was reaching its end and the local recording industry was just taking off, it was estimated that there could be as many as 1 million phonographs in Australia. Four years later, record sales in Finland were close to 1 million copies, at a time when the population of the country barely surpassed the 3 million mark (Johnson 2002, p. 37). By the end of the 1920s, between a third and a half of the households in North America and Europe had a talking machine, and there were some cities in the United States in which such figure reached 60%. And certainly not only among middle or upper classes. In 1924, 23% of working-class homes in Muncie (Illinois) reported that they had a phonograph, while a survey made in rural Alabama in 1930 indicated that more than 50% of the houses did not have pipelines but 12% had a phonograph (Suisman 2009, p. 249; Barnett 2020, pp. 5–8).

Yet numbers provide us only with a partial insight into the growth of the recording industry. Behind and beyond those numbers, there are countless stories pertaining both the imperial outreach of recording companies and the extent to which phonograph culture, as an unprecedented social phenomenon, grew and gained currency around the world in the early twentieth century. While most histories of the acoustic phonograph and the early recording industry have focused on the initiatives of the executive heads of the companies and the operations of the companies themselves—somewhat in abstraction—I am interested in the heterogeneity of narratives and actors that contributed to the blossoming of the business, from recording scouts to the listeners. In the remainder of this chapter, I unearth some of those stories pertaining to the production of acoustic recordings in itinerant scenarios. Elsewhere I have studied a different set of narratives and actors in relation to the circulation and consumption of these records (Ospina Romero 2021). By engaging with the minutiae of the recording ledgers and other material vestiges of the scouts' journeys, I will focus on some episodes in the recording expeditions set by the Victor Talking Machine Company through Latin America and East Asia in the 1910s, in order to analyze the scouts' improvisations on the ground.

These improvisations, I argue, are traces of the extemporaneous and imperial character of both the recording industry and the United States at the time. The global expansion of recorded sound entailed the consolidation of media empires such as that of the Victor company, defined, in my view, by the intersection of commercial agendas and new audible regimes (De Grazia 2005; Radano and Olaniyan 2016). Nevertheless, rather than orderly, logical, or controlled entities, these media empires were messy formations, constituted and sustained in conditions of incoherence, unevenness, and even anarchy as well as across improvisations around recording procedures, repertoires, personnel, marketing, and organizational structures (Kaplan 2002; Mann 2003; Stoler 2010). While setting up makeshift recording laboratories, these recording scouts faced multiple challenges, including identifying local talent, negotiating copyright deals, and sometimes wrangling tardy, drunken performers into the studio. It is clear that these recording scouts were attempting to follow executive master plans to open up new markets for the phonograph. Yet, it was up to them and the people they worked with everywhere to figure out how to put such plans into practice. Some procedures in relation to the operation of the technology were somewhat foreshadowed as well as certain guidelines and expectations set by the companies. Nevertheless, the expeditions implied an unpredictable array of spontaneous decisions. For the most part, just as some of the musicians they brought in front of the recording horns, the scouts were playing by ear.

Thus, while exploring the quotidian challenges of recording scouts, this chapter is also a study of the imperial dynamics and the (neo)colonial practices that shaped the recording business and propelled its global ventures in the early twentieth century. The everyday situations in the expeditions were, I believe, the actual playground of imperial dominance and cultural resistance in the international dealings of recording companies. After inquiring into some pioneering transnational recording ventures in the early 1900s, I will examine the unfolding of Victor's expeditions and the scouts' improvisations in matters of social interactions and technology. At the end, I will come back to the relation between coloniality, empire, and the scouts' multifaceted labor.

Sending phonographs and recording experts abroad

In 1878, after having filled the patent for his newest invention, Thomas A. Edison established the Edison Speaking Phonograph Company to publicize his machine, which he initially did through circus-like demonstrations "on a stage where enthralled crowds would hear voices recorded in various languages and even dogs barking" (Cross and Proctor 2014, pp. 134–5). By the late 1880s and early 1890s, these kinds of exhibitions had become somewhat frequent in various places around the world. Already in 1892, for example, public phonographic demonstrations were taking place in Santiago and Valparaiso in Chile, and similar spectacles proliferated around the same time in Spain; as a matter of fact, in 1899 one of the most popular acts in the Teatro Apolo, in Madrid, was the zarzuela *El fonógrafo ambulante* ("The Itinerant Phonograph") which entailed a live demonstration of one of such machines during the performance (González and Chapí 1899; González and Rolle 2003, p. 90; Moreda Rodríguez 2019). Although in 1902 the stores of *Casa Edison* in São Paulo made grandiose announcements of new records with Brazilian music, the truth is that Brazilian audiences had been acquainted at this point with phonographic merchandise—including local musics—for over two decades (Pérez González 2018). Thus, as commercial ventures expanded and the recording business settled, recording experts, working inside stationary studios or touring the world in search of novel repertories, became a crucial component in the productive loop of the emerging companies.

One of the first traveling recording experts was Adalbert Theo Edward Wangemann (1855–1906), who began working for Edison in the late 1880s. Having been a pioneer in the development of recording techniques in the United States, Wangemann's early interventions on musicians' dispositions overseas for the sake of the phonograph are prototypical and somewhat exemplary of the kind of interventions that recording scouts would make all over the world in the next few decades. According to Patrick Feaster:

> By the time Wangemann went to Europe in June 1889, he was already accustomed to rearranging performers around recording horns to achieve superior phonograms, so that when he set about recording the German Emperor's royal orchestra in Berlin, he "suggested certain changes in the position of the instruments which experience had convinced him were more favorable to the blending and recording of sound than their ordinary disposition." The conductor at first refused to rearrange his orchestra, but when Wangemann went ahead and recorded it in its usual configuration, the Emperor was so dismayed upon listening to the phonogram that he ordered everything to be redone according to Wangemann's instructions. "The result," it was reported, "so pleased the emperor that at the next royal concert the strings, wood-wind and brass were placed 'à la phonograph.'"
>
> (Feaster 2007, p. 157)

Fred Gaisberg (1873–1951) was undoubtedly the most emblematic and the most remembered traveling expert of his generation. As the foremost overseas agent of the Gramophone Co., he toured through Italy, Russia, India, Singapore, China, Japan, Thailand, and Burma, recruiting local performers and bringing to the spotlight some of the first recording celebrities of the era, including Enrico Caruso, Fyodor Chaliapin, Ignace Jan Pederewski, and Gauhurjan. His diaries and memories are a rich testimony of the portability and the extemporaneous character of acoustic recording. Making sometimes as many as 60 or 70 recordings in a single day, Gaisberg was a pioneer in the art of setting makeshift studios in almost any imaginable location or circumstance. Some years before the labor division between technical experts and music directors, and many years before the emergence of music producers and managers proper, all these roles were encompassed in a single individual like Fred Gaisberg (Gaisberg 1942; Moore 1999; Eisenberg 2005; Strötbaum 2010a, b). And that was also the case with a host of similar recording scouts in the acoustic era—including Odeon's John Daniel Smoot, who by 1906 had toured through North Africa, Turkey, Greece, and East Asia, and Victor agents like the Sooy brothers, George Cheney, or Charles Althouse—although with less visibility and corporate muscle than

Gaisberg (Vernon 1997; Fischer 2012). Like Gaisberg, these scouts had to deal with the puzzling materiality of the acoustic equipment and operated with an ample degree of autonomy when selecting performers and making decisions overseas on behalf of their companies. Unlike Gaisberg, however, they did not necessarily hasten making recordings to overachieve their own expectations, but often times worked under the pressure of predetermined goals of productivity set by their employers.

Figure 1.1 Guitarist in recording session, Mexico, 1905 (Colección Archivo Casasola, Fototeca INAH).

Between 1903 and 1928, the Victor Talking Machine Company organized more than 20 recording fieldtrips to various cities in Latin America. Almost 7,000 selections were recorded—including both musical and nonmusical performances—most of which became commercial records within months.[2] Typically, two recording scouts were deployed. Their luggage included a portable recording machine, several wax discs, recording horns of various sizes and shapes, sound boxes, spring motors, and dynamos; everything packed in multiple trunks and transported across the hemisphere in transoceanic steamships. Going on an expedition was an exceptional assignment. For the most part, the scouts worked as recording experts in Victor's studios in Camden, New Jersey, and thus their technical expertise making recordings at Victor's headquarters was put to the test when facing the unpredictable conditions of the various locations overseas in which they had to set up makeshift "laboratories"—as studios were known at the time (Brock-Nannestad 1997; Copeland 2008; Barnett 2020, p. 54; Ospina Romero forthcoming).

The expeditions began in 1903 with a trip to Mexico City, followed by another visit to the same city two years later. In 1907 and 1908, Victor set expeditions to Cuba, Mexico, Brazil, and Argentina. Early in 1910 the scouts went again to Cuba, and in November, on the onset of the Mexican Revolution, they made recordings in Mexico City. Havana was one of the most common destinations. Besides the trips in 1907 and 1910, the company set expeditions to the island almost every year between 1911 and 1927. Some excursions entailed a single trip to a particular country while others implied a journey through two or more nations. In the first semester of 1912, for example, the scouts went to Buenos Aires and Rio de Janeiro; in the second half of 1913, they visited Lima and Bogotá; and in the summer and fall of 1914, they traveled through Cuba and Trinidad. The outbreak of the Great War in Europe seems to have put Victor's transoceanic travels on hold, but not for long; by mid-October 1916, a team was already making recordings in Havana. The long excursion I mentioned at the beginning of the chapter and that I will revisit later—in which a pair of scouts visited seven countries in ten months—took place in 1917. This was, apparently, the last transnational excursion. From 1918 and through the 1920s, the company focused its international campaigns on Cuba, Mexico, Argentina, and Brazil, taking advantage of the satellite offices, studios, and factories it had established there. Yet Victor did not neglect the music *from* nor the market *in* the other countries of the Americas. Recordings of Latin American music kept taking place in Victor's laboratories in New York and New Jersey, either by Latin American musicians visiting the United States or by North American performers playing arranged versions of music scores collected from various places in the hemisphere (Victor Recording Ledgers 1905–1917; *Discography of American Historical Recordings*; Cañardo 2017).

Despite the arrangements and contacts that were made in preparation for each trip, going on a recording expedition was in itself a journey into unpredictable situations. Sometimes, a representative of the company would travel in advance to line up the performers and set other things ready before the arrival of the scouts. Eventually, local dealers, musicians, or other intermediaries could be appointed with the same mission. More often than not, however, the scouts seemed to have departed without major preparations in place. But even with logistical provisions taken care of in advance, a recording tour entailed, almost by definition, an unforeseen array of events—as one can appreciate through the multiple annotations made in the recording ledgers.

Victor's recording ventures in the 1910s[3]

On July 13, 1913, Frank Rambo and Charles Althouse sailed for Lima, Peru, via the Panama Canal. That was the first tour Victor commissioned to the northern west coast of South America. Victor's strategy implied pursuing connections with key individuals or local institutions—such as music stores, schools, and publishers—in order to get access to musicians and repertoire that would be popular or characteristic of local sounds and aesthetic tastes. This strategy implied a whole chain of intermediaries. Frank Rambo connected with Casa Castellanos and with Rogelio Soto, a Peruvian music producer, who, in turn, connected the scouts with local musicians Miguel Almeneiro and Alejandro Ayarza, who eventually facilitated the access to other performers. As a matter of fact, the house of Miguel Almeneiro functioned as a recording laboratory for some days (Borras and Rohner 2013). In Lima, Rambo and Althouse recorded 202 pieces in three weeks. Around 15 different artists and groups were part of these sessions, including solo instrumentalists like Alejandro Gómez Morón, vocal duets such as the Hermanas Gastelú, and diverse ensembles like the Estudiantina Chalaca or La Banda del Regimiento de Gendarmes de Lima. Seemingly, the original plan was to record only Peruvian selections. In the end, though, the scouts also gathered Ecuadorian music in Lima, and instead of returning directly to the United States, they stopped in Panama, made a shipment of records to New Jersey for manufacture, changed steamships, and navigated up the Colombian Magdalena River toward Bogotá. It looks like it was during the layover in Panama that in communication via telegram with Harry Sooy and other employees at Camden, it was decided to extend the tour and visit Colombia in order to make "records of the natives for that part of the world" (Sooy, H. 1925, p. 56).

In Bogotá they recorded, in 16 days, 120 pieces performed by 20 different artists and small orchestras, including musical numbers by ensembles like Union Musical, Quinteto Rubiano, the duet of Alejandro Wills and Alberto Escobar, and the Terceto Sánchez-Calvo as well as a variety of spoken performances—from historical reenactments to comedies—like the recordings made by Jorge Andrade Hewitt and the duet of Pinillos and Villamarín. In order to recruit local talent, and more particularly, in assessing which

Figure 1.2 Recording experts featured in the silent film *The Immortal Voice* (The Bray Studios, 1923).

local artists represented the best investment for the phonographic business, the participation of Manuel Gaitán, the owner of one of the biggest music stores in Bogotá at the time, seems to have been crucial as well as the intervention of the musician Jorge Rubiano. Likewise, the artistic circles of the National Music Conservatory, the city's main Cathedral, and the public venues for popular entertainment were particularly influential. Indeed, it was a collection of performers that participated—often times simultaneously, given their working networks—in the various musical realms of the city: from classical and religious music to the popular offerings in cafés, theaters, and clandestine gatherings (Bermúdez 2000, pp. 115–23; Cortés Polanía 2004, p. 154; Ospina Romero 2017, pp. 97–106; Bolaños 2020, pp. 135–7). Just as some of their colleagues had done in previous expeditions, Rambo and Althouse probably visited some of these public and private venues themselves as part of their talent scouting ventures. Although they took advantage of the mediation of people like Gaitán and Rubiano, they assessed directly, as much as they could, the popularity and suitability of each artist and recording event before summoning them to the studio.

Victor and Columbia had made recordings of Trinidadian music in 1912, when the ensemble led by George R. L. Baillie (a.k.a Lovey) toured the United States under the name of Trinidad Dance Orchestra, although the records came out as Lovey's Trinidad String Band (Cowley 1996). Following suit on the commercial success of Lovey's Band records, Victor sent its recording experts in the summer of 1914. This time, Althouse was paired with George Cheney, making the team that would lead most of the expeditions in the next few years. A Victor representative named Theodore Terry arrived in the island two weeks before with the mission of arranging the performers and having "everything in readiness so that Mr. Cheney may begin his work at once," as a local newspaper in Port of Spain announced it. The same newspaper described their visit as a "special trip to Trinidad for the purpose of recording a complete repertoire of Trinidadian music including the Pasillos, Spanish Waltz and Two steps by well-known Bands; also

Carnival and Patois songs and East Indian selections by local talent" (*Port of Spain Gazette*, August 28, 1914). Another newspaper informed about the recording sessions, pointing out the anxiety it was causing on some musicians: "We understand that Mr. Henry Julian [a.k.a Iron Duke] (...) has been practicing assiduously for the above purpose and that several other bands and performers have been engaged" (Cowley 1996, p. 192). Except for one day, Cheney and Althouse held recording sessions in Port of Spain every day for almost two weeks. Besides the indefatigable artistry of Henry Julian, they recorded the famous orchestra of Lionel Belasco and other popular performers in the local scene such as Jules Sims, Gellum Hossein, and the Orquesta Venezolana de Chargo—an ensemble apparently made up of a combination of Trinidadian creoles and immigrants from Venezuela. Although Victor did not release commercially many of the 83 recordings made in this trip, it made sure to have some records ready in time for the Carnival season of 1915 (Victor Recording Ledgers 1914; Cowley 1996, pp. 192–3).

By then, Cheney and Althouse were getting ready—if not already en route—for an expedition through China, Korea, and Japan that motivated a long article in the Spanish edition of *The Voice of the Victor*, the company's trade journal. Featuring a series of photographs taken by Althouse himself and the experts' chronicle of their cultural impressions of those remote lands and peoples, the article celebrated the exceptionality of the recordings as well as the efforts made by Cheney and Althouse to complete their mission abroad. The scouts had a hard time at the beginning trying to communicate their "desires" to the Chinese performers, not only due to the language barrier but also because of the musicians' unfamiliarity with the recording technology. Hence, the services of a Mr. Hsu were essential. Rather than being merely a translator, "he served with great enthusiasm as a mediator between the Chinese artists (...) and the technicians," helping also to bridge the gap between the stylistic features of their musical performances and the material possibilities of the equipment ("La Compañía Victor ha grabado un magnífico repertorio en el Lejano Oriente." *The Voice of the Victor* [Spanish edition], Vol. 2, No. 2. June 1916, pp. 15–18). In Korea, the scouts were amazed by the ease with which their local assistants, in spite of their short height, were able to carry trunks as heavy as 135 kilos. Unapologetically, they describe them as "dwarfs." By the same token of exoticism, the scouts accounted for the attires and other "peculiarities" of the Chinese theater, including the way in which men impersonated women, the surprisingly perfect English of the Korean translator, and even a cyclone that attacked the region during their stay. Following another trip to Cuba toward the end of 1916, to which Theodore Terry also came along, these two recording experts embarked the next year on what was the longest expedition they ever made.

During the long expedition of 1917—that took them across multiple countries in the Caribbean and South America—Cheney and Althouse kept a daily record in the ledgers of the times in which they held the recording sessions. In general, the time frames invested in the laboratory did not show any particular pattern. They usually began the sessions between nine and ten in the morning, but there were days in which they had their laboratory already set up much earlier. A recording session with a single performer or ensemble could take as little as two hours or as long as six hours or more. Two or three recording blocks took place each day, having regularly one in the morning and another (or two more) in either or both the afternoon and the evening. Some days, however, recording sessions began as late as two or three in the afternoon, lasting only two or three hours, while other days they recorded only at night, and yet others they had intense journeys that began early in the evening and kept going until way past midnight. In short, the scouts had to accommodate their work-time to the quotidian circumstances of each city (or each performer), just as they had to arrange and rearrange the various components of their recording equipment according to the characteristics of each musical number and the acoustic conditions of each place they had to turn into a makeshift recording studio.

More often than not, things did not go according to plan—scheduled musicians would not show up or forgot their instruments and parts; quite frequently, they were not prepared enough to perform flawlessly or to adapt their art to the capturing limitations of the technology. And neither were their instruments, since the scouts sometimes had to intervene in their material physiognomy in order to guarantee an acceptable sonic rendition, as it was the case one day for the recording of a traditional trio in Venezuela ("native harp, cuatro [and] maracas"). As they put it, "Mr. Cheney took seeds out of the maracas and replaced [them with] steel ball bearings" (Victor Recording Ledgers, January 27, 1917). Hence, recording sessions usually took longer than expected. When performing live, time was not a major constraint; but in the laboratory, performers had to cut or add sections, play faster or slower, change the tempo at different spots, alter dynamics, modify lyrics, insert sudden cadences, or improvise arrangements. And so did, in their own way, Cheney and Althouse. But the scouts did not only have to deal with the musicians. Local dealers and other intermediaries sometimes had a say—either solicited or not—about the selection of the performers, the quality of the recordings, or even the administration of the recording sessions.

Between July 29 and August 1 (Sunday to Wednesday), the scouts spent most of the time traveling, from La Paz to Guaqui (in Bolivia), and then to Puno and Arequipa (in Peru). On Thursday, they set the laboratory, and on Friday they expressed their frustration for the derelict preparations made by a local music merchant: "Riega says [there is] no talent. Done nothing. Ha[d] two months notice" (Victor Recording Ledgers, August 3, 1917). On the next Tuesday, either because Riega figured something out or the scouts recruited some performers on their own, the sessions in Arequipa finally started off. But complications with Riega kept surfacing. On Wednesday, the circumstances surrounding the recording of a comedian resulted more confusing than entertaining:

Riega brough[t] man to lab. to make comic records. Said he would like four [done] by AM. After he heard this man[']s stuff in lab. he acted very peculiarly. Left laboratory for one hour and then wrote [a] note to Mr. Cheney, saying he did not want any records of this man.(Did not tell Cheney in person—but left lab.)

(Victor Recording Ledgers, August 8, 1917)

It appears that the comedian, a "Sr. Valdivia," was not really amusing—or at least not that morning—but Riega realized about that only while the recordings were being made. Althouse was presumably proficient in Spanish but not enough as to being able to judge the either comical or dull potential of Mr. Valdivia's performances. Upset but still clueless, the recording experts did not comment any further. Riega kept changing performers, bringing people he barely knew, trying to persuade musicians to return and make more recordings, or even mocking around with his *quena* (Victor Recording Ledgers, August 9, 1917).

It was not only about lining up reliable artists and setting up the recording equipment efficiently. Sometimes the scouts even had to figure out how to get the musicians in a suitable physical condition to perform. On October 23, for example, Cheney and Althouse were making recordings in Guayaquil, Ecuador, the last station in their transnational excursion of that year. They were expecting a "Band," seemingly one of the ensembles of either the Police or the Military, for a session that was supposed to begin at 8 a.m. Nevertheless, at 9:30 a.m. the scouts called the Band headquarters to report that out of the 25 men expected, only ten had showed up. They could not make the scheduled recording, but not only because of the lack of personnel. In the ledgers, the scouts wrote: "Holiday yesterday and the majority are intoxicated, Commander said." Both the musicians who did not show up and the ones who did were apparently drunk. Unable to play their instruments, they hung out in the studio, coping with their hangovers while the scouts scrounged up some food for them: "Had 100 B.B., large pot of soup, sandwiches, etc. ordered" (Victor Recording Ledgers, October 23, 1917).

The ledgers also show that the scouts had apparently different standards of compensation for the various people they interacted with. It looks like the monetary value of their talent, if any, was determined on a case-by-case basis—scaling usually from paying nothing to paying a little. At the high-end of the payment spectrum, for example, Cheney and Althouse paid $100 pesos to the Chilean tenor Ludovico Muzzio for 19 performances recorded in Santiago, over the course of six recording sessions in June 1917. Moreover, the scouts secured not only his recorded voice but also his exclusivity for Victor: "The artist commits also to not sing for any other talking machine company for a period of 24 months (…) in consideration to the amount of $100 local currency" (Victor Recording Ledgers, June 14, 1917; González and Rolle 2003, p. 183). But the $100 Chilean pesos were far from being a fortune. Roughly, it was equivalent to the wages a field laborer in Chile would receive for ten days of work—as it is possible to conclude from available documentation on work-related incidents—and certainly it was just a small fraction of the income of a qualified worker at the time.[4] All things considered, though, Muzzio's case was probably an exception in the contractual arrangements between local performers in Latin America and the Victor company, or the scouts for the same matter. Most likely, for the majority of them, a monetary compensation was never part of the deal when recruiting them for a recording session—a symptom of the power imbalances and neo-colonial maneuvers that informed Victor's operations throughout its global media empire, and in which the labor and salaries of recording scouts were also contingent upon the same practices of capitalist exploitation (Ospina Romero, forthcoming).[5]

The making of acoustic recordings in itinerant scenarios

In general, the intended setting of recording studios during the fieldtrips was consistent with the standards of the companies' laboratories at their headquarters in the United States and Europe. That is apparent, among other things, when considering the bulk of equipment taken by the scouts and the adaptation of the physical spaces they found along the way. Likewise, the way in which the scouts had to rearrange performers and ensembles before the recording horns and the various musical interventions they fostered were not, in principle, very different from the kind of adjustments they routinely had to make when working in Camden, New York, Paris, or London. Nonetheless, the recording expeditions implied an encounter with a multiplicity of unforeseen physical and musical scenarios. Although being on tour was rationalized as the replication of metropolitan standards along a colonial circuit, the dynamics of such mobilization made more apparent the non-standard character of those standards. For example, Victor boasted that in the fieldtrips things were done just as in its studios in Camden; but often times that was simply impossible due to the contingency and unpredictability of the musics and the physical spaces they found throughout the tours.

According to George Brock-Nannestad, Victor had fewer traveling recording experts than the Gramophone Co., and the latter company engaged in more and more frequent expeditions than the first. Apparently, not only Gramophone's equipment was more portable than Victor's but the different approach each company had toward recording ventures overseas made the luggage of the British scouts much lighter than that of their US counterparts. Indeed, the frequency and simultaneity of Gramophone's travels throughout Europe and Asia allowed them to store locally provisions of horns and other items, unlike Victor's employees who had to carry all the gear with them each time they traveled. The heaviest part of the cargo was the crates that carried the blank wax masters. Each master weighted usually between 10 and 11 pounds, so that a single three-month expedition could easily add up to half of a ton. Furthermore, whereas the Gramophone Co. managed to reduce that weight (and the number of crates) by shaving discarded masters to be reused within the same trip, Victor usually "played it safe," that is, it aimed for a more durable (and arguably better sounding) master record. Such an approach implied, evidently, the transportation of as many masters back and forth as recordings were intended or made (Brock-Nannestad 1997).

Setting up temporary recording laboratories was a permanent test for the scouts' imagination. As some sketches in the ledgers show, the goal was to replicate the same layout of two adjacent rooms used at Victor's laboratory in New Jersey. Every new place implied specific arrangements in order to reproduce that layout or to procure something similar (Figure 1.3). The recording machine was regularly concealed in one room and only its horn breached through the wall into the performers' room. Quite too often, however, in the makeshift studios they had to set up during the tours, the room was partitioned merely by a curtain (Barrell 1958, p. 41). The recording ledgers included, just as the same documents did in the Camden laboratory, detailed, almost cryptic annotations about the material configuration of the recording equipment. These annotations appeared usually in three columns. The first two columns referred, respectively, to the type of sound box—the small device between the horn and the wax plates—and the kind of recording horns used for each recording. The third column included information about the devices used to connect various horns at the same time, an issue to which I will come back later. While the notes about sound boxes consist mostly of single annotations, as if keeping a record of the kind used for each piece, the horns appear in a multiplicity of combinations, indicating the various arrangements needed to accommodate for expected and unexpected

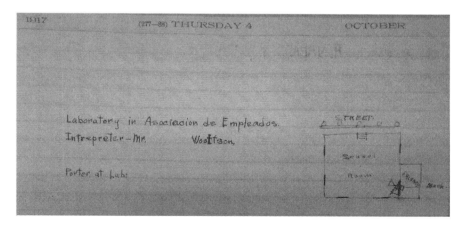

Figure 1.3 Drawing of a recording laboratory in Guayaquil, Ecuador, made presumably by Charles Althouse (Recording Ledgers, Victor Talking Machine Company, October 4, 1917. Courtesy of SONY Music).

changes in instrumentation, acoustic properties, space, and place. Even if the material arrangements for making acoustic recordings were somewhat established by then, the tours posed a series of unpredictable challenges that demanded variable doses of improvisation. Before dealing with the performers, or while dealing with them, the scouts had to ensure the optimal operation of the machine. That depended, to begin with, on the proper assemblage of the different parts of the equipment, namely the motor, the turntable, the wax masters, the cutting needle, the sound box, and the horns.

There were different kinds of horns available, and the scouts carried between 6 and 12 with them during the tours. For the sake of its specific use, the three most significant features in a horn were its material, its dimensions, and its shape. Recording technicians experimented with a variety of materials for the horns during the acoustic era, including glass and wood, but metal horns—made of brass, tin, copper, or aluminum—were the most used throughout. While straight, conical horns with a circular mouth were frequently used for recording voices, elongated, angled, or elliptical horns were tried sometimes for grand pianos or violins in view of the directionality of their sound waves and their relative positions in the studio layout (Brock-Nannestad 1997; Copeland 2008, pp. 249–74).[6] Victor scouts frequently recorded with two or more horns simultaneously, somewhat of an extended practice in recording laboratories at the time, but particularly challenging in the nomadic scenario of the recording expeditions. The link was possible by means of a special Y-shaped brass connector or "joint" among other devices. The scouts used short rubber tubes to connect the horns and the sound box with each of the joint's prongs. For this matter, both the horns and the sound box ended also in tubes of the same diameter as the prongs (Brock-Nannestad 1997; Leech-Wilkinson 2009). Besides the challenge of achieving an accurate connectivity, the scouts had to make sure that the sound waves were transmitted with enough strength in order to guarantee the completion of the recording process in the cutting surface. Generally, connecting two horns helped channel more sound waves from different places in the recording room into the sound box. It was also useful to avoid sound refraction and sound leakage, and if done properly, it could potentially increase the volume of the recording. At the same time, however, chances were that instead of getting good vibrations, sound energy could be lost, absorbed, reflected, turned into heat, or that the sound waves coming through one horn could actually escape through the other (Copeland 2008, pp. 262–3).

Clearly, managing the various components of the recording equipment implied its own set of challenges, experiments, and improvisations. For instance, on August 29, 1917, in Lima, Cheney and Althouse recorded the Banda del Batallón Gendarmes, an ensemble that included eight clarinets, one piccolo, one flute, three cornets, three flugelhorns, four saxophones, two tenor horns, four French horns, four trombones, two baritone horns, two tubas, bass, and drums. It was certainly quite a challenge in sound-capturing.

For each one of the six pieces they recorded that day, the scouts rearranged most of the items of the recording equipment, namely the horns, the vibrating diaphragms that commanded the motion of the needles, and the devices they used to connect multiple horns at the same time. As for the horns, they alternated between five different kinds—most of them being straight horns but with different lengths and diameters—depending on the specific instruments to be featured more prominently, and sometimes having up to three horns connected simultaneously. All of this as if experimenting which material combination would yield the best results for such an ensemble. And the effort would eventually pay off, considering the quality and the various nuances achieved in some of those recordings.[7]

Recording scouts, improvisation, and media empires

Recording experts in the acoustic era worked mostly behind the scenes—and often times literally behind curtains, walls, and glass barriers. Thus, from the onset of their careers, their efforts, contributions, and interventions were unacknowledged and frequently regarded as non-transcendental, merely technical and ordinary, or simply taken for granted. As Paul Fischer puts it, based on the testimonies left by some of them, "[t]heir work turned them into international travelers, befriended by some of the world's great artists and political figures, but to many whose work they captured, they were merely the mysterious 'faces in the window'" (Fischer 2012). Their daily actions, particularly in the context of their scouting activities overseas, were instrumental for the global expansion of recorded sound. Through a series of improvisatory strategies and collaborations with local people, these recording experts—turned by such commissions into talent and recording scouts—participated in the configuration of novel commercial categories, such as "foreign" and "ethnic" records, as well as in the development of transnational networks for the ongoing extraction, marketing, and distribution of musical sounds.

Recording experts were part of top-down power structures in light of their position as subordinate agents of multinational corporations with massive resources and political influence. Nevertheless, the very nature of their assignments implied a substantial degree of autonomy to act on behalf of the company. To begin with, they got to decide what was recorded and what not out of a considerable pool of musical possibilities. Even if other personnel in the company eventually took over the production of the records, such process was built upon the materials picked by the scouts and the way in which they mediated, in the first place, between local music and their mass dissemination. Indeed, they were the ones shaping the repertoires that would eventually flood the companies' catalogs, and even had a say when determining which and how many records were produced as well as about the potential marketing of certain recordings in places other than those where they were originally made.

But recording scouts were more than recording experts on tour. As they ventured overseas, they had to assume unpredictable roles. They acted as business representatives, legal advisors, cultural mediators, translators, vocal coaches, talent scouts, music producers, journalists, and even lobbyists. As the ledgers show, they had to deal with a variety of copyright issues while specifying the terms of the agreement between Victor and each performer. In other words, the labor division by virtue of which there was a logistical distinction between the roles of a company representative, a music director, a local dealer, a talent scout, and a recording expert, was just apparent. Not only these roles were not necessarily mutually exclusive, but more often than not, they were encapsulated in a single individual like Gaisberg, Rambo, Cheney, or Althouse. By the same token, it was not only their technical knowledge what was invested in the expeditions, but their cultural capital, their language skills, and their ability to interact and negotiate a myriad of issues with various sorts of peoples. For the scouts, the recording expeditions did not only entail the potential encounter with unfamiliar music, whether or not pleasant to their ears, it was also the engagement in a cross-cultural journey in which almost anything could happen. And considering the ample range of selections captured—from operatic renditions to all sorts of popular music to recitations, comic sketches, and jokes—it was also a journey of discovery in which almost anything could become a good-selling record. Furthermore, capturing local music numbers on wax implied the eventual circulation of these recordings far beyond their local audiences and traditional performance venues (Ospina Romero 2021). Yet, rather than allowing for the portability of all kinds of vernacular musics, the scouts' improvisatory interventions implied significant doses of arbitration in the globalizing ventures of the music industry. Who made it to the studio and what repertoires turned out to be massively disseminated depended on the aesthetic and acoustic judgment of the scouts, the frequently random selection of musical numbers, and the convoluted networks of local artistic circles that informed the organization of the recording sessions.

Inasmuch as they functioned as performances of spontaneity, the scouts' improvisations in matters of language, technical procedures, marketing categories, or musical selectivity functioned pretty much within the parameters of structured spontaneity similar to those of jazz improvisation, social mobilization, and entrepreneurial initiatives—as examined by scholars in the fields of jazz, critical improvisation studies, and music management studies (Fischlin, Heble, and Lipsitz 2013; Lewis and Piekut 2016; Chapman 2018). That is, rather than random or indiscriminate arrangements, their off-the-cuff decisions and procedures were most of the time intentional, calculated, and rested on the basis of their technical knowledge and expertise in the affairs of the nascent music industry. Furthermore, the scouts' improvisations in particular, and those of the recording industry at large, operated on the basis of the inconspicuous yet expanding force of the US market empire: the strategic accommodation to local scenarios for the sake of consumer culture

(De Grazia 2005). In this respect, Stephen Greenblatt's notion of improvisation is illuminating. He writes:

> by [*improvisation*] I mean the ability to both capitalize on the unforeseen and transform given materials into one's own scenario. The 'spur of the moment' quality of improvisation is not as critical here as the opportunistic grasp of that which seems fixed and established.
>
> (Greenblatt 1980, p. 60)

Notwithstanding the perks of Victor's recording incursions for local musicians and entrepreneurs, these recording campaigns were grounded on unequal power relations as well as on (neo)colonial structures of domination.

Recording companies like Victor, Pathé, Gramophone, and Odeon created empires of their own in tandem with the configuration of a new imperial age fostered by the (neo)colonial enterprises of the United States, France, Britain, and Germany in various parts of the planet. By virtue of explicit and implicit alliances with their political counterparts, recording companies took advantage of imperial resources and networks while providing, at the same time, other networks and resources for the colonial agendas of modern political empires. The extemporaneous scenarios of the expeditions and the scouts' improvisations around random events and material dispositions are symptoms, in my view, of the disjointedness that sustained the quotidian operation of media empires. Besides, the accelerated mechanization of the music industry responded to the unprecedented demand *for* and mass consumption *of* portable recorded music. The imperative demand for musical novelty mirrored the increasing demand for more copies of the same recordings and the talking machines to reproduce them. In manifold ways, such "machine-ism" and the modern imperial configuration of the world in the early twentieth century are two sides of the same coin. In short, as this "machine-age imperialism" unfolded, to use Jeremy Lane's expression, so did the recorded music industry (Lane 2013).

The labor of recording scouts like Rambo, Cheney, and Althouse was essential for the purposes of the industry and played a crucial role in shaping the contours of the recording business. The everyday activities of the scouts offer an alternative to the historical narratives in which the globalization of recorded music is explained, explicitly or implicitly, by the driving impulse of either the companies' heads or the corporations themselves, in abstraction. These top-down narratives, widespread in several accounts about the history of the phonograph, are usually wrapped up in uncritical phrases like "Edison did," "Columbia recorded," or "Victor accomplished." But who was actually Edison, Columbia, and Victor? I believe that by paying attention to the specific actions of specific individuals, in different positions throughout the corporate ladder, we can appreciate more clearly the extemporaneous— and often cluttered and anarchic—interplay that shaped the configuration of modern media empires. At the same time, challenging top-down histories hints at the complication of simplistic narratives of cultural imperialism. Although the companies' executives had significant power in the administration of the business, more often than not their agency relied on—or at least was informed by—the interventions of their employees and the artists they met in the here-and-now of music-and-record making as well as in the everyday of marketing, retailing, cultural exchange, and imperial representation.

Notes

1 Recording Ledgers of the Victor Talking Machine Company (1917). Special Collections Archive of the University of California in Santa Barbara and SONY Music Archives in New York City.
2 The database of the *Discography of American Historical Recordings*, administered by the University of California in Santa Barbara, include references about recording matrixes, released and unreleased recordings, and other contextual information pertaining the operations of Victor, Columbia, Edison, Gramophone, OKeh, and other companies in the early twentieth century, see https://adp.library.ucsb.edu/
3 In this section, I present a few episodes associated with three of Victor's recording scouts: Frank Rambo, Charles Althouse, and George Cheney. Frank S. Rambo (1884–1917), a native from Philadelphia, was the son of a merchant/milk dealer. He participated in two recording expeditions in 1913: Cuba (with Harry Sooy) and Peru-Colombia (with Charles Althouse). He could not go to any more tours afterwards due to health issues and passed away in 1917, just a few days after his 33rd birthday. George Cheney assumed his position. Charles S. Althouse (1894–1968) was born in Philadelphia, and by the time he was 20 he was already working for Victor. His father seems to have been a storekeeper in a shipyard. Althouse, who apparently was fluent enough in Spanish, partook in at least eight expeditions—many of them with Cheney: 1912 (Argentina and Brazil), 1913 (Peru and Colombia), 1914 (Cuba and Trinidad), 1915 (China, Korea, and Japan), 1916 (Cuba), 1917 (the long expedition across the continent), and 1919, 1920 and 1925 (Cuba). In 1923, Althouse worked at the Pan American Recording Company (the name of Victor's factory in Argentina), but his mission ended suddenly after he was accidently hit by a car in Buenos Aires. George K. Cheney (1871–1937) grew up in upstate New York, the son of a relatively well-known house painter in the area. At the turn of the century, Cheney was already working on (and patenting) mechanical improvements in the recording mechanism and directed a recording laboratory for the Universal Talking Machine Company—which would be eventually purchased by Victor. Cheney also worked as a recording technician for the Zonophone Company, in which role he apparently went to China in 1906. He joined the Victor company in May of 1914, led most of the subsequent expeditions, and also helped with Victor's factory in Argentina in 1923 and 1925. For a complete chronology of Victor's expeditions through Latin America and biographical references of the company's ten recording scouts I have identified so far; see Appendixes 1 and 2 in Ospina Romero, forthcoming.
4 "Denuncia de Accidentes de Trabajo" (Report of accidents in the workplace), Valparaiso, Chile, March 7, 2018. I thank Josh Savala for providing me with this historical document.
5 Through the memories of Raymond Sooy, also part of the Victor staff of recording experts/scouts, we know that in 1904 he signed his first contract with the company for $936 annually—roughly equivalent to $27,000 today—plus

additional profit bonuses. But after the first six months, he only collected a dividend payment of $26.64, about $750 today (Sooy, R., 1925).

6 See "Mechanical Appliances," *Talking Machine News*, July (1903), pp. 37–38; "Taking Instrumental Records," *TMN*, August (1903), pp. 57–58; "Band Records," *TMN* September (1903), pp. 77–78; "Voice Records," *TMN*, October (1903), pp. 100. I appreciate the support of George Brock-Nannestad for the clarification of some of these issues.

7 An interesting example of these achievements in matters of dynamics was the piece "Los aires," recorded by the Banda del Batallón Gendarmes two days later. This and many other recordings from the acoustic era are now available for online streaming through *National Jukebox. Historical Recordings from the Library of Congress*, http://www.loc.gov/jukebox.

References

Barnett, K. (2020) *Record Cultures. The Transformation of the U.S. Recording Industry*. Ann Arbor: University of Michigan Press.

Barnum, F.O. (1991) *"His Master's Voice" in America: Ninety Years of Communications Pioneering and Progress: Victor Talking Machine Company, Radio Corporation of America, General Electric Company*. Camden: General Electric Co.

Barrell, W. S. (1958) I Was There. *The Gramophone*, June 1958, p. 41.

Bermúdez, E. (2000) *Historia de la música en Santafé y Bogotá, 1538–1938*. Bogotá: Fundación de Música.

Bolaños, L.P. (2020) *Cine Silente: una historia de Hollywood en Colombia (1910–1930)*. Medellín: La Carreta Editores.

Borras, G. and F. Rohner (2013) *La música popular peruana. Lima-Arequipa (1913–1917). Los archivos de la Victor Talking Machine*. [Liner notes]. Instituto Frances de Estudios Andinos, Instituto de Etnomusicología, Pontificia Universidad Católica del Perú.

Brady, E. (1999) *A Spiral Way: How the Phonograph Changed Ethnography*. Jackson: University Press of Mississippi.

Brock-Nannestad, G. (1997) The Objective Basis for the Production of High-Quality Transfers from Pre-1925 Sound Recordings. *Audio Engineering Society Convention* 103, pp. 1–29.

Cañardo, M. (2017) *Fábricas de músicas: comienzos de la industria discográfica en la Argentina (1919–1930)*. Buenos Aires: Gourmet Musical Ediciones.

Chapman, D. (2018) *The Jazz Bubble: Neoclassical Jazz in Neoliberal Culture*. Stanford: University of California Press.

Copeland, P. (2008) *Manual of Analogue Sound Restoration Techniques*. London: The British Library.

Cortés Polanía, J. (2004) *La música nacional y popular colombiana en la colección mundo al día: 1924–1938*. Bogotá: Universidad Nacional de Colombia.

Cowley, J. (1996) *Carnival, Canboulay and Calypso: Traditions in the making*. Cambridge: Cambridge University Press.

Cross, G. and R. Proctor (2014) *Packaged Pleasures. How Technology and Marketing Revolutionized Desire*. Chicago: The University of Chicago Press.

De Grazia, V. (2005) *Irresistible Empire: America's Advance through Twentieth-Century Europe*. Cambridge: Belknap Press of Harvard University Press.

Denning, M. (2015) *Noise Uprising: The Audiopolitics of a World Musical Revolution*. London; Brooklyn: Verso.

38   *Sergio Ospina Romero*

Discography of American Historical Recordings. University of California at Santa Barbara Library, available at: https://adp.library.ucsb.edu/index.php

Eisenberg, E. (2005) *The Recording Angel: Music, Records and Culture from Aristotle to Zappa,* 2nd ed. New Haven: Yale University Press.

Feaster, P. (2007) *"The Following Record": Making Sense of Phonographic Performance, 1877–1908.* Ph.D. Indiana University.

Fischer, P.D. (2012) The Sooy Dynasty of Camden, New Jersey: Victor's First Family of Recording. *Journal on the Art of Record Production,* available at: http://www.arpjournal.com/asarpwp/the-sooy-dynasty-of-camden-new-jersey-victor's-first-family-of-recording/

Fischlin, D., A. Heble and G. Lipsitz (2013) *The Fierce Urgency of Now: Improvisation, Rights, and the Ethics of Co-Creation.* Durham: Duke University Press.

Gaisberg, F.W. (1942) *The Music Goes Round.* New York: Macmillan Co.

González, J. (libretto) and R. Chapí. 1899. *El fonógrafo ambulante. Zarzuela en un acto y tres cuadros, en prosa.* Madrid: Arregui y Aruej, eds; R. Velasco, printer.

González, J.P. and C. Rolle (2003) *Historia social de la música popular en Chile, 1890–1950.* Santiago: Ediciones Universidad Católica de Chile.

Greenblatt, S. 1980. Improvisation and Power. In: Said, E. (ed.) *Literature and Society. Selected Papers from the English Institute, 1978.* Baltimore: Johns Hopkins University Press, pp. 57–99.

Gronow, P. (1982). Ethnic Recordings: An Introduction. In: American Folklife Center (ed.) *Ethnic Recordings in America: A Neglected Heritage.* Washington, DC: Library of Congress, pp. 1–49.

Gronow, P. (1983). The Record Industry: The Growth of a Mass Medium. *Popular Music,* 3, pp. 53–75.

Gronow, P. (1998). *An International History of the Recording Industry.* London; New York: Cassell.

Hochman, B. (2014). *Savage Preservation: The Ethnographic Origins of Modern Media Technology.* Minneapolis: University of Minnesota Press.

Johnson, B. (2002) The Jazz Diaspora. In: Horn, D., and M. Cook (eds.) *The Cambridge Companion to Jazz.* Cambridge: Cambridge University Press, pp. 33–54.

Kaplan, A. (2002). *The Anarchy of Empire in the Making of U.S. Culture.* Cambridge: Harvard University Press.

Lane, J. (2013). *Jazz and Machine-Age Imperialism: Music, "Race," and Intellectuals in France, 1918–1945.* Ann Arbor: The University of Michigan Press.

Leech-Wilkinson, D. (2009). *The Changing Sound of Music: Approaches to Studying Recorded Musical Performance.* London: CHARM.

Lewis, G., and B. Piekut (eds.) (2016) *The Oxford Handbook of Critical Improvisation Studies.* Nueva York: Oxford University Press.

Liebersohn, H. (2019) *Music and the New Global Culture. From the Great Exhibitions to the Jazz Age.* Chicago: The University of Chicago Press.

Mann, M. (2003). *Incoherent Empire.* London: Verso.

Martland, P. (2013). *Recording History: The British Record Industry, 1888–1931.* Lanham: Scarecrow Press.

Moore, J.N. (1999). *Sound Revolutions: A Biography of Fred Gaisberg, Founding Father of Commercial Sound Recording.* London: Sanctuary.

Moreda Rodríguez, E. (2019). Travelling Phonographs in Fin de Siècle Spain: Recording Technologies and National Regeneration in Ruperto Chapí's El Fonógrafo Ambulante. *Journal of Spanish Cultural Studies* 20(3), pp. 241–55.

Ospina Romero, S. (2017). *Dolor que canta. La vida y la música de Luis A. Calvo en la sociedad colombiana de comienzos del siglo XX*. Bogotá: Instituto Colombiano de Antropología e Historia.

Ospina Romero, S. (2021). The Transnational Circulations of Sound Recordings in the Era of the Acoustic Phonograph. In: Beaster-Jones, J. and K.E. Goldschmitt (eds.) *Oxford Handbook of Global Music Industry Studies*. New York: Oxford University Press.

Ospina Romero, S. (forthcoming) *Fonógrafos ambulantes. Música y globalización en las expediciones de la Victor Talking Machine Company por América Latina y el Caribe, 1903–1926*. Buenos Aires: Gourmet Musical.

Pérez González, J. (2018) El espectáculo público de las "maquinas parlantes". Fonografía en São Paulo, 1878–1902. *Ensayos. Historia y teoría del arte*, 22(35), 109–32.

Radano, R., and T. Olaniyan (eds.) (2016) *Audible Empire: Music, Global Politics, Critique*. Durham: Duke University Press.

Sooy, H. (1925) *Memoir of My Career at Victor Talking Machine Company, 1898–1925*. Unpublished manuscript.

Sooy, R. (1925) *Memoirs of My Recording and Traveling Experiences for the Victor Talking Machine Company*. Unpublished manuscript.

Stoler, A. (2010) *Carnal Knowledge and Imperial Power: Race and the Intimate in Colonial Rule*. Berkeley: University of California Press.

Strötbaum, H. (ed.) (2010a) *The Fred Gaisberg Diaries. Part 1: USA and Europe (1898–1902)*.

Strötbaum, H. (ed.) (2010b) *The Fred Gaisberg Diaries. Part 2: Going East (1902–1903)*.

Suisman, D. (2009) *Selling Sounds: The Commercial Revolution in American Music*. Cambridge: Harvard University Press.

Vernon, P. (1997) Odeon Records. Their "ethnic" output. *The Magazine for Traditional Music throughout the World*, available at: http://www.mustrad.org.uk/articles/odeon.htm [Accessed 1 June 2020].

2 Global transfer, local realities

Early phonographic practices and challenges in China (1900–1914)

Andreas Steen

The phonograph travelled quickly after Edison had announced his new invention on November 21, 1877. In the case of China, this can be illustrated by two examples: first, when the high official Guo Songtao was appointed China's first ambassador to the United Kingdom in 1877, and in the following year also to France. He saw the phonograph at an exhibition at the South Kensington Museum on May 5, 1878, described it briefly, and by October had chosen a direct phonetic translation to name it, mentioning the "fang-luo-ge-na-fu" together with the "mai-ge-luo-feng" (microphone) (Guo 1982, 675). Second, four months later the invention also arrived in Shanghai, the largest extraterritorial treaty port in China. In an article filed under "Miscellaneous" and entitled "The Phonograph in Shanghai," the *North-China Herald* (NCH) wrote on August 31, 1878:

> The instrument shewn [sic] us was, like the microphone, a very rough looking affair, and being but a trial model, had suffered severely in appearance from alterations in design and modification of details. Closer inspection, however, proved that the greatest possible care had been exercised where necessary, and in some parts the work was most highly and accurately finished.
>
> (p. 222)

Both examples are mere snapshots, yet they were early signs of increasing global transfer, technical knowledge exchange and forthcoming sonic possibilities against the background of colonial expansion, as observed with curiosity by a Chinese envoy in London and by a group of foreign expats in Shanghai.

In China, the ruling Qing dynasty (1644–1911) had been forced to open a growing number of treaty ports since the First Opium War (1839–1842), and the phonograph accompanied a new period in foreign-Chinese diplomacy, later joined by the gramophone, which Emile Berliner patented in 1887. Both inventions were embedded in a larger (scientific) discourse on Western technologies and modernity, obsessed "with the four major categories of modern technology: sound (*sheng*), light (*guang*), chemistry (*hua*),

DOI: 10.4324/9781003006497-4

and electricity (*dian*)" (Lee, 2000, p. 35). At the turn of the century, "this in-genious and beautiful toy made a great sensation" at an all-male "Smoking Concert" for foreigners in Tianjin (NCH, 1898). Simultaneously, Chinese audiences enjoyed the combination of opera performance and (foreign) gramophone concert in teahouse theatres. Accustomed to its noisy environ-ment, urbanite Chinese listeners were less concerned with the sound qual-ity and, as Xu Peng (2017, p. 20) argues, "embraced the talking machine wholeheartedly from the very beginning and reckoned with its musical force within the paradigm of high-class art."

Phonograph and gramophone were seen (and presented) as expressions of Western modernity, if not superiority, yet "in concert" they created sites and moments of musical entertainment and enjoyment for different audiences in China's treaty ports. The examples above indicate that the new medium – which by the turn of the century was given the name "liu-sheng-ji" (save-sound-machine) – travelled with almost no time delay from the imperialist centre to the semi-colonial treaty ports. Global networks of business and transport allowed the almost simultaneous rise of a gramophone culture at both places, writes Jones (2001, p. 57), and concludes that "[t]he "history of the record industry in Shanghai belies the assumption of "belated moder-nity" ..." (ibid.).[1]

This chapter looks into the first decade of Chinese gramophone culture, when the market was "relatively chaotic" (*bijiao hunluan*) (Gu, 2015, p. 90). It began after the Victor Talking Machine Co. and the Columbia Grapho-phone Co. had reached an agreement over record patent rights (1902), and "competition shifted from hardware to software or, better put, to the musi-cal content of the phonograms" (Tschmuck, 2006, p. 15).

How did this competition affect new, culturally complex and still unex-plored large markets such as China? In China, to begin with, the record industry arrived in an atmosphere characterized by political conflict, anti-foreign sentiment and a simultaneous desire for Western modernity and national strength. In 1900, the Eight-Allied Army had defeated the Boxer Uprising, looted Beijing and its surroundings and forced China to sign the Boxer Protocol (1901). While the foreign powers insisted on extending their privileges in China, an increasing anti-Manchu nationalism succeeded to overthrow the Qing Dynasty and establish the Republic of China in 1912. Two years later, the First World War (1914–1918), travel and material restric-tions as well as the need to engage in war production at home ended this period of global recording expeditions.

As everywhere in the world, China's recording history began with the ar-rival of foreign phonograph company scouts, whose "reactions in the field were [often] driven by their assumptions about music, race and primitivism." Miller (2006, pp. 172–3) even discovered that "artists or music that challenged scouts' understanding of the dichotomy between primitivism and civiliza-tion rarely got recorded." In China, however, the challenges were different, mostly because the foreign scouts had to team up with experts who pursued their own goals when engaging in this new territory of transcultural inter-action. I argue that the company scout's lack of local cultural knowledge and linguistic competence created a significant space for Chinese agency in a moment of political uncertainty and cultural reform. Central to this agency was the middleman (Chinese manager, *comprador*), who usually was an amateur performer (*piaoyou*), embedded in the networks of the Peking opera world.[2] Motivated by commercial incentives, he selected artists and repertoire, and stood at the junction between foreign profit and local artistic recognition, fame and failure.

I will focus on Peking opera, which around 1900 was the most popular musical genre in China, while also paying attention to other popular folk art forms (*quyi*).[3] The famous *laosheng* actor Tan Xinpei (1847–1917) provides a well-documented example to illustrate local agency and global competi-tion over musical content. Geographically, this leads us to Beijing and two international treaty ports, Shanghai and Tianjin, because their triangular relationship of dynamic artist exchange also defined the early activities of the recording companies.

Peking opera around 1900: networks, stars and mobility

Peking opera (*jingju*) was born in 1790, when the Four Great Companies from Anhui province performed in Beijing to celebrate the 80th birthday of the opera-loving Qianlong emperor.[4] They performed the *pihuang* style, a synthesis of different dramatic and melodic styles that was also welcomed by audiences in the capital. The Peking opera developed as one of more than 300 local operas (*xiju*) and saw its first blossoming period between 1870 and 1910. It was performed by men, who were trained in the role types of *sheng* (man), *dan* (woman), *hualian* (painted face), *chou* (clown) and *wu* (acrobatics) or *wen* (civil; stress on singing). In those decades, the old male (*laosheng*) ad-vanced to become the most popular, caused also by a general militarization of popular culture from the Taiping Rebellion (1850–1864) to the two Opium Wars and the Sino-Japanese War (1894–1895).

Later emperors, however, were not as passionate about opera plays, and even banned opera troupes within the Beijing city walls (Yeh, 2014, p. 77). Opera theatres provided low-class entertainment, and to officials, the world of opera was a nuisance that needed to be controlled. Actors and actresses, although admired, were assigned the lowest social status and prohibited to mingle with the rest of society. The situation improved in 1883, when Empress Dowager Cixi, herself an avid Peking opera fan, lifted the ban on inviting external actors into the Forbidden City, thereby raising both the reputation of this entertainment form and the social prestige of its actors. Most famous became the *laosheng* actor Tan Xinpei, who was born into a family of actors and also known under his artist name Xiao Jiaotian. His unique style is:

usually described as overcast and mournful. He was above all an innovator of new and intricate arias, snatching up brilliant scraps of melodies from throughout the Chinese musical universe (he was famous
for borrowing melodies from *bangzi* and *dagu*) and weaving them into
unpredictable but fluent passages of song.

(Goldstein, 2007, p. 51)

Peking opera is a sonic and visual spectacle, combining singing, acting,
dancing, acrobatics and music. The content refers to famous events and moments in Chinese history, to heroes and battles, war strategies, intrigues,
love stories, anecdotes and so on. Plays and performances were often based
on episodes from popular classical novels, such as *All Men are Brothers*
(*Shuihu zhuan*), *Journey to the West* (*Xiyouji*) and *The Romance of the Three
Kingdoms* (*Sanguo yanyi*), expressing Confucian values of loyalty, righteous-
ness, benevolence and filial piety. Until 1900, when fire destroyed most of
the teahouse theatres during the suppression of the Boxer Uprising, opera
performances in Beijing relied on customs and a rotation system of actors
and troupes, without any "headlines or advertisements" (Goldstein, 2007,
p. 31). Great opera stars had their own schools and amateur-players (*piaoyou*)
associated with them. Their close ties to actors, their networks and expertise, together with their motivation to preserve, study and promote the art
of their idols turned them into ideal and indispensable partners for the recording companies.

Shanghai, the prospering treaty port south of the Yangzi river, first invited the "capital drama troupes" (*jingxiban*) in 1867. Since the 1870s, it
became "common for Beijing's *pihuang* actors to journey by steamboat to
Shanghai, performing for a few months or even years in the bourgeoning
metropolis" (Goldstein, 2007, p. 43). Shanghai's theatres were commercial
businesses that ran on a star system, which profited from the popularity
of the specially invited guest (*kechuan*), who was accompanied by a local
troupe. Since a rotation system did not exist, advertisements played a crucial role to attract audiences from an early time – the first Chinese-language
newspaper, *Shenbao*, began printing daily performance schedules in 1872.
Already in the 1880s, an actor like Tan Xinpei was making around ¥ 30 a
month in Beijing, but received about ¥ 200 in Shanghai (Goldstein, 2007,
p. 48). Due to increasing demand and rising salaries in the treaty ports, Beijing's actors would not only regularly perform in Tianjin and Shanghai, they
also filled the gossip of newspapers about actors, actresses and courtesans.
As a prospering foreign treaty port, Shanghai attracted a wide range of artists and audiences, which created space for innovation and experiment: in
1894, the *Meixian* Teahouse opened as the first venue for female Peking opera actors, who often were invited from Tianjin. The northern actresses were
extremely popular in Shanghai, and some perceived their success as a threat
to the city's male actors.[5]

After 1900, Beijing opera's reorganized system preferred individual contracts and a salary based on the actor's popularity. Shanghai, also known for its dignified treatment of actors, became even more attractive to artists from Beijing (Yeh, 2014, p. 91). In 1900, *laosheng* actor Sun Juxian (1841–1931) had negotiated a share of the daily profits and earned an unprecedented ¥ 2,000 in one month in Shanghai. One year later, Tan Xinpei earned the same amount in a month, which he thought was too low compared to the overall profit the theatre had made: "by 1912 he reached $15,000, and in his last visit in 1915 he received $8,000 for a ten-day visit. At the same time, the theater grossed $30,000 during these ten days."[6] Commercial incentives and modern venues, advertisements, periodicals and the mobility of actors had created a star system that focused on the individual performer, and some of them had started to demand an opera reform.

Early recordings

In spring 1903, Frederick William Gaisberg (1873–1951), an experienced recording expert who had been active all over Europe and arranged the famous records of Caruso in 1902, arrived in Shanghai to make the first Chinese recordings for the British Gramophone & Typewriter (G&T), London. Acknowledging his cultural ignorance, he approached the British music house S. Moutrie & Co. (*Moudeli yanghang*), established in 1847, with offices in Kobe, Yokohama and Hong Kong. On Monday, March 16, he met Xu Qianlin (1862–1951), the company's Chinese manager. Xu, who had been working for S. Moutrie & Co. since 1882, obviously knew Shanghai's musical field and the popular artists currently residing in the city. Two days later, Gaisberg (1942, p. 62) noted in his diary:

> we made our first records. About 15 Chinamen had come, including the band to accompany. As a Chinaman yells at the top of his power when he sings, he can only sing two songs an evening – then his throat is hoarse. Their idea of music is a tremendous clash and bang. With the assistance of a drum, three pairs of huge gongs, a pair of clappers, a sort of banjo, a squacky fiddle of bamboo & some bagpipe-sounding instruments, besides the yelling of the singer, their idea of music was recorded on the Gramophone. On the first day, after making ten records we had to stop: the din had so paralysed my wits that I could not think.

Until March 27, Gaisberg made 325 records in Shanghai, and, as he noted, "the differences between the tunes of any two records were too slight for me to detect" (Gaisberg, 1942, p. 63). Gaisberg and his team moved on to Hong Kong, where the songs were "not nearly so interesting" and altogether recorded 470 Chinese matrices during this journey.[7]

A look into G&T's *Catalogue of Chinese Gramophone Records* (1904), the earliest surviving Chinese record catalogue, reveals that Gaisberg had been well advised over the period of nine days. Xu Qianlin quickly grasped the new business opportunity and managed to arrange recording sessions with a wide range of Peking opera actors and female artists in Shanghai.[8] Divided into Cantonese and Mandarin records, male and female voices, the catalogue's largest categories are "Songs by Male Voices" (113/77), followed by "Songs by Female Voices" (55/28) and "Songs by Male Voices, Cantonese" (51/32).[9] The artist selection reflects the trend of the times, namely that the powerful "old man" (*laosheng*) role type was most popular in Shanghai, followed by the "female" (*dansheng*) role type, which was performed by male actors. Gaisberg's catalogue offered records of famous *laosheng* stars such as Xiao Jiaotian (Tan Xinpei, 3), Zhou Fenglin (4), Wang Guifen (4), Wang Hongshou (2) and Bai Wenkui (7).

Particularly motivated were three actors, who already engaged in the opera reform: Feng Zihe (1888–1941), the young and new rising star on Shanghai's opera stage, recorded 15 numbers. Feng had been trained by his father to perform the *dan* role and quickly became famous after his debut at the age of 12. His career was still in its early stage, yet he was open to Western influences, strived for the modernization of opera and became an important pioneer for the Peking opera in the Shanghai style (*haipai jingju*). In 1904, he began to study English, Western music and dance during the daytime. He performed in the evenings, was radical and experimental, adapted Western plays for Peking opera, even sang in English and truly was an avant-garde actor (Li, 2019, pp. 137–40; Ming Chi, 1999, pp. 503–8).

Wang Xiaonong (1858–1918), son of an elite Manchu family, had received a fine education and served as a magistrate, but was expelled from the post due to conflicts with the local gentry. Frustrated over the world of officialdom, he joined the world of opera and specialized in *laosheng* roles. "He was a tempestuous fellow, a notoriously heavy drinker and debaucher, but his sincere passion and intellect enlivened his performances and moved the audience" (Goldstein, 2007, p. 95). Wang also was a prolific writer and innovator with a patriotic heart, who with *Dang ren bei* (Party Member Monument) wrote his first critical opera play. The play referred to a political struggle in the Northern Song Dynasty (960–1127) and the *Yuanyou* Party Stele, on which conservative members that were against the New Policies had been inscribed and denounced. Wang used the story to bemoan the failure of the Reform Movement (1898) and the murder of Tan Sitong (1865–1898) and other martyrs. First performed in 1901, it became very popular and was one of his signature plays, still performed in Shanghai in 1918 (Li, 2019, p. 289; Wang/Du, 2017, p. 151). For G&T, however, he recorded 12 records of traditional opera, including the popular piece *Dingjun shan* (Dingjun Mountain).

Lin Buqing (1862–1918), born in Danyang, Jiangsu province, was famous in and around Shanghai and a popular artist who excelled in the Suzhou style of storytelling in rhymed verse (*tanhuang*). He sang in dialect mimicry and parodic ballads, and Gaisberg managed to invite him for 15 recordings of his classical repertoire under the role type *xiao chou* (Little Clown). *Tanhuang* was widely considered as low culture and often banned from performing, because it was associated with immoral allusions and content (Wang/

Du, 2017, pp. 65 and 164). There is no precise answer why the three actors had less inhibitions when Xu Qianlin invited them to a recording session, although perhaps they already sensed that it could increase their popularity and become a promotional tool for their art and other messages.

Reform, records and resistance

By then, Chinese intellectuals already initiated a new discourse about opera. Chen Duxiu, for example, "credited opera and opera performers as the educators of the people," and in 1904 complained that "only in China [...] performing operas is considered a mean occupation" (Li, 2019, p. 56). In the same year, Wang Xiaonong and critic Chen Qubing published Shanghai's first opera journal *Ershi shiji dawutai* (*The Great Stage of the Twentieth Century*). The journal provided the platform to debate and promote the opera reform and the so-called "civilized theatre" (*wenming xi*), a new hybrid form of Chinese and Western elements to educate and enlighten the audience – also about Han Chinese unity and anti-Manchu activism. One year later, the journal was closed for subversion, but the new plays were popular, even among students, who were further inspired by a wave of translated works that introduced them to "the rising and falling of nations as well as the struggles and revolutions of the people" (Yue, 2006, p. 115). In 1908, the Xia brothers revolutionized the opera experience with the "The New Stage" (*Xin wutai*), a western-style theatre, part of a "bold agenda for drama reform aimed to raise both popular drama and actors, as a social group, to new heights of social and cultural respectability" (Goldstein, 2007, p. 76). In practice, these activities led to creative experiments with patriotic stories and conflicts based on foreign historical events, though commercial incentives later also encouraged the combination with vulgar content and visual sensations (Su Yi, 1995, p. 213).

This was the cultural atmosphere in 1904, when the Columbia Graphophone Co. sent its engineer Charles W. Carson to Shanghai, selecting as its agent the Swiss company J. Ullmann & Co., "Manufacturers of Chronometers, Watches, Clocks and Musical Boxes," with offices in Hong Kong (1871), Shanghai and Tianjin. In the following year, the Victor Talking Machine Record Co. sent recording engineer George Kenny Cheney, who like Gaisberg approached the music house S. Moutrie & Co. We can assume that the Chinese manager and the artist jointly agreed on the record content. Interestingly, and after being acquainted with the new medium, the above-mentioned recording stars became more courageous.

Wang Xiaonong not only recorded *Party Member Monument* for Columbia (1905) and Victor (1906), but also *Gua zhong lan yin* (The Fall of Poland; Columbia 1905). The latter opera was inspired by the popular book *Bolan shuaiwang zhanshi* (*The History of Poland's Demise*), written in Japanese by author Shibue Tamotsu (Tokyo 1895) and published in its second Chinese translation in Shanghai in 1904. The book tells the story of Poland's partition in the eighteenth century, and the heroic but unsuccessful battle of independence against Russia, Prussia and Austria. It quickly became popular among Chinese revolutionaries, inspired historical fiction writing and Wang's opera play (1904). The use of the popular "melon metaphor" (*gua*) in its title and its implied reference to the foreign powers' China policy of "cutting up a melon" made the anti-foreign critique very explicit.[10]

Another example of political critique offered Lin Buqing, the master of *tanhuang* and folk art forms (*quyi*). In 1906, he recorded *Dizhi Mei huo* (Boycott American Products) for the Victor label, and two years later, *Jin Mei huo* (Ban American Products) for the International Talking Machine G.m.b.H. (Odeon).[11] The background of these records was America's "Chinese Exclusion Act" (1882), which was renewed with the Geary Act (1892) and again in 1902 with no termination date. Opposition against Chinese discrimination was strong in Shanghai, and after the US Congress approved the Extension of the Chinese Exclusion Act in 1904, it culminated in a boycott against American goods and services under the leadership of the Shanghai Chamber of Commerce in May 1905. The boycott activities spread over ten provinces and lasted into 1906, the year of Lin's recording (Gerth, 2003, p. 128).

Lin Buqing addressed several critical issues in his repertoire. In his *tanhuang* piece *Shanghai nao gongtang* (Shanghai's Troublesome Court; Columbia 1907), he referred to a disputed case at the Mixed Court of the International Settlement of Shanghai. In *Tianzu hui* (Natural Feet Society; Columbia 1907), Lin focused on the Natural Feet Society, founded in 1901 by Alicia Ellen Neve Bewicke, better known as Mrs. Archibald Little, together with her husband. She was widely regarded as the leading European voice against foot binding in China. Her goal to abolish this practice was shared by all modernizers and reformers, and now also addressed in a modern *tanhuang* opera.

Figure 2.1 Lin Buqing: "Boycott American Products" (1908) (Courtesy: Wang Gang).

Wang Xiaonong and Lin Buqing are only two examples of reform-oriented patriotic artists, whose sonic activism translated into a new form of circulating political messages. Did Columbia's and Victor's agents know that Lin Buqing sang "Boycott American Goods"? They probably did, but they also knew that the foreign companies ignored local politics and lyrics of inscrutable content, to concentrate on repertoire variety and sales instead.

Recording all dialects, all of China

In 1906, the Victor Talking Machine Co. presented itself as highly satisfied and confident regarding its business in China. It did so by praising its cooperation with agent S. Moutrie & Co. and comprador Mr. Yuen Sing Foong, emphasized in an article and a photograph in the trade magazines *The Talking Machine World* and *The Music Trade Review*:

> Mr. Yuen Sing Foong has been many years connected with the talking machine business, and has established throughout China for the S. Moutrie Co. many branches, and has sold Victor talking machines and records to dealers in every city and large town in the Chinese Empire. Mr. Yuen speaks good English, although he has never been out of China. He is a great scholar, and speaks most of the different dialects spoken in China. It was through his influence that Geo. K. Cheney was able to secure for the Victor Co. the best talent in China. The records taken in China turned out so satisfactory that the S. Moutrie Co. have placed orders for thousands of them. In China there are many dialects spoken, and Mr. Cheney took records of all the principal dialects. Mr. Cheney, who recently returned from the Far East, said to The World that "the Chinese take great interest in the talking machine. In towns which are not large enough to support a theatre they use the Victor machine as an entertainer, charging a small admission, which enables all to hear songs sung by some of the most noted actors in China.[12]

Mr. Yuen Sing Foong is introduced as the ideal cooperation partner to whom the Victor Talking Machine Co. owes most of its success in China. This triple-honour, in text and image, and in foreign magazines, was highly unusual, since record companies and their engineers normally avoided revealing their Chinese middlemen. We can interpret this as a demonstration of Victor's self-confidence; it can also be read as a much-needed sign of honour to Mr. Yuen to secure his service and skills to continue recording "all of China" for the Victor label in an increasingly competitive environment.

Founded by Heinrich Bumb in Berlin in 1904, for example, the German Beka-Record GmbH had also organized a recording expedition, spending the period from February to early April 1906 in Hong Kong and Shanghai. Bumb's route was similar to Gaisberg's, and so was his experience. He published a detailed report in ten successive numbers of the Berlin trade journal

Die Phonographische Zeitschrift.[13] The Beka team recorded about 200 record sides (numbers) in China, which were released as Beka-Grand-Records with a dragon on a yellow label. Among them was the Xin Fu theatrical troupe, which previously had made recordings of Peking opera for Columbia (Du, 2015, p. 86). However, Bumb did not reveal his middleman, and the advice he provided is seen as sceptical today: The repertoire "lacks the works of well-known artists, especially Peking opera records, not few are the recordings of amateur *piaoyou*. Among the Cantonese records are some experts,…" (Wang/Du, 2017, p. 121).

The records were advertised together with the other "Asiatic Records" in the *Talking Machine World* in November 1906, promoting "Indian records in 6 different languages, Chinese records in 5 different languages as well as Japanese and Malay records." In the winter of 1907/1908, Beka arranged a second tour to China, and the team went to Beijing and Tianjin, mostly recording Peking opera, clapper opera (*bangzi*) and *quyi*. On this occasion, Beka recorded *laosheng* Yu Shuyan (1890–1943) and Tan Xinpei, which I will return to later. In 1908, ads such as "Beka Record – The Best Record in the World" promised a "Repertoire Always Up-To-Date," and had six Chinese languages in the programme: Swatow, Guakau, Pekinese, Shansinese, Kiangnanese and Cantonese.[14]

By then, the market had become very competitive, because companies realized that "[t]he chief end of the phonograph business is the sale of records. […] The growth and profit are in records" (*Talking Machine News* 1909). Victor and the Gramophone Co. already agreed in 1907 to minimize

Figure 2.2 The *Xinfu* theatrical troupe, group photo in Shanghai, recorded for Columbia. (*The Music Trade Review*, Vol. XLII, No. 11, 17.03.1906).

costs and challenges by dividing the market: Victor engaged in North and South America, China and Japan; the Gramophone Co. in Europe, India and other Asian countries (Miller, 2006, p. 168). Maybe this information motivated Harry L. Marker (1876–1966), who had only recently returned from a world recording tour for Columbia, to report his successes in China, where he had spent "a year divided between Pekin, Shanghai, Hong Kong and Tientsin," realizing that the "Chinese actors like to sing for the talking machine, for they are well paid and the sale of their records increases their popularity." *The Music Trades* (1908) further wrote that he:

> had records made for the Columbia by the great actors of the Empire and some of the most famous of the sing-song girls, who, by the way, are in many instances extremely pretty and in all instances extremely chic. Some of the actors who sang for the phonograph are men who appear before the Emperor only. How the Columbia Company secured their services is a feat which the export department of the company is not divulging.
>
> (p. 38)

Marker boasted about what we can call "sonic trophies," but kept silent about his local contacts. He was, however, the only recording engineer who mentioned the complex translation process from opera performance to musical record and the indispensable competence of the Chinese expert:

> When Mr. Marker learned that the operas ran easily along for more months than the talking machine record does minutes, he naturally was rather perplexed to know how he was going to get that music on the graphophone. It is there all right. Native experts decide just what are the chef's d'oeuvre of these "operas" and the singers render these selections. The music sounds pretty much all alike to the American.
>
> (ibid)

Until 1912:

> Columbia's recording experts explored several cities, moving back and forth to Shanghai, Hong Kong, Tianjin, Beijing, Xiamen, Shantou, Singapore etc. Altogether they recorded more than 2000 sides of Chinese records, which turned Columbia into a powerful rival to the Victor Talking Machine Co.
>
> (Wang/Du, 2017, p. 92)

In 1913, the latter's repertoire was published in the thick catalogue of *Victor Records in Chinese Mandarin, Cantonese, Amoy, Foochow and Swatow Dialects*.

Fame, fakes and actresses

Harry L. Marker's claim to have recorded "the most famous of the sing-song girls" is difficult to verify, since no catalogue of the Columbia-Marconi Velvet Tone records survived, yet the popularity of female singers is undisputed and also documented in an 80-page catalogue published by Pathé-Phono-Cinema Chine (*Baidai jiqi zhuanpan*). Experts place the publication year between 1906 and 1909 (Gu, 2015, p. 85). This outstanding catalogue not only criticized a problematic business practice from those years, it also illustrates Pathé's intelligent entry into China's record market.

The French company Société Pathé Frères, founded 1896 in Paris and specializing in phonographs and film equipment, approached Shanghai in 1900 to sell its products, which soon also included Chinese phonograph cylinders. Motivated by increasing prospects, the company "Pathé Phono-Cinema Chine" was registered in Paris in August 1907. Branch offices were opened in Shanghai, Tianjin and Hankou as well as in Calcutta, Jakarta and Singapore. In August 1908 the first Chinese records were advertised in Shanghai under the company branch name *Baide yanghang*. Records had been made in Beijing (*xiqu, quyi*, 560 sides) and in Guangzhou/Hong Kong (Cantonese Opera and songs, 200 sides).[15] Thus, the catalogue is divided into the two categories "Beijing Records" and "Canton Records." I will focus on the "Beijing Records," which take up two-thirds of the catalogue.

The attractive visual design of this catalogue derives from the professional and respectful photographs of nearly each actor and actress, which were taken during the recording period (Wu Xiaoling, 2006, p. 112). Even in Europe, this expensive format was rarely seen, reminding us that Pathé was the latecomer on the Chinese recording market, eager to challenge its competitors. Pathé and its Chinese representative Du Kai had noticed the popularity of northern actors and actresses. In order to approach them properly, they first contacted the famous and influential amateur performers (*mingpiao*) Qiao Jinchen (see FN 3) and Wang Yutian in Beijing, both of whom practiced the Tan (Xinpei) style (Ming Chi, 1999, p. 200).

The repertoire presented in the catalogue consists of four sections: Peking opera and local clapper opera, popular songs (*shidiao xiaoqu*) and brothel tunes (*yaodiao*), music of Peking opera and *quyi* and Cantonese opera (*yueju*). Wu Xiaoling (2006, p. 113) praises Du Kai for this selection, because he not only understood the musical preferences of different social consumer groups, but also "turned his view to the purse of overseas Chinese" by recording Cantonese opera. Most important, however, was the first page of the catalogue, which announced three numbers recorded by Tan Xinpei: *Hongyang dong* (Hongyang Grotto) and *Mai ma* (Selling Horses, 1 & 2). The records were promoted with a handwritten and signed statement by the artist, in which he certified the authenticity of his recordings and praised Qiao Jinchen's role for introducing Pathé to Beijing's opera actors. This presentation of an artist was extraordinary, and it was as much a critique of counterfeit records as it was a clever marketing strategy.

Counterfeit records not only reflect the global competition over musical content and big stars, they further illustrate the middleman's individual agency and his inexperience, if not unwillingness to consider the cultural (artistic) consequences of his actions. The majority of fake records was released by Moutrie & Co., write Wu Xiaoru (1995, pp. 785–96) and Zhao Bingxiang (2016, p. 114). Its Chinese manager, Xu Qianlin, who worked for G&T and Victor, is said to have argued that:

> honesty with regard to records is unnecessary. It is enough to invite some troupes of famous opera schools for singing and paste a famous name on the label. This is easy and comfortable, and saves costs while achieving the same sales.
>
> (Luo, 1996, p. 398)

Gaisberg's 1904 catalogue mentioned three records of Xiao Jiaotian – all fakes! From the German Beka, we know that "a few records were labelled with Tan Xin Pei, a famous Peking opera actor…, but the recordings were in fact sung by others" (Du, 2015, pp. 86).[16] The "other" usually was an unknown *piaoyou*, imitating the "King of Actors," who for various reasons may have ignored recording.

Several actors feared to lose their voice once they "sung into" the machine, writes Chen (1965, p. 114). Also, Tan had no financial interests, as he was paid outstanding salaries for sold-out performances in Shanghai – his performance art was also honoured in the first Chinese movie production (1905). Naturally, he questioned the medium's ability to adequately record the nuances of his voice. And didn't recording reduce the opera enjoyment of his art to only the sonic aspect? Furthermore, performance was also improvization, but a recording would set a standard, and above-all gave the *piaoyou* community a tool to carefully study and compare his singing art.[17] However, it is said that Pathé's middlemen finally dispersed his doubts with a chunk of opium, and that when he agreed to record, other actors in Beijing followed, as demonstrated by the excellent repertoire in the catalogue (Ge, 2008, p. 27; Gu, 2015, p. 90). In the end, Tan's proof of authenticity greatly enhanced Pathé's reputation in the world of Peking opera, and it surely was a sign of gratitude that both Qiao Jinchen and Wang Yutian were listed with 8 and 14 record numbers in this catalogue. When Wang's star began to rise with the circulation of his records, this again inspired actors such as Yu Shuyan to take the medium seriously (Zhao, 2016, p. 122).

Under the rubric "Beijing Records," the catalogue also included 224 titles recorded by 24 female singers. Some of them were mentioned with an impressive number of records, for example, Yingui (36), Guifeng (28), Guixi (16), Lishun (16) and Da Yunqing (10). They performed opera pieces, songs and the popular genres of drum songs (*dagu*) and clapper opera (*bangzi*)

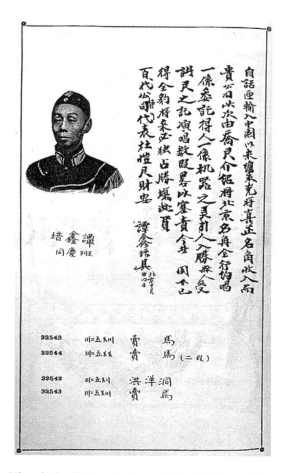

Figure 2.3 Tan Xinpei: the "King of Actors". (*Pathé Phono-Cinema-Chine: Opera Catalogue*, 1909).

(Steen, 2006, p. 147). Drum song girls "became wildly popular in Tianjin and Beijing in the 1910s and 1920s.... The most spectacularly popular and best documented stage art for women in this period was the clapper opera (*bangzi qiang*)" (Cheng Weikun, 1996, pp. 201 and 203).

The rise of female artists from the teahouses to the big stages characterizes the dynamic transformation of China's musical world in this period. When Gaisberg arrived in Shanghai in 1903, Xu Qianlin had established contacts to nine female artists who agreed to join recording sessions, the most famous being Lin Daiyu (3), Lin Guifen (2) and Jin Xiaobao (1).[18] Their names were accompanied by the explanation "prostitute" (*jinü*), to signify social status and distinguish them from "female voices" sung by men. Few

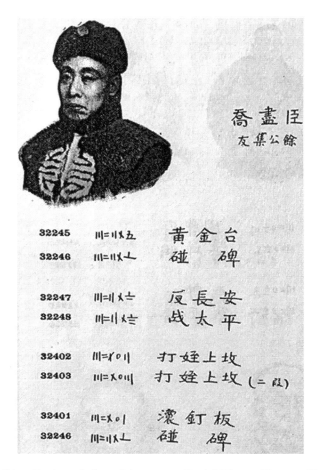

Figure 2.4 Qiao Jinchen: influential *piaoyou* (Pathé Phono-Cinema-Chine: Opera
Catalogue, 1909).

years later, Pathé used the term "girl" (*guniang*) and combined it with a
photograph, next to those of male artists. This shift in representation was
necessary to raise their social status and recognition of their art, yet it was
also a new step towards commodification.

With this catalogue, and in a moment of increasing competition, Pathé
had insisted on proving its product's authenticity and rose to fame. Around
1910, the company sent its expert Edgard Labansat (?–1939), who previously
had "established branch offices for his firm in India, the Strait Settlements,
Indo-China and Hong Kong" (NCH, 1939, p. 504). The company changed
its Chinese name to *Baidai* (Pathé) and Labansat, together with his Chinese
manager Zhang Changfu, a *piaoyou* from Ningbo, could rely on the same
opera network to win Tan Xinpei for a second set of six records in 1912

(Zhao, 2016, p. 115). One year later, Victor published its catalogue of records in five Chinese languages, featuring female singers from Tianjin, but also eight "fakes" of Tan Xinpei (Steen, 2006, p. 136).

Tan Xinpei and the materiality of sound

Tan visited Shanghai as guest performer in 1912, when the new trend was not to be ignored: female voices, actresses and dan actors had conquered the theatres and stages; the rising star was Mei Lanfang (1894–1961), who in 1913 gave his debut in Shanghai. One year later, writes Goldstein (2007, p. 111), the female star "Liu Xifen arrived from Tianjin and for a time was more popular than either Tan Xinpei or Mei Lanfang." Meanwhile, Tan's records had travelled to Europe and the USA. As a small note in the *Henan ribao* (*Henan Daily*, 1914) revealed, experts were fascinated with his "clear and melodious, really special" tone, and a big company prepared to invite Tan to the USA. It would cover the costs, but also expressed the fear that Tan rejects the offer due to his age and health. He would have been the first Beijing opera actor to perform abroad. In 1915, he went to Shanghai instead and excited the city by performing for ten days at the New Stage (*Xin wutai*) (Ming Chi, 1999, p. 208). When he died two years later at the age of 70, an era had come to an end.

Pathé, however, had preserved the real sound of the King of Actors, realized the promotional value of his records and benefited from the company's positive reputation. In 1919, obviously convinced of its future prospects in China, the company began to build China's first record pressing plant in Shanghai's French Concession. One year later, it made the first records with the new star Mei Lanfang. Pathé-Orient, as it was now called, became China's leading record company during the 1920s, and for many years to come placed Tan's records on the first page of its catalogues.

In conclusion, it is apt to say that the music industries' global expansion led to competition over musical content early in China. The first decade of recording in China was a dynamic period of cooperation and transcultural interaction between foreign record scouts and local middlemen, mostly *piaoyou*. Educated and individually different, at best informed and well connected, the latter quickly understood the commercial value of recording, but also realized their freedom, if not power, to select the repertoire. They chose the popular actors and genres of those days, included counterfeits of famous actors, supported political messages and capitalized on the popularity of actresses and female singers. Selection, however, was not only a matter of interest and motivation, but also of networks and possibilities. The downfall of the Qing empire seemed not to have affected these networks and the foreign record business in China, yet it was this influential and diverse group of experts that defined the sonic repertoire of an increasingly popular medium and thereby actively helped to integrate it into China's cultural and political context. Foreign record scouts, however, came with the monetary and technical "power to record," though all of them felt inclined to express little if any understanding of what was recorded. Educated and socialized in America and Europe, they shared the "aesthetic requirements of a music industry keen on providing entertainment" (Tschmuck, 2006, p. 39), but failed to grasp the cultural and political dynamics in China. The fact that Chinese music was not seen as a challenge to Western superiority may have inspired ignorance, when – in combination with the missing cultural and linguistic competence – putting the business in the hands of a hopefully trustworthy middleman. For all involved, however, this was a decade of experience and cooperation, learning and improvement, which came to an end with the First World War, and laid the foundation for the new gramophone culture of the 1920s.

Notes

1 For a general overview of the pre-1949 recording industry in China, see Ge Tao, 2009; Jones, 2001; Steen, 2006, 2015b.
2 The *piaoyou* (literally, ticket friend) was an amateur actor or what we call an "active fan" today. He studied the style of a specific actor and was also engaged in performing and promoting it. Some *piaoyou* became famous actors themselves. Qiao Jinchen (1863–1926), for example, was a talented and influential *piaoyou* in Beijing. He had learned English, worked as interpreter for the Danish embassy and later in a Chinese-Russian bank. He then became comprador for several foreign companies, and also excelled in writing opera plays and published opera critiques. *Piaoyou* were organized in *piaofang* (literally, ticket house), which functioned like clubs, arranged according to actor and/or opera style. See Ming Chi, 1999, pp. 195–204; Su Yi, 1995, pp. 60–1.
3 *Quyi* = folk art forms of different local regions, including ballad singing, storytelling, comic dialogues, clapper talk, cross-talk and so on.
4 On the history of Peking opera, see Goldstein, 2007; Hsu Tao-ching, 1985; Li Hsiao-t'I, 2019; Ming Chi, 1999.
5 Goldstein, 2007, p. 110. On Peking opera in Shanghai, see Li, 2019; on early female performers, actresses and their art in Beijing and Tianjin, see Cheng Weikun, 1996, 2003.
6 Yeh, 2014, p. 82. On the opera business and salaries, see Goldstein, 2007, pp. 48–9; Yeh, 2014.
7 On the early period of record production in Guangdong and Hong Kong, see Rong, 2006.
8 Xu Qianlin was not only a businessman, but also a socially and politically engaged citizen of Shanghai. Later he organized the Chapei Volunteer Corps during the 1911 Revolution, promoted the Anti-Kidnapping Society at Shanghai with branch offices in various ports, founded the International Famine Relief Committee Shanghai in 1913 and served on the International War Relief Committee 1915, among others. See, *The China Weekly Review*, 1925.
9 The numbers refer to different sizes: 7-inch and 10-inch records.
10 See the details by Wang/Du, 2017, pp. 150–5. On the "melon metaphor" and Wang's opera, see Wagner, 2017, p. 104; on the "sound" of Wang Xiaonong, see Qian Nairong, 2014, pp. 48–9; on his opera plays, see Yue Meng, 2006, pp. 112–19.
11 On Lin Buqing's records, see Wang/Du, 2017, pp. 164–74.

12 The Talking Machine World, 1906. See also *The Music Trade Review* (1906); for a reprint of Mr. Yuen's photo, see Lubinski/Steen, 2017, p. 287.
13 On Beka's recording expedition, see Bumb 1906; on his stay in China, see Steen, 2015a.
14 See The Talking Machine World, 4:10, 15.10.1908. Since neither Beka nor Odeon published a Chinese catalogue that survived until today, the repertoire can only be evaluated from the records themselves.
15 On the catalogue, see Steen, 2006, pp. 127–30; Wang/Du, 2017, pp. 114–15. On the early history of Pathé-Orient, see also Ge Tao, 2008; Wang/Du, 2016.
16 On Tan's records, see Ge Tao, 2008, p. 27; Qian Nairong, 2014, pp. 23–5; Steen, 2006, pp. 134–43, 2017; Wu Xiaoru, 1995; Zhao, 2016.
17 On Tan Xinpei's career, see Steen, 2006, pp. 133–43.
18 A list of early Peking opera actresses in Beijing, Tianjin and so on offers Ming Chi, 1999, pp. 284–93.

References

Catalogues

Gramophone & Typewriter: Catalogue of Chinese Gramophone Records, 1904.
Pathé Phono-Cinema-Chine 百代机器唱盘电片公司: 法商戏目录: 百代机器转盘, 北京, 广东 (Opera Catalogue: Pathé Gramophone Records: Beijing, Canton), ca. 1906–1909.
Victor/Moutrie & Co.: 役挫公司中国曲调: 北京音, 广东省城音, 厦门音, 福州音, 汕头音 (Victor Records in Chinese Mandarin, Cantonese, Amoy, Foochow and Swatow Dialects.), ca. 1913.

Literature

Bumb, H. (1906) Unsere Reise um die Erde: Skizzen von der großen 'Beka'-Aufnahme-Expedition. *Phonographische Zeitschrift*. 7 (27–37). (available also on recordingpioneers.com).
Chen Zhuoying 陈卓莹 (1965) 解放前唱片公司概述 (Overview of Record Companies in China before 1949), 广东文史资料. *Guangdong Historical and Cultural Material*. 18, pp. 113–20.
Cheng, W. (1996) The Challenge of the Modern Actresses: Female Performers and Cultural Alternatives in Early Twentieth Century Beijing and Tianjin. *Modern China*. 22(2), pp. 197–233.
Cheng, W. (2003) Women in Public Spaces: Theater, Modernity, and Actresses in Early Twentieth-Century Beijing. *Asian Journal of Women Studies*. 9(3), pp. 7–45.
China Weekly Review, The (ed.) (1925) *Who's Who in China (Biographies of Chinese)*, Shanghai.
Du Junmin (2015) Beka Chinese Records (1906–1949). In: Gronow, P., Hoger, C. & Wonneberg, F. *The Lindström Project: Contributions to the History of the Record Industry*, Vol. 6. Vienna: Gesellschaft für Historische Tonträger, pp. 86–121.
Gaisberg, F. (1942) *The Music Goes Round*. New York: Macmillan Company.
Ge Tao 葛涛(2008) 百代浮沉 / 近代上海百代唱片公司盛衰纪 (The Rise and Fall of the Pathé/EMI (China) Record Company in Modern Shanghai), 史林 (*Historical Review*). 5, pp. 26–41 & 127.
Ge Tao 葛涛 (2009) 唱片与近代上海社会生活 (*Music Records and Social Life in Modern Shanghai*). Shanghai: Cishu Publishing House.

Gerth, K. (2003) *China Made. Consumer Culture and the Creation of a Nation*. Cambridge; London: Harvard University Press.

Goldstein, J. (2007) *Drama Kings. Players and Publics in the Re-creation of Peking Opera, 1870–1937*. Berkeley: University of California Press.

Gu Shuguang 谷曙光 (2015)京剧唱片学中的珍稀史料 – 北京唱盘研究(Valuable Material of Beijing Record Studies – "Beijing Records" Research), 中国戏曲学院学报 (*Journal of National Academy of Chinese Theatre Arts*). 63(2), pp. 84–92.

Guo Songtao 郭嵩涛 (1982) 郭嵩涛日记 (*Guo Songtao: Diary*). Changsha: Hunan People's Publishing House.

Henan Ribao 河南日报 (Henan Daily) (1914)谭鑫培声播欧美(Tan Xinpei's Voice spreads to Europe and America), 17 July, p. 1.

Hsu Tao-ching (1985) *The Chinese Conception of the Theatre*. Seattle: University of Washington Press.

Jones, A. (2001) *Yellow Music. Media Culture and Colonial Modernity in the Chinese Jazz Age*. Durham; London: Duke University Press.

Lee, L. (2000) The Cultural Construction of Modernity in Urban Shanghai: Some Preliminary Explorations. In: Yeh, W. (ed.), *Becoming Chinese. Passages to Modernity and Beyond*. Berkeley: University of California Press, pp. 31–61.

Li, H. (2019) *Opera, Society, and Politics in Modern China*. Boston: Harvard University Asia Center.

Luo Liangsheng 罗亮生 (1996 [1986])戏曲唱片史话(Historical Account of Beijing-Opera Records). 京剧谈往录三编 (*Beijing Opera Stories and Memories*). 3, pp. 397–416.

Miller, K.H. (2006) Talking Machine World: Selling the Local in the Global Music Industry, 1900–20. In: Hopkins, A. G. (ed.) *Global History: Interactions between the Universal and the Local*. Houndmills; Basingstoke: Palgrave Macmillan, pp. 160–90.

Ming Chi 鸣迟 et alii (ed.) (1999) 中国京剧史 (*History of China's Peking Opera*), 4 Vols. Beijing: China Opera Publishing House.

NCH (1898) Smoking Concerts, 21 February, p. 275.

NCH (1939) Obituaries: M.E. Labansat, 22 March, p. 504.

North-China Herald (NCH) (1878) The Phonograph in Shanghai, 31 March, p. 222.

Qian, N. 钱乃荣 (2014) 上海唱片 1903–1949 (*Shanghai Music Records 1903–1949*). Shanghai: People's Publishing House.

Rong, S. 容世成 (2006) 唱片工业与广东曲艺 1903–1953 (*The Recording Industry and Cantonese Folk Vocal Art Forms*). Hong Kong: Cosmos Books.

Steen, A. (2006) *Zwischen Unterhaltung und Revolution: Grammophone, Schallplatten und die Anfänge der Musikindustrie in Shanghai, 1878–1937*. Wiesbaden: Harrassowitz.

Steen, A. (2015a) Heinrich Bumb and Beka in China: A Strange Artistic Experience. In: Gronow, P., Hoger, C. & Wonneberg, F. *The Lindström Project: Contributions to the History of the Record Industry*, Vol. 6. Vienna: Gesellschaft für Historische Tonträger, pp. 122–29.

Steen, A. (2015b) 在娱乐与革命之间: 留声机唱片与上海音乐工业的初期 (*Between Entertainment and Revolution: Gramophones, Records, and the Early Days of Shanghai's Music Industry*). Shanghai: Cishu Publishing House.

Steen, A. (2017) (with Christina Lubinski) Travelling Entrepreneurs, Traveling Sounds: The Early Gramophone Business in India and China, *Itenerario (International Journal on the History of European Expansion and Global Interaction)*. 41(2), pp. 275–303.

Su Yi. 苏移 (1995) 京剧二百年概况 (*200 Years of Beijing Opera: An Overview*). Beijing: Yanshan Publishing House.

Talking Machine News (1909) The Talking Machine Industry. It's Marvellous Development. Some American Observations. 7(89), p. 72.

The Music Trade Review (1906) Talking Machines in China. 42(20), p. 86.

The Music Trades (1908) Making Columbia Records in Famous Jap Palaces, 4 January, p. 38.

The Talking Machine World (1906) Talking Machines in China. 2(6), p. 35.

Tschmuck, P. (2006) *Creativity and Innovation in the Music Industry*. Dordrecht: Springer.

Wagner, R. G. (2017) Dividing up the Chinese Melon, "guafen": The Fate of a Transcultural Metaphor in the Formation of National Myth, *Transcultural Studies*. 1, pp. 9–122.

Wang Gang 王钢/Du Junmin 杜军民 (2016) 百代公司在中国的发端 (The Early Days of the Pathé Record Co. in China). In: 中华艺术论丛 (*Essays on Chinese Art, no. 17*). Shanghai: Shanghai University Publishing House, pp. 1–26.

Wang Gang 王钢 / Du Junmin 杜军民 (2017) 孙中山及辛亥革命音频文献 (*Audio Documents of Sun Yatsen and the Xinhai Revolution* [1911]). Zhengzhou: Wenxin Publishing House.

Wu Xiaoling 吴晓铃 (2006) 82年前的声响记录 北京唱盘 (Sound Recordings 82 Years Ago: Beijing Records). In: 吴晓铃集 (*Wu Xiaoling: Collected Works*), Vol. 3. Shijiazhuang: Hebei Education Publishing House, pp. 112–15.

Wu Xiaoru 吴晓如 (1995) 吴小如戏曲文录 (*Wu Xiaoru: Essays on Chinese Opera*). Beijing: Beijing University Publishing House.

Xu, P. (2017) Hearing the Opera: "Teahouse Mimesis" and the Aesthetics of Noise in Early Jingju Recordings, 1890s-1910s. *Chinoperl*. 36(1), pp. 1–21.

Yeh, C.V. (2014) Where is the Center of Cultural Production? The Rise of the Actor to National Stardom and the Beijing / Shanghai Challenge (1860s – 1910s). *Late Imperial China*. 25(2), pp. 74–118.

Yue, M. (2006) *Shanghai and the Edges of Empires*. Minneapolis: University of Minnesota Press.

Zhao Bingxiang 赵炳翔 (2016) 民国年间上海京剧唱片概论 (A Study of Peking Opera Records in Shanghai in the Republican Period). 上海戏剧学院学报 (*Journal of the Shanghai Opera Institute*). 3, pp. 112–23.

3 Settler colonial soundscapes

Phonograph demonstrations in 1890s Australia

Henry Reese

There is a growing recognition that the talking machine 'travelled in the footsteps of imperialist expansion and colonial politics' (Lubinski and Steen, 2017, p. 277). The technology of sound recording moved along the networks and circuits of empire. In turn, cultures of recorded sound were shaped on the ground by interactions between the transnational agents of the recording industry and diverse local peoples. The overtly imperialistic rhetoric that surrounded the early phonograph—discourses of conquest, capture and annexation—has been well demonstrated (Picker, 2003, p. 113). But the culture of sound recording also contributed to a subtler process of settler place-making. In this chapter, I argue that the constituent features of an Australian settler colonial soundscape are evident in the recording choices of the pioneers of the phonograph in the colonies and in the enthusiastic public reception of these recordings. By rereading the repertoire of the first demonstrators of the phonograph in Australia in the early 1890s, I demonstrate that this early technological spectacle was used to reanimate and perform the socially significant sounds of widely dispersed British settler communities in Australia. By technologically highlighting culturally meaningful aspects of local and distant soundscapes alike, the phonographic demonstrators encouraged their audiences to attend to and remark on their sonic environments. The effect of this is to demonstrate the importance of background sound, of soundscape, to the creation of European place in Indigenous spaces.

While most of the work on early phonographic performances has focused on American, European and Asian contexts, I argue that a distinctive soundscape of settler colonial order and modernity is evident through the recording practice of the first demonstrators of recorded sound in Australia. Accordingly, I offer an interpretation of the early phonograph demonstration as an opportunity for settlers to take stock of and celebrate the significant elements of their local and wider colonial soundscapes, at a time of self-conscious settler nationalist ferment, historical consciousness and colonial modernity. I use recordings of bells—a popular subject for early recordists and a recognisable feature of the local soundscapes through which they moved—as a case study. The celebration of bell sounds was one element of a wider process of settler place-making through sound, a gridlike imposition

DOI: 10.4324/9781003006497-5

of European sound worlds onto deeper, subtler Indigenous space. Recovering this long-lost genre of popular entertainment requires close reading of newspaper reviews of phonograph performances, in order to take seriously the meanings of these performances in their own cultural context.

My argument benefits from and contributes to a growing understanding that settler colonialism represented the imposition of a distinctive spatial order. Settler colonialism was and is a 'historical process of remaking space,' involving the creation and assertion of new meanings by settlers over existing and enduring Indigenous spaces (Banivanua Mar and Edmonds, 2010). This is a permanent and world-changing imposition; the settlers came to *stay* (Wolfe, 2006, p. 388). As Europeans appropriated and changed Indigenous lands, they imposed powerful new meanings and understandings on it. The settler imaginary refashioned space in service of claims to progress, commerce, modernity and history (Banivanua Mar and Edmonds, 2010). This was an embodied process, and the 'entire human sensorium was engaged in the acts of making and accommodating and resisting empire' (Rotter, 2011, p. 4). A powerful seam of scholarship has explored the manifold ways in which imperial encounters were figured and shaped on an intimate, quotidian scale, through bodily and sensory encounters (Ballantyne and Burton, 2005, 2009). The colonial world was the crucible of embodied knowledge that contributed to both the construction and the challenging of notions of difference and hierarchy (Erlmann, 2004, p. 10).

Several studies have demonstrated that the processes of settler colonial expansion, conquest and encounter were alive with sound (Collins, 2006; Keyes, 2009). The soundscapes of conquest, exploration and frontier violence were tempered with subtler resonances, as spatial preferences and forms of affective attachment developed as part of the process by which Europeans made themselves at home in their unfamiliar environments. In the Australian context, the well-noted eeriness of Antipodean nature slowly gave way to familiarity and appropriation as British settlers established a presence there. By the late nineteenth century, settler nationalism had come to co-opt distinctive 'Australian' sounds for its own ends. Here, the sounds of native flora and fauna as well as Aboriginal speech and music were incorporated into the wider claims to legitimacy of the settler state, especially in the fervent decades of nation-building that book-ended the turn of the century.

A number of scholars have begun to explore the depth of Australian settler place attachments through sound (Harper, 2000; Bandt, Duffy and MacKinnon, 2007; Richards, 2007; Thomas, 2007; Collins, 2011; Harris, 2014). To date, however, I have offered the only systematic treatment of the relationship between recorded sound and wider soundscape consciousness in Australia. As the first cultural history of recorded sound in Australia, my doctoral dissertation demonstrated that affective engagement with the Australian soundscape developed in tandem with an understanding and appreciation of the technology and possibility of sound (Reese, 2019). The early phonograph is important as source material into colonial soundscape consciousness, because it provoked early listeners to reflect upon their local soundscapes and on how their wider worlds sound. Demonstrations of recorded sound provided a shared framework by which the intimate processes of everyday emplacement were performed and affected in public. The early phonograph, I argue, affords the historian of sound a rare opportunity to explore a colonial audience making explicit its sonic preferences in public.

These preferences had a distinct impact upon the shape of settler colonial expansion and appropriation of the Australian environment. The strikingly 'British' character of the Australian urban environment was one of the most important impositions of the late nineteenth century. The soundscapes of settler colonialism in Australia were primarily imported from Britain. From the foundations of European colonisation in Australia, a British rural soundscape ideal—a preference for the quiet, ordered hum of agricultural productivity which implied social order and hierarchy—was imported and imposed upon territory that was produced at the very moment that this land was conquered, surveyed and opened to pastoralism and agriculture (Denney, 2012). I argue here that an *urban* soundscape ideal also pervaded Australian settler culture, and that some of the primary features of this are evident in the recording choices of early phonograph exhibitors in the 1890s. This recognition fits well alongside Radano and Olaniyan's rethinking of the relationship between empire, space and the 'transnational ecology of music creation' (Radano and Olaniyan, 2016, p. 15).

After situating the early phonographic demonstrations in the cultural context of colonial modernity, I explore how recordings were used to animate an ordered, affectively charged soundscape, which deepened settler place-attachment and ultimately contributed to the ongoing dispossession of Indigenous peoples in Australia. Bell recordings in particular offer clear evidence of the self-conscious celebration and attention to the spatialising process of European sound-making in settler colonial Australia. In terms of sources, the recordings I discuss herein are knowable only through their written traces. None of the earliest Australian sound recordings I discuss here have survived. The records of popular stage performances in this period are also notoriously elusive (Bellanta, 2012c). As such, I have had to rely on newspaper advertisements, reviews and the occasional interview to reassemble the lost world of the phonographic exhibition. Through extensive research into the colonial newspaper record, it is possible to recompose the actions, progress and reception of the early phonograph demonstrators in late colonial Australia. Reading the records of the early phonograph demonstrations affords an opportunity to explore the meanings of recorded sound in settlers' own words, but these sources must also be read critically in light of the general tendency for hyperbole and sensation that pervaded reports on the colonial stage at the time.

Settler society, mobility and colonial modernity

As a mass cultural phenomenon, the phonograph demonstrations of the late nineteenth century tapped into some of the deepest cultural preoccupations of colonial Australia. This section sets out some of the common cultural themes in settler society at this time, which were all evident in the content of the phonograph performances. My argument—that the phonograph demonstrations of the 1890s emerged at a crucial stage in the formation of settler identity and place attachment—depends upon a specific set of historical factors. The common features of urban settler society must be understood in relation to the urban boom that provided the material backdrop to the cultural phenomena catalysed by the phonograph demonstrators. My discussion chimes with recent approaches to the transnational entanglements of modern settler culture in Australia (Vernon, 2016). I will therefore outline the colonies' place in the British Empire and racial and national imaginings in late nineteenth century Australia, before outlining the common spatial factors that provided the contextual basis for the Australian soundscape of the era. I will then demonstrate how these themes were embedded in the popular performance cultures that provided the contextual frame necessary for making sense of the phonograph demonstration in colonial culture.

Mobility was the defining feature of the modern in Australia. While the experience of travel was by no means unique to Australia, the unique combination of 'continental scale, perceived isolation, migratory histories, maritime geographies, relative affluence, and the unceasing process of settler colonial dispossession' loomed large in the national imaginary (Rees, 2017, p. 3). A set of common cultural preoccupations pervaded the settler communities across this region. As Alan Atkinson has argued, the final quarter of the nineteenth century witnessed the rise of a settler *mentalité*, a revolution in thought and practice that 'coped with vastness': high literacy and massive migration, increased mobility and migration facilitated by transport and communications revolutions, mass democracy and an expanded scope of governance made possible by an imaginative inhabitation and appropriation of the enormous spaces of the continent. The Europeans in Australia 'wrestled with puzzles of space and distance,' striving to anchor 'European civilisation in Australian space' (Atkinson, 2014, pp. 68–74 and 96–7).

This spirit or sentiment contributed to the decade-long project of Federation of the Australian colonies, which sprang to prominence as a political movement in 1889 and remained prominent throughout the 1890s (Hirst, 2000). The rise of a settler historical consciousness, especially after the Centennial of European settlement in the Antipodes in 1888, contributed to a deepening sense of place attachment, especially among those 'pioneers' who remembered the extraordinary dynamism of the nineteenth century settler project (Griffiths, 1996). The colonies also enjoyed a reputation as social laboratories, places of progressive thought and democratic participation—'working men's paradises' (White, 1981). Racial imagination was a crucial ingredient here. The animation of a discourse of whiteness, construed in both biological and cultural terms, provided a deep cultural anchor in the Antipodean space. To colonial nationalists, Australia and New Zealand were the model 'white man's countries,' a bastion of the 'English-speaking' race that drew on and influenced transnational projects of racial exclusion (Anderson, 2005; Lake and Reynolds, 2008). The experiences of migration and a shared Britishness remained important cultural and material touchstones (Magee and Thompson, 2010, pp. 5–21). It has long been accepted in Australian historiography that sentimental commitment to Empire and Britishness was not incompatible with the rise of colonial nationalism (Meaney, 2001). But this was not the only referent. British settler identity was entangled in complex ways with the emergence by the early twentieth century of a 'shared Anglo-Saxonism,' an 'Anglo-worldwide imagined community' that encompassed white Americans as well as Australians (Belich, 2009, p. 480).

This was a dynamic time for white settlers living in Australasia. The arrival of the phonograph into the Antipodes coincided with the apogee of a boom period in settler society, and persisted during its collapse into economic depression from 1891 (Belich, 2009, p. 548). In the economically vibrant 20 years to 1891, parts of Western Australia, Tasmania, South Australia and New South Wales boomed, along with New Zealand and Queensland as a whole. Massive influxes of British capital underwrote enormous growth in infrastructure (especially railways), housing and farming and their associated speculations and support industries (Belich, 2009, pp. 357–8). The colonies were becoming increasingly interconnected. The city of Melbourne was the centre of Australia's explosive growth in the 1870s and 1880s, growing to a metropolis of nearly half a million by 1890 (Belich, 2009, p. 84). The Victorian capital was the economic and cultural centre of Australia, at least 30% larger than Sydney, its nearest competitor. While the depression that set in from 1891 permanently took the shine out of the southern city, it remained the locus of political life in the new nation after Federation of the colonies in 1901 (Belich, 2009, pp. 360–1).

Spatially, Australasia was dominated by a handful of sprawling cities and country towns servicing enormous pastoral hinterlands. By 1890, extensive railway and steamship networks interlinked the continent tightly (Blainey, 2001, pp. 248–57). Despite the centrality of pastoralism, agriculture and mining to the economies of the settler colonies and of the rural idealism of the bush to settler culture, Australia and New Zealand were also heavily urbanised regions (Davison, 1995). British visitors in the late nineteenth century were regularly struck with the similarity of the colonies' cities in look, feel and sound to those of Britain. The Australian city was widely understood as 'a provincial adaptation of predominately English styles and ways of life' (Davison, 2001, p. 779). As Asa Briggs has influentially noted, 'in many ways—socially, culturally and physically—nineteenth century Melbourne was a provincial British city overseas' (Briggs, 1990, pp. 277–310). Its suburban form and building stock were strongly influenced by British and Irish cities built at a comparable time, and Melbourne was 'constructed by builders and developers whose ideas about urban life, as well as their craft skills, were learnt in their home countries before they came to Australia' (O'Hanlon, 2014, pp. 132–3). At the same time, the low-density suburban sprawl of Melbourne and many other Antipodean frontier cities (prototypically Adelaide, Perth and Auckland) resembled a broader Pacific system of settler urbanisation. A common urban form—rectilinear, low density, suburban, businesslike, fuelled by a sprawling pastoral and agricultural sector—developed quickly across the American west, Canadian prairie and Antipodes alike in this period of rapid settler expansion (Hamer, 1990; Frost, 1991, pp. 18–28).

A common, recognisable spatial order pervaded the wider settler world. In this sense, the corporeal underpinnings of the nineteenth-century urban experience were distinct (Bijsterveld, 2013, p. 16; Kenny, 2014, p. 29). Settlers themselves were well aware of a common mood, a spirit of bustle, a hum of activity and busyness, during boom times in regions of recent settlement (Belich, 2009, pp. 195–8 and 548). The modern Antipodean settler city was a place with a vibrant street life in which commerce, entertainment, governance, social disorder and resistance intermingled (Swain, 1985; Brown-May, 1998). The settler city was also the site of distinctive class, gendered and ethnic tensions. The urban soundscape was contested by several kinds of actors, particularly the linguistically diverse inhabitants of the city (Rhook, 2014, 2015). Gangs of 'larrikins' or rough working-class youth were also an integral ingredient of the soundscape of the colonial Australian scene (Bellanta, 2012a). Working class women's public presence was often contested and criminalised in the late nineteenth-century Australian city (Piper, 2015; Minchinton, 2020). Another constitutive feature of the 'urbanising frontier' was the dispossession and marginalisation of Indigenous peoples from larger settler cities across the settler world (Edmonds, 2010).

The 1890s in Australia witnessed a mix of local and transnational influences in popular culture. Emerging mass cultural productions—Tin Pan Alley songs, new dance crazes, phonograph and cinema exhibitions and touring vaudeville shows—all became widely popular in the 1890s (Bellanta, 2013, p. 257). Despite the privations of economic depression that set in as the decade advanced, settlers enjoyed a relatively high standard of living and continued to spend their hard-earned cash on commercial entertainments, spectator sports and the popular press. These themes coexisted with other well-known preoccupations of the period such as nationalism, the rise of a political labour movement, immigration restriction and the attainment of universal suffrage (Bellanta, 2012b, pp. 151–3).

Touring entertainers and theatrical companies were some of the most mobile commercial actors in Australia at this time, following well-worn networks and itineraries across the colonies (Davison, McCarty and McLeary, 1987). Australia and New Zealand formed one cohesive Australasian circuit for the purposes of the transnational entertainment industry, and several prominent Australian and British companies regularly hosted the brightest local, British and European talent (Kelly, 2009, pp. 1–18). The region was also increasingly encompassed in a wider Pacific circuit for American troupes that treated the Australasian stage as an extension of the American West (Wittmann, 2010). Visiting observers and theatrical entrepreneurs noted that Australian audiences had high standards for their entertainments and felt themselves to have a cosmopolitan cultural outlook (Matthews, 2005, pp. 47–8). Distance, mobility and imaginary journeys were central to popular culture. Audiences were comfortable with a wide variety of representations of exotic times and places, and these were all reflected onstage (Kelly, 2009, pp. 6–13).

Phonograph demonstrations in colonial Australia

The phonographic demonstrators of the early 1890s encountered an Australasian stage that was not as firmly 'bifurcated' between high- and low-brow, 'legitimate' and 'popular' as in Britain and the United States at this time (Waterhouse, 1995, p. 33). While cultural hierarchy still mattered in a society cross-cut with class tensions, many forms of entertainments were notable for their cross-class appeal. The phonograph performance shared much with the 'wonder show,' a hybrid genre of entertainment that played on the technological sublime, wherein science and technology were used to 'create surprise then pleasure in the spectator whose day-to-day perceptions are shattered and opened to new realms of possibility' (Nadis, 2005, pp. xi–xiv). This magical quality cut across colonial hierarchies, ensuring that the pioneering Australian exhibitors were as comfortable performing in the drawing rooms of the New South Wales governor as at Melbourne's grand Athenæum Theatre and the more sensational Melbourne Waxworks, the first three venues of Douglas Archibald's iconic 1890 phonograph tour (Reese, 2017). The pioneering phonograph performers discussed in this section most commonly performed at such respectable yet democratic venues as town halls, mechanics' institutes and agricultural shows, as they traversed the theatrical networks of the colonies.

Following the invention of an 'improved' phonograph in the late 1880s, a wave of popular demonstrations immediately preceded the wholesale commercialisation of the technology. This was an integral phase in the cultural history of recorded sound. Previous demonstrations had occurred in the 1870s, but as Gustavus Stadler (2010) has emphasised, the content of the 1890s phonograph recordings is what made early demonstrations so culturally meaningful. What was on show was no longer merely 'the quasi-magical fact of sound reproduction.' Recordings carried an ideological and cultural charge, which was heightened by the strong claim on the 'real' that these records made in the minds of their audiences. While the 1890s recordings are often dismissed by historians of recorded sound on the grounds of supposedly low fidelity, the clarity, reality and importance of early phonograph cylinders was obvious to listeners at the time (Stadler, 2010). Specific sounds and recordings subjects mattered. 'Modern' aurality relied on the construction of sound as 'an object of knowledge in its own right: where speech, music, and other human sounds were reduced to special categories of noises that could be studied by the sciences of sound' (Sterne, 2003, p. 43). Early exhibitors of the phonograph guided audiences towards a recognition of the socially significant sounds of their local and wider soundscapes, from the grand tenor of political speech to the quotidian, like the chime of a bell.

The early phonograph was a 'partial machine,' a participatory medium in which meaning was produced through performance (Sterne, 2003, p. 247; Böstrom, 2011). Performances of recorded sound took place in a *fin-de-siècle* context, in which audiences were encouraged to reflect on their shared heritage and its relationship to the restless changes of modernity (Kenney, 1999, p. 26). Technological modernity and the broader rhetoric of the 'modern wonder' pervaded the early medium (Rieger, 2005, pp. 20–50). John M. Picker has noted the distinctly Victorian themes that adhered to the first British performances of the technology that occurred under the auspices of the Thomas Edison's London agent, the eccentric Colonel George Gouraud, from 1888. Recorded sound was both humanised and animated through performances and promotional rhetoric that emphasised the medium's ability to preserve the voice long after the death of the speaker, and to connect far-flung peoples through the intimacy and affectivity of the human voice. Recorded sound collapsed and truncated both space and time in a manner that spoke to particularly modern anxieties. This was a genre that modulated between the middle-class respectability of science and rational recreation and the mystical, sensational atmosphere of the popular stage (Picker, 2003, pp. 110–42). These metropolitan preoccupations were acutely felt in settler societies spatially distant from the imperial centre and obsessed with the historical consciousness outlined above.

Spatially, Lisa Gitelman has underscored the modulation between local and global that adhered to early phonograph performances, noting the peculiar ability of these spectacles to unite a dispersed audience in its very 'recordability' (Gitelman, 2006, p. 34). While her comments relate to the first wave of demonstrations in the 1870s, this quality applied even more in the 1890s, when the durability, mobility and content of phonograph cylinders was central to the medium. 'Early phonograph performances,' Gitelman argues, were local experiences—many audience members probably knew each other—yet they had extralocal significance. Like the exchange columns and wire stories of the local press, phonograph exhibitions pointed outward, toward an impersonal public sphere comprised of similarly private subjects. Audiences in the meanest church basements were recorded just like audiences in the grand concert halls of New York, Chicago and New Orleans. In their very recordability, people were connected. Audience members might imagine themselves as part of an up-to-date, recordable community, an 'us' (as opposed to some imagined and impoverished 'them'), formed with similarly up-to-date recordable people they didn't know (2006, p. 34).

The early phonograph demonstrations were led by the handful of companies that pioneered the technology. By the late 1880s, company representatives strove to spread their technology throughout the world. Thomas Edison had established an American agent, Everett Frazar, in China from

1889 (Lubinski and Steen, 2017, p. 277). Several agents had travelled to India from this time. In Australia and New Zealand, several figures made a convincing claim to be the 'introducers' of the phonograph to the colonial public at this time. The most prominent of these were the New South Wales businessman-turned-politician Charles Garland, the Victorian theatrical impresario James MacMahon, the American-born, Sydney-based scientific lecturer William H.H. Lane and the flamboyant English meteorologist-turned-performer Douglas Archibald.

Each of these pioneering demonstrators established relationships with the Edison representatives in Britain and/or America, all participated in public lectures with the phonograph from early 1890 and each represented himself in the colonial press as the pioneer of the talking machine in the Antipodes. All travelled widely throughout the well-established theatrical networks of the country and together they performed hundreds of times in every sizeable town in the colonies. Their journeys were covered widely in the popular press (Reese, 2019, Ch.3). Of these pioneers, Douglas Archibald was by far the most prolific and popular. From his arrival in Melbourne in early 1890 until his departure some three years later, the restless traveller enjoyed a moderate celebrity across the colonies. I have elsewhere provided a detailed account of Archibald's biography, preoccupations and touring itinerary (Reese, 2017). His performances in Ceylon, the Dutch East Indies (Indonesia) and Singapore have also attracted some recognition as prominent events in local media cultures (Suryadi, 2006; Wickramasinghe, 2014, pp. 81–90; Tofighian, 2017).

A typical phonograph performance involved a short lecture whereby the phonograph impresario would introduce audiences to the scientific principles behind sound recording; then would follow a demonstration of the talking machine. Musical selections would be reproduced and descriptions

Figure 3.1 Sir George Grey (centre) records a message on Douglas Archibald's (left) phonograph, as Auckland mayor J.H. Upton (right) looks on. Auckland, New Zealand, 1891. Reference: AEGA 18982 PC4 1891/4 Archives New Zealand Te Rua Mahara o te Kāwanatanga.

would be offered of the context from which the cylinders were recorded. Political speeches were very popular; this was an era of performative oratory, and the voices of such transnational political icons as William Gladstone and George Grey were central to the appeal of the phonographic lecturers (Scalmer, 2017, Ch.5)

Local dignitaries would also often be invited on stage to commit a few words to posterity. Many adopted a self-consciously historic mode in so doing, and dreams of the unity of English-speaking peoples across the seas—the phonograph as a medium of affective connection across vast distance, an agent of imperial unity—were particularly popular (Reese, 2017). 'Popular prices,' typically ranging from one to three shillings, depending on the seat, ensured an audience that was broadly representative of mainstream colonial society at this time. Women and children were especially encouraged to attend phonograph demonstrations, and many of the lecturers held special matinée shows to facilitate family attendance. While some newspaper reports suggest the presence of Indigenous attendees at some performances, the audiences were predominantly white (Reese, 2019, Ch.3).

Another crucial feature of early Australian phonograph demonstrations was the proto-field recording practice of the performers. Wherever they travelled, the phonographic lecturers made cylinder recordings of significant, notable or interesting sounds. As such, the phonograph tour had an iterative quality. Audiences were encouraged to participate in the global mobility of the performers (Reese, 2017). A rare and unique collection of recordings was central to the appeal of a phonograph lecturer. By 1891, when the Victorian impresario James MacMahon started to compete with Douglas Archibald, he boasted that he possessed 'a collection of phonograms which cannot be duplicated the world over' (*New York Times*, 23 February 1891, p. 8). Systematic recording was the key to an attractive record collection. A New Zealand newspaper noted of James MacMahon and his brother Joseph that:

> ever since they have been in this city they have been collecting the voices of professionals and prominent men and women, and they have now on hand several boxes filled with the voice photographs of actors, actresses, singers, and statesmen.
>
> (*Grey River Argus*, 13 May 1891, p. 4)

Douglas Archibald was also a prolific recordist. Among his collection of field recordings were:

> a London street penny whistle performance, selections by the Melbourne waxworks band, bugle calls, the chimes of the bells at Trinity Church, New Zealand, and a flute and pianoforte duet played in Edison's laboratory in America at the beginning of the present year.
>
> (Maryborough *Advertiser*, 22 September 1890)

He also featured other more 'exotic' recordings, such as Indian 'nautch' songs, declamations in Māori and possibly the words of the Kaurna and Ngarrindjeri residents of Raukkan mission in South Australia (Brisbane *Courier*, 2 September 1892, p. 5; *Poverty Bay Herald*, 1 December 1892, p. 4; Adelaide *Advertiser*, 27 November 1890). Audiences seem to have been more interested in more familiar soundscapes; however, the excitement of recognising local sounds helped to highlight the reality of the science of recording, demonstrating that the wondrous new technology had a place in local life. Archibald's choice of subjects also included ambient sounds, elements drawn from the everyday texture of his acoustic environment. Take, for example, Archibald's description of his recording practice in the city of Napier on New Zealand's North Island: 'the bagpipes have been waking the echoes of the night and early morning. Professor Archibald could not sleep for the noise, and so took two records of bagpipe music' (*Poverty Bay Herald*, 2 February 1891, p. 2).

Bells and the colonial soundscape

Bells were a strikingly common choice for field recording by the early exhibitors. The ubiquity of the bell in the Australian environment provides a representative case study of a familiar, celebrated environmental sound that was used by the phonograph demonstrators to highlight the affective elements of the colonial soundscape. Douglas Archibald even used a bell analogy to describe the mechanism of the ear: 'In the ear these movements cause certain bones to vibrate which are attached to nerve fibres, acting like bell ropes upon the brain' (Launceston *Colonist*, 15 November 1890, p. 17). Bells were one of the many imported structures by which settlers strove to impose order on Indigenous space. They rightly occupy a prominent space in histories of sound, characterised by Alain Corbin's iconic treatment of the construction and maintenance of acoustic community (Corbin, 1998, Ch.4). While the sonic habitus that Corbin describes was specific to the communities surveyed, bells were constitutive of social order, authority and ceremony in many other nineteenth-century communities (Smith, 2001, 9, p. 58).

In colonial Australia too, bells long functioned as the 'metronome[s] of the local community' (Davison, 1993, p. 33). The construction of church and civic belfries was a priority for early colonists. By the 1850s, urban planners and architects were noting that bells were a common feature of the colonial landscape (Davison, 1993, p. 79). Bells of all kinds were ubiquitous in Melbourne by 1890 (Belich, 2009, 357). As well as the post office and church bells, urban life was punctuated by the clang of the auctioneer's handbell, the handbells of hawkers and travelling salespeople advertising their presence, the clangour of bullock teams as they dragged drays of goods to port and market and (from the 1880s) the signals of Melbourne's iconic trams. In 1845, the City Council passed a by-law regulating the ringing of bells on the streets, and routinely declined citizens' applications to act as official Council bellmen from the 1860s through to the 1910s (Brown-May, 1998, p. 81). There were too many bells on the streets already, the town clerk thought.

There is ample evidence that colonial citizens oriented themselves by the bells of the city. In 1884, journalist and urban explorer John Stanley James, better known as the 'Vagabond,' called for some regulation of the sound-scape. As he wrote in 1884, 'In this country where everyman has a watch and every house two or three clocks, I think church bells should not be allowed, unless musical' (Davison, 1993, p. 65). In Fergus Hume's sensational 1886 novel *The Mystery of a Hansom Cab*, witnesses in a Melbourne murder case are able to locate themselves accurately in time throughout the night, across the city, by the striking of the post office clock on Bourke Street (Hume, 2012, p. 212). As late as 1915, a Melbourne workingman wrote to the Town Clerk, complaining that the Town Hall clock was always a little bit behind time. This was a problem because his employers marked time according to the chimes of the Town Hall clock. To this man's annoyance, when his fore-man rang the six o'clock bell to dismiss the workers at the end of the work-day, he would routinely be late for his train. The railway's time was more punctual than that of his factory (Davison, 1993, pp. 41 and 46). Bells were unstable yet omnipresent arbiters of public and private time.

The supply of bells from British foundries provides a valuable 'export study' of the spread of common soundmarks across the British world (Ban-field, 2007). Civic bells were heavy, expensive and rare. They required great expertise and cost to cast, transport and install, and their movement around the world is indicative of the spread of British sonic preferences. The ven-erable Whitechapel foundry of Mears and Stainbank, for instance, was responsible for distributing a common type of religious sound throughout the British Empire. The foundry's 1885 catalogue notes that they had sup-plied peals of bells to churches and cathedrals in India, Hong Kong, South Africa, Jamaica, Trinidad and Canada. Their Australian clients included congregations in the colonial capitals of Melbourne, Sydney and Hobart as well as the Victorian regional centres of Geelong, Ballarat and Sandhurst (Whitechapel Bell Foundry, 1885, pp. 8–13 and 41–4).

By 1890, there were three sets of cathedral bells in Melbourne: the six bells of St. James' 'Old Cathedral' hung in 1852, the eight bells of St. Patrick's hung in 1868 and the 13 bells of the central St. Paul's, first heard in 1889. In the boom years of the 1870s, the bells of St. Patrick's Catholic cathedral in Fitzroy could be heard from as far away as Heidelberg, some ten kilometres away, then on the north-eastern bush fringe of the city. The City Council provided a salary to a team of ringers to ring the bells of St. Paul's every Sunday and on important civic occasions. At his New Year's Day service at St. Paul's in 1890, a Melbourne bishop waxed lyrical about the importance of bells in colonial society. Bells, he stated, 'mingled themselves with all the greatest and most important events of life from the cradle to the grave' (Pettet and Doggett, 2001, pp. 5–17). By now, talk of Federation was in the air, and the Bishop claimed that civic ceremonies, led by bells, 'tended in a measure to bring about what, as patriotic citizens, they desired to witness—Australian Federation' (Pettet and Doggett, 2001, p. 17).

The phonographic performers were keen to capitalise on this slew of cultural associations. Alongside his numerous musical items, William Lane's records included the following descriptive specialties and soundscape recordings: 'imitations of English birds,' the calls of Australian birds, including the kookaburra, and recordings of local clock bells (Sydney *Evening News*, 29 October 1890, p. 1). Douglas Archibald was an even more prolific recordist of local and famous bells on his phonograph tour. This was a common strategy that he imported wholesale from his initial tours across England in 1888–1889. In Sunderland, great 'amusement was caused by the reproduction of the announcements of sales by the town criers of Spalding and Leamington, their voices mingling naturally with the sounds of the bells which they carried' (Sunderland *Daily Echo*, 20 September 1889, p. 3). Archibald did the same in Lancaster, where the voice and bell of Thomas Dawson, the local bellman, was 'reproduced with wonderful accuracy' (Lancaster *Gazette*, 13 July 1889).

In Australia, Archibald regularly demonstrated the sounds of church bells from Auckland (Maryborough *Advertiser*, 22 September 1890). More common were recordings of local town criers. In Ballarat, the audience delighted at a record:

> by J. Wood, the Bellman, who rang his bell into the receiver, and then announced a sale to be held by Messrs Brokenshire and Coltman on Tuesday next. An error in the date, corrected in the next breath, was most faithfully reproduced, to the amusement and delight of the audience.
>
> (Ballarat *Star*, 24 September 1890, p. 4)

In Western Australia, he made a recording of Tommy Hopkins, the town crier in the port city of Fremantle:

> which was so realistic that no one who has heard the celebrity, whose voice Mr. Archibald has immortalised, could fail to recognise him. The ringing of the bell was particularly realistic; and it was difficult to realise that the clanging accompaniment to the announcement of the auction emanated from the machine.
>
> (Geraldton *Victorian Express*, 28 August 1891, p. 5)

Archibald also collected bell sounds as he travelled widely across South and Southeast Asia. For instance, in Bombay, he scaled the Rajabai Tower to record the sound of its famous bells. As a review in Singapore noted of a performance in May 1892, '[t]he big bells in the Rajabai Tower, Bombay, gave a tremendous clang, too soon over to be more than suggestive of the real sound. On the other hand, the Bellman and Crier of Perth was splendidly rendered' (Singapore *Free Press*, 6 May 1892, p. 3). Reviews of these bell recordings commonly emphasised the shock of recognition, the delight of audiences in hearing their local soundmarks reframed onstage and the hilarity and surprise that came with this. Given that town criers were still a common presence in Australian cities at this time, albeit one associated with the old world, the village and the community—all nostalgic presences in settler modernity—the moment of recognition engendered by these recordings was one that served to highlight a crucial feature of the colonial soundscape (Doggett, 2012).

Conclusion: reframing colonial soundscapes

This essay has demonstrated the subtle ways in which the recording practice of early Australian phonograph demonstrations could contribute to a dominant colonial soundscape during a period of self-conscious colonial modernity and mobility. The selection and recontextualisation of colonial soundmarks underscores the deep imposition of European sound-making traditions onto Indigenous spaces. This practice has deeper implications. The supplanting of Aboriginal sound-worlds with a British urban soundscape ideal was one ingredient in the broader processes of settler dispossession. The fact that the phonograph demonstrators could move seamlessly through very different colonial spaces and British enclaves suggests that a common sonic ideal underpinned their activities. Given the importance of audiences in the construction of the meanings of these early 'partial machines,' these moments of recognition highlight the importance of everyday European sounds in the construction of settler place attachment. Recorded sound simultaneously produced and mediated settler place attachment. The fact that this settler colonial soundscape could be rendered audible through such a fleeting and unusual genre of performance as the phonograph demonstration serves as a valuable demonstration of the fragility and subtlety of the historical soundscape and the close reading of historical evidence required to reconstruct such a world.

My case study of bells represents merely one kind of European sound that was part of the imposition and celebration of a settler auditory ideal on Antipodean space. Other possible subjects include urban or pastoral soundscapes, musical cultures and traditions of oratory and language. As such, this study demonstrates one of the ways in which settler colonial space was also made through sound. As the example of the phonograph demonstrations demonstrates, the trans-imperial flow of technology could be deployed in service of the spatialising process of settler colonialism. The creation and privileging of everyday soundscapes reflected normative European attitudes and dispositions towards how the world ought to sound. On the one hand, recorded sound allowed settlers to familiarise or appropriate their surroundings; on the other, it contributed to highlight the surroundings' racial difference. A vibrant tradition of Indigenous sound-making has long provided a counterpoint to the dominant settler soundscape outlined herein

(Thomas, 2007). To move towards a postcolonial soundscape is to strive to recognise the deep entanglement of modernity, place attachment and the colonial sensorium, and to listen more deeply for voices that were marginalised by the clangour of the settler state.

References

Anderson, W. (2005) *The Cultivation of Whiteness: Science, Health and Racial Destiny in Australia*. Melbourne: Melbourne University Press.
Atkinson, A. (2014) *The Europeans in Australia*, Vol. 3. Sydney: UNSW Press.
Ballantyne, T. and A. Burton. (2005) Introduction: Bodies, Empires, and World Histories. In: Ballantyne, T. and A. Burton. (eds.) *Bodies in Contact: Rethinking Colonial Encounters in World History*. Durham: Duke University Press, pp. 1–15.
Ballantyne, T. and A. Burton (2009) Introduction: The Politics of Intimacy in an Age of Empire. In: Ballantyne, T. and A. Burton (eds.) *Moving Subjects: Gender, Mobility, and Intimacy in an Age of Global Empire*. Urbana: University of Illinois Press, pp. 1–28.
Bandt, R., M. Duffy and D. MacKinnon (eds.) (2007) *Hearing Places: Sound Place Time Culture*. Newcastle-Upon-Tyne: Cambridge Scholars Publishing.
Banfield, S. (2007) Towards A History of Music in the British Empire: Three Export Studies. In: Darian-Smith, K., P. Grimshaw and S. Macintyre (eds.) *Britishness Abroad: Transnational Movements and Imperial Cultures*. Melbourne: Melbourne University Press, pp. 63–89.
Banivanua Mar, T. and P. Edmonds (2010) Introduction: Making Space in Settler Colonies. In: Banivanua Mar, T. and P. Edmonds (eds.) *Making Settler Colonial Space: Perspectives on Race, Place and Identity*. Basingstoke and New York: Palgrave Macmillan, pp. 1–24.
Belich, J. (2009) *Replenishing the Earth: The Settler Revolution and the Rise of the Anglo-World, 1783–1939*. Oxford and New York: Oxford University Press.
Bellanta, M. (2012a) *Larrikins: A History*. Brisbane: University of Queensland Press.
Bellanta, M. (2012b) Naughty and Gay? Revisiting the Nineties in the Australian Colonies. *History Australia*, 9(1), 136–54.
Bellanta, M. (2012c) Australian Masculinities and Popular Song: The Songs of Sentimental Blokes 1900–1930s. *Australian Historical Studies*, 43(3), 412–28.
Bellanta, M. (2013) Rethinking the 1890s. In: Bashford, A. and S. Macintyre (eds.) *The Cambridge History of Australia*. Cambridge and New York: Cambridge University Press, pp. 218–41.
Bijsterveld, K. (2013) Introduction. In: Bijsterveld, K. (ed.) *Soundscapes of the Urban Past. Staged Sound as Mediated Cultural Heritage*. Bielefeld: Transcript, pp. 11–28.
Blainey, G. (2001) *The Tyranny of Distance: How Distance Shaped Australia's History*. 21st Century ed. Sydney: Pan MacMillan.
Böstrom, M. (2011) Creating Audiences, Making Participants: The Cylinder Phonograph in Ethnographic Fieldwork. In: Ekström, A. et al. (eds.) *History of Participatory Media: Politics and Publics, 1750–2000*. New York: Routledge, pp. 49–62.
Briggs, A. (1963/1990) *Victorian Cities*. London: Penguin.
Brown-May, A. (1998) *Melbourne Street Life: The Itinerary of Our Days*. Melbourne: Australian Scholarly/Arcadia.

Collins, D. (2006) Acoustic Journeys: Exploration and the Search for an Aural History of Australia. *Australian Historical Studies*, 37(128), 1–17.

Collins, D. (2011) The "Voice" of Nature? Kookaburras, Culture and Australian Sound. *Journal of Australian Studies*, 35(3), 281–95.

Corbin, A. (1998) *Village Bells: Sound and Meaning in the 19th-Century French Countryside*. Translated by M. Thom. New York: Columbia University Press.

Davison, G. (1993) *The Unforgiving Minute: How Australia Learned to Tell the Time*. Melbourne: Oxford University Press.

Davison, G. (1995) Australia: The First Suburban Nation? *Journal of Urban History*, 22(1), 40–74.

Davison, G. (2001) The European City in Australia. *Journal of Urban History*, 27(6), 779–93.

Davison, G., J.W. McCarty, J.W. and A. McLeary (eds.) (1987) People Moving. In: *Australians, 1888*. Sydney: Fairfax, Syme & Weldon, pp. 228–53.

Denney, P. (2012) Picturesque Farming: The Sound of "Happy Britannia" in Colonial Australia. *Cultural Studies Review*, 18(3), 85–108.

Doggett, A. (2012) Crying in the Colonies: The Bellmen of Early Australia. *Journal of Australian Colonial History*, 14, 49–68.

Edmonds, P. (2010) *Urbanizing Frontiers: Indigenous Peoples and Settlers in 19th-century Pacific Rim Cities*. Vancouver: UBC Press.

Erlmann, V. (2004) But What of the Ethnographic Ear? Anthropology, Sound, and the Senses. In: Erlmann, V. (ed.) *Hearing Cultures: Essays on Sound, Listening and Modernity*. Oxford and New York: Berg, pp. 1–20.

Frost, L. (1991) *The New Urban Frontier: Urbanisation and City-Building in Australasia and the American West*. Sydney: New South Wales University Press.

Gitelman, L. (2006) *Always Already New: Media, History, and the Data of Culture*. Cambridge and London: MIT Press.

Griffiths, T. (1996) *Hunters and Collectors: The Antiquarian Imagination in Australia*. Cambridge and Melbourne: Cambridge University Press.

Hamer, D. (1990) *New Towns in the New World: Images and Perceptions of the Nineteenth-Century Urban Frontier*. New York: Columbia University Press.

Harper, M. (2000) Sensuality in Sandshoes: Representations of the Bush in the Walking and Writing of John Le Gay Brereton and Percy Grainger. *Australian Historical Studies*, 31(115), 287–303.

Harris, A. (2014) Hearing Aboriginal Music Making in Non-Indigenous Accounts of the Bush from the Mid-Twentieth Century. In: Harris, A. (ed.) *Circulating Cultures: Exchanges of Australian Indigenous Music, Dance and Media*. Canberra: ANU E-Press, pp. 73–97.

Hirst, J. (2000) *The Sentimental Nation: The Making of the Australian Commonwealth*. Oxford and New York: Oxford University Press.

Hume, F. (2012) *The Mystery of a Hansom Cab*. Melbourne: Text Classics.

Kelly, V. (2009) *The Empire Actors: Stars of Australasian Costume Drama, 1890s–1920s*. Sydney: Currency Press.

Kenney, W.H. (1999) *Recorded Music in American Life: The Phonograph and Popular Memory, 1890–1945*. New York and Oxford: Oxford University Press.

Kenny, N. (2014) *The Feel of the City: Experiences of Urban Transformation*. Toronto and London: University of Toronto Press.

Keyes, S. (2009) "Like a Roaring Lion": The Overland Trail as a Sonic Conquest. *Journal of American History*, 96(1), 19–43.

Lake, M. and H. Reynolds (2008) *Drawing the Global Colour Line: White Men's Countries and the International Challenge of Racial Equality.* Cambridge and New York: Cambridge University Press.

Lubinski, C. and A. Steen (2017) Traveling Entrepreneurs, Traveling Sounds: The Early Gramophone Business in India and China. *Itinerario,* 41(2), 275–303.

Magee, G.B. and A.S. Thompson (2010) *Empire and Globalisation: Networks of People, Goods and Capital in the British World, c.1850–1914.* Cambridge and New York: Cambridge University Press.

Matthews, J.J. (2005) *Dance Hall & Picture Palace: Sydney's Romance with Modernity.* Sydney: Currency Press.

Meaney, N. (2001) Britishness and Australian Identity: The Problem of Nationalism in Australian History and Historiography. *Australian Historical Studies,* 32(116), 76–90.

Minchinton, B. (2020) Female Crews: Sex Workers in Nineteenth-Century Melbourne. *History Australia,* 17(2), 346–64.

Nadis, F. (2005) *Wonder Shows: Performing Science, Magic, and Religion in America.* New Brunswick and London: Rutgers University Press.

O'Hanlon, S. (2014) A Little Bit of Europe in Australia: Jews, Immigrants, Flats and Urban and Cultural Change in Melbourne, c.1935–1975. *History Australia,* 11(3), 116–33.

Pettet, H. and A. Doggett (2001) *The Bells are Ringing! A Celebration of Melbourne Life through the Story of Her Bells.* Melbourne: Helen Pettet and Anne Doggett.

Picker, J.M. (2003) *Victorian Soundscapes.* Oxford: Oxford University Press.

Piper, A. (2015) Women's Work: The Professionalisation and Policing of Fortune-Telling in Australia. *Labour History,* 108, 37–52.

Radano, R. and T. Olaniyan (2016) Hearing Empire—Imperial Listening. In Radano, R. and T. Olaniyan (eds.) *Audible Empire: Music, Global Politics, Critique.* Durham: Duke University Press, pp. 1–22.

Rees, Y. (2017) Reading Australian Modernity: Unsettled Settlers and Cultures of Mobility. *History Compass,* 15(3), 1–13.

Reese, H. (2017) "The World Wanderings of a Voice": Exhibiting the Cylinder Phonograph in Australasia. In: Damousi, J. and P. Hamilton (eds.) *A Cultural History of Sound, Memory and the Senses.* New York and London: Routledge, pp. 25–39.

Reese, H. (2019) *Colonial Soundscapes: A Cultural History of Sound Recording in Australia, 1880–1930.* Doctoral dissertation, University of Melbourne.

Rhook, N. (2014) Listen to Nodes of Empire: Speech and Whiteness in Victorian Hawker's License Courts. *Journal of Colonialism and Colonial History,* 15(2), 1–15.

Rhook, N. (2015) "The Chief Chinese Interpreter" Charles Hodges: Mapping the Aurality of Race and Governance in Colonial Melbourne. *Postcolonial Studies,* 18(1), 1–18.

Richards, F. (ed.) (2007) *The Soundscapes of Australia: Music, Place and Spirituality.* Aldershot: Ashgate.

Rieger, B. (2005) *Technology and the Culture of Modernity in Britain and Germany, 1890–1945.* Cambridge and New York: Cambridge University Press.

Rotter, A.J. (2011) Empires of the Senses: How Seeing, Hearing, Smelling, Tasting, and Touching Shaped Imperial Encounters. *Diplomatic History,* 35(1), 3–19.

Scalmer, S. (2017) *On the Stump: Campaign Oratory and Democracy in the United States, Britain, and Australia.* Philadelphia: Temple University Press.

Smith, M.M. (2001) *Listening to Nineteenth-Century America*. Chapel Hill and London: University of North Carolina Press.

Stadler, G. (2010) Never Heard Such a Thing: Lynching and Phonographic Modernity. *Social Text*, 28(1), 87–105.

Sterne, J. (2003) *The Audible Past: Cultural Origins of Sound Reproduction*. Durham and London: Duke University Press.

Suryadi (2006) The "Talking Machine" Comes to the Dutch East Indies: The Arrival of Western Media Technology in Southeast Asia. *Bijdragen tot de Taal-, Land- en Volkenkunde*, 162(2/3), 269–305.

Swain, S. (1985) The Poor People of Melbourne. In: Davison, G., D. Dunstan and C. McConville (eds.) *The Outcasts of Melbourne: Essays in Social History*. Sydney: Allen and Unwin, pp. 91–112.

Thomas, M. (2007) The Rush to Record: Transmitting the Sound of Aboriginal Culture. *Journal of Australian Studies*, 31(90), 107–21.

Tofighian, N. (2017) Watching the Astonishment of the Native: Early Audio-visual Technology and Colonial Discourse. *Early Popular Visual Culture*, 15(1), 26–43.

Vernon, J. (2016). The History of Britain is Dead: Long Live a Global History of Britain. *History Australia*, 13(1), 19–34.

Waterhouse, R. (1995) *Private Pleasures, Public Leisure: A History of Australian Popular Culture since 1788*. Melbourne: Longman.

White, R. (1981) *Inventing Australia: Images and Identity 1688–1980*. Sydney and London: George Allen & Unwin.

Whitechapel Bell Foundry (1885) *Catalogue of Peals and Bells from the Foundry*. London: Mears & Stainbank.

Wickramasinghe, N. (2014) *Metallic Modern: Everyday Machines in Colonial Sri Lanka*. New York and Oxford: Berghahn.

Wittmann, M.W. (2010) *Empire of Culture: U.S. Entertainers and the Making of the Pacific Circuit, 1850–1890*. PhD Thesis, University of Michigan.

Wolfe, P. (2006) Settler Colonialism and the Elimination of the Native. *Journal of Genocide Research*, 8(4), 387–409.

Part II

Repertoires, auditory practices and the shaping of new listening identities

4 Portugal and mechanical music in the early phonographic era

An intermedial approach

João Silva

This chapter studies mechanical music in Portugal and how it impacted the circulation of repertoires in the early phonographic era. Mechanical music comprises recorded sound and mechanical instruments such as the player piano, innovations that transformed the ways people interacted with music in the late nineteenth century. These goods reflect the penetration of mass-produced objects in the domestic space where Victorian intimacy ruled. People adjusted player mechanisms to their parlour piano and bought phonographs and gramophones, as music rolls, discs, and cylinders became part of everyday life. Portugal is an interesting case study because it illustrates how a small rural nation incorporated mechanical music into the daily lives of urban audiences, which contrasts with large industrialized countries, and shows how pliable mechanical music was in penetrating different contexts (Losa, 2013). Since Portugal lacked record pressing facilities and had one small manufacturer of player pianos and music rolls, its market depended on imported products. As in many places, music drawn from operettas, *zarzuelas*, and musical revues dominated the Portuguese stages and set the scene for an articulated system of musical commodities as piano rolls, cylinders, and discs added to the sheet music in making these repertoires ubiquitous (Silva, 2016).

The complex articulation between local agents and foreign ventures in the early phonographic period resonates with other countries. Recording technicians from multinational companies captured local artists while local tinkerers played a fundamental role in making mechanical music fashionable. This dialectic was crucial to establish what would become a transnational market for mechanical music. Products emanated from the theatre and crossed boundaries between the stage, the street, the café, and the home. Librettos, postcards, and sheet music extended the influence of the stage show and penetrated other territories. Discs, cylinders, and music rolls widened the scope of these goods and reinforced the presence of theatrical music in everyday life. Moreover, they reconfigured the constellation of music commodities throughout the Westernised World.

This chapter tries to understand mechanical music through the lens of intermediality, the way different media interconnect and articulate.

DOI: 10.4324/9781003006497-7

Multimedia stage shows were fragmented in products storing different types of information as the processes of 'remediation' increased and enhanced their appeal to a wide range of everyday situations. I will present *Fado do 31* as a case study for remediation. This song, one of the hits of the 1913 revue *O 31*, is still performed today. *Fado do 31* generated a set of commodities in Portugal and Spain, which comprised sheet music, sound recordings, and music rolls. These goods demonstrate the piece's success and contributed to its ubiquity.

Mechanical music in Portugal at the dawn of the twentieth century

> With an audience comprising doctors, jurisconsults, and journalists, Monteiro de Souza started Edison's phonograph.[1] The machine began by introducing itself and greeting the audience. We heard Pinheiro Chagas praising Edison's great invention, and listened to: the royal anthem and a military march performed by the wind band of the Regiment of Artillery n.º 1, a bugle concerto recorded in London, a part of *Carmen* by Francisco de Andrade in a London theatre, and two pieces of the opera *Flavia*, by the maestro Sauvinet accompanying himself on piano.[2] These phonograms were reproduced with the utmost clarity and sufficient sharpness to be appreciated through direct listening, *i.e.*, through small rubber ear tubes.
>
> ('Thomaz Edison', 1889, p. 228)

This account of a demonstration of Edison's phonograph in Portugal focuses on repertoire and sound quality. Capturing the sound waves of performances and reproducing them in different places and times embodied sonic modernity and reshaped the music business. The Portuguese listened to Caruso in their parlours without him ever performing in the country. This commodification of music intensified toward the end of the nineteenth century as fixed sounds became tradable (Scott, 2008; Chion, 2016). From then on, everyday life integrated local and transnational genres that circulated effortlessly. Theatrical shows, sheet music, sound recordings, and piano rolls coexisted and infiltrated different places, linking stages, streets, and homes. The ubiquity of music in everyday life transformed the way people musicked as multinational companies and local enterprises established a market for sound recordings. A new set of competing technologies, strategies, and repertoires became the staple of everyday life. However, making mechanical music profitable in a small-scale market such as Portugal followed a path that required inventiveness and combined novelty with firmly established models.

The magician Bargeon de Viverols carried out the first public demonstrations of the 'talking phonograph' in the intermissions of the plays performed at Lisbon's Teatro da Trindade in 1879 ('Carteira dos theatros', 1879, p. 1). He showed the machine in Spain during the same period, which illustrates the proximity of the Iberian entertainment circuits (Moreda Rodríguez, personal communication August 2020). However, a few years went by before these demonstrations gave way to a steady market created by multinational companies, such as The Gramophone Company and Pathé, and Portuguese enthusiasts.

Francisco Santos Diniz traded in mechanical instruments, bicycles, and clocks. Two phonographic patents were granted to him between 1898 and 1902, covering his brand Audiophone and an improvement on the gramophone (Losa and Belchior, 2010, p. 7). Furthermore, Diniz sold his talking machine 'O Gigante' in his downtown Lisbon store alongside flat records by the Gramophone Company and the German-based Odeon. Moreover, he recorded cylinders of prominent performers. A few years after the death of his son Alberto in 1903, Diniz liquidated his company. Joaquim Duarte Ferreira, an early enthusiast, filed a patent to make and to record discs and cylinders in 1904. The company Pinto & Meirelles traded in wax cylinders and contested Ferreira's application, a move that hampered the Portuguese industry and made local ventures dependent on foreign production facilities for the next 50 years. The introduction of mechanical organs and pianos in Portugal helped to set the stage to a small market for mechanical music. Music from operas and operettas played by organ grinders infiltrated the local soundscape while prestigious piano stores began trading in player mechanisms. Around 1907, entrepreneur Abel Ferreira da Silva established a small factory to build mechanical instruments and punch rolls in Oporto.

The major international companies trading in Portugal were The Gramophone Company and Pathé. They shared a similar strategy, which relied on vertical integration. However, their products were different. The Gramophone Company worked under Emile Berliner's patents and traded on gramophones and discs. Pathé operated under Edison's patents and sold phonographs, gramophones, flat records, and cylinders. Thus, their recordings were unplayable in the competitor's machines. This lack of technological standardisation fed rival catalogues that featured the same performers and repertoire.

The British-based Gramophone Company secured a dominant role by creating subsidiary companies and marketing branches in Germany, Italy, France, Russia, Austria-Hungary, and Australia. By 1899, Alfred Clark, a former American associate of Edison, established the Compagnie Française du Gramophone in Paris, which worked as a sales agency for Gramophone. As its manager and partial owner, he became responsible for recording music from the places the company oversaw, including Portugal. Toward the end of 1903, the Compagnie Française du Gramophone relied on local agents, like Santos Diniz and Carlos Calderon (in Lisbon) and Artur Barbedo (in Oporto). Later, they opened a store in Lisbon's commercial district that traded exclusively in its products and carried out an aggressive advertising campaign. However, the shop closed in 1906 as Francesco Stella became the local agent for the company (Companhia Franceza do Gramophone, 1910).

The earliest Portuguese discs for The Gramophone Company were cut in Oporto between late October and early November 1900 and predate the company's establishment in the country. The American technician William Sinkler Darby led an expedition that resulted in 70 pressings of local artists, including wind bands, fados, traditional songs, pieces from operettas and revues, and piano solos (Belchior, 2010, p. 15). Despite the absence of reliable information about Gramophone's local recordings between this journey and 1905, Alfred Clark informed the mother company that 'of the discs sold in Portugal about two-fifths are Italian, two-fifths Spanish, and one-fifth Portuguese' (Clark, 1904). Since most Italian records featured opera, this letter shows that the talking machines aimed at the well-to-do who bought more 'sophisticated' repertoires. Later, the company advertised the 'popular gramophone', an affordable player that became accessible to more people as music from revues, *zarzuelas*, and operettas dominated the Portuguese catalogues. Nevertheless, phonographic products were still expensive for most Portuguese.

Paris incarnated modernity and cosmopolitanism throughout Europe and Pathé was its phonographic equivalent. The French-based company operated in Portugal as early as 1906 keeping a store in Oporto and an office in Lisbon. It traded in a variety of goods, such as phonographs, gramophones, blank and recorded cylinders, and parts and accessories for their machines. Moreover, Pathé ran a recording room in the Oporto premises to capture and replicate its local pieces. The company sold standard and large cylinders (probably the Salon or Stentor), and discs. However, despite the reliance of Pathé on cylinders, flat records dominated the Portuguese market from an early stage.

Smaller local traders relied on German companies to record their Portuguese catalogues. These tendencies contrast with Spain where, apart from Odeon, there was an overwhelming presence of British and French companies, suggesting that large-scale markets concentrated the attention of the majors, leaving smaller countries more open to other players. The entrepreneur José Castelo Branco created the record label Simplex at the beginning of the twentieth century, evidencing this tendency. He owned a store in Lisbon and imported Dutch bicycles; the Sociedade Fabricante de Discos – Disco Simplex C. B. began to advertise discs and talking machines in 1905. In November 1909, Castelo Branco gave away 125 talking machines as part of an advertising campaign (*Illustração portugueza*, 25 October 1909). He understood that people would buy his records if they had the devices to play them.

The store sold discs by the local Simplex and the German Odeon, Beka, and Homophon. Since Portugal depended on imported goods and technicians, local traders faced severe constraints, which fostered the establishment of symbiotic relationships between small ventures and foreign companies.

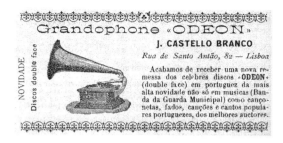

Figure 4.1 Advertisement for the store run by José Castelo Branco, *Tiro e Sport*, 15 December 1905, p. 9 (Hemeroteca Municipal de Lisboa).

Local dealers played a fundamental role in selecting which music to record, and people like Castelo Branco profited from the shared interests between Portuguese and foreign businesses.

Competitors issued the same performers and songs as artists and repertoires overlapped, since exclusivity was unusual in a period that preceded technological standardisation. The core of the Portuguese business comprised music that was familiar to the audience as prominent artists recorded popular hits, showing the importance of the stage for the phonographic industry. Entrepreneurs hired famous performers while technicians looked for singers whose voices could record well, as technical limitations privileged the ability to project sound clearly and an efficient delivery over a trained singing voice. 'Only full, even voices of sustained power could be utilised, and all nuances, such as pianissimo effects, were omitted' (Gaisberg, 1942, p. 85). Most artists were famous actors who recorded popular songs associated with their stage performances.

Recording famous people from the music theatre was a pervasive tendency in early phonography (Gronow and Englund, 2007). Portuguese and Brazilian catalogues reflect the weight of the popular stage and evidence an intense transatlantic relationship. In Portugal, companies concentrated on issuing compositions from operettas, *zarzuelas*, and musical revues. *Cançonetas* performed by comic actors followed these songs. Most *cançonetas* were loose narrative pieces that commented on everyday life. They filled set changes and became so popular that advertisements promoted them alongside the main play. People like Baptista Diniz wrote *cançonetas* for recording purposes, such as the songs included in the 1908 catalogue of the Companhia Francesa do Gramophone (Companhia Franceza do Gramophone, 1908). A large number of local fados and traditional songs feature extensively in catalogues. At the time, 'fado' designated varied repertoires that spanned from urban popular songs to rural pieces. Some recordings used Portuguese guitars to assert their authenticity. Local song collectors published songbooks aimed at the bourgeois parlour. These transcriptions, usually for voice and piano, became a prominent source for recording traditional music. Wind bands cut overtures, dances, marches, and anthems. In some cases, they played arrangements of theatrical songs. The local repertoires also included comic monologues and sketches, which were sometimes called 'eccentric'.

In short, the theatrical song prevailed in the Portuguese entertainment market as its ubiquity traversed boundaries between spaces, classes, people, and machines. Issuing hits from stage productions in several formats and media paralleled many countries (Scott, 2008). Cosmopolitan repertoires, like the French operetta, coexisted with genres prized by the Portuguese, such as fado, *maxixe*, and *vira*. Bolter and Grusin developed a remediation theory, showing the ways different media interact in the digital world (Bolter and Grusin, 2000). Despite focusing on 'new' media at the end of the twentieth century, their ideas help to illuminate the media ecology of the early phonographic period. Mechanical music transformed the cultural landscape of the late nineteenth century by bringing in media that 'are always introduced into a pattern of tension created by the coexistence of old and new' (Marvin, 1988, p. 8). This disruption is visible when studying the different embodiments of commodified music, since sound recordings and music rolls coexisted with sheet music and frequently drew from it.

Remediation followed several paths to reach a wider audience. The same piece of music was performed in the theatre, played at home during a *soirée*, integrated into the city's soundscape by an organ grinder, and heard in the bandstands on Sunday afternoon concerts. Efficient remediation transformed the musical materials significantly to amplify the music's impact across media. Furthermore, 'because all mediations are both real and mediations of the real, remediation can also be understood as a process of reforming reality as well' (Bolter and Grusin, 2000, p. 56).

Intermediality, technology, and commodified music

The notion of intertextuality emerged from the work of literary theorists whose thought was influenced by structuralism. Kristeva poses the '"literary word" as an intersection of textual surfaces rather than a point (a fixed meaning), as a dialogue among several writings: that of the writer, the addressee (or the character), and the contemporary or earlier cultural context' (Kristeva, 1980, p. 65). This formulation ascribes dynamism to a strict structuralist approach and indicates that texts are shaped by a plural relationship with other texts, which makes meaning fleeting and provisional. Therefore, capturing 'absolute meaning' is a fiction since meaning is relational and depends on the variable articulation between texts. Kristeva's concept was expanded by Gérard Genette, who coined the term 'transtextuality' (Genette, 1997). Intertextuality became 'the relation of co-presence between two or more texts, that is, the effective presence of one text in another which takes place by means of plagiarism, quotation or allusion' (Alfaro,

1996, p. 280). However, transtextuality is not limited to the free circulation of texts. Serge Lacasse coined the term 'transphonography' to describe the connection between sound recordings and focused on the relationships between recorded sounds, which can be enlightening when studying music based on sampling (Lacasse, 2010). However, the constellation of theatrical commodities in the early twentieth century comprises much more than sounds. Texts, costumes, photographs, and sheet music interacted with new goods such as sound recordings and piano rolls. Using transphonography, a theory developed when disembodied sound dominated, to address the early phonographic period obfuscates relevant aspects of intermediality.

Therefore, I will focus on intermediality to highlight the variety of media through which music became part of everyday life and how they intersect a range of skills and materials. Intertextuality 'acknowledges the circulation and interplay of meaning across numerous signifying practices (music, literature, film, the visual arts and so on)' (Scott, 2009, p. 10). Tangible objects that 'exist in time and space' contain immaterial sounds and 'may function as personal or collective memory objects', embedding materiality in the ways people relate to phonography (Roy, 2015, p. 142). The stage show is a successful embodiment of modernity and intermediality since it comprises texts, visual arts, dance, music, and sometimes film. Moreover, theatricalising these shows linked and transformed different practices and media since several forms of expression participate in the construction of its meaning (Wolf, 1999, p. 1; Kattenbelt, 2006). With the industrialisation of the late nineteenth-century production of leisure, the stage show became 'a multilayered communication medium that connected to other media' (Scott, 2019, p. 191). Grosch and Stahrenberg argue that this 'symbiotic mesh' allowed for products associated with the musical theatre to transcend spatial and social boundaries, segmenting this process in primary, secondary, and tertiary media (2014, pp. 187–200). They pose the stage show as the primary medium, followed by secondary media such as sheet music and broadsheets, and by tertiary media, recorded music. A chain of material objects that radiates from the stage but fosters different forms of engagement by audiences was in place.

This threefold segmentation is insightful, but boundaries were porous and flexible, which created multiple access points to the products associated with the popular theatre. Naturally, theatrical commodities emanate from stage performance. However, their distribution was not straightforward. New spaces opened in small towns, welcoming professional touring companies during the summer and amateur companies for the rest of the year. These venues evidence how different agents took part in disseminating the plays. Lisbon and Oporto concentrated theatrical activity: most shows took place in Portugal's largest cities, but people contacted with the music through other channels. Travelling musicians carried these songs to rural populations while urban audiences who did not attend the theatre heard them played by barrel organs in the streets of Portuguese cities and towns

('Musicos ambulantes', 1896). Furthermore, placing sound recordings as a tertiary medium is problematic because many recordings did not rely on secondary media such as sheet music.

Despite the significant role played by sheet music in piano and voice recordings, there were other conventions in place during the early phonographic period. Members of the cast often recorded with small orchestras. It is not possible to ascertain if these used the materials from the play or if musicians made new arrangements for recording purposes. The latter seems more plausible. The recording pioneer Fred Gaisberg argued that 'there was no pretence of using the composer's score' since 'the inadequacy of the accompaniments to the lovely vocal records made in the Acoustic Age was their great weakness' (Gaisberg, 1942, p. 85).

Thus, a simple partition of media concerning the musical theatre is often problematic since these developed simultaneously as part of an articulated production system. Basing an approach on the proximity with the 'real' show may obscure other paths through which people accessed the commodities generated by the play. The ubiquity of theatrical music is a consequence of its ability to be transformed to penetrate successfully in different cultural spheres. Instead of a hierarchical approach based on ontology, I propose that products from the popular theatre are qualitatively different goods that follow different itineraries of dissemination and whose connection with the 'original' show is variable.

Commodification was instrumental in establishing a cosmopolitan popular culture that transcended national borders, in which music played a fundamental role (Scott, 2008, p. 44). Cultural goods connected to the theatre were a significant part of everyday life and a staple of modern cosmopolitanism. Stage shows, librettos, postcards, sheet music, music rolls, and sound recordings were the most relevant. As the initial stage for intermediality, the show merges text, visual arts, dance, and music. It is then segmented in commodities that capture partial aspects of the play. Printing the librettos and *coplas* of successful shows made them both attainable and desirable. However, it was frequent for performers to improvise in musical revues, establishing a direct rapport with the audience and changing the play's text. Occasionally, shows included music from other productions as the Portuguese parodied Italian operas and Spanish *zarzuelas* and revues. For example, the revue *Vistorias do diabo*, staged in 1884, includes musical *contrafacta* from the 1879 *zarzuela La salsa de Aniceta*. Using precomposed pieces evidences the omnivorous tendencies of the revue, highlights the connection between Portugal and Spain, and generates another layer of intermediality. Moreover, singing popular songs with other lyrics for satirical purposes was frequent and generated new intermedial objects.

Stationaries and advertisers printed theatrical postcards that soon became tradable collectables. Many were fabricated and aimed to recreate scenes of the show while others were studio portraits of the leading performers. An incipient star system displayed how the gendered body, especially of female artists, became commodified to attract the audience with modern technologies that remediated the stage presence of prominent performers (Farfan, 2012). The press frequently reproduced the same photographs, which indicates the reinterpretation of a product in the market for cultural goods. A snapshot published in a newspaper was ephemeral and perishable but became a collectable if printed on a postcard.

Music commodities such as sheet music, music rolls, and sound recordings embody different tendencies of modernity. The second half of the nineteenth century witnessed the spread of sheet music. Given its reliance on music literacy, it shows the importance of domestic music-making for the Portuguese middle and upper classes. People gathered around the family piano to perform hits from operettas and revues. Romantic beliefs fostered types of music-making that relied on face-to-face interaction and were instrumental in developing an 'imagined musical community' that was 'reinforced by music participation within the family or immediate (non-imagined) community' (Brackett, 2016, p. 44). Cheap, easy to sing and play, and widely accessible, sheet music reflects the place occupied by the piano as the privileged vehicle for domestic music-making. However, their relationship with the theatrical show is not straightforward. Most pianists were amateurs and the household piano was not the pit orchestra. Thus, publishers adapted the pieces to its intended audience by keeping the essential aspects of the song (melodic contour, lyrics, harmony, and rhythm). Sheet music covers had the mnemonic power of evoking the show, often including a photograph of the stage performer. They frequently used the play's success as an advertisement and pointed to other products associated with the show (sheet music of similar pieces, printed *coplas* or librettos, or sound recordings).

The player piano shows how the mechanisation of music penetrated the household. It hijacked a symbol of bourgeois nineteenth-century culture and allowed for the mechanical reproduction of music. This instrument included expressive devices that relied on human skill to convey successful performances, focusing on the interaction between people and machines. Mechanical music was a novelty entering people's homes with the music roll as one of its Trojan horses. Mechanical instruments established their particular space in everyday life in the early twentieth century (Taylor, 2007; Suisman, 2010). Sheet music and the perforated roll used paper, which instigated legal battles between sheet music publishing companies and music roll manufacturers (Gitelman, 2004). However, different media may share a raw material, but reflect distinct social practices as users transformed them (Herzogenrath, 2012). The information stored in sheet music and piano rolls differs significantly: the first relies upon notation for human decoding while the latter contains instructions to be read by a machine. Many 'metronomic' or 'arranged' rolls relied on sheet music, revealing the intermediality that was in place in the early twentieth century. This type of roll stood between sheet music and sound recording. Later, the reproducing piano recorded performances by famous artists in special rolls, which are closer to phonography since they capture more nuances and transfer the performance skills to the apparatus. In this process, the music roll poses relevant questions concerning intermediality. Is it a secondary or a tertiary medium? Should we interpret it as parallel to sheet music by placing it as a secondary medium? What do music rolls capture of the 'real' show? Should we address it as a tertiary medium, given that many rolls relied upon a secondary medium? Should we distribute them between both categories according to their making, 'metronomic' versus 'recorded'?

The last set of music commodities, sound recordings, inscribed the sound waves of a live performance. However, they did not capture the live show as the sonic world of the recording isolates sound. Costumes, sets, gestures, and dances were not part of early phonography, in which a 'new kind of real in which the purity of hearing alone was distilled' (Weidman, 2003, p. 464). In addition to this, recorded sound preserved 'the trace of events: or, rather, its testimony is given in an indexical voice' (Rothenbuhler and Peters, 1997, p. 252). Thus, placing stage shows alongside the theatrical songs that dominated the phonographic market is complicated. Recording aimed to recreate the stage presence of the singers facing the audience, traversing boundaries between stage and domestic space. They included 'the mechanical inscription of sound, the musical configuration or dramatic narrative of the sound event, and the production of phonographic artificiality' (Ospina-Romero, 2019, p. 240). Multinational and local phonographic companies issued a large number of pieces from operettas and revues and contributed to their ubiquity in everyday modern life. Many recordings featured the stage performer, relying upon the artist's prominence as a marketing strategy. Thus, people recorded the music that the audience associated with them. However, there were exceptions. Duarte Silva, an actor with a good voice but with a physical impairment that limited his acting, developed a significant recording career. Silva was not a star, but he played secondary roles and recorded pieces whose lyrics and music were published, feeding the intermedial constellation of theatrical products.

Early phonography poses relevant questions concerning media ecology. Like sheet music, recordings transformed the materials (Suisman, 2010). The replacement of instruments that did not record well acoustically makes the phonogram an unreliable inscription of the stage show. Recording sessions were events specifically created to capture a given piece 'for the explicit purpose of its reproduction' and were independent of theatrical performance (Sterne, 2003, p. 41). Thus, phonograms are associated with the show but do not reflect what happened on stage, standing-in as a sonic reduction of a multimedia spectacle. A discussion that permeated early phonography was fidelity. Would discs and cylinders be taken as indexical mnemonics of the theatrical performance for someone who attended it? Would recordings be the only contact some people had with the piece, becoming their 'master'? Would an early record sound the same today as it did for its buyers 100 years ago? Recreating the original context in which early recordings circulated is impossible. First, the materials that make both machines and recordings have endured a century and time transformed them. Second, the first listeners heard the records as a novelty whose fidelity relied on the belief in which technology worked as a 'vanishing mediator' that placed the inscription as a stand-in for reality (Sterne, 2003, p. 285). Third, accounts of listeners are scarce, and many survived as a part of advertisements praising sound fidelity. Therefore, a connection between a live stage show and a recording was tenuous, but sustained a complex network that linked people, music, and machines.

Remediation in practice: *Fado do 31*

The ubiquity of musical commodities as part of a group of mass-produced goods in the early phonographic period is a consequence of remediation. For Bolter and Grusin, 'what is new about new media comes from the particular ways in which they refashion older media and the ways in which older media refashion themselves to answer the challenges of new media' (Bolter and Grusin, 2000, p. 15). This tension resonates with the early days of mechanical music when music rolls and sound recordings changed the ways the Portuguese musicked. Piano sellers began trading on music rolls, phonography remediated theatrical repertoires, and sheet music contained pieces that had become successful through recordings.

The transformation of ephemeral moments of stage shows into lasting products was instrumental in creating a collective musical memory. Moreover, remediation followed distinct paths to reach audiences with different routines. Mechanical music transformed profoundly early twentieth-century everyday life, as new media had to be widely accepted and fashion themselves as 'modern' to replace or supplement older media (Bolter and Grusin, 2000, p. 19). Thus, mechanical music strived to improve people's experience, automating everyday life and reconfiguring the human understanding of both space and time (Suisman, 2010).

The musical revue is a satirical genre that relied on current events, such as the everydayness of the Portuguese Republic established in 1910. The new regime and the changes it strived to carry out were frequently mocked in the theatre (Bastos and Vasconcelos, 2004). Moreover, songs from the revue dominated Portuguese sound recordings. To exemplify the remediation of stage music in Portugal, I chose 'Fado do 31'. This song was part of the revue *O 31*, premièred on the Teatro Avenida, Lisbon, on 26 June 1913. The play's reviews were enthusiastic, highlighting the 'way its authors had filled it with zest and the good rendition of its performers' (*O thalassa* 1913, p. 7). The revue ran for over a year and was frequently reprised in Portuguese and Brazilian stages the following decade, incorporating other sketches and casting new performers. Its title is based on a pun since '31' is still used as a slang term to designate a complicated situation, and Portugal's instability was a '31'. *O 31* was updated several times, while its hit song is still part of the Portuguese collective memory. 'Fado do 31' is a satire of the country's circumstances in a politically charged revue and its presence in multiple formats such as sheet music, sound recording, and music rolls reflected and amplified its popular appeal. The writer Pereira Coelho (1879–1963) and the composer Alves Coelho (1882–1931), then proficient authors in Lisbon's theatres, penned the song. Its form alternates verse and a chorus, a convention associated with the theatrical *fado-canção* while the lyrics incorporate Lisbon slang. The piece was published in Portugal and Spain, making it ideal to understand how the commodity form crossed national borders and the transformations it underwent to appeal to foreign audiences. 'Fado do 31' became so popular that Canadian soldiers fighting in the Western Front of the Great War learned it from their Portuguese peers (Pontes, 1917, p. 1). Moreover, the remediations of 'Fado do 31' illustrate the place occupied by the song in the market for cultural goods.

As the representative of the 'old' media, sheet music aimed at domestic consumption by musically literate people and Portuguese and Spanish editions reflected the success of 'Fado do 31' (Antunes de Oliveira, Losa and Silva, 2008). I will examine two Portuguese issues and one Spanish edition by Sassetti, a music store and printer established in Lisbon in 1848, and a Spanish printing by Unión Musical Española. Sassetti's Portuguese editions used the same plates but had different covers. What appears to be the earliest has a plain cover page with the title, its authors, the publisher, and copyright notice (Coelho; Coelho n.d.). The other printing bears the same information, states that it is the seventh edition and shows a photograph of the singer Maria Vitória (1888–1915) in costume (Coelho; Coelho *c*.1913). Vitória, one of the first fado singers to traverse the boundary between the tavern and the stage, starred in the show. Products used the image of the early stars for promotion, evidencing the intermedial economy in which 'performers negotiated and explored contemporary technological developments, the evolution of fandom and star culture, and the increasing commmodification of art and entertainment' (Simonson, 2013, p. 2). Printings of 'Fado do 31' marketed goods sold by Sassetti, such as instruments and sheet music. The earliest edition advertised fados by Duarte Silva and Reinaldo Varela, two recording pioneers, while the other includes a *morna* from Cape Verde. Biorito y Ribé penned a Spanish version of 'Fado do 31'. Despite the similarity of the lyrics between the two languages, the Spanish version avoids slang. Ribé changed the words, recasting it into a love song that placed the character as born in Vila Real (Northeast Portugal), which made the piece more understandable for Spanish audiences.

The Spanish versions share the printing plates and the back cover containing advertisements to Sassetti's Portuguese songs. Their front cover is similar and includes a photograph of Purita Mignon, a singer and dancer who 'created' it on stage. Moreover, the Sassetti piece includes Unión Musical Española's stamp, evidencing shared commercial interests and cooperation between Iberian companies and outlining the transnational nature of the music industry.

Figure 4.2 First page of *Fado 31: Canción Portuguesa*. Madrid: Unión Musical Española (Biblioteca Nacional de España).

Portuguese and Spanish companies issued music rolls containing 'Fado do 31'. The roll punched by the Oporto firm Indústria Portuguesa shows the proximity between published music and mechanical instruments, given its similarity with Sassetti's sheet music (Coelho n.d. [140]). With the tempo

Figure 4.3 Piano roll label of *Fado: da Revista 'O 31'*. Oporto: Industria Portugueza (140) (Biblioteca Nacional de España).

indication 'Andante', the roll appears to be a direct transcription or remediation of the sheet music. However, it contains slight differences, like the recapitulation of the introduction at the end of the piece.

The Spanish editions are substantially different. Published by Diana (Madrid) and Rollos Victoria (Barcelona), they remediated 'Fado do 31' to enhance the possibilities of the player piano. Thus, the publishers added notes, arpeggios, and chords to create a thicker sound without significantly altering the song. Both examples contain metronome marks and tempo, giving important performance indications. Diana published the piece as 'Allegretto moderato' with a 90 metronome mark while Rollos Victoria included an 80 metronome and 'Allegretto'.

Phonographic companies recorded Portuguese and Spanish versions of 'Fado do 31'. I will examine the Portuguese recordings made by Maria Litaly and Isabel Costa and the Spanish versions by La Colombia and La Goyita (Pepita Ramos). Maria Litaly performed in the stage show and recorded 'Fado do 31' for Simplex accompanied by the piano (Litaly *c.*1913). Here, the pianist emulates the Portuguese guitar, reinforcing the local atmosphere of the song. Thus, this arrangement stresses the strong association between an instrument and a genre, evoking an idea of authenticity. Authenticity is especially important in the period when fado adjusted to the moral restrictions of the legitimate stage by relinquishing its association with the marginal sectors of Lisbon's population (including outcasts such as pimps, prostitutes, and drunkards). Thus, a few musemes identified the genre in the global commodity form of the theatrical song, a strategy partaken by music from other countries. Isabel Costa, a Portuguese pioneer who cut records in the early phonographic period, recorded 'Fado do 31' for Homokord with an ensemble of strings and winds, in which the latter predominate (Costa *c*.1922). Here, the arpeggiated accompaniment supports some instruments doubling the melody, which contrasts with the sheet music arrangement, aimed at the amateur pianist. The recording emulates the sheet music in the syncopated introduction, the chorus, and the solo parts, while the voice resonates with the conventions of early phonography that privilege the clear enunciation of the words.

In May 1917, the variety singer and dancer La Colombia recorded 'Fado do 31' for Compañía del Gramófono, an enterprise associated with The Gramophone Company (La Colombia 1917). Juan Martínez Abades (1862–1920) wrote the lyrics, which stand much closer to the Portuguese slang than the sheet music version by Biorito y Ribé (La Colombia 1917). However, the arrangement does not have the arpeggiated figurations of Costa's recording, and La Colombia doubles the orchestra with wordless vocals at the reprise of the introduction. The distinguished *cupletista* La Goyita (Pepita Ramos) recorded Biorito y Ribé's version of 'Fado do 31' for the German company International Talking Machine Co. (La Goyita *c*.1917). This vertical arrangement resembles La Colombia's performance, as the ensemble appears to be constituted exclusively by wind instruments. Thus, the versions differ, which illustrates the variety of processes associated with remediation in the early phonographic period.

Fado do 31 has been frequently revisited well into the twenty-first century. The Portuguese dance critic Manoel de Sousa Pinto remarked that the piece was very successful in Spain and inspired local composers to write fados with numbers in their title thinking the Portuguese did the same (Pinto, 1921, p. 537). Moreover, 'many Spanish dancers perform the well-known Fado do 31', with a choreography inspired by the Parisian Apache dance, 'without a trace of the Portuguese spirit' (Pinto, 1921, p. 537). People danced a Portuguese song in Spain using French moves, which reveals the complex and ever-changing processes through which audiences remediated music in the early twentieth century.

Conclusions

The introduction of mechanical music in Portugal reflected the intense competition between media and manufacturers. Music stores established in the nineteenth century sold instruments and sheet music when the piano was a well-known site for the embodiment of cultural capital associated with bourgeois self-accomplishment. Thus, sheet music celebrated music literacy as a part of the domestic life. Street organs were ubiquitous in the urban soundscape, carrying operatic melodies from the elegant theatre to other spaces, and phonography was taking off. The player piano became a piece of furniture in homes, in theatres, in cinemas, and in cafés, transforming the ways in which people interacted with mechanical music. The introduction of phonography into the circuit of competing media began by showing it as a novelty, a magical amusement. Later, it became a sound and entertainment carrier, which shook the media network. However, the repertoires, dominated by theatrical songs, overlapped across media.

Sheet music targeted amateur musicians and had to be accessible to its intended audiences. Therefore, many songs stand as a simplified version of the stage song. Punching 'metronomic' music rolls based on sheet music was frequent. Nonetheless, many tended to rework the piece to enhance the possibilities of the mechanism, reflecting a quasi-orchestral perspective on the music. Sound recordings varied, using the piano or employing a large ensemble, as many famous performers recreated their stage hits on wax and shellac. They fed and relied upon an early star system and reinforced the ubiquity of theatrical songs in the emergent forms of automated entertainment. Mechanical music expanded face-to-face music-making and transformed the sociability routines of the wealthy Portuguese since phonography was not accessible to large parts of the population. Local companies sold cheaper machines and records, which featured music from the operetta, the *zarzuela*, the revue, or fado, local marching bands, and folk songs. These objects circulated in the entertainment market and evidenced how the success of new media depended on local repertoires. Thus, stage show, sheet music, music roll, and sound recording were part of a complex and articulated network of auditory experiences. Moreover, remediation highlighted the advantages of each medium to enhance its appeal. The different ways sound and music permeated Portuguese everyday life linked Romanticism and modernity, art and entertainment, the old and the new, the urban and the rural, the tangible and the intangible, the transnational and the local, and the public and the private.

Notes

1 Carlos Monteiro de Souza was Edison's representative in Brazil, stopping over in Lisbon in his return trip from the Exposition Universelle.
2 Pinheiro Chagas was a Portuguese writer, journalist, and politician; Francisco de Andrade was an internationally acclaimed Portuguese opera singer; Adolpho Sauvinet was a Portuguese composer.

References

Antunes de Oliveira, G.L. Losa and J. Silva (2008) A edição de música impressa e a mediatização do fado: o caso do "Fado do 31", *Etno-Folk: Revista Galega de Etnomusicoloxía*, 12, 55–67.
Bastos, G. and A.I. Vasconcelos (2004) O *Teatro em Lisboa no tempo da Primeira República*. Lisbon: Museu Nacional do Teatro.
Belchior, S. (2010) Sinkler Darby's 1900 Expedition for the Gramophone Company in Portugal. In: Gronow, P. and C. Hofer (eds) *Contributions to the History of the Record Industry: Beiträge zur Geschichte der Schallplattenindustrie,* vol. 5. Vienna: Gesellschaft für Historische Tonträger, pp. 9–18.

Bolter, J.D. and R. Grusin (2000) *Remediation: Understanding New Media.* Cambridge: The MIT Press.

Brackett, D. (2016) *Categorizing Sound: Genre and Twentieth-Century Popular Music.* Berkeley: University of California Press.

'Carteira dos theatros,' (1879) *Diário Illustrado,* 20 October, 1.

Chion, M. (2016) *Sound: An Acoulogical Treatise.* Durham: Duke University Press.

Clark, A. (1904) Letter to the Compagnie Française du Gramophone, and the Gramophone & Typewriter's offices in London, 5 May.

Companhia Franceza do Gramophone (1908) *Novo catalogo de discos portuguezes.* Lisbon: n.p.

Companhia Franceza do Gramophone (1910) *Catalogo geral dos discos.* Lisbon: Companhia Franceza do Gramophone.

Farfan, P. (2012) 'The Picture Postcard Is a Sign of the Times:' Theatre Postcards and Modernism. *Theatre History Studies,* 32, 93–119.

Gaisberg, F. (1942) *The Music Goes Round.* New York: MacMillan Press.

Genette, G. (1997) *Palimpsests: Literature in the Second Degree.* Lincoln: University of Nebraska Press.

Gitelman, L. (2004) Media, Materiality, and the Measure of the Digital; or, the Case of Sheet Music and the Problem of Piano Rolls. In: Rabinoviz, L. and A. Geil (eds.) *Memory Bytes: History, Technology, and Digital Culture.* Durham: Duke University Press, 199–217.

Gronow, P. and B. Englung (2007) Inventing Recorded Music: The Recorded Repertoire in Scandinavia 1899–1925, *Popular Music,* 26(2), 281–304.

Grosch, N. and C. Stahrenberg (2014) The Transculturality of Stage, Song and Other Media: Intermediality in Popular Musical Theatre. In: Platt, L., T. Becker and D. Lindon (eds.) *Popular Musical Theatre in London and Berlin: 1890–1939.* Cambridge: Cambridge University Press, 187–200.

Herzogenrath, B. (2012) Introduction. In Herzogenrath, B. (ed.) *Travels in Intermedia[lity]: Reblurring the Boundaries.* Lebanon: Dartmouth College Press, 1–14.

Illustração portugueza, (1909) 25 October [advertising pages].

Kattenbelt, C. (2006) Theatre as the Art of the Performer and the Stage of Intermediality. In: Chapple, F. and C. Kattenbelt (eds.), *Intermediality in Theatre and Performance.* Amsterdam: Rodopi, pp. 29–39.

Kristeva, J. (1980) Word, Dialogue, and Novel. In: Roudiez, L.S. (ed.) *Desire in Language: A Semiotic Approach to Literature and Art.* New York: Columbia University Press, pp. 64–91.

Lacasse, S. (2010) Une introduction à la transphonographie. *Volume,* 7(2), 31–57.

Losa, L. (2013) *Machinas fallantes: A música gravada em Portugal no início do século XX.* Lisbon: Tinta da China.

Losa, L. and S. Belchior (2010) The Introduction of Phonogram Market in Portugal: Lindström Labels and Local Traders (1879–1925). In: Gronow, P. and C. Hofer (eds.) *The Lindström Project: Contributions to the History of the Record Industry: Beiträge zur Geschichte der Schallplattenindustrie,* vol. 2. Vienna: Gesellschaft für Historische Tonträger, 2010, pp. 7–11.

Martínez Alfaro, M.J. (1996) Intertextuality: Origins and Development of the Concept. *Atlantis* 18(1–2), pp. 268–85.

Marvin, C. (1988) *When Old Technologies Were New: Thinking about Electric Communication in the Late Nineteenth Century.* Oxford: Oxford University Press.

'Musicos ambulantes' (1896) *O Occidente,* 25 November, 258–9.

O thalassa (1913) 26 September, 7.

Ospina-Romero, S. (2019) Recording Studios on Tour: The Expeditions of the Victor Talking Machine Company through Latin America, 1903–1926. [Doctoral dissertation, Cornell University, Ithaca].

Pinto, M. de Sousa (1921) Pela dança portuguesa: motivos, *Ilustração portuguesa*, 31 December, 535–7.

Pontes, J. (1917) A verdadeira aliança: tocando guitarra e jogando o pau. *A Capital*, 1 September, 1.

Rothenbuhler, E.W. and J.D. Peters (1997) Defining Phonography: An Experiment in Theory. *Musical Quarterly*, 81(2), 242–64.

Roy, E.A. (2015) *Media, Materiality and Memory: Grounding the Groove*. New York and Oxford: Routledge.

Scott, D.B. (2008) *Sounds of the Metropolis: The 19th-Century Popular Music Revolution in London, New York, Paris and Vienna*. New York and Oxford: Oxford University Press.

Scott, D.B. (2009) Introduction. In: Scott, D.B. (ed.) *The Ashgate Research Companion to Popular Musicology*. Farnham: Ashgate.

Scott, D.B. (2019) *German Operetta on Broadway and in the West End, 1900–1940*. Cambridge, Cambridge University Press.

Silva J. (2016) *Entertaining Lisbon: Music, Theater, and Modern Life in the Late 19th Century*. New York and Oxford: Oxford University Press.

Simonson, M. (2013) *Body Knowledge: Performance, Intermediality, and American Entertainment at the Turn of the Twentieth Century*. New York and Oxford: Oxford University Press.

Sterne, J. (2003) *The Audible Past: Cultural Origins of Sound Reproduction*. Durham: Duke University Press.

Suisman, D. (2010) Sound, Knowledge, and the "Immanence of Human Failure. *Social Text 102*, 28(1), 13–34.

Taylor, T.D. (2007) The Commodification of Music at the Dawn of the Era of "Mechanical Music. *Ethnomusicology*, 51(2), 281–305.

'Thomaz Edison: Auctor do phonographo' (1889) *O Occidente*, 11 October, 227–8.

Weidman, A. (2003) Guru and Gramophone: Fantasies of Fidelity and Modern Technologies of the Real. *Public Culture*, 15(3), 453–76.

Wolf, W. (1999) *The Musicalization of Fiction: A Study in the Theory and History of Intermediality*. Amsterdam: Rodopi.

Sheet music

Coelho Pereira; Alves Coelho (n.d.) *Fado da revista 'O 31,' cantado por Maria Vitória*. Lisbon: Sassetti, [7th edition].

Coelho, Pereira; Alves Coelho (*c.* 1913) *Fado da revista 'O 31.'* Lisbon: Sassetti.

Ribé, Biorito y; Alves Coelho (n.d.) *Fado 31: Canción Portuguesa*. Lisbon: Sassetti.

Ribé, Biorito y; Alves Coelho (n.d.a) *Fado 31: Canción Portuguesa*. Madrid: Unión Musical Española.

Music rolls (available at Biblioteca Digital Hispánica)

Coelho, Alves (n.d.) *Fado: da Revista 'O 31.'* Oporto: Industria Portugueza [140].

Coelho, Alves (n.d.) *Fado: De la revista 31.* Barcelona: Rollos Victoria [5107].

Fado de la revista 31 (*c.*1916) Madrid: Diana [303].

Discography

Costa, Isabel (*c*.1922) *Fado do 31.* Homokord [9526].

La Colombia (1917) *Fado 31.* Barcelona: Compañía del Gramófono [W 263563].

La Goyita (*c*.1917) *Fado 31.* Weissensee, International Talking Machine Co [A 138306].

Litaly, Maria (*c*.1913) *O fado do 31.* Simplex [48511].

5 Discòfils

Notes on the birth of the record club and the record listener in 1930s Barcelona

Eva Moreda Rodríguez

The early history of recording technologies is full of inventions. During these decades, a multiplicity of technological innovations were developed and patented by multinational companies and local inventors, often working in stern competition with each other and among themselves. Other inventions, however, were less tangible, with no exact date and not clearly identifiable inventor: I am referring here to the gradual development of new concepts and practices borne out of complex interactions and frictions between the technological, the commercial, the social, the cultural and the artistic interact over a period of years or even decades, involving local, regional, national and transnational dimensions. One such invention is the idea of recorded music itself, as elegantly put in the title of a widely cited article by Gronow and Englund (2007) that refers to the decades-long process which led from Edison's first phonograph in 1877 to its widespread, practically exclusive use as a music playback machine.[1] This process involved technological and commercial developments, but also social and cultural negotiations that were in many cases place- or country-specific.

While recorded music in the above sense might be regarded as the key invention in the earlier history of recording technologies, further crucial developments took place throughout the 1920s and 1930s. It was at this time that new modes of listening specific to recorded music as well as the concept of the record listener were "invented". These transformations, in the words of Sophie Maisonneuve, resulted from a combination of "materialities and sociabilities" (2002, pp. 44–5): the "materialities" (mostly the dissemination of electrical recording from 1925 onwards, which substantially improved the kinds of acoustic data that could be captured in a record) shaped and were in turn shaped by the "sociabilities" (ever-evolving practices and cultural discourses around music, sound, listening and technologies).

Maisonneuve has also examined what was innovative about these new understandings of the record listener and of record listening, stating that listening was longer, limited by what was being performed in nearby venues, but instead dictated by personal preference, with the home and not the concert hall becoming the main listening centre for many (Maisonneuve 2006, p. 27, 2009, pp. 241–55). Listening also became purely acousmatic, without

DOI: 10.4324/9781003006497-8

recourse to visual elements (Maisonneuve 2006, p. 24). This, together with the improved technical capabilities of electrical recording, allowed new modes of listening focused on acoustic elements and details such as colours and timbres that may have gone unnoticed in a concert hall (Maisonneuve 2007, pp. 54–6). New understandings of listening gave rise to new social practices and artifacts, including the proliferation of record magazines and record reviews in more general publications (Maisonneuve 2002, pp. 45 and 59), increasing the numbers of critical repertoires and guides for record collectors (Maisonneuve 2006, p. 30) and the development of record clubs (Maisonneuve 2002, p. 45), on which this chapter intends to expand further. Ludovic Tournès, while agreeing with Maisonneuve on most of the characteristics of "discophilie", as listed above, traces back the roots of these developments to new understandings of time emerging from the Industrial Revolution, whereby time became rationalized, linear, quantified and mathematical (2006, p. 6).

While Maisonneuve's and Tournès's approach is sociological, aimed at documenting widespread social change through a focus on industrialized nations such as France and the United Kingdom (where recorded music was relatively accessible to the middle and upper classes of the population), in this chapter I propose a more minimalistic, context-sensitive approach to some of the same kinds of developments. I will be focusing on one single record club, Discòfils, operative in Barcelona for a year and a half between late 1934 and mid-1936. There are three main reasons why Discòfils makes for a noteworthy case study to interrogate the practices and artifacts described by Maisonneuve and Tournès. The first of these reasons is of an eminently practical nature. Unlike with other informal record clubs (certainly in Spain, where no other record club is known to have existed around this time, but also worldwide), Discòfils has left us a substantial archive consisting of programmes, meeting minutes, correspondence and other documents. These allow us to obtain valuable and unique insights into how the group organized themselves, what their motivations were, what sorts of listening practices they developed, how they understood recorded music and what sorts of frictions or negotiations they faced in doing so. The archive is held by the Biblioteca de Catalunya in Barcelona as part of the papers of local engineer Ricard Gomis, a founder of the group, under the sub-heading "Subfons Discòfils". Gomis's extensive collection of 78rpm discs and disc catalogues was donated to the library in 1994, the year following Gomis's death, but the materials pertaining to Discòfils only arrived there in 2011, after the library decided to organize an exhibition focusing on the record club.[2] The level of detail of the Discòfils documentation and the fact that Gomis decided to keep it until his death suggests that he and other members of the club had at the time an uncommon awareness that what they were doing was unique and innovative.

The second reason to study Discòfils is that record clubs from the time have not yet been extensively studied[3]; and yet, as one of the key social practices developed around recorded music in the 1930s, they can provide unique, "on-the-field" insights into how audiences interacted with the increasing amounts of recorded music being available to them and how these complemented or disrupted their listening practices. In this respect, Discòfils also provides it with a rather unique example. The society shared some characteristics with the best-known record clubs of the time such as *The Gramophone* in Britain (founded in 1923). Indeed, as in the British "gramophone recitals", the members of Discòfils regularly met up to listen to recordings together, which – as will be discussed later – significantly shaped the listening experience. But, whereas *The Gramophone* also offered its members the opportunity to be part of a larger community and to become acquainted with new understandings of listening through their own magazine, operating a "top-down" business model, Discòfils remained decidedly "bottom-up": its membership was deliberately limited, as will be discussed later, so as to keep the group manageable and socially viable, and even though the club had plans to develop outside Barcelona and Catalonia, perhaps eventually establishing a model comparable to *The Gramophone*, such plans never materialized.

Third, an even cursory examination of the Discòfils materials soon makes it clear that they are better interpreted through a context-sensitive lens: whereas it is certainly possible to see most of the developments identified by Maisonneuve reflected in the practices adopted by Discòfils, we also need to look at place-specific discourses around technology, recorded music and modernity that had developed in Barcelona, Catalonia and Spain for the preceding 40 years. These discourses influenced the types of repertoires covered by Discòfils as well as the very fact that an innovative initiative like Discòfils had developed in Barcelona and not in any other Spanish city. This chapter therefore intends to demonstrate that the processes by which the record listener and record listening were invented were heavily influenced by national, regional and local frictions and negotiations, and an understanding of these is fundamental to refine our understanding of the processes Maisonneuve describes. Accordingly, in the conclusion, I will discuss what lessons we can draw from Discòfils to inform further research on record clubs and on the birth of the record listener in other contexts.

Understandings of modernity in Spain, Catalonia and Barcelona

Key to understanding the development of Discòfils is the various discourses that developed around modernity in Spain from the later decades of the nineteenth century onwards. I understand "modernity" here in the sense of Peter Osborne: not as a project or an empirical category, but rather as a new understanding of temporality where the past is totalized from the point of view of the present, understood as constantly evolving and transitory (1995, pp. 1–2). This new temporality centres the notion of progress as the key narrative of the history of the nation-state (Balibrea 2006, p. 163). From the 1870s onwards, a key pillar of the new understanding of modernity developing in Spain was *regeneracionismo*, encompassing a range of individuals and groups, across a number of social classes and political ideologies, who sought to "regenerate" Spain from the crisis it was allegedly in after the loss of its overseas colonies and its inability to adapt itself to the new world order (Swyngedouw 2015, pp. 3–4). Although the solutions proposed by the *regeneracionistas* to solve Spain's crisis were enormously diverse, originating from instances as disparate as the Catholic Church and the nascent women's movement, there was a general sense that scientific research, particularly applied research and technology, were crucial to solve Spain's crisis (Andrés-Gallego 1998, p. 242).

Unsurprisingly, some of the discourses around science, technology, national identity and modernity advanced by the *regeneracionista* movement influenced how recording technologies were received in Spain in the late nineteenth century. When phonograph demonstrations proliferated throughout the 1890s, advertisements and accounts often presented them as a scientific and cultural occasion rather than as musical events or as mere entertainment (Moreda Rodríguez 2019a, pp. 242–6). After the introduction of Edison's Spring Motor, Home and Standard phonographs between 1896 and 1898, the first Spanish recording labels – the *gabinetes fonográficos* – started to open, selling imported phonographs but also recorded cylinders they produced themselves employing mostly local singers. *Gabinetes* thrived mostly in Madrid, where some of their owners adopted a rhetoric heavily reminiscent of *regeneracionismo*, claiming that their ventures offered eminently rational entertainment, always grounded upon the latest advances of science. They also claimed that by importing and exporting the newest recording technologies, they were helping revitalize the Spanish economy (Moreda Rodríguez 2020a).

While the connection between recording technologies and modernity discourses that underpins the birth of Discòfils can be tracked down to these earlier years, the cultural landscape in 1900 was still significantly different to the one that gave rise to the record club in 1934. First, in 1900 Madrid was at the centre of the nascent Spanish recording industry, and such discourses of modernity were produced and disseminated predominantly there (Moreda Rodríguez 2020a). The Barcelona *gabinetes* were much less active in this respect. Indeed, there were fewer *gabinetes* in Barcelona than in Madrid and they typically stayed open for shorter periods of time. Moreover, in contrast with Madrid's *Boletín fonográfico*, no publications existed at the time in Barcelona focusing on recording technologies, meaning that opportunities to promote the new devices and establish discourses around them were more limited. Second, while the *gabinetes* – both in Madrid and Barcelona – did understand that the future of the phonograph was inextricably tied to music, their owners were not composers or musicians, and most came from commerce or applied science backgrounds. When they decided what types of music and repertoires to record, they were driven by a mixture of technological limitations and market preferences. For example, they recorded brass band music extensively but very few chamber music involving strings, because the former instruments were easier to record than the latter, but also because brass music was at the time popular in Spain, while chamber music only attracted limited audiences (Moreda Rodríguez 2020b). Opera and *zarzuela* were recorded extensively, with a focus on the latest successes or repertoire works that were performed regularly; however, the idea of the phonograph being a means to access less familiar or unknown repertoires did not feature very heavily, if at all, in the discourse of the *gabinetes*. For Spanish composers active at the time, recording technologies were not a pressing concern either: Enrique Granados and Isaac Albéniz both left a very small number of non-commercial recordings, but did not otherwise demonstrate much interest in the potential impact of recording technologies on the circulation of music. *Zarzuela* composers, however, were more concerned with regulating the hiring of their scores for the purposes of live performance; this, and not recordings, was still the main means they had available of making their works known and financially profitable.

Two key cultural and social changes, however, took place between the era of the *gabinetes* and the birth of Discòfils. First, the Spanish recording industry underwent a geographical restructuring. In 1903, through its subsidiary Compagnie Française du Gramophone, The Gramophone Co. Ltd. opened an office in Barcelona (Torrent i Marqués 2002, p. 8). Within two years, the thriving *gabinete* industry in Madrid had died down: some establishments closed their doors and others became Gramophone resellers (Moreda Rodríguez 2020b). It is not known why Gramophone decided to open a branch in Barcelona and not in Madrid, but it is likely that Barcelona being closer than Madrid to Paris and the rest of Europe played a role. Similar reasons can be cited to explain the French label Odeon opening a branch in Barcelona in 1906 (Torrent i Marqués 2002, p. 9). With the advent of the gramophone, record production was no longer in the hands of a large number of small producers, as was the case with the *gabinetes*, but rather concentrated in the hands of a few multinationals operating through complex networks of branches and subsidiaries. In this context, record shops played an important role in terms of articulating a community focused around record collecting and listening in local contexts, as was the case with the ten or so record shops active in Barcelona from the mid-to-late 1900s (Torrent i Marqués 2004).

The second key shift that facilitated the birth of Discòfils has to do with the emergence of a new generation of classically trained composers readier to engage with moving image and audio technologies as the possibilities of these became more promising. Manuel de Falla (born in 1876) was the first major Spanish composer to record (as a pianist and harpsichordist) several of his own works, but it was not until the 1920s that young composers engaged with technologies more thoroughly, particularly in Madrid and

Barcelona. Such engagement must be understood side by side with these composers' commitment to renovating Spanish (or Catalan) music, bringing it in line with modernist currents elsewhere (Palacios 2008, pp. 11–14).

This commitment to modernization as well as engagement with moving image and audio technologies expressed itself in different ways. The Grupo de los Ocho in Madrid and the Grup dels Vuit in Barcelona (both translate as the "Group of Eight"; this is, however, a coincidence and the groups operated independently) have traditionally been identified as the main poles of this movement of musical renovation, but neither group was homogeneous in terms of the musical styles they cultivated (ranging from impressionism to neoclassicism to 12-tone technique) or their long-term vision for Spanish or Catalan national music. In which concerns engagement with technologies, the radio attracted attention in both cities, with Grupo de los Ocho's composer Salvador Bacarisse undertaking an ambitious programme of dissemination of canonic and new music through Unión Radio in Madrid (Moreda Rodríguez 2019b) and German-born critic and musicologist Otto Mayer repeatedly defending the potential of the radio to democratize music (Alonso Tomás 2019). On the other hand, the Madrid composers and critics engaged with cinema in a more sustained way than those in Barcelona, whereas the latter were more interested in recording technologies – presumably as a result of the different spread of both industries in each of the cities. While Mayer and critic J.G. published record reviews with some regularity in the culture and arts magazine *Mirador*, the Madrid music criticism scene was mostly disinterested in recordings. It is indeed Mayer's and J.G.'s reviews, together with other written commentary on recorded music published in magazines and newspapers, which suggest that certain discourses surrounding recording technologies and its connections to modernity had already started to circulate in Barcelona before the birth of Discòfils. Both critics regarded recordings as a mean of disseminating canonic works rather than "frivolous genres" (J.G. 1933, p. 8). Their articles also speak of a nascent understanding of how record listening differed from listening in live contexts (J.G. 1933, p. 8) and of a focus on previously neglected aspects of the listening experience as described by Maisonneuve above (Mayer 1935, p. 8).

Setting up Discòfils

Four key documents from the Discòfils archive offer valuable insights into how the association was set up, how their members saw themselves and how these views evolved over time, suggesting that new understandings of recorded music and of record listening had started to develop among the membership. The earliest of these documents is likely to be an undated piece of writing, listing the aims of the future association (Discòfils, ca. 1934a) and presumably drafted by its future founders Gomis and Joan Prats (an art promoter and close collaborator of painter Joan Miró). The document articulates what would then become the main aim of Discòfils: to offer their members an opportunity to listen to "musical works of the utmost value" that were never or rarely heard in Barcelona. In order to do so, the club proposed to use recordings of "unknown and masterful works" from private collections in Barcelona. From this, we can infer that such collections would have been gradually developing since the advent of electrical recording and the subsequent expansion of recorded repertoires (Maisonneuve 2006, p. 37). Discòfils therefore presented itself as a member-driven association very closely connected to its milieu – as it would remain throughout its existence. However, although disseminating "unknown and masterful works" would always stay the main aim of Discòfils, the association subsequently redefined and expanded its role in some ways, as will be discussed subsequently.

The second relevant document is the association's rules (*estatutos*), issued on 29 December 1934 and signed by Gomis and Prats (Discòfils 1934b). It described the aims of the association as follows:

> The main aim of the association is to disseminate music through recordings. The association will make use of any means that can make its aim more effective: listening sessions, sometimes accompanied by talks; organization of record collections; publication of books and magazines; it will also stimulate the production and dissemination of the record.

As I will discuss subsequently, however, listening sessions (*audicions*) remained the main and practically the only structured activity of the group throughout its existence – probably because its short lifespan prevented its members from tackling more ambitious initiatives. Whereas the notion that recording technologies should be used to increase familiarity with a range of repertoires is consonant with what was happening in other contexts around this time (LeMahieu 1982, p. 391; Maisonneuve 2002, p. 54), what is conspicuously absent from the *estatutos* of Discòfils is an interest in technology *qua* technology. This would remain so throughout the life of the club, and is particularly intriguing considering Gomis's engineering background.

Two further aspects of the *estatutos* help us understand the intimate connection of the new association to local artistic and intellectual circles. First, the *estatutos* were written in Spanish – a legal requirement at the time, given that Spanish was the only official language in Spain – but all others Discòfils' papers suggest that the group's day-to-day business was conducted in Catalan. This is consonant with the background of their founders, and presumably with that of their intended membership too. Both Gomis and Prats came from the Catalan bourgeoisie, which, from the early twentieth century onwards, embraced Catalan nationalism (*catalanisme*) replacing Spanish with Catalan as the *langue de culture* (Ferrando Francés and Nicolás Amorós 2011, p. 314). Torrent i Marqués suggests that throughout the early decades of the twentieth century, Barcelona record shops conducted their business in Spanish, which they and their customers saw as a higher-status language (2004, p. 6). If that was the case, then Discòfils' decision to use Catalan would have signalled a desire to encompass recording technologies under the Catalan bourgeoisie's aspirations of economic prosperity and cultural modernity.

The second noteworthy aspect of the *estatutos* is the fact that membership was limited, in the first instance, to 20 "active members" (*socios activos*) who were obliged to actively help run the club. Once the limit had been reached, other applicants could join as "associate members" (*socios adheridos*) with no organizational duties. *Activos* paid 36 pesetas per year, while *adheridos* contributed 12, suggesting that the club was geared to the bourgeoisie and upper classes in the first instance.[4] This membership structure differentiates Discòfils from record clubs organized by record labels or structured around a magazine, where members would not normally have duties other than paying their fees. This suggests that Prats and Gomis did not necessarily aim at setting up an ambitious, geographically diverse infrastructure like that of *The Gramophone*; on the contrary, their preference was for a small association where all members knew each other and were strongly committed to furthering the association's aims. Agreements were struck later on with commercial establishments; record shops César Vicente and Unión Musical Casa Werner acted as hubs where potential applicants could obtain information and submit their membership application (Discòfils 1935c), and the Barcelona branch of Gramophone provided discs to be used at listening sessions after artistic director Robert Gerhard approached them (Discòfils ca. 1935b; Gerhard ca. 1935a).

The third key document is the minute of the association's first meeting, held on 25 January 1935 (Discòfils 1935a).[5] On this occasion, the group chose a governing board composed of nine individuals (including three women, which was remarkable in the typically male-dominated world of record collecting) and featuring several prominent names from Barcelona's bourgeoisie and cultural life. These included cultural activist and impresario Manuel Clausells Vilasaló, violinist and musicologist Enric Roig Masriera (also a very keen collector, who was appointed "technical advisor" to the club) and Isabel Llorach d'Olsa, a very active sponsor of the arts in Barcelona. Composer Robert Gerhard[6] was appointed as "artistic advisor", initially for a one-year term which was then extended (Gerhard ca. 1935e). Gerhard's duties included giving several talks per year and overseeing the programmes that would be played back at listening sessions. Originally from Valls (Tarragona), Gerhard studied in Berlin and Vienna with Arnold Schoenberg between 1923 and 1928 (Alonso Tomás 2013). Back in Barcelona, he worked at the Biblioteca de Catalunya on eighteenth-century music under musicologist Higini Anglès. He also wrote music criticism, translated music books from the German, organized concerts (often featuring the music of his teacher and other Second Viennese School composer) and was a member of the Grup de Vuit (Perry 2013, pp. 15–18). Gerhard is not known to have been a keen collector or an experienced technologist in those years.

Instead, it is likely that he was approached by Prats and Gomis because of his background as a composer and familiarity with new music. Gerhard's appointment as well as the rather generous salary he received from the association (and the fact that his was a salaried position at all)[7] further confirms that Discòfils' main focus was on disseminating the musical canon rather than on technological matters per se.

The fourth key document is a manifesto launched at an indeterminate date, but possibly several months after the club had been formally set up. The manifesto itself reveals that by that point, membership had grown to 29 members, most of them coming from Barcelona's artistic, scientific and financial elite, such as painter Joan Miró, physiologist August Pi i Sunyer, industrial engineer Josep Maria Lamaña and poet Carles Riba. Musicians were also well represented, including Higini Anglès, composers-conductors Ricard Lamote de Grignon and Eduard Toldrá and soprano Conxita Badia (Discòfils ca. 1935d).

Apart from growing its membership, the group was now able to articulate their understanding of recorded music and of listening in more complex ways than had been the case so far. It is indeed in the manifesto that the link between understandings of recorded music and modernity in the sense of Osborne above first became explicit. The manifesto defined a *discòfil* not by their expertise with recording technologies or the size of their record collection (in fact, the manifesto claimed that one could be a *discòfil* without owning a single record), but rather by a shared sensitivity concerning the connection between the record and music history. A *discòfil* was someone who, like the founders of the association, had understood "long ago" that "the modern disc" had revolutionary potential in transforming one's relationship with music by opening up access to a wide range of repertoires, including "the classical works of the great masters, the most representative examples of contemporary music, exotic music, the folklore of the various countries, the music of faraway civilizations". The manifesto therefore proposed a new conceptualization of the musical past made possible precisely by the progress-driven, transitory nature of the present (which is, as I have discussed earlier, a characteristic of modernity). Moreover, the focus was decidedly on members (as opposed to companies) as the main actors and beneficiaries of these new conceptualizations. This can be seen in the club's plan to issue a series of "discophile" records in limited numbers; through these, members would become acquainted with works of exceptionally high musical value. Companies, however, would not benefit substantially, as the leadership of Discòfils candidly admitted that such records would be commercially unprofitable.[8]

The manifesto also suggests that new sensibilities were emerging in regard to listening practices, in the sense of Maisonneuve above. It claimed that records not only allowed discophiles to become acquainted with unknown repertoires, but also to listen to music in a more nuanced, complex way. It compared records to score-reading, claiming that in the past, listeners could only get to know a work closely by learning how to read music – which was time-consuming and laborious. Instead, thanks to the record listeners, they could now "multiply their perception abilities, refine their critical eye and sensitiveness, acquire confidence and style in their personal style", thus democratizing music, which adds a further dimension to the group's commitment to modernity.

The manifesto in practice

The programme of activities undertaken by Discòfils allows us to consider how the aims and views expressed in the documents I have discussed above translated into practice. As I have advanced earlier, out of the various initiatives mentioned by Discòfils in their *estatuto* and manifesto, only one unquestionably came to fruition –listening sessions. Although there is no conclusive evidence for this, we can presume that these sessions also provided an opportunity to advance some of the more general aims named in the *estatutos* and manifesto, such as helping members develop their private collections and disseminating information about new disc releases, which Gerhard kept on top of (Gerhard ca. 1935d).

During its first season (January to June 1935), Discòfils organized listening sessions on a monthly basis at the bookstore Llibreria Catalònia; in the second one, they increased to two per month, which suggests that this was a successful format (Discòfils 1935c). In their summary of activities for the 1935–1936 season (Discòfils 1935c), the organizers discriminated between "audicions-conferèncias" (including a detailed talk about the works programmed) and "audicions-exposició" (introducing new records, preceded by a very brief introductory commentary). Whereas the former type of sessions (on which more later) is consonant with the central role that Discòfils accorded detailed and nuanced music listening, the latter suggests a nascent interest in the recording industry *qua* recording industry that is also typical of new understandings of the record (Maisonneuve 2002, p. 58).

While in practice all listening sessions were simply labelled "audicions", from the titles and content of individual events as well as from press reviews, we can presume that most events fell under the "audicions-exposició" format. The talks were sometimes given by guest speakers, presumably invited by Gerhard himself: composer and critic Josep Palau spoke on Mendelssohn and composer Baltasar Samper on jazz (probably the only session to focus on non-Western classical music, despite the association's claims in its manifesto) (anonymous 1935a, p. 7) and Adolfo Salazar visited Barcelona from Madrid to talk to Discòfils about Russian music (Petit 1936, 8).[9] Unfortunately, none of the talks have reached us and press reviews offer only minimal information without detailing the historical and/or analytical aspects discussed, which could have shed further light on the sorts of listening that Discòfils encouraged. We know, however, that both the technical and the presentation aspects were given utmost attention by the organizers, with Gerhard and Gomis corresponding about the types of playback devices available, how they should be arranged in the room, what the written programme accompanying the listening sessions should include and how many sides should be played back so as to keep the audience's attention (Gerhard thought it should be a maximum of eight, as opposed to ten) (Gerhard 1935c). This further hints at the development of new listening practices oriented towards gaining an intimate understanding of the formal aspects of the work.

The selection of works, however, is testimony to how understandings of recorded music and listening practices changed since recording technologies arrived in Spain in the late nineteenth century. Significantly, Discòfils did not include any opera or *zarzuela* in their listening sessions, as these would be readily available to bourgeois audiences in theatres throughout Barcelona. Similarly, orchestral music from the classical and romantic period – which made up the bulk of the programmes of the Orquestra Pau Casals, then the main orchestra in Barcelona – was rarely included. Opportunities to listen live to chamber music from these same periods, however, were scarcer in Barcelona, and so Discòfils sometimes featured such works in its listening sessions too, including an indeterminate Mendelssohn quartet in Palau's talk (anonymous 1935a) as well as Mozart's Quintet in C major and Schubert's *Six German Dances* in Anton Webern's recent arrangement for chamber orchestra (anonymous 1935e; Discòfils 1935c).

Most of the repertoire presented by Discòfils, however, focused on two areas that were less well represented in live music events, and also in other record clubs elsewhere in the world: early and contemporary music. Neither was completely absent from Barcelona's concert life, but neither can be regarded as mainstream in the sense that the Orquestra Pau Casals and the Teatre del Liceu were. During its first season, Discòfils presented recorded music by Dufay, Josquin, Lasso, Palestrina, Victoria, Venosa, Morley, Gibbons, John Bull, Farnaby, Hassler, Gabrieli, Monteverdi, Bach, Handel, Vivaldi, Scarlatti and Couperin (Discòfils 1935c). In which concerns new music, Gerhard did by no means limit himself to the music of his teacher Arnold Schoenberg and his disciples; he did programme *Verklärte Nacht*, but also Sibelius's fifth symphony and Bela Bartók's second string quartet. In one of the listening sessions, he programmed Hindemith's *Mathis der Maler* symphony and Stravinsky's *Histoire du soldat* side by side, presenting them as embodying "the most fundamental musical values of today" (anonymous 1935c, 1935d). Debussy, however, is a conspicuous absence in the group's programmes,[10] but he was, among contemporary composers, remarkably well represented in live programmes in Barcelona and Madrid, and it is therefore likely that Gerhard preferred to focus on less frequently played composers.

This section has thus far discussed the impact of Discòfils among its rather small circle of members. The club did have some impact on broader musical circles in Barcelona and Catalonia, although evidence suggests that this was limited. Only two publications regularly covered the activities organized by Discòfils, both of which had a pre-existing specific interest in audio technologies: *Mirador* and *L'instant*, a short-lived evening newspaper closely connected to Radio Associació de Catalunya. One piece of evidence suggests that Discòfils might have even excited some rivalry in these circles. Otto Mayer, one of the critics at *Mirador*, organized a listening session of Hindemith's *Mathis der Maler* at the Ateneu Polytechnicum[11] in April 1935, just a few days before Gerhard's talk on the same work with Discòfils (anonymous 1935b). Although we do not know his reasons for doing so, it might be that he wanted to scoop Gerhard.

Outside Barcelona, Discòfils attracted attention from music societies in Catalonia, which wrote in to enquire whether the association could help them organize listening sessions (Discòfils 1935b). In response, Discòfils drafted a project, which however never came to fruition (Discòfils ca. 1935e). The terms of the arrangement would be as follows: interested local music societies should provide a suitable playback device (with Discòfils liaising with Gramophone on their behalf if necessary), and Discòfils would organize a series of one-hour sessions spread throughout the year, consisting of eight to ten disc sides each and accompanying introductions delivered by Josep Palau. The fact that listening sessions were offered as a package rather than as one-off events further hints at the group's commitment to systematically transform listening practices through close engagement with records and the practice of discophilia. The draft project only provides one sample programme for a potential listening session, covering Mozart's and Schubert's Lieder, which suggests that the group were sensitive to the fact that some of the repertoires that were commonplace in Barcelona were less accessible in other areas of Catalonia. Ultimately, Discòfils aimed at opening several branches throughout the region, which "could be truly transcendental for musical life in Catalonia" (Discòfils ca. 1935e). This confirms that they conceived of their modernizing project in national terms, with Catalonia (as opposed to Spain) being the national frame of reference.

Conclusion

The Discòfils documentation can certainly be interpreted in the context of the grand narratives of the birth of the record listener and of new record listening practices throughout the 1920s and 1930s. What we find here, however, is a fascinating wealth of detail that suggests that such narratives need to be particularized through a context-sensitive approach that acknowledges the local, regional or national practices and discourses that contributed to shaping the invention of the record listener.

There are several noteworthy aspects in the Discòfils activities that open up avenues of enquiry for the detailed study of record clubs elsewhere. The

first of those concerns the varying paces at which the developments identified by Maisonneuve and Tournès imposed themselves in different parts
of the world, depending on local, national or regional variations. The evidence from Discòfils suggests a long period of incubation lasting almost ten
years from the advent of electrical recording, during which a relatively small
number of isolated collectors became acquainted with the technology and
subsequently reflected how this was changing their listening practices. This
relatively long period of incubation relative to the record clubs discussed by
Maisonneuve (2002) and LeMahieu (1982) can be attributed to the smaller
size of the Spanish market compared to France or the United Kingdom, but
further studies in other peripheral contexts might help nuance this claim
further. Once Discòfils was established, however, its development was rapid:
even in the space of a year and a half, their members' understanding of recorded sound and music changed perceptibly over this time. We can hypothesize that such changes might have also impacted on the listening practices
of individual members.

The second of these aspects concerns the local, regional and national contexts that made it possible for an initiative of this kind to develop, that is,
the context-specific "materialities and sociabilities" at play here. The "materialities" would be primarily the relatively active network of record shops
operating in Barcelona from the early 1900s to 1935, which we can presume
helped normalize record consumption to an extent, providing future members of Discòfils with a constant supply of new records and opportunities to
informally socialize with each other in a physical space. The "sociabilities"
are more diffuse, and they would include the dissemination of certain national or regional discourses concerning science, technology and modernity
in both Spain and in Catalonia, interfacing with the more general discourses
discussed by Maisonneuve and Tournès. For example, in the case of Discòfils, we might hypothesize that the almost exclusive focus on the knowledge of music (as opposed to the purely technological qualities of the disc)
is down to the fact that from the early 1920s onwards, it was composers and
music critics who led the way in promoting new technologies as a way of
disseminating and popularizing classical music.

Finally, another reason why the Discòfils case study is fascinating is that
it ended abruptly, leaving us to speculate as to how the cultural shifts documented in their archive might have suffered further transformations after the association disbanded. With no formal notice of the dissolution of
Discòfils, we can only presume that the start of the Spanish Civil War on
18 July 1936 made it impossible for the group to undertake a third season.
Manuel Clausells was murdered in the first weeks of the war by uncontrolled
anti-fascist activists, whereas Anglès (who was a priest) moved to Munich
fleeing similar outbursts of anti-clerical violence; Conxita Badia left for
Buenos Aires; and Robert Gerhard was now absorbed by his work at the
Biblioteca de Catalunya and at the culture and propaganda services of the

Generalitat de Catalunya. After the Civil War ended and the Franco regime started, with Gerhard in exile in Cambridge and pro-Catalan cultural activities severely paired down, it is not surprising that Discòfils failed to re-emerge, cutting a historical process short as it started to develop.

Notes

1   Some of the bibliography that has covered some of these processes (often in specific cultural contexts) includes Feaster (2001), Feaster (2007), Gauß (2009), Kennedy (1999) and Stern (2003).
2   Biblioteca de Catalunya, "Gomis, Ricard", https://www.bnc.cat/Fons-i-colleccions/Cerca-Fons-i-col-leccions/Gomis-Ricard
3   Exceptions include Maisonneuve (2002) and LeMahieu (1982).
4   Thirty-six pesetas was indeed around the weekly salary of a Catalan textile worker at this time (Llonch Casanovas 2004, 137–9).
5   Although an association's *llibre d'actes* (minutes' book) would typically be updated regularly after each meeting, Discòfils' book only contains a minute of their first meeting.
6   Throughout this chapter, I will be using the Catalan form of Gerhard's first name as this was the name he used at the time. In exile in Cambridge (UK), Gerhard started signing as Roberto (presumably to dispel suspicions that he was of German origin), and this is the name that he is commonly known under nowadays.
7   During his first season as an artistic director (which effectively ran only from January to June 1935), Gerhard received a lump sum of 500 pesetas (Discòfils ca.1935b). During his second season (November 1935–June 1936), Gerhard was paid 300 pesetas per month (Gomis and Prats ca. 1935). Gerhard's salary (particularly considering that his duties to Discòfils were on a part-time basis) compares rather favourably to university professors' at the time, who started on about 667 pesetas per month.
8   There is no evidence however that this ever came into fruition, probably because it required financial and organizational resources that Discòfils was not able to amass. There is no indication either of the sorts of works or composers that the club planned to include in these records.
9   Salazar spoke about Stravinsky's *Duo concertant* and *Apollon musagète*, Prokofiev's *Le pas d'acier*, Alexander Mossolov's *The iron foundry* and Julius Ehrlich's *Dnieprostroi*.
10 Gerhard noted down the Pathé recording of *Sirènes* in a list of recent records (Gerhard 1935d), but there is no evidence that it was included in the listening sessions.
11 The Ateneu, together with other institutions, offered courses in Estudis Universitaris Catalans: Catalan-language, degree-level courses that could not be taught officially at the University of Barcelona since the Spanish Ministry for Education demanded Spanish as the language of instruction.

Primary sources from the Subfons Discòfils

Note: Several of the Discòfils' sources are undated; tentative dates are preceded by "ca.". Such approximations are my own (and explained wherever possible in the chapter), and may not always coincide with the dates given to the same documents by the Biblioteca de Catalunya.

114   *Eva Moreda Rodríguez*

Discòfils (ca. 1934a). *Untitled Piece of Writing Listing the Future Aims of Discòfils* [Manuscript]. Held at: Barcelona: Biblioteca de Catalunya. Arxiu BC 31.56 3.8.
Discòfils (1934b). *Estatutos* [Manuscript]. Held at: Barcelona: Biblioteca de Catalunya. Arxiu BC 3156 1.1.
Discòfils (1935a). *Llibre d'actes de Discòfils, Associació Pro-Música oficial.* [Manuscript]. Held at: Barcelona: Biblioteca de Catalunya. Arxiu BC 3156, 1.3.
Discòfils (ca. 1935b). *Acta Discòfils* [Manuscript]. Held at: Barcelona: Biblioteca de Catalunya. Arxiu BC 3156 2.3.
Discòfils (1935c). *Anunci de l'activitat per al curs 1935–1936* [Manuscript]. Held at: Barcelona: Biblioteca de Catalunya. Arxiu BC 3156 1.2.
Discòfils (ca. 1935d). *Manifest de Discòfils.* [Manuscript]. Held at: Barcelona: Biblioteca de Catalunya. Arxiu BC 3156 3.3.
Discòfils (ca. 1935e). *Avantprojecte [de creació].* [Manuscript]. Held at: Barcelona: Biblioteca de Catalunya. Arxiu BC 3156 2.1.
Gerhard, R. (ca. 1935a). *Letter to Ricard Gomis.* [Manuscript]. Held at: Barcelona: Biblioteca de Catalunya. Arxiu BC3156 3.1
Gerhard, R. (ca. 1935b). *Letter to Ricard Gomis.* [Manuscript]. Held at: Barcelona: Biblioteca de Catalunya. Arxiu BC 3156 2.15.
Gerhard, R. (ca. 1935c). *Letter to Ricard Gomis.* [Manuscript]. Held at: Barcelona: Biblioteca de Catalunya. Arxiu BC 3256 2.14
Gerhard, R. (ca. 1935d). *Columbia History of Music.* [Manuscript]. Held at: Barcelona: Biblioteca de Catalunya. Arxiu BC 3156 3.7.
Gerhard, R. (1935e). *Letter to Ricard Gomis, 12th October.* [Manuscript]. Held at: Barcelona: Biblioteca de Catalunya. Arxiu BC 3156 2.13.
Gomis, R. & Prats, J. (ca. 1935). *Letter to Robert Gerhard.* [Manuscript]. Held at: Barcelona: Biblioteca de Catalunya. Arxiu BC 3156 2.15.

Secondary bibliography

Alonso Tomás, D. (2013) 'Unquestionably decisive': Roberto Gerhard's Studies with Arnold Schoenberg. In: Adkins, M. (ed.) *The Roberto Gerhard Companion.* Farnham: Ashgate, pp. 25–47.
Alonso Tomás, D. (2019) From the People to the People: The Reception of Hanns Eisler's Critical Theory of Music in Spain through the Writings of Otto Mayer-Serra. *Musicologica Austriaca*, 5, available at http://www.musau.org/parts/neue-article-page/view/76?fbclid=IwAR0I1KyGsfuLavj7PLt_dMBJyCsjWExx0033vBF4lLUWGiqkfE-OAscYkb4 (last accessed: March 2020).
Andrés-Gallego, J. (1998) *Un 98 distinto. Regeneración, desastre, regeneracionismo.* Madrid: Ediciones Encuentro.
Anonymous (1935a) Discòfils. *L'instant*, 5 February, p. 7.
Anonymous (1935b) Sessió Hindemith. *Mirador*, 4 April, p. 8.
Anonymous (1935c) La sessió de Discòfils de demà: Hindemith i Strawinsky. *L'instant*, 11 April, p. 5.
Anonymous (1935d) Hindemith, Strawinsky. *L'instant*, 13 April 1935, p. 7.
Anonymous (1935e) Discòfils. *L'instant*, 31 October, p. 7.
Balibrea, M. P. (2006) Max Aub y el espacio-tiempo de la nación. In: Aznar Soler, M. (ed.) *Escritoras, editoriales y revistas del exilio republicano de 1939.* Sevilla: Renacimiento, 2006, pp. 163–9.

Feaster, P. (2001) Framing the Mechanical Voice: Generic Conventions of Early Sound Recording. *Folklore Forum*. 32, pp, 57–102.

Feaster, P. (2007) *"The Following Record": Making Sense of Phonographic Performance, 1877–1908*. Doctoral dissertation. Indiana University.

Ferrando Francés, A. and Nicolás Amorós, M. (2011) *Història de la llengua catalana*. Barcelona: Universitat Oberta de Catalunya.

Gauß, S. (2009) *Nadel, Rille, Trichter: Kulturgeschichte des Phonographen und des Grammophons in Deutschland (1900–1940)*. Vienna and Cologne: Böhlau.

Gronow, P. & Englund, B. (2007) Inventing Recorded Music: The Recorded Repertoire in Scandinavia 1899–1925. *Popular Music*. 26(2), pp. 281–304.

J.G. (1933) 'Els artistes i els discos'. *Mirador*, 30 November, p. 8.

Kennedy, W.H. (1999) *Recorded Music in American Life: The Phonograph and Popular Memory, 1890–1945*. New York and Oxford, Oxford University Press.

LeMahieu, D.L. (1982) The Gramophone: Recorded Music and the Cultivated Mind in Britain between the Wars. *Technology and Culture*. 23(3), pp. 372–391.

Llonch Casanovas, M. (2004) Jornada, salarios y costes laborales en el sector textil catalán (1891–1936). *Revista de Historia Industrial*. 26, pp. 100–141.

Maisonneuve, S. (2002) La constitution d'une culture et d'une écoute musicale nouvelles: Le disque et ses sociabilités comme agents de changement culturel dans les années 1920 et 1930 en Grande-Bretagne. *Revue de Musicologie*. 88(1), pp. 43–66.

Maisonneuve, S. (2006) De la machine parlante au disque: Une innovation technique, commerciale et culturelle. *Vingtième Siècle. Revue d'histoire*. 92, pp. 17–31.

Maisonneuve, S. (2007) La Voix de son Maître: entre corps et technique, l'avènement d'une écoute musicale nouvelle au XXe siècle. *Communications*. 81, pp. 47–59.

Maisonneuve, S. (2009) *L'invention du disque 1877–1949: genèse de l'usage des médias musicaux*. Paris: Éditions des Archives Contemporaines.

Mayer, O. (1935) La nostra discoteca. *Mirador*, 21 February, p. 8.

Moreda Rodríguez, E. (2019a) Travelling Phonographs in fin de siècle Spain: Recording Technologies and National Regeneration in Ruperto Chapí's *El fonógrafo ambulante*. *Journal of Spanish Cultural Studies*. 20(3), pp. 241–255.

Moreda Rodríguez, E. (2019b) Outreach, Entertainment, Innovation: Exiled Spanish Composers and European Radio. *Contemporary Music Review*. 38(1–2), pp. 7–23.

Moreda Rodríguez, E. (2020a) Amateur Recording on the Phonograph in *fin-de-siècle* Barcelona: Practices, Repertoires and Performers in the Regordosa-Turull Wax Cylinder Collection. *Journal of the Royal Music Association*. 145(2), pp. 385–415.

Moreda Rodríguez, E. (2020b) Reconstructing *zarzuela* performance practices ca. 1900: Wax Cylinder and Gramophone Disc Recordings of *Gigantes y cabezudos*. *Journal of Musicology*. 137(4), pp. 459–487.

Osborne, P. (1995) *The Politics of Time. Modernity and Avant-garde*. London: Verso Books.

Perry, M.E. (2013) Early Works and Life of Roberto Gerhard. In: Adkins, M. (ed.) *The Roberto Gerhard Companion*. Farnham: Ashgate, pp. 9–23.

Petit, J. (1936) Salazar a Discòfils. *Mirador*, 20 January, p. 8.

Palacios, M. (2008) *La renovación musical en Madrid durante la dictadura de Primo de Rivera. El Grupo de los Ocho (1923–1931)*. Madrid, Sociedad Española de Musicología.

Sterne, J. (2003) *The Audible Past. Cultural Origins of Sound Reproduction*. Durham and London: Duke University Press.

Swyngedouw, E. (2015) *Liquid Power Contested. Hydro-Modernities in Twentieth-Century Spain*. Cambridge: MIT Press.

Torrent i Marqués, A. (2002) Visió europea del naixement de l'enregistrament sonor. *Girant a 78rpm*. 1(1), pp. 5–9.

Torrent i Marqués, A. (2004) Efectes secundaris dels discs a 78 rpm. *Girant a 78 rpm*. 2(4), pp. 5–12.

Tournès, L. (2006) Le temps maîtrisé. L'enregistrement sonore et les mutations de la sensibilité musicale. *Vingtième Siècle. Revue d'histoire*. 92, pp. 5–15.

6 Mediatization of music, musicalization of everyday life

New ways of listening to recorded sound in Sweden during the interwar years, 1919–1939

Ulrik Volgsten

Music has undergone a tremendous mediatization the last 100 years. Electrification and, later on, the digitization of music media have exposed music to an increased dissemination, both spatially – it can be heard almost everywhere – and temporally – one can listen to music almost anytime. This increased spatial and temporal dissemination can be likened to a democratization of music. Anyone can listen to anything at anytime and anywhere. The claim is an exaggeration, of course (music is subject to both political and commercial constraints), but from a historical perspective the purely quantitative aspect of music's mediatization has been enormous. Even more important is the qualitative aspect of music's mediatization. The mediatization of music has affected our relation to music, not only how we sing, play and "create" it, but also how we listen, appreciate and understand it. As will be shown, there is support to the claim that music – at least in the West – is not the same today as it was 100 years ago. The general perception of what music *is* changed in fundamental ways during the twentieth century, from being essentially something one did together with others, a communal activity, to becoming an object, a personalized commodity intended for individual consumption in private detachment through new media systems such as records, players and home speakers or shielding earphones.

Mediatization is a concept borrowed from the media sciences. The phenomenon it refers to has been described as a long-term process where people in their communication both use and refer to media in such ways that "media in the long run increasingly become important for the social construction of everyday life, society and culture as a whole" (Krotz, 2009, p. 24). However, in the study of media's role for music in culture and everyday life, it is important also to speak about a musicalization – both of the media and of everyday life. While mediatization is about the media's long-term impact on everyday practices and communication in areas that were previously relatively unaffected by media, musicalization refers to a long-term process characterized by an increasing presence of music affecting our everyday

DOI: 10.4324/9781003006497-9

lives and ourselves. Hence the process of musicalization is intimately connected with new technological conditions and forms of mediation as well as with socio-cultural processes such as individualization, commercialization and globalization. In its broadest sense, the concept captures the gradually changing place of music in social life, from technologically non-mediated forms of music in pre-modern societies to the ubiquity of music in today's digitalized and globalized world (Pontara and Volgsten, 2017a).

The macro level changes and transformations described by the concepts of mediatization and musicalization nevertheless depend on what happens at meso and micro levels. While the mentioned changes and transformations of music may seem obvious from a twenty-first-century retrospect, they were not always so at the time of their occurrence. To the extent they were (limiting the scope to the twentieth century), old customs and everyday practices were soon forgotten, vaporized by the swirls of progress and overshadowed by the catastrophes of World Wars. This does not mean that all changed. Some of the old remained and some merely retreated into the background. The aim of this chapter is therefore to highlight and detail some fundamental changes and important transformations and displacements in everyday listening to recorded music as they first emerged. More specifically the period of time is limited to the interwar years from 1919 to 1939, when such changes were particularly significant. And the focus is on changes and transformations in the way music – both classical and popular – was understood, i.e. in the general perception of what music *is*.[1]

As a case the study focuses on Sweden, while assuming that the observed changes and transformations occurred similarly in other countries throughout the Western world (cf. e.g. Ashby, 2010; Katz, 2004). In terms of technology, Sweden was at the forefront in many respects, with national campaigns promoting many modern innovations such as domestic use of electricity.[2] In cultural matters it was hardly leading, although it was quick to absorb novelties from countries such as Germany, France, Great Britain and the United States. Considering record production, Sweden was at the frontier in the Scandinavian and Baltic regions (along with Denmark and Latvia; see Gronow, 2010; Gronow and Englund, 2007), and it is quite likely that the same can be said about the reception of recorded music.

Sources for the inquiry are various types of press coverage, such as entertainment and celebrity columns. In particular there will be focus on the journalistic novelty of the period, the record review. Partly constitutive of a public audience, the public criticism in the dailies can be taken as a valid indication of what many listeners heard when they listened to recorded music and how they made sense of it (cf. Volgsten, 2015a). An important proviso, however, is that the two dailies under scrutiny are Stockholm-centered, which may be seen as an urban centeredness at the cost of countryside periphery.

I have shown elsewhere that listening to recorded music changed in Sweden during the first half of the twentieth century (Volgsten, 2019). This transformation of listening involves three, partly overlapping phases, each characterized by a different approach to or view of the recording medium. During the first phase, the gramophone and its records are treated as a mechanical instrument, replacing not only "real" instruments, but also "real" musicians (anyone can play the gramophone). This approach alternates with a view of the record as a medium documenting a past event of music-playing, i.e. what one hears is a sort of aural picture of the past. Both views or approaches are finally overshadowed (although never eradicated) by a third view, according to which the recording medium is perceived as a generic aesthetic expression (cf. Maisonneuve, 2009, p. 151), somehow representing "real" music in the here-and-now. The first of these three mesophases of change will be briefly described below (for further detail, see Volgsten, 2019), after which the focus will be set on more specific micro aspects of change that ultimately paved the way for the third approach. The findings are finally considered with regard to their long-term effects and roles, i.e. in terms of mediatization and musicalization.

Playing the gramophone before the 1920s

Recorded music in Sweden during the early decades of the century met with a "utilitarian" approach among audiences (Volgsten, 2019). During this initial phase, the music played on the gramophone should be good to dance to, and the records should play the songs the socially gathered like to hear.[3] The same approach characterized consumers irrespective of whether the recorded music was played outdoors at countryside fairs, in the background at small town cafés, for dance at weekend or wedding parties or together with small string orchestras performing "gramophone concerts" at posh restaurants in the capital.[4] The records were *played* rather than listened to. And the gramophone was regarded more or less as a mechanical instrument, like a music box or a barrel organ – even when the recorded sound was a singing voice.

This utilitarian approach also accounts for the marked aversion against the record player encountered in the country's upper-class *salong*. A machine and a technological innovation, the gramophone mechanically imitated music and thus signalled a culture in decay. Although luxurious cabinet gramophone models, the so-called *salongsgrammofon*, were marketed in Stockholm already in 1917, they did not make it into the heart of the upper-class residences. "Real" music was an edifying activity in which one participated together; in one way or another, not a passive entertainment. Records and gramophones were too obviously tied to mass cultural expressions – anaesthetics of pleasure, to use a phrase from 1910 by the Swedish civilization critic Vitalis Norström – to be accepted by the cultural establishment.[5]

A third area dominated by the utilitarian approach was that of the producers and manufacturers. That the recording technology and its products were regarded somehow as mechanical instruments without regard to the artistry of the recorded performer was a view held even by Thomas A. Edison, the inventor of the phonograph, according to whom "[w]e care nothing for the reputation of the artists, singers, or instrumentalists. ... All that we desire is that the voice shall be as perfect as possible" (quoted in Suisman, 2009, p. 128). The statement, in a 1912 letter, shows an indifference towards the recorded artists typical of the time also in Sweden. It can be seen, for instance, in commercial advertisements of the Favorite label in 1905, marketing its records by only mentioning the song titles in its repertoire, and the Pathéfon label, who as late as 1916 announced records for the summer's dance occasions mentioning neither artist nor tune.[6]

Summing up the first decades of the twentieth century, irrespective of whether the verdict was positive or negative, the gramophone was regarded as a mechanical instrument to be *played* rather than *listened to*. It is not until after the 1920s that descriptions occur of the gramophone and its records as something to be listened to rather than played. However, a change can be observed already at the outset of the decade.

From playing together to solitary listening: record reviews, listening booths and living rooms

A change in attitude towards the gramophone and records can be noticed in Sweden around 1920. From a historical perspective, one of the most striking signs of this change is a review of a recording issued by His Master's Voice of Tchaikowsky's *Symphonie Pathétique*, performed by The Royal Albert Hall Orchestra. Published in the daily *Svenska Dagbladet* on December 12, 1923, and thus one of the country's first record reviews, it is quite likely inspired by the review of the same recording in the British *Gramophone* journal earlier the same year (the reviews are not identical). The review had been preceded in the same daily a few months earlier by an editorial report on new recordings, both classical and popular. However, the first report contained no critical judgment as did the second. It would take few more years before critical record reviews were more systematically presented in *Svenska Dagbladet* under headings such as *Grammofonnytt* ("Gramophone news") from 1926 on and *Grammofonrevy* ("Grammophone Review") in the 1930s.[7]

The emergence of record reviews in the press is important for the transformation of listening. Similar to the traditional concert review, the record review adds an aura of seriousness to the recording medium, in that the review shows that the music recording deserves serious discussion. A good example is the series of comprehensive record reviews entitled *Grammofonmusik under kritik* ("Gramophone music under criticism") in the same daily paper in 1928. It starts on November 9 with a critical discussion of the cultural and entertaining advantages of both serious and popular music, and concludes on February 8 the following year with an introduction of the new electronic recording and playback technology (electronically recorded discs had been commercially available in Sweden since early 1926). Whereas electronic recording enabled registration of a richer palette of details than did the earlier acoustic recordings, the new playback technologies with electric pickups and loudspeakers enabled the reproduction of a broader frequency range and a smoother balance between registers. As put in the rival daily *Aftonbladet* on March 31, 1926, the new electric technology offers "a clear and strong tone distinctly reproducing all the nuances of a recording".

The mentioned series of record reviews in *Svenska Dagbladet* was headed by the composer and critic of classical music Moses Pergament, who undoubtedly added a professional status to the undertaking.[8] Besides modern music by composers like Schoenberg and Stravinsky, Pergament took popular music, including jazz, seriously (although not without reservations). Similarly, he took a serious and critical interest in gramophone records, to an extent that exceeds many of his contemporary composer colleagues. Although reviews in other dailies may have been less ambitious than in *Svenska Dagbladet*, and of course not all records were positively judged, the overall impact on the readers of record reviews is likely to have been in favor of recorded music. The record reviews thus work against the negative attitude expressed by the relative absence of phonographs and gramophones in the upper-class *salong*. Yet another aspect of the review is important to bring forth. In addition to adding seriousness and cultural prestige to the recording medium, the record review carries an implicit reference to private and solitary listening. The record review is assumedly or explicitly based on repeated listening at will by the reviewer, even short sections of the recording, which is hardly possible in public settings and quite disturbing when listening with friends.

Thomas Mann's famous depiction of solitary listening in his 1924 novel *Der Zauberberg* (*The Magic Mountain*) may easily be (mis-)taken as an indication of a widespread practice (cf. Chanan, 1995, p. 41ff.; Gauß, 2009, p. 314ff.). Mann's listener is hospitalized in a distant sanatorium shielded by the mountains of the Swiss Alps, listening alone at night when the other patients are at sleep. For matters of historical plausibility, however, Mann's scene should be contrasted to the more overtly ironic one described in a 1923 issue of the British journal *Gramophone*. In the latter, solitary listening to recorded music is likened to abnormal activities such as "sniffing cocaine, emptying a bottle of whisky, or plaiting straws in [one's] hair" (Williams, quoted in Katz, 2004, p. 20). In other words, one can assume that Mann's description of solitary listening is more fictional than documentary of a widespread practice, and that solitary listening to either classical or popular music was, in Sweden as elsewhere, a radically new way of listening, emerging and consolidating in the interwar period.

Besides being a prerequisite for in-depth record reviews, solitary listening requires a shielded and undisturbed space.[9] The cloistered environment suitable for solitary listening described by Mann got a more prosaic and everyday equivalent not in the *salong*, but in the new living rooms of the modern family apartments presented at various housing exhibitions. For instance, a national housing exhibition in Stockholm in 1926 shows a plan of a small flat wherein the small living room accords a specially designated space for a gramophone. However, the flat of 40 square meters designed for a family of four persons indicates that the undisturbed space for solitary listening was more of an ideal than a reality for most people (Volgsten, 2019). As an ideal, it was nevertheless strengthened by not only the listening practice implied by the mentioned record reviews, but also by the specially designed listening booths, "furnished according to English/American principles", which the Stockholm retailers began to advertise around 1923.[10]

In the first decades of the century, records were sold by retailers of sheet music and musical instruments,[11] but records could also be sold by tobacconists, watchmakers and even by bicycle dealers. The first store to be devoted mainly to selling records appears to have been *Musikhörnan* ("The Music Corner") in Stockholm, starting in 1932 (Sörhuus, 2018, p. 8). However, the music stores boasting listening booths that cropped up in the 1920s usually had a separate department or section for their record sales. And rather than selling a small number of records together with the players, all manufactured by the same company, records were now sold individually to the customer's own taste and preference. The listening booths thus came to fulfill a function that differed from earlier displays of the technology's ability to represent recorded sounds as "natural" as possible. Instead, the booths were advertised as "comfortable listening rooms where each and everyone in peace and quiet and in a pleasant environment can make their own choice"[12] – a choice that nourished individual preference on the part of the consumer as well as a focus on the particular record release, i.e. the objective commodity form into which music was steadily turning.

The solitary listening situation offered by the new record stores' shielded booths thus differed radically from that of, for instance, the old countryside fairs, where one could pay to listen to recorded sound (music, speech, etc.) through rubber tubes. Listening at an outdoor fair had been a collective display in which the listening act and reactions of the listeners were part of the spectacle. Likewise, the public phonograph parlors, *gabinetes fonográficos*, and the *salons du phonographe* that could be found in the big cities of the Western world already around the turn of the century had been social venues (cf. Kenney, 1999, p. 26; Maisonneuve, 2009, p. 37; Moreda Rodriguez, 2017). In this approach, they differ from their solipsistic successors of the 1920s. Although the record store itself was a public venue, its shielded booths simulated the secluded listening space of the private living room. But what, more specifically, did the change in listening consist in?

Figure 6.1 Advertisement for record store with listening booths, *Svenska Dagbladet*, April 19, 1929.

Record reviews and the work of classical music

Reviews become regular strands towards the end of the 1920s not only in daily papers, but also in popularly oriented journals and periodicals such as *Scenen, Våra nöjen, Charme* and *Populär Radio*. The change in attitude that the reviews conveyed can be contrasted to Edison's concern with the truthful reproduction of the human voice. The phonograph and the gramophone had competed in terms of the respective technology's ability to reproduce sound and music as "naturally" and "life-like" as possible. From the outset, "naturalness" was a scientific criterion, although it would soon be promoted as an aesthetic value. As a value articulated against its binary opposite "artificial", this focus on the "natural" entered a conceptual space structuring a new aesthetics of listening through evaluative terms such as "active/passive", "communal/individual", "human/mechanical", "original/copy" – all grouped under the more dominant dichotomy "true/false".

In many ways, the change in attitude towards the gramophone and recorded music (both classical and popular) that can be traced in the reviews corresponds to transformations within this conceptual space. Evaluations and judgments change between terms, turning the formerly positive into the dismissed negative and vice versa, or simply to the discarding of certain dichotomies in favor of others. For instance, what was formerly dismissed as mechanical becomes regarded as human, whereas at the same time, the individual is changed into a positive marker to the detriment of the communal. How the dynamics of such a conceptual space may structure aesthetic imagination can be observed in a series of classical reviews published between February 1938 and July 1939 in *Svenska Dagbladet* under the headline *Inspelat och avlyssnat* ("Recorded and monitored") by music critic Kajsa Rootzén. Like Pergament, Rootzén had a thorough interest also for the modernists of the new century as well as for popular music (she had a candidate degree in musicology). The April 17 review starts with a lengthy introduction that merits full quotation:

> Serious gramophiles must – inasmuch as they do not live in their own villa – be something of a haunting for their neighbors. Their daily agenda usually consists of playing with full orchestra, and, if one is to go from some open-hearted confessions in the trade press, some of them go so far as to say that they prefer music in canned form rather than in the natural form of the concert hall. Thus, they have ended up in what from several perspectives can be described as a conceptual confusion. They have elevated the surrogate to an intrinsic value, the means to the end, and thereby overlooked, among other things, such an important fact as that the music of the great symphonic tradition was created for the big room, the public auditorium, and not for a private "cozy corner". [...] As study material, such recordings are utterly praiseworthy, but adequate as reproductions they are not, and as conserves they do not disclose

the whole truth about an individual impression. It is not just a certain spiritual dimension that is missing. There is still also this "one-eared-ness" in the impression that technicians are struggling to remedy, i.e. in that what we hear mediated through the microphone sounds as if the immediately present music were being listened to with one ear clogged. And precisely in the case of orchestral sound-complexes, this deficiency makes itself particularly noticeable. Even in circumstances of perfect recordings and even if it is a Toscanini who conducted the performance. The Italian maestro has an ability like maybe no other to make the air vibrate with intensity around a gramophone record [...] but equal to what he can bestow in terms of clarity and novelty at the concert podium it will not be.

What we see here, first, is that the previously dominant utilitarian approach towards the gramophone as a mechanical instrument has been replaced by a new attitude, according to which the recording is heard as "mediation [*för-medling*] through microphones" of an actual performance, a documentation of a previous event. But as such, the recording is inferior and the inferiority is threefold. First, it is a technical issue, a "one-eared-ness that technicians are struggling to remedy". But it is also a social issue. Rootzén uses the word "canned", a metaphor coined by John Philip Sousa in 1906. Sousa's metaphor was primarily directed towards what he saw as an impoverish-ment of domestic singing and playing (corresponding to the aversion in the early decades to grant entry to the gramophone in the upper-class *salong*). In Rootzén's review, the critique is, if not softened, directed instead towards the threat against public participation in the "public auditorium". Finally, there is what can be described as a spiritual issue, "a certain spiritual di-mension that is missing", which apparently seems so obvious to the reviewer it hardly merits further explanation: "equal to what [a Toscanini] can bestow in terms of clarity and novelty at the concert podium it will not be".

Now this may seem as if Rootzén, although regarding the gramophone record as a medium (not a music box or mechanical instrument), would de-spise it altogether as an invalid aesthetic form of communication, retaining it only for the utility of musical studies and training. The technical, social and spiritual limitations of the recording would, according to such a stance, add up to the view that the recording is a mere copy and not an original, not the real thing. That Rootzén does not unambiguously do so becomes clear in the other reviews in the series, in which the aforementioned transforma-tion and displacement of values and concepts shine forth in a remarkably clear way.

On April 24, Rootzén reviews Brahms' Violin Sonata in d minor, re-corded by Columbia, with Joseph Szigeti on the violin and Egon Petri on the piano. Although the gramophone is a mere "mediation" unable to communicate the "essence" of the music, Brahms is said to be "more of a chamber musician than a symphonist" in temper and mood, without "the genuine symphonist's need to communicate to a mass of listeners – not even when expressing himself symphonically" (Brahms, known for his low self-esteem, did not finish his first symphony until the age of 43). Thus, his music is "particularly suitable for private company". What these quotations indicate is an obvious reservation, if not negation, of the technology's supposed social inferiority. Rather, given the right music and careful listening, the gramophone record will provide an "increasing yield". The mechanical is not so un-natural after all. The music of a composer like Brahms, Rootzén goes on to say, may even provide "consolation and security, uplifting and support". In other words, as a means for individual mood regulation and self-boosting, solitary listening to music on record need not be dismissed as asocial behavior.[13]

An equally interesting revision of values can be seen in a review published on August 28, of Arthur Honegger's *Concertino* for piano and orchestra, on His Master's Voice, with Eugen Ormandy conducting the Minneapolis Symphony and Eunice Norton as soloist. The "composition" – not the performance-as-event – is "eminently recorded", and similarly so is the *Serenata in Vano* by Carl Nielsen, also on His Master's Voice. By thus speaking of the recording of the composition (rather than of its recorded performance), Rootzén indirectly questions the relevance of the distinction between the gramophone record as a recording of an event and as a mechanical instrument, in favor of what can at least in retrospect be interpreted as a recognition of the recording as a mode of aesthetic expression in its own right. Of course, Rootzén's wordings may be no more than linguistic short-hands for the view that gramophone records are recordings of events, but the fact that this shift in language passes without notice suggests a corresponding conceptual displacement.

The clearest manifestation of the view that the recording is heard as an aesthetic expression in its own right appears in a review on March 13, 1938. Here, Rootzén focuses on the première recording of Robert Schumann's Violin concerto in d minor on Telefunken, with Georg Kulenkampff as soloist and the Berlin Philharmonic Orchestra conducted by Hans Schmidt-Isserstedt. This last work by the then delirious composer (Schumann died in a mental asylum in 1856) had been withheld from the public domain since its conception, and its recent publication was not without objections. However, Rootzén's review is enthusiastic. The critic describes her own listening experience, when "lowering the needle into the outermost groove of the first record", how it has "something of the teasing excitement of sensation". In other words, the listening situation and the accompanying experience quite clearly involve playing the record, which could be understood as a manifestation of the older approach to the medium. But as she goes on, one understands that Rootzén is neither merely playing the gramophone, neither studying a documentation or a representation of a past performance-event. She is experiencing Schumann's Violin sonata in the presence of the situation: "as soon as one has gotten a bit into the work, a worthier attitude takes over and after a few more minutes one is capable of listening to the whole several rounds with composure and a more well-tempered mood". The crucial word is the "the work". The review continues as a critical comment on the musical work, a work that is being performed in front of the listener in that particular moment.

In this case, Rootzén listens directly to the work. The performance is reduced to an intermediate, serving the "essence" of the music. This rather extreme approach is in line with the attitude expressed by the conductor Ernest Ansermet in an interview by Rootzén on March 22, 1936. Ansermet speaks about the conductor's duty of not standing in the way of the work, but reproducing it "in a and for itself". Rootzén's verdict on Ansermet's achievements is "clarity – self-restraint – nobility". The interview is even introduced with a quote of Igor Stravinsky famously stating that, in the vein of the prevailing *neue Sachlichkeit* movement, "a conductor's value is exclusively revealed by his [sic] ability to see what is really in the score", i.e. the notational signs of the musical work purged of contingent interpretation.

Taken together, the reviews published by Rootzén over the course of 15 months in the late 1930s indicate a transformation of the approach towards the gramophone and its records.[14] Gone are any signs of the older approach towards the gramophone as a mechanical instrument to be played (one now "listens" comfortably in one's living room's "cozy corner", without having to crank up the gramophone with one's own hand power, since the traction is electric). The signs of transformation rather concern a change from regarding the recording as a "natural" documentation of a performance event to an approach to the recording medium as a generic aesthetic expression. The record represents a musical work to the listener, which can be repeatedly performed to the listener in a state of immediate presence.

This transformative process involves a change of the evaluative distinctions on several points. First, the social (active/passive, communal/individual) retreats into the background, more or less neutralized. Second, the technical (human/mechanical) and the spiritual (profound/trivial) both shift from the medium to the mediated. In other words, what is human/mechanical and profound/trivial are not issues of the gramophone and its records anymore, but of the recorded music, the musical work.

Personality, movie stars and priestesses of intimate art

Turning to reviews of popular music recordings, one may get the impression that not much is happening in terms of change during the interwar years. Artists are mentioned by name, but not much is said in detail about their respective contributions. Moreover, record reviews remain sorted under companies' labels at least until the mid-1930s. Reviews of popular music are also far less ambitious than are reviews of classical music. This goes for reviews in *Svenska Dagbladet* and even more so if one looks at competing dailies in the capital. Common in all papers is the increased mention of artist's names, which indicates a move away from the view of gramophones and records as mechanical instruments. However, the change seems to halt at the view of records as documentations of past events. The new records are repeatedly mentioned in terms of the artists having made a recording, which in Swedish is expressed with either of the words *inspelning, insjungning* or *upptagning* (appr. "in-playing", "in-singing" or "up-taking") – all referring to the past event in the studio rather than to the present event of listening to the record and experiencing the artist perform the music here-and-now.

There are of course exceptions, some of which warrant mentioning since they suggest a more profound transformation. In a May 27, 1934, "gramophone Review" in *Svenska Dagbladet*, the classical critic Moses Pergament reviews a recording on Columbia by "French gramophone singer" Lucienne Boyer, who reportedly has a "finesse and charm that radiates old culture". And as the critic goes on to say, "one is enchanted as much by her pleasantly toned-down but nevertheless intensive rendering as by her richly nuanced half-voice. Lucienne Boyer sings – figuratively speaking – in dampened light". Pergament's position as composer and critic of classical music in one of the capital's major dailies adds, as already suggested, status to the reviews. In addition, it is noteworthy that he – although generalized as "one" rather than "I" in the foregoing quote – admits being "enchanted" (*man tjusas*) by Boyer's voice, which is obviously experienced in the moment of listening to the record. And given that the critic also mentions the French titles of the songs, *J'ai rêvé de t'aimer* ("I've dreamt of loving you") and *L'étoile d'amour* ("The love star"), one may even guess that the listening experience has a vaguely erotic tinge, not least as it occurs in a metaphorically "dampened light".[15]

A different exception can be found in the daily *Aftonbladet*, which published reviews under the heading *Grammofonnytt* ("Gramophone news") sporadically from the end of the 1920s and weekly between 1935 and 1937 under the heading *Veckans skivor* ("Records of the week"). In a comment by signature "Miss Hot" on October 10, 1935, the "very beautiful" voice of the "naturally talented" singer Folke Anderson (recorded on His Master's Voice) would obtain optimal result if there were "a director behind the voice, just as there is one at the theatre and elsewhere". Not only does this comment anticipate the emergence of the record producer's role from mid-century on, but "the theatre and elsewhere" also nods to other areas of popular culture. In particular, the sound film (the most obvious "elsewhere" of the quote) turns out to have a close relationship with popular music and recording. Notably, there was an exchange of performers – singing actors and acting vocalists – since the pioneering sound film *The Jazz Singer* in 1927. The 1930s saw an international boom of musical films starring crossover artists such as Fred Astaire, Marlene Dietrich, Bing Crosby, Maurice Chevalier and Swedish singer-actor Zarah Leander. In the context of the daily press, this motivates a widening of attention. But rather than focusing on film reviews, it is celebrity coverage that tends to allow more musing comments on recordings and recording artists.

For instance, in a celebrity column in *Aftonbladet* on April 4, 1937, it is said that the same Boyer "has a capability of letting her charming personality reach through even something as unpersonal as the gramophone". Boyer, the reader is told on another occasion (October 23, 1932), "interprets the authentic femininity ... She is not a *grande dame* [sic] with a pied past and a dubious future – she is just a young woman that has become disappointed about love but expects everything of love". What these comments convey is something that the brief reviews of new recordings (of popular music) do not admit in their attempts at focusing on the product, namely the perceived personality of the artist and the authenticity of his or her voice. Neither are these qualities easily attained by the artist. As remarked by signature "Kid" in *Aftonbladet* on May 20, 1935:

> Some of the city's young singing voices right now do their best to sound exactly like Lucienne Boyer or Sophie Tucker or sometimes Zarah Leander. Which is a mistake since anyone can buy the original on record at any time they want, and since the originals are usually better, at any rate more similar to themselves.

A final example. This time the subject is not Boyer, but the Austrian "gramophone star Greta Keller" who has formed "a school for singing types with sensuous tremble of the voice" (*Aftonbladet* September 19, 1935). In a commentary in *Svenska Dagbladet* on September 13, 1936, by the signature "Dixie", on the occasion of her recent concert, Keller's voice is compared to that of Leander. Whereas Leander has "conquered Vienna" with her voice on stage, Keller has made a deep "impression" on the Stockholm audience even before visiting the city – through her recordings. But whereas Leander "is the Diva who dominates the stage from the minute she makes her entrance until she exits ... she is not intimate". Keller, by contrast, Dixie goes on to say,

> is the priestess of intimate art. She is simple but noble and withdrawn in her appearance. She stands absolutely still by her microphone and sings her songs without gesticulation – the expression of the voice and the face is all. Her dark tone is so soft that it barely reaches the back of the Odéon hall, or even above the orchestra, which by the way has faced a remarkably tough task in appropriating the discrete delicacy necessary for Greta Keller's accompanists. [...] A more intimate and elegant setting would have been more in the style with her entire person and a more tactful and adaptable accompaniment would have made justice to her delivery. The Greta Keller, who in her individual way gets close to us when her voice whispers with melancholy from the gramophone or the radio, one cannot obtain from the cabaret scene. Isn't this a paradox?

> (*Svenska Dagbladet*, September 13)

Now, if we read these record reviews and celebrity columns together (as the readers of the papers assumedly did – they were published side by side on the same pages in the papers) and compare them with the record reviews of classical music, we see interesting similarities and parallels as well as differences. For instance, it is striking that the popular music reviews so often remain sorted under the companies' labels. This is undoubtedly a remnant from earlier decades and indicates that the change is gradual. The new may overshadow the old, but never erases it. However, as we turn to the celebrity columns and their occupation with movie stars along with occasional comments on music (besides music films), we find that the evaluative opposition between active and passive is more or less gone. The listener is not assumed to be acknowledged in or partake in music-making to any considerable extent. The listener is non-active just like the movie spectator, but listening is no longer articulated against or contrasted with its opposite playing and singing (or, as would be the case in film, acting).

The distinction between the communal and the individual remains, but is rather shifted to the unquestioned advantage of the individual. The star is an individual articulated in contrast to the everyday woman and man, turning the communal into an inarticulate mass. The listener is invited to escape the everyday by being personally invited by the star. This can be observed on two accounts. The listener is addressed as an individual by the artist on record. The listener is invited to become the "you" of the songs, as in Boyer's *J'ai rêvé de t'aimer*. This effect is heightened by the new "whispering" vocal technique made possible by the electric microphone in the late 1920s, and is widely embraced by the new "gramophone singers", who also embraced the particular attitude of addressing its audience. As put by a Swedish radio producer; "it's not a great auditorium they're addressing, its *one single* individual" (quoted in Strand, 2019, p. 122). And correspondingly, as becomes abundantly clear in comments such as those on Boyer's past and future, the listener's interest is increasingly focused on the individual artist, on the artist's history and individual *personality*.

This focus on personality quite obviously differs from what Rootzén describes in her reviews of classical music. Listening to the music of a Brahms, for instance – reportedly suitable for "private company" – is directed towards the *work* (e.g. Brahms' Violin Sonata in d minor). No doubt, Rootzén pays due attention to musicians and conductors too; but rather than their personality, her interest lay in the universal human character expressed by the work of music (cf. Pontara and Volgsten, 2017b; Volgsten, 2021).

The paradox reported by Dixie in her column has to do with exactly this focus on personality (rather than character), perceived by the individual listener as a private and intimate experience: how can it be that the artist seems to get closer to the listener "from the gramophone or the radio" than live on stage? Part of the answer is of course the increased solitary listening, made possible by an increase of available private space at home, such as the modern living room with its electric power outlets. Solitary listening was also implicitly promoted by the activity of the record reviewer and the availability of shielded listening booths in the new record stores, where one could freely choose and listen to records by artists whose personal voices one found attractive. But how can the voice heard through the mechanic apparatus be humanly expressive, and even more so than the face-to-face encounter?

The solution to the paradox can be found in the same source material, which inverts the distinction between original and copy. Despite the references to the records as recordings (i.e. *inspelning, insjungning* or *upptagning*), it is the record and not the past performance event that constitutes the original. In the words of signature "Kid", "[A]nyone can buy the original on record", the latter of which can thus be repeatedly played and listened to. The statement may seem to be a single occurrence of an odd attitude. However, the close relation between popular music and sound film is obvious when it comes to how it was reported in the press. And experiencing the visual presentation of film as a fictional reality should be no more difficult than hearing the aural presentation of records as one.

There are further indications that the solution to the paradox is to be found in relation to experiencing film. For instance, in Svenska Dagbladet on September 15, 1935, the signature Z-a. criticizes a Danish film actress who is marketed as one-of-a-kind with the *diseuses* (speaking actresses influencing the cabaret tradition) Boyer and Keller, but who in contrast to the named song stars entirely lacks "personality". The word is written in English (not Swedish) on two occasions in the column, which indicates that "personality" may be an imported quality, a stylistic trait from Hollywood. Nevertheless, that personality would be a fictional trait, a rehearsed *persona*, does not seem to be a problem. The technique of cinematically constructing a sense of "reality" is even brought to the fore explicitly in a lengthy essay in *Svenska Dagbladet* on May 24, 1933, devoted to the recently published study *Film als Kunst* ("Film as Art") by the German scholar Rudolf Arnheim.

In other words, the readers of the dailies can be assumed to be at least slightly familiar with the artificiality of the sense of "reality" appearing on screen in a fictional present tense. And it is not unlikely that this voyeur-auditeur approach had an impact on the new way of listening to and experiencing music.[16] This is not to say that sound film would in any way be a necessary condition for listening to recorded music. What can be inferred is that popular music recordings, like their classical counterparts albeit in distinct ways, were increasingly heard by their listeners as generic aesthetic expressions.[17]

Mediatization of presence, musicalization of everyday life

The journalistic coverage of classical and popular music, found in reviews and celebrity columns of the Swedish daily press during the interwar years, differ in their subject matter. Reviews of classical music tend to focus on a fictional (or at least, ontologically problematic) object, the musical work (cf. Volgsten, 2015b). Popular music coverage significantly attends to the personal voice, the voice of a personality equally fictional, the artist's persona. However, both types of coverage recognize a new mode of musical communication through the generic aesthetic expression of the recording medium, a mode distinguished by a peculiar sense of presence. This is a kind of phonographic presence "here-and-now" in need of further study (metaphysically, phenomenologically and ideologically), which involves both temporal and spatial aspects. By contrast, the presence of the early century's mechanical instrument was not mediated, it was face to face (and the civilization critic of the upper-class *salong* would not face a machine). The documented performance, on the contrary, did not distinguish itself by the presence of the performance at all, but by its absence, its past tense.

In terms of long-term mediatization processes, by which Sweden exemplifies how a country can be peripheral in cultural respect without being ignorant or backward (in many technical matters it was, or was soon to become, among the leading), one can see both how the recording technology changed the way music was perceived and listened to during the twentieth century, and how everyday use changed the technology and its use. The interwar matters are particularly significant. On the one hand, passive listening to recorded sound by necessity places active playing and singing in the back seat. On the other hand, non-technological, everyday factors such as living rooms and record reviews in daily papers invite solitary listening at the expense of collective face-to-face participation.[18] And as the century continues, this solitary listening spawns a continuing demand for specially designed home equipment and mobile listening devices (teenage-room record players, cassette radios, the Walkman etc.; see Volgsten, 2021).

On a more abstract level of the medium, the natural grooves of the phonogram record are carriers of both immaterial form and its sounding materialization (a dual message that the phonogram transports as an enclosed sign from sender to receiver; see Volgsten, 2015b), affording the conspicuously twentieth-century notion of an abstract Platonic work. Less abstract but technically advanced, the electric microphone enables the intimate whispering vocal technique that seemed to bring the personal singer of the interwar years in private contact with its listener. After the Second World War, the technology would consecutively open up for the imaginative work of the sound producer and the creation of all sorts of ambiences, atmospheres and sonorous effects. At the same time, classical and popular music will both affect each other in terms of work aesthetics as well as personalized modes of listening.

The long-term musicalization, in turn, has to do with how music through these media increasingly becomes part of everyday life. As a commodity with a certain phonographic presence, music becomes available for purposes that were previously virtually unthinkable. While the accessibility is unquestionably a side of music's mediatization, musicalization refers to the parts of the transformation process that are irreducibly musical. It is a completely new role that the music has come to play in the private sphere, where undisturbed listening to an increasingly personal selection of artists and genres not only becomes possible but fully normal. And as the reviews and columns of the daily press during the interwar years indicate, music increasingly comes to function as a constantly available means for individual mood regulation, self-reflexivity and identification (DeNora, 2000; Pontara and Volgsten, 2017a, 2017b; Volgsten, 2021). Together with the work as aesthetic object, with which it recurrently conflicts, this notion of music as "self-object" accounts for what music has very much become since the interwar years of the twentieth century. Music is not so much a collective activity as it is a private object.

Notes

1 This amounts to a more profound transformation than merely of "the way we listen to music and the way music is performed" (Day, 2000, p. ix).
2 By 1918, Stockholm had its own hydropower station located 132 km north of the city, supplying the whole city with electricity at the beginning of the 1920s. By contrast, in a country where more than 80% of the population resided in rural areas, only 65% of the countryside households had electricity by 1939 (Hallerdt and Lindroth, 1992). Nevertheless, wherever it was available, new electric playback equipment could freeload off power supplies intended for more "useful" devices in the home such as lights, stoves, refrigerators etc.
3 The gramophone was introduced in Sweden in 1903 and soon replaced the phonograph, the sales of which had ceased by 1905 (Franzén et al., 2008, p. 144f.).
4 To address larger audiences, pneumatic gramophones were used, as witness advertisements throughout the 1910s of the so-called Auxetophone Concerts.
5 See Norström (1910). The negative attitude towards the gramophone can be inferred from its almost total absence in a contemporary posh journal such as *Svenska hem i ord och bilder* ("Swedish homes in words and pictures"), and by the almost exclusively negative comments it received in the daily papers during the first decades of the century (see Volgsten, 2019).
6 Pathéfon was the Swedish spelling used in advertisements for the French Pathéphone. The Swedish market was dominated by foreign companies, some of which like the Gramophone Company had a Swedish subsidiary (e.g. Skandinaviska Grammophon). The first major Swedish record company, relying mainly on Swedish artists, was Sonora, founded in 1932.
7 Record reviews were published on a more regular basis in the French daily *Le Temps* from 1920 on, and in the British *Times* from 1924 on (Maisonneuve, 2009, p. 210).
8 In many respects, Pergament was a pioneer, with a modernist approach that was still exceptional in the mostly national romantic climate in Swedish culture.
9 Solitary listening should thus not be confused with attentive listening, which it may facilitate but for which it is not necessary; attentive listening may be collective and public and (needless to say) solitary listening may be distracted.
10 Quote from advertisement in the journal *Scenen*, 20 1925. Stefan Gauß mentions in passing that the Lindström company had *Vorführkabinen* in one of their Berlin retail stores in the early 1920s (Gauß, 2009, p. 87). Jonathan Sterne mentions the telephone booth as formative for the "audile technique" required for solitary listening (Sterne, 2001, p. 158); however, when it comes to listening to recorded music, the record stores' booths are likely to have had an equal if not stronger impact.

11 In the United States it took until 1951 before the profits of record sales surpassed that of sheet music (Mundy, 1999, p. 79). In Sweden, it most likely happened later.
12 Quote from advertisement in the journal *Scenen*, 20 1925.
13 On recorded music's role as mood regulator and self-technology, see Volgsten (2021).
14 This is not to say that Rootzén underwent some kind of mindset-change during this relatively short time period, but rather that the reviews display a conceptual tension that indicates the transformation going on at a public level of discourse. That old ideas may linger on is exemplified by the conductor Christopher Hogwood likening a recording to "a photograph of an event" in 1985 (quoted in Day, 2000, p. 34).
15 That this is not only a case of male (heterosexual) fantasies thriving on the new technology and vocal technique is shown in McCracken (2000), Strand (2019) and Volgsten (2021).
16 Arguing from the point of view of the industry, it has been said that after the success of *The Jazz Singer* in 1927, "the meaning of popular music would always to some extent be dependent on its visual economy" (Mundy, 1999, p. 51).
17 It is worth pointing out that several critics that shine forth here were women: Kajsa Rootzén, Dixie (pen name for Ellen Liliedahl) and Kid (Ingrid Bruncrona). Like her male colleague Pergament, Rootzén can be seen as a pioneer record reviewer, although unique in being a woman. Liliedahl, by contrast, was one among many female film reviewers in the interwar years, a circumstance that changed to its opposite after the Second World War, when film criticism became established as "serious" and male dominated cultural journalism (Werner, 1976).
18 On the persistence of collective modes of music listening other than face to face, see Pontara and Volgsten (2017b).

References

Ashby, A. (2010) *Absolute Music, Mechanical Reproduction*. Berkeley: University of California Press.
Chanan, M. (1995) *Repeated Takes: A Short History of Recording and Its Effects on Music*. London and New York: Verso.
Day, T. (2000) *A Century of Recorded Music. Listening to Musical History*. New Haven and London: Yale University Press.
DeNora, T. (2000) *Music in Everyday Life*. Cambridge: Cambridge University Press.
Franzén, T., G. Sundberg and L. Thelander (2008) *Den talande maskinen. De första inspelade ljuden i Sverige och Norden*. Helsinki: Suomen Äänitearkisto/Finlands ljudarkiv.
Gauß, S. (2009) *Nadel, Rille, Trichter. Kulturgeschichte des Phonographen und des Grammophons in Deutschland (1900–1940)*. Köln: Böhlau Verlag.
Gronow, P. (2010) The Emergence of a National Record Industry in the Baltic Region. Paper presented at *The 2010 Baltic Audiovisual Archival Council Conference, Riga*.
Gronow, P. and Englund B. (2007) Inventing Recorded Music: The Recorded Repertoire in Scandinavia 1899–1925. *Popular Music*, 26(2), pp. 201–304.
Hallerdt, B. and Lindroth, C. (1992) *Ljus, kraft, värme: energiförsörjning i Stockholm 1853–1992. Stockholms tekniska historia 5*. Solna: Seelig.
Katz, M. (2004) *Capturing Sound. How Technology Has Changed Music*. Berkeley: University of California Press.

Kenney, W. H. (1999) *Recorded Music in American Life. The Phonograph and Popular Memory, 1890–1945*. Oxford: Oxford University Press.

Krotz, F. (2009) Mediatization: A Concept with Which to Grasp Media and Societal Change. In: Lundby, K. (ed.) *Mediatization. Concept, Changes, Consequences*. New York: Peter Lang, pp. 21–40.

Maisonneuve, S. (2009) *L'invention du disque 1877–1949. Genèse de l'usage des médias musicaux contemporains*. Paris: Éditions des archives contemporaines.

McCracken, A. (2000) 'Gods Gift to Us Girls': Crooning, Gender, and the Re-creation of American Popular Song, 1928–1933. *American Music*, 17(4), 365–95.

Moreda Rodriguez, E. (2017) Prefiguring the Spanish Recording Diva: How gabinetes fonográficos (Phonography Studios) Changed Listening Practices, 1898–1905. In: Barlow, H. and D. Rowland (eds.) *Listening to Music: People, Practices and Experiences*. Milton Keynes: Open University Press. https://ledbooks.org/proceedings2017/2017/02/27/prefiguring-the-spanish-recording-diva-how-gabinetes-fonograficos-changedlistening-practices-1898-1905/ (accessed 16 August 2020).

Mundy, J. (1999) *Popular Music on Screen: From the Hollywood Musical to Music Video*. Manchester: Manchester University Press.

Nortsröm, V. (1910) *Masskultur*. Stockholm: Idun.

Pontara, T. and Volgsten, U. (2017a) Musicalization and Mediatization. In: Driessens, O., G. Bolin, A. Hepp and S. Hjarvard (eds.) *Dynamics of Mediatization: Institutional Change and Everyday Transformations in a Digital Age*. Cham: Palgrave MacMillan, pp. 247–69.

Pontara, T. and Volgsten, U. (2017b) Domestic Space, Music Technology and the Emergence of Solitary Listening: Tracing the Roots of Solipsistic Sound Culture in the Digital Age. *Swedish Journal of Music Research*, 1, 105–23.

Sterne, J. (2001) *The Audible Past. Cultural Origins of Sound Reproduction*. Durham and London: Duke University Press.

Strand, K. (2019) Mikrofonsångaren: Sven-Olof Sandberg och gestaltningen av närhet och distans i de tidiga elektriska ljudmedierna. In: Volgsten, U. (ed.) *Musikens medialisering och musikaliseringen av medier och vardagsliv i Sverige* (Lund: Mediehistoriskt arkiv), pp. 107–28.

Sörhuus, T. (2018) *Stockholms skivaffärer & skivbörsar: en 100-årig historia*. Stockholm: Premium Publishing.

Suisman, W. (2009) *Selling Sounds: The Commercial Revolution in American Music*. Cambridge: Harvard University Press.

Volgsten U. (2015a) Between Critic and Public. Listening to the Musical Work in Stockholm during the long 19th Century. *Swedish Journal of Music Research*, 97, 1–25.

Volgsten, U. (2015b) Work, Form and Phonogram: On the Significance of the Concept of *Communication* for the Modern Western Concept of Music. *IRASM: International Review of the Aesthetics and Sociology of Music*, 46, 207–32.

Volgsten, U. (2019) A Technology and Its Vicissitudes: Playing the Gramophone in Sweden 1903–1945. *Popular Music*, 38, 219–36.

Volgsten, U. (2021) Extending the Sonic Bubble: Solitary Listening as a Technology of the Self. In: Nathaus, K. and M. Rempe (eds.) *Musicking in 20th Century Europe*. Berlin: De Gruyter. pp. 281–300.

Werner, G. (1976) Kvinnor pionjärer i svensk filmkritik. *Svenska Dagbladet*, March 5, p. 2.

Part III
Phonography as ideology
The reordering of knowledge
and sensibilities

7 Recording music, making business

The Russian recording industry at the beginning of the twentieth century

Karina Zybina

In 1878, *Niva* (Grainfield), one of the most popular Russian magazines,[1] informed its readers about Thomas Alva Edison's sensational invention: the phonograph.[2] An anonymous correspondent[3] described it as "a device which is able to record and preserve the sounds of our voice for a long time",[4] designed with the purpose:

> to *automatically* imprint and prolong the human voice, and reproduce spoken words at will. It means that even the sounds of the human voice become in a way immortal, speaking to our brain and heart for long, similar to writing.[5]

The comprehensive and accurate description of its technical features, accompanied by a couple of clear illustrations, demonstrated the extreme simplicity of this device that, according to the article's author, was "a general property of all devices that mark an era".[6] In fact, the article itself marked the beginning of a new epoch in the history of Russian music: the era of the sound recording industry.

A decisive step in the process of integration of this invention into the Russian market was made in 1880, as the prominent Russian publisher and librarian Florenty Pavlenkov,[7] in cooperation with his close childhood friend Vladimir Cherkasov,[8] issued a word-for-word translation of the influential book *The telephone, the microphone and the phonograph*[9] by French "scientific journalist" and inventor[10] Théodore du Moncel (1821–1884), who introduced the phonograph to European audiences. Provided with Edison's list of the phonograph's potential *faits accomplis*,[11] it briefly referred to the ability of this device to capture not only the human speech, as was stated before, but also "singing with or without the knowledge or consent of the source of their origin".[12] In doing so, the book made it very clear that the phonograph would soon have an impact on the entire world of music as well as familiar daily routines.[13]

This chapter chronicles and analyzes the first gusts of this strong wind of changes by tracing the history of Russian music recording business from its beginning up to 1917. It investigates the ways the recordings were integrated

DOI: 10.4324/9781003006497-11

into the Russian daily life by exploring the remaining printed sources (newspapers, magazines, posters, and libretti); it also scrutinizes repertoire politics and artistic selection and formulates how a global idea of recorded music was turned into a local business.

"An amusing toy, but nothing else"? The phonograph, 1889–99

The first phonograph, a newly produced "Spectacle" Class M model,[14] reached Russia in August 1889. It was brought by Edison's official representative and close friend, Julius H. Block (1858–1932). News about the arrival of this cutting-edge technological wonder spread fast, leading to a series of non-commercial, formal and informal, presentations of this curiosity spanning over the course of about five years. The first event in this series was initiated by the Czar Alexander III[15] and took place in November 1889 at the Gatchina Palace near St. Petersburg.[16] During this semi-official demonstration, some attendees, including the Empress, recorded their voices; Block himself reproduced musical samples, among others, a cornet solo for the Czar, himself an amateur cornet performer.[17]

On 31 October, an official presentation of the phonograph was organized in the St. Petersburg hotel Frantsiia (France). As the *Niva* magazine reported:

> Julius I. Block showed [...] the newest model of the *phonograph* invented by Edison, presented to him by the inventor himself during Mr Block's last stay in America, for scientific purposes only. The demonstration of this phonograph in the hotel Frantsiia was held with the attendance of a large number of scientists and writers invited by Mr Block [...] Using the phonograph, Mr Block reproduced not only musical pieces performed by different instruments and a human voice, industrial noises etc., but also a human speech – poem recitations etc.[18]

Soon thereafter, in 1890, Block received an invitation from the prominent Russian physicist Alexander Stoletov to deliver a three-day series of public lectures on the phonograph to his students and colleagues[19] at the Moscow University.[20] The lectures encouraged the active participation of the audience members, who were allowed to suggest pieces they would like the phonograph to record, and met with overwhelming success that could have hardly been envisioned even by the organizer himself. Stoletov called the public reception as "nechto nebyvaloe" (something unheard-of), and left the following description of the lectures in one of his letters to his colleague, Professor Vladimir Michelson:

> Imagine a lecture hall fully packed with people. I start with a short explanation (about 30 minutes), with attached illustrations. Then the following sounds are made: a clarinet solo, Yuzhin's declamation,[21] Nikita's singing,[22] an English scene with whistle and laughter, etc.,

etc. Then we start creating new phonograms: a female singer sings a romance, the count Tolstoĭ (a student) plays balalaika, students sing 'Down the river mother Volga' and 'Gaudeamus', we record and reproduce it in turns. As a conclusion, I shouted a phonogram for Edison, in English (it will be delivered to him) and sent him a telegram on behalf of professors and students. During these three evenings (8 to 11 pm), the lecture hall presented an astonishing scene. Boundless enthusiasm; both me and Block got enough of it! Now we've made some noise in Moscow; during the last evenings, [even] strangers tried to force their way [into the building]. But the device is really magical![23]

At some later date in 1890, Julius Block also took part in a similar event at the St. Petersburg Conservatoire[24] and other institutions located in St. Petersburg.[25] Apart from that, he also introduced the device to a number of distinguished musicians who either lived or passed through Moscow and St. Petersburg at the time, setting a number of private "tests" aimed at showing a diversity of the phonograph's functions and features. In order to document these events, he asked his respondents to leave a comment on the machine in an album,[26] managing to collect 17 holograph-signed testimonials, among others, by Pyotr Ilyich Tchaikovsky, Sergei Ivanovich Taneyev, and Nikolai Andreyevich Rimsky-Korsakov.[27]

Additionally, he organized a series of "test recording sessions", which eventually grew to an extensive collection of recorded music. Some of these recordings were offered for discussion to a large number of musicians in order to evaluate the device's quality and future prospects. Thus, in 1893, the young Leonid Sabaneev, alongside the brothers Pyotr, Modest, and Anatoly Tchaikovsky and the composer Taneyev, attended a presentation of several recently made recordings in Block's shop in Moscow. Their discussion focused on Paul Pabst's *Paraphrase on Tchaikovsky's Sleeping Beauty* (op. 66) and Anton Stepanovich Arensky's interpretation of a few excerpts from his own Trio in D minor (op. 32)[28] with the violinist Jan Hřímalý and the cellist Alfred von Glenn. According to Sabaneev, the attendees first listened to the music recorded on the wax cylinder, using three headphones in turns, then sat down in a circle and carefully discussed all pros and cons. The conclusions they came up with were quite different:

> Taneyev [...] was rather sceptical and pointed out that the invention meant nothing for the art and we needed to wait for improvements. Tchaikovsky, on the contrary, looked rather joyful and optimistic, and expressed his hope that the phonograph could well become very helpful for learning music.[29] In general, everyone agreed that this is an amusing toy, but nothing else.[30]

By 1899, when Block moved from Russia to Germany, he built up an impressive phonogram library that included "treasures"[31] such as Sergei

Taneyev's and Anna Yesipova's piano performances, Maria Klimentova-Muromtseva's, Yelizaveta Lavrovskaya's, and Nikolai Figner's voice samples, and many other curious items.[32] In doing so, Block acted as a collector[33] and not as a businessman, however: none of these recordings were made for commercial purposes.[34]

The only commercial activity around the phonograph was undertaken in 1890, when a group operating under the name *European Phonograph Tournée [Travel] Co.* organized a series of phonograph presentations in the theatre of George Paradise in Moscow[35] and the Hotel Europe in St. Petersburg. Led by Arnold Gillin as well as certain Mr Drehs[36] and Mr Coal,[37] the group advertised itself as Edison's representatives whose aim was to demonstrate "Edison's latest model [...] by means of a RUPOR [Megaphone] or 'Phono', allowing the phonograph's sounds (phonogram) to be heard simultaneously by any number of the public".[38]

The first sequence of presentations took place from 2nd to 4th March and was followed by two exhibitions on 26th and 29th of March; all events included the reproduction of circa 19 recordings, among others, seven orchestral pieces (mostly marches performed by different military orchestra as well as Mikhail Glinka's *Kamarinskaya* and a *Lydia Polka* by a certain Bauer), five solo items for different instruments (a Potpourri from the Charles Gounod's *Faust*, a gipsy song "Oh, Moscow, Moscow" for the oboe, a *Kamarinskaya* for the clarinet, an unknown solo on the piston cornet, and a beat of the drums), and four vocal pieces (an Aria from Giacomo Meyerbeer's *L'Africaine*, couplets from Karl Millöcker's operetta *Vice-Admiral*, a romantic song "Moscow", and an Aria from Johann Strauss' *Gypsy Baron*). Performed by a number of prominent Russian artists, the majority of them were made specifically for this demonstration. Typically, the orchestral version of the Russian National Hymn "God Save the Czar", performed by the military orchestra of the third Grenadier Petrovsky Regiment, served as the true highlight of the event.[39]

The reception of these events was rather cool, however. Julius Block, who attended the whole "Moscow series", characterized them as "an act of profanation", deeply criticizing the recording techniques and the results. According to his letter to Edison written on 15 March 1890, the presenters:

> did not speak into the phonograph, nor did they shout, they roared, so that I thought they would break the glass. When this yelling was reproduced, it came out so faint, that it was difficult to discern the words. A Cornet Solo of Mr. Levy's was announced. When this was given, I became completely disgusted ... many notes [were] chocked ... I was near despairing when I saw the crowd satisfied with this parody of reproduction, because they know of nothing better.[40]

A review with the catchy heading *The Phonograph With a Bad Cold* published in the *St. Petersburg Gazette* (*The St. Petersburg Newspaper*) after the "St. Petersburg series" was even more critical. Mentioning the lack of the interest in these events ("not many people were present ... ladies of uncertain age predominated"), an anonymous correspondent referred to Block's presentations, arguing that:

> those, who had occasion to witness the demonstration of the phonograph of Mr. Block, last winter, could readily conclude, that Mr. Gillin's phonograph very strikingly differs ... [it] brings forth continuously sounds, which remind you of Punch and Judy ... Mr. G. explained that the phonograph had travelled a long distance & the phonograms had grown damp!!! Goodness me! Exclaimed a sensitive lady, the phonograph has the influenza!! All the reproductions were so "grippy", that it seriously endangered the health of Edison's last child ... Well, we could not stand it any longer. When the phonograph gave a tremendous sneeze, we wished it good health, from all our heart and hurried off home.[41]

Between 1893 and 1894, the Moscow Museum of Applied Knowledge hosted the next documented series of phonograph presentations, moderated by the director of the applied physic department, Albert Repman.[42] Towards the end of the century, however, the strong interest in this device gradually waned. Still unavailable for sale, the phonograph remained "an amusing toy, but nothing else" for the absolute majority of the Russian population. As a consequence, the Russian recording industry was small and scarcely visible. Only the rise of the gramophone and gramophone discs in the Russian market dramatically changed this situation.

"As necessary as a sewing machine": Gramophone and pathephone (1899–1907)

In 1898, the founder of the *United State Gramophone Company* Emile Berliner sold his patents to a group of investors based in Europe. Headed by Trevor Williams, the group that founded the *Gramophone Company* strived to have the European monopoly on the new product: recorded music. According to its advertisement, the company would bring to homes of their potential costumers "the actual voices of orators, singers, comedians and story-tellers", stating that "no sooner does an artist become a popular favourite than he or she is invited to sing and play for us, into a Gramophone".[43]

In 1899, Sophia Medvedeva's vocal ensemble recorded a sample of Russian folk songs issued by the *E. Berliner Gramophone* company in London. While on tour in the UK,[44] the ensemble recorded about 100 gramophone discs, mostly Russian folk songs and romances, among others, the famous *Ochi chërnye* ("The black eyes").[45] Importantly, all discs were intended for sale in Russia.[46]

Immediately after this recording session in London, two Berliner's representatives, William Sinkler Darby and Fredrick William Gaisberg, were sent to Russia in order to produce a new series of Russian discs.[47] Travelling by train from Eidkunen (Germany), they gave gramophone concerts at their stops held to "the amusement of the natives".[48] A one-month session[49] that took place in St. Petersburg brought about an impressive collection of 239 new gramophone discs, recorded by a number of Russian opera and romance singers, a balalaika player, and the Finliandsky Guard Regiment orchestra. Soon thereafter, the discs were prepared for launch and went for sale.[50]

In 1901, the society *Grammofon v Rossii* (Gramophone in Russia) was established in St. Petersburg;[51] in 1902, the *Gramophone* company opened a branch office in Riga with the purpose to cover all Russian-speaking territories with the official Gramophone production: *Otdelenie fabriki plastinok russkogo repertuara* (A branch office of the disc factory with the Russian repertoire). It is not surprising therefore that in 1902, the newly launched magazine *Grammofon i fonograf* (*Gramophone and phonograph*) stated that:

> gramophone and phonograph are not just technical devices; like clocks, which were unavailable to the middle class in the past, gramophones have been in the same position until very recently. Now that the technical advancements of gramophone and phonograph pushed down prices, their range of activities has widened to such a degree that they breached the wall and became as necessary for every cultured citizen as a sewing machine.[52]

Between 1901 and 1902, the St. Petersburg branch organized a special recording session with distinguished artists such as the tenors Leonid Sobinov and Nikolai Figner, the soprano Medea Figner, and the bass Feodor Chaliapin. Noticeably, every recording made by an opera "celebrity" was handsomely paid. As the *Grammophone i fonograph* reported:

> the famous artist of the Imperial Opera House Feodor I. Chaliapin sang for the gramophone "Le veau d'or est toujours debout" from the opera *Faust* (catalogue number 22823), Susanin's aria from the opera *A life for the tsar* (22892), and six romances: "When the King went forth to war" by Feodor Koenemann (22820), "Ah thou red Sun" by Mikhail Slonov (22821), "Elegy" by Gennariĭ Karganov (22822), "Disappointment" by Tchaikovsky (22824), "The Night", a Russian song (22891), "The nightingale" by Tchaikovsky (22825) [...] The singer was paid 2,000 rubles for each aria and romance that he sang. As we know, Chaliapin refused another offer made to him last October by the Zonophone company, but has apparently succumbed to the temptation now. Supposedly,
>
> > Le veau d'or est toujours debout;
> > On encense sa puissance
> > On encense sa puissance
> > D'un bout du monde à l'autre bout!
>
> By the way, Nikolai N. Figner, too, solemnly stated in his letter, published in "The New Times" two years ago, that he *never* sang and would *never* ever sing for the gramophone or phonograph because this would

be a profanation of art. But tempora mutantur, et nos mutamur cum illis, so Figner ... changed his mind about gramophones and sang several
dozens of pieces.[53]

Despite this barely concealed criticism from the journalist, this session was
of crucial importance: it led to a production of Tchaikovsky's earliest recorded compositions. Some of these recordings are now preserved in the
collection of the Russian State Archive of Recordings (these recordings are
listed in Table 7.1 with their reference numbers).[54]

By 1903, both the gramophone and gramophone discs drove the phonograph and cylinders out of the Russian market.[55] As the 1903 Gramophone
Catalogue stated:

> until recently, just 5 years ago, the gramophone was a novelty in Russia.
> It was seen as a curious device, and his inventor was considered by the
> technical world as someone who compiled and transformed the inven-
> tion designed by someone else. But what do we see right now? The gram-
> ophone drove the phonograph fully out. From a curiosity, it turned into
> a necessity for every educated family. The gramophone serves for en-
> tertaining, learning, it trains ear and aesthetic taste. The gramophone
> distracts people from drinking.[56]

At nearly the same time, the *Grammofon i fonograph* noted that "the record
company Pathé [based] in Paris expressed its desire to enrich us with more
information from France"[57] and so to enter the Russian recording market and to reach the potential Russian audience as well. In 1904, the same
source stated that:

> the Paris company Pathé made a Russian recording on wax cylinders.
> The best and distinguished artists were invited, and a lot of numbers
> were recorded. The representative office is given to Mr Iakob and the
> ex-agent of the Pathé company Mr Filips, who established a special
> warehouse in Moscow on a cooperative basis. Personally, we have not
> heard these cylinders yet.[58]

In March 1904, the same magazine mentioned a recording session undertaken by the Pathé company in St. Petersburg and listed the recorded
compositions, the majority of which were written by Russian composers
such as Alexander Nikolayevich Serov, Tchaikovsky, and Glinka.[59] In August 1904, it informed its readers that the discs were already available "in
stock in St. Petersburg".[60] In 1907, a new recording machine was launched,
named after the Pathé company: the pathephone. According to the an-
nouncement published in *The Gramophone News* magazine, the device was
able to reproduce music without styluses, noises, hissing, and inconvenient
sounds, being "the only speaking machine that has a diaphragm with a

Table 7.1 Gramophone recordings of Tchaikovsky's works made between 1901 and 1902; the collection of the Russian State Archive of Recordings (RGAFD)

Shelfmark	Recording date	Recording title	Performer
4/63453 (Nr. M10–45309)	1901	Lensky's arioso "Ia lublu vas, Ol'ga" ("I love you, Ol'ga") from "Eugene Onegin"	Leonid Sobinov with piano accompaniment
4/63453 (Nr. M10–45309)	1901	Lensky's arioso "V vashem dome" ("In your house") from "Eugene Onegin"	Leonid Sobinov with piano accompaniment
4/63453 (Nr. M10–45309)	1901	Lensky's aria "Kuda, kuda vy udalilis" ("Where have you gone, O golden days of my spring?") from "Eugene Onegin"	Leonid Sobinov with piano accompaniment
4/63455 (Nr. M10–45314 (22549))	1901	Andrei's aria "Kak pered Bogom" ("Like before God") from "Mazeppa"	Nikolai Figner with piano accompaniment
4/63455 (Nr. M10–45314 (22618))	1901	German's arioso "Prosti, nebesnoe sozdan'e" ("Forgive me, celestial creature")	Nikolai Figner with piano accompaniment
4/op. 10 "G"/38 (Nr. M10–45191 (23135))	1901	Liza's aria "Ah, istomilas' ia gorem" ("I am worn out by grief")	Medea Figner with piano accompaniment
4/63453 (Nr. M10–45310)	1901	"Za oknom v teni mel'kaet" ("Outside in the shadows"), op. 60 Nr. 10	Leonid Sobinov with piano accompaniment
4/63455 (Nr. M10–45314)	1901	"Strashnaia minuta" ("A terrible moment") op. 28, Nr. 6	Nikolai Figner with piano accompaniment
4/63468 (Nr. M10–45415 (22824))	1902	"Razocharovanie" ("Disappointment") op. 65, Nr. 2	Feodor Chaliapin with piano accompaniment
540/op. 35 "g"/203 (Nr. 36561)	1902	"Solovei" ("Nightingale") op. 60 Nr. 4	Feodor Chaliapin with piano accompaniment

Figure 7.1 Advertisement for the pathéphone in *The Gramophone News* magazine (*Novosti grammofona* 1 (1908)).

permanent sapphire".[61] The breaking character of this novelty was intensified by an illustration showing a discobolus, who throws a gramophone disc (see Figure 7.1).

Afterwards, Pathé gradually turned into the main recording company in Russia; in 1907, it opened its factory in Moscow, then new branches in St. Petersburg, Rostov-on-Don, and Odessa.[62]

"More popular than in other countries": The audience and its response (1907–1917)

In 1907, one of the editors of *The Gramophone News*, A. Emte, placed the following address on the first page of the April issue:

> It is hard to imagine how fast the gramophone has spread throughout the whole world, even though not much time has passed since its invention. This wide and fast dissemination of speaking machines may at first glance seem even more impressive, if one takes into account relatively high prices

for these devices and discs, a short life span of these discs on the one hand and the common tendency to renew their repertoire constantly on the other. All this requires considerable, sometimes even great, expenditures. [...] Nonetheless, however strange it may seem at first glance, the gramophone has become more widespread in Russia than in other countries.[63]

The enormous popularity of both the gramophone and the pathephone is further confirmed by the fact that by 1910, there were around 80 recording companies active in Russia.[64] They regularly supplied the recording market with new discs, mostly recorded by distinguished Russian artists.[65] Vocal music – opera excerpts, songs, romances, and Russian folk songs – constituted by far the greatest part of these productions. For instance, the 1912 poster published by the Pathé company advertised two different series of newly made recordings marked "with the yellow etiquette" and "with the red etiquette" (see Figure 7.2). The "yellow" list (12 discs, see the left side of the poster) consisted exclusively of classical music and included a number of vocal and instrumental solos; the "red" list (35 discs) contained numerous Russian folk songs, choir performances, and several orchestral compositions played by the Pathé orchestra. Twenty discs – slightly more than one-half of the entire collection – were dedicated to vocal compositions.

Significantly, Pathé's focus on folk music might be based on an observation made by Pathé's representative Theobald Noble during his recording trip to Russia in 1911–1912. Describing his experience in the *Talking Machine World* magazine, he noticed the interest of illiterate majority of the Russian population in the recorded music, arguing that:

> Russia will eventually outdo the United States as regards the number of records sold yearly. At present the population of Russia is in a state of emancipation, which is slowly but surely making progress. There is a musical population of something like two hundred millions. The great majority are at present illiterate and still the yearly sales of the combined talking companies reach any number over ten millions per year.[66]

Opera excerpts were taken from works composed both by Russian and foreign composers; they were often printed together with their texts, the so-called *Libretti*, which also appeared separately either in various magazines or as single volumes. Texts in foreign languages were normally translated into Russian. These translations sometimes replaced original texts in the actual performance of the piece. One example of this kind comes from an overview of some new *Gramophone* recordings published anonymously in 1907:

> Mr Karenzin sang Alfred's aria from the *Traviata* for us (catalogue number 2–22966). It was not bad at all. When Russian artists embark on a performance of Italian arias, they always take risks. After Italians, with their divine bel canto and charming mezzo voce, it is nearly impossible to listen to Russian singers in the same arias. An exception

Figure 7.2 Poster published by the Pathé company in August 1912, courtesy of
the Russian State Library named after Vladimir I. Lenin, shelfmark
IZO P0 I №9/3.

must be made only for Sobinov and his Italian voice. Mr Karenzin has a
clear and resonant, but a little bit flat, tenor, and he was able to succeed
in this aria. He performs it very clearly on this disc. Nevertheless, we

can explain the tendency of the *Gramophone* company to record Italian arias performed by Russian singers only by its desire to meet the wishes of the Russian audience to listen to Italian arias in Russian.[67]

The enormous popularity of recording machines in pre-revolutionary Russia can be seen in the same light: they fulfilled the desire of a wide Russian audience – coming mostly from the countryside – to become active participants in musical life, which was only available for the educated class before.[68] Numerous opera excerpts taken from the works written by Russian and European composers, but sung predominantly in Russian, opened the gate to the cultural life that had for so long remained closed and "secretive". At the same time, the Russification of foreign compositions blurred the line between "the Self" (what constituted the national "identity") and "the Other": Glinka and Mozart, Tchaikovsky and Wagner all became part of a more abstract idea of universal (and global) music. Significantly, the numerous libretti accompanying the newly issued recordings were categorized by (1) catalogue numbers and (2) performers' names; composers' names and work titles appeared in small print and were nearly unnoticeable for casual observers.

Moreover, the growing recording business stimulated an appropriation of the Western church music. The most impressive example is the 1911 catalogue that covered all the discs published in and for Russia by the Pathé company,[69] among which were single pieces by Russian composers such as Dmitri Stepanovich Bortniansky, Alexander Tikhonovich Gretchaninov, and Tchaikovsky. The large catalogue section "Duhovnoe horovoe penie" ("Sacred Choir Singing") also lists the "Lacrimosa" from Wolfgang Amadeus Mozart's unfinished *Requiem* Mass KV 626 (catalogue number 27520; see Table 7.2).[70] Sung in Russian, it was performed by the Iukhov Choir,

Table 7.2 Excerpt from the 1911 Pathé Records Catalogue, section "Duhovnoe horovoe penie" ("Sacred Choir Singing") (p. 149)

Choir led by I. I. Iukhov

Catalogue number	Title	Composer
27535	Sovet prevechnyi	
27536	Tebe Boga hvalim	Bortniansky
27539	Blazhen muzh	Tchaikowsky
27541	Svete tihii	Tchaikowsky
27516	Gospodi, pomilui	Voskresenskii
27528	Raduitesya Bogu	Bortniansky
27534	Hvalite imia Gospodne	Andreev
27542	Ot iunosti	
27517	Vidish moiu skorb'?	Astaf'ev
27520	Lacrimosa	Mozart
27514	Otche nash	Ivanov
27515	Veruiu	Gretchaninov

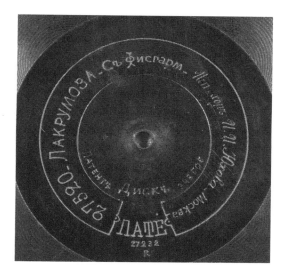

Figure 7.3 W. A. Mozart, *Lacrimosa*, performed by Iukhin Choir, Pathé recording
disc, catalogue number 27520.

a salaried employee of numerous Moscow churches, appreciated for its interpretations of Russian church music.[71]

Significantly, the inscription on the disc mentions the recording company,
the catalogue number of the recording, the work title ("Lacrymosa"), and
the performers ("performed by I. I. Iukhov Choir, Moscow, accompanied
by the pump organ"; see Figure 7.3), but omits the name of the composer.
Given the surrounding context, Mozart's music could well have been perceived by the audience as written by one of the Russian composers.

The recording industry that emerged so forcefully at the beginning of the
twentieth century played a decisive role in shaping this new world of music and changing the direction of its history. What started as a mere game,
"an amusing toy, but nothing else", gradually turned into a successful local
business deliberately aimed at the wide Russian audience, but also into a
powerful tool that made deep marks and incisions in the reception history
of classical and popular music.

Notes

1 Regularly issued from 1870 to 1918, it positioned itself as "an illustrated journal of literature, politics and modern life" ("иллюстрированный журнал
литературы, политики и современной жизни"). All translations in this article
are mine, unless noted otherwise. Transliterations are based on the Modified Library of Congress system, excerpt for already established names and titles (e.g.,
Pyotr Tchaikovsky instead of Pëtr Chaikovski).

2 The publication was a part of a massive international advertising campaign which started in 1877; the original report, provided with a simple illustration, appeared on 22 December 1877 in the American popular science magazine *Scientific American* (pp. 384–385) and was followed by a sequence of reports and advertisements worldwide; a representative selection from these publications is offered in Roland Gelatt's influential book (1955, pp. 25–30). Similar to other European countries, the phonograph first entered Russia through printed sources; see more about it in Elodie Roy's recent paper (2016).

3 At the end of the article, only the abbreviation "St. P. H." is given.

4 Russian: "Аппарат, записывающий и сохраняющий звуки нашего голоса".

5 Russian: "назначение этого аппарата состоит в том, чтобы автоматически закреплять и делать более продолжительною человеческую речь и, по произволу, автоматически повторять сказанные слова. Это значит: самыя звуки человеческого голоса делаются так сказать бессмертными, на долгое время говорящими нашему уму и сердцу, подобно письменам"; see St. P. H. (1878, p. 90).

6 Russian: "общее свойство всех устройств, делающих эпоху"; ibid.

7 Pavlenkov is also known as the founder of the series "Biograficheskaia biblioteka: Zhizn′ zamechatel'nykh liudei" ("The Biographical Library: Lives of Remarkable People") that still enjoys nationwide popularity in Russia; see more about his activity in this field in Trigos and Ueland (2018).

8 Ibid. (p. 49). After Pavlenkov's death, Cherkasov wrote the first official biography of his friend; see Cherkasov (1907).

9 The original French version served as a basis for this translation; Du Moncel (1878).

10 The characteristics given him in the obituary published in the British journal *Nature* 22 February 1884 (pp. 412–413).

11 The list was first published in the newspaper *The North American Review*; significantly, the phonograph's ability to record and to reproduce music was listed nearly at the very end as one of the additional features, but not the dominant one; see more about it in Jüttenmann (1979, p. 32).

12 Du Moncel (1880, p. 296). The translation is adopted from 1879 American edition; Du Moncel (1879, p. 258). In the English-speaking version, this passage lacks any reference to music, the signal words "chants" and "penie" (singing) in the French- and Russian-speaking version, respectively.

13 As Anna Fishzon stated, recording machines, integrated into the daily life, were able to redraw boundaries between "private and public, work and leisure" (2011, p. 807), for, according to Evan Eisenberg, "it is possible to play records while [eating, shaving, writing, and falling asleep], and for many people it was impossible not to" (2005, p. 38). To mention is also John Philip Sousa's 1906 prophecy that "it will be simply a question of time, when the amateur disappears entirely" (1906, p. 280); for more about the changing world of music, see Katz (2011).

14 A distinguish feature of the Class M model was a built-in electric motor which enabled an accurate speed adjustment. However, the model suffered from a serious disadvantage: it was about 22 kilos in weight; see more about this machine in Jüttenmann (1979, p. 48).

15 In doing so, Alexander III continued the tradition of "royal presentations" given in Europe from 1888 onwards. One of the most famous royal events took place in 1888 in the presence of the aged Queen Victoria and resulted in the unique recording of her voice; see more about it in Dash (2011).

16 Presumably, the presentation took place on 10 November: the so-called cablegram with the reference to this event was sent by Block to Edison on 11 November; see Block to TAE, 11 November 1889 (D8958AAT; TAEM 127:615). All quotations from Edison's correspondence are taken from the digital edition

provided by the Rutgers School of Arts and Science and given according its citation rules; see http://edison.rutgers.edu/citationinst.htm (accessed 11 January 2021).

17 According to the information given in Koenigsberg (1992, p. 3). Inspired by this presentation, Alexander III urgently requested his own device. In order to response to this request, Edison sent to him a not yet for sale "Water Power" phonograph model which was received on 7 April 1890 (according to the information given in Block's letter to Edison, see Block to TAE, 11 April 1890 (D9055AAP; TAEM 130:176)); see about it also in Denisov (2016, p. 135).

18 Russian: "Ю.И. Блок показывал [...] новейший тип изобретенного Эдисоном фонографа, врученного ему лично изобретателем, – во время последнего пребывания г. Блока в Америке, – исключительно для научных целей. Демонстрирование этого фонографа в гостинице Франция произведено в присутствии приглашенного г. Блоком, многочисленного общества ученых и писателей [...] Кроме воспроизведения музыкальных пьес, исполненных на различных инструментах и человеческим голосом, фабричного шума и пр., г. Блок воспроизвел на фонографе человеческую речь – декламирование стихов и пр"; see Anonymous (1889, p. 1167). It is still noticeable that the phonograph's main function as a music recording machine hadn't been established yet; demonstrations featured a range of sounds.

19 According to Block, the event was attended by at least "80 professors of the university"; see Block to TAE, 28 February 1890 (D9055AAI; TAEM 130:155).

20 Block erroneously locates this event in the Imperial Technical Society; see ibid.

21 Alexander I. Yuzhin, the artist of the Maly Theatre in Moscow.

22 Under the pseudonym Madamoiselle Nikita was known the soprano Louisa Margaret Nicholson.

23 Russian: "Успех вышел колоссальный—нечто небывалое. Представьте себе битком набитую аудиторию. Начинаю я кратким объяснением (около получаса), с рисунками в приложении. Затем перед ними поочередно раздаются — соло на кларнете, декламация Южина, пение Nikita, английская сцена со свистом и хохотом и пр., пр. Затем начинаем творить новые фонограммы: певица поет романс, граф Толстой (студент) играет на балалайке, студены поют 'Вниз по матушке по Волге' и 'Gaudeamus', все это по очереди записываем и воспроизводим. В заключение всего я прокричал по-английски фонограмму к Эдисону (она будет ему переслана) и отправил от имени профессоров и студентов телеграмму ему же. Удивительное зрелище представляла аудитория в эти три вечера (8-11 ч.). Энтузиазм беспредельный; досталось и Блоху и мне! Теперь мы нашумели на всю Москву; последние вечера к нам ломились уже посторонние лица. А снаряд действительно волшебный!", quoted from Tepliakov and Kudriavtsev (1996, p. 70). Some sources link this description to an unidentified 1879 event in the Moscow Museum of Applied Knowledge; I was unable to find any clue about it, however. The first documented series of phonograph presentations hosted by the Museum took place between 1893 and 1894 and was moderated by the director of the applied physic department, Albert Repman. A short reference to these events contains an anonymously published book *25 let muzeia prikladnyh znaniĭ v Moskve: 30oe noiabria 1872–30oe noiabria 1897* (*25 Years of the Museum of Applied Knowledge in Moscow*) (1898, p. 66).

24 The event was organized by the director of the conservatoire, Anton Rubinstein; see more about it in Vaidman (2003, p. 395).

25 The full list of institutions is given in Block's letter to Edison; see Block to TAE, 28 February 1890 (D9055AAI; TAEM 130:155).

26 The so-called "Edison Album" is now preserved in the New York Public Library (shelfmark JPG 09-2); a digital version is available at https://digital collections.nypl.org/items/72acd4a0-f116-0136-83ba-55c0e7ffbfd0 (last accessed 27 December 2020).

27 Most comments were left between 1899 and 1894 in St. Petersburg and Moscow; only Arthur Nikisch's testimonial is dated 1900, Berlin.

28 The whole *Trio* was finished in 1894.

29 Tchaikovsky's enthusiasm for the phonograph confirms his entry in Block's "Edison Album". Dated back to 14 (26) October 1889, Tchaikovsky's characteristic was as follows: "The Phonograph is undoubtedly the most astonishing, the most beautiful, the most interesting invention amongst all those which do honour to the 19th century! Glory to the great inventor Edison!" ("Le Phonographe est certainement l'invention la plus surprenante, la plus belle, la plus intéressante parmi toutes celles qui honorent le 19-me Siècle! Gloire au grand inventeur Edisson!"), the translation is provided by the digital platform Tchaikovsky Research; see "Endorsement of Thomas Edison's "Phonograph" at http://en.tchaikovsky-research.net/pages/Endorsement_of_Thomas_Edison%27s_%22Phonograph%22#cite_note-note2-2 (last accessed 8 November 2020). According to Block, Tchaikovsky also considered the idea of making "experiments in using the phonograph for composition"; see Block to Batchelor, 19 October 1889 (D8958AAN; TAEM 127:610).

30 Russian: "Танеев, как помню, был скептически настроен и выразил мнение, что это изобретение для искусства не имеет никакого значения и что надо ждать усовершенствований. Чайковский, напротив, был настроен скорее радостно и оптимистически – выражал надежду, что этот фонограф может быть хорошим подспорьем при изучении музыки. В общем, все сходились на том, что это – занятная игрушка, но не более", in Sabaneev (2005, p. 80).

31 Block's own characteristic, quoted from the Booklet text that accompanies the first edition of Block's recording collection; Maltese, J.A., Benko, G. (2008) 'History of the Block Cylinders in *The Dawn of Recording. The Julius Block Cylinders*, Marston Records, catalogue number 53011-2, available online at the official homepage of the Marston company: https://www.marstonrecords. com/products/block#:~:text=Starting%20in%201889%2C%20what%20is, Russia%2C%20Germany%2C%20and%20Switzerland (last accessed 8 November 2020).

32 Provided with a handwritten catalogue (the so-called "Phonogram-mothek"), Block's collection of the wax cylinders was partly donated to the Phonogramm-Archiv of the Ethnologisches Museum in Berlin and supposed to be completely destroyed during World War II. In fact, some of them miraculously survived and were transferred to Leningrad; currently, they are preserved in the phonogram collection of the St. Petersburg Institute of Russian Literature, Pushkin House (Pushkinsky Dom); in 2008, the recordings were published by the Marston Records company. For a detailed description of the history of Block's collection, see Denisov (2016); Kopytova (2009, pp. 63–65).

33 A term used in his own letter to Edison of 14 February 1890: "I now commence to collecting good musical phonograms"; see Block to TAE, 14 February 1890 (D9055AAF; TAEM 130:151).

34 As he stated in a letter to Charles W. Batchelor, Edison's associate, his desire was "to KEEP a phonogram of each of the celebrities"; see Block to Batchelor, 19 October 1889 (D8958AAN; TAEM 127:610).

35 Now Mayakovsky Theatre. Koenigsberg erroneously locates it in St. Petersburg; see Koenigsberg (1992, p. 4).

36 According to Koenigsberg (1992, p. 5), it could also be a certain Droese.

37 F.C.B. Cole; see Koenigsberg (1992, p. 5).

38 Quoted from Koenigsberg (1992, p. 5). The description of this event can also be found in Block's letter to Edison; see Block to TAE, 27 March 1890 (D9055AAN; TAEM 130:160).

39 According to the poster published in Koenigsberg (1992, pp. 6–7).

40 Quoted from Koenigsberg (1992, p. 5).

41 Quoted from Koenigsberg (1992, p. 8).

42 A short reference to these events contains an anonymously published book *25 let muzeia prikladnyh znanii v Moskve* (1898, p. 66).

43 Quoted from Gronow and Englund (2007, p. 282). As the easiest and the most practical instrument to record, the voice was the principal object of the Gramophone activity; see about it in Fishzon (2011, p. 808).

44 The exact purpose of their visit is unknown, however; see Grunberg and Ialin (2002, p. 228).

45 The *Berliner Gramophone* company provided the recordings with the catalogue numbers 11000–11097; see ibid., p. 228.

46 According to the catalogue published in 1901, the recordings were available in Burchard store in St. Petersburg; see *Grammofonnoe libretto* (1901).

47 Their visit was initiated by August Burchard, a businessman and the official representative of the *Berliner Gramophone* in Russia.

48 The entry in Gaisberg's diary from 8 March 1900; see Strötbaum (2010, p. 52). In reality, Gaisberg's and Darby's "concerts" were preceded by the first Russian "gramophone tour" undertaken in 1898 by Iosif Mueller, a businessman based in Moscow; a reference to this tour can be found in the 1909 issue of the magazine *Ofitsial'nye izvestiia aktsionernogo obtschestva Grammofon* (1909, p. 6).

49 The first (unsuccessful) recording was made on 12 March and the last on 12 April; see Strötbaum (2010, pp. 55–61).

50 The publication process was marked by a conflict between Burchard and his partner, Ippolit Rapgof, who insisted on excluding a number of recordings with a poor artistic quality. Interested mostly in financial profits, Burchard denied these charges. As Rapgof stated, he "requested [Burchard], in the interests of artists, to bring for sale high-quality discs only; Mr Burchard, however, as a man of business who is not interested in the Russian art, rejected my request" (Russian: "Я требовал, в интересах артистов, чтобы в продажу поступали одни лишь удачные пластинки, на что г. Бурхард как человек коммерции, которому так чужды интересы русского искусства, вовсе не согласился"); see Rapgof (1900, p. 4). In the *Berliner Gramophone* catalogue, these disks covered numbers 20000–20903; see the list in Grunberg and Ialin (2002, pp. 233–240).

51 See *Grammofonnaia ghizn'* (1912, p. 20); Gronow (1981, p. 255).

52 Russian: "Граммофон и фонограф не только аппараты технического свойства; подобно часам, когда-то недоступным лицам со средним достатком, и граммофоны находились до последнего времени в таком же положении. В настоящее время граммофоны и фонографы настолько упали в цене благодаря усовершенствованиям, их круг деятельности настолько расширился, что эти аппараты пробили брешь и стали настолько же необходимыми для каждого интеллигентного обывателя, как швейная машина"; see *Grammofon i fonograf* (1902, p. 1).

53 Russian: "Известный артист императорской оперы в Москве Ф.И. Шаляпин, спел для граммофона 'Песнь о золотом тельце' из оперы Фауст (22823), Арию Сусанина из оперы 'Жизнь за царя' (22892) и шесть романсов: 'Как король шел на войну', Кеннеман (22820), 'Ах ты солнце, солнце красное' Слонова (22821), Элегия, музыка Карганова (22822), 'Разочарование' Чайковского (22824), 'Ноченька', русская песнь (22891), 'Соловей' Чайковского (22825). [...] Певцу уплачено было за арию и каждый пропетый романс по 2000 рублей. Как нам известно, Шаляпин на предложение, сделанное ему в октябре прошлого года "Обществом Зонофон", отвечал отказом, но, очевидно и он в конце концов не устоял перед искушением. Очевидно, что

На земле весь род людской
Чтит один кумир священный,
Он царит над всей вселенной
Тот кумир телец златой!…
Кстати здесь сказать, что и Н.Н. Фигнер года два тому назад торжественно заявлял в письме, помещенном в "Новом Времени", что никогда не пел и петь не будет для граммофона и фонографа, что такой поступок был бы профанацией искусства. Но ведь tempora mutantur et nos mutamur cum illis и поэтому Фигнер … изменил свой взгляд на граммофон и спел несколько десятков номеров"; in *Grammofon i fonograf* (1902, p. 9).

54 The information is given according to the catalogue *Tvorchestvo kompositora P. I. Tchaikovskogo v fonodokumentah RGAFD* (2020).

55 Officially, the production of wax cylinders was stopped in 1911; see Grunberg and Ialin (2002, p. 17).

56 Russian: "Еще так недавно, всего пять лет тому назад, граммофон являлся новинкой в России. На него смотрели как на любопытный аппарат, а на изобретателя, технический мир взглянул как на компилятора и трансформатора чужого изобретения. Что же мы видим теперь? Граммофон совершенно вытеснил фонограф. Из предмета любопытства граммофон стал предметом необходимости каждой интеллигентной семьи. Граммофон служит предметом развлечения, поучения, развивает слух, эстетический вкус. Граммофон отвлекает народ от пьянства"; in *Katalog izbrannyh p'es dlya grammofona* (1903, p. IV).

57 Russian: "Акционерное общество Пате в Париже изъявило желание обогащать нас сведениями из Франции"; see *Grammofon i fonograf* (1902, p. 2).

58 Russian: "Парижская фирма Пате произвела на фонографических валиках русскую запись. Были приглашены лучшие выдающиеся артисты, и записано очень много номеров. Представительство передано г. Якобу и бывшему вояжеру фирмы Пате г-ну Филипсу, которые на компанейских началах учредили в Москве специальный склад. Нам еще не привелось лично слышать этих валиков"; quoted from *Grammofon i fonograf* (1904, p. 24).

59 *Grammofon i fonograf* (1904, p. 112–114).

60 *Grammofon i fonograf* (1904, p. 272–275).

61 Russian: "единственная говорящая машина, имеющая мембрану с постоянным сапфиром", see *Novosti grammofona* (1908). On pathephone, see also Grunberg and Ialin (2002, p. 18).

62 See the advertisement published in *Novosti grammophona* (1907).

63 Russian: "Трудно себе представить, с какой стремительной быстротой граммофон распространился по всему миру, несмотря на то, что со дня его изобретения прошло сравнительно еще немного времени. Широкое и быстрое распространение говорящих машин станет на первый взгляд еще более поразительным, если принять во внимание сравнительно высокие цены на аппараты и пластинки, недолговечность пластинок с одной стороны и постоянное стремление обновлять свой репертуар – с другой. Все это требует больших, а подчас даже крупных затрат […] Тем не менее, как это не покажется на первый взгляд странным, граммофон распространен в России более, чем в других странах"; in Emte (1907, p. 3).

64 The full list of these companies is provided by the Internet platform *The Russian Records*; see https://www.russian-records.com/categories.php?cat_id=1&l=russian (last accessed 8 November 2020). See also Grunberg and Ialin.

65 There are few exceptions. For instance, the Orpheon record company issued recordings both of Russian and foreign artists, among others, of Enrico Caruso. See the appendix that overviews activities of the most important pre-revolutionary Russian recording companies.

66 Noble (1913, p. 52).
67 Russian: "Г. Карензин спел нам арию Альфреда из 'Травиаты'. (нр. 2–22966). Вышло очень недурно. Когда русские артисты берутся за исполнение итальянских арий, это всегда бывает рискованно. После итальянцев с их божественным bel canto и обаятельным mezzo voce, слушать в этих же ариях Русских певцов почти нельзя. Исключение составляет только Собинов со своим итальянским голосом. Исполняет он ее на пластинке очень отчетливо. Все-таки мы можем объяснить стремление О-ва Граммофон записывать итальянские арии в исполнении русских певцов только желанием пойти на встречу желанию русской публики слушать итальянские арии на русском языке"; in *Novosti grammofona* (1907, pp. 30–32).
68 To mention just one of the Pathé advertisements described by Anna Fishzon: it "featured three sisters whose dull existence in a provincial backwater was enlivened when their father bought a gramophone"; see Fishzon (2011, p. 804).
69 *Polnyi katalog dvustoronnih plastinok* (1911).
70 The recording was made between 1907 and 1910; the exact recording date is unknown; see Grunberg and Ialin (2002, p. 34).
71 The choir was founded in 1900 by the peasant Ivan Iukhov; by 1910, it was one of the most popular and frequently performing choirs in Moscow; see more about the activity of this ensemble in Tevosian (2008).

References

Anonymous. (1877) "The Talking Phonograph", *Scientific American*, 22 December, pp. 384–385.
Anonymous. (1884) "Obituary", *Nature*, 22 February, pp. 412–413.
Anonymous. (1889) "Smes' (Miscellanies)", *Niva* (Grainfield), 46, pp. 1167–1168.
Anonymous. (1898) *25 let muzeia prikladnyh znanii v Moskve: 30oe noiabria 1872–30oe noiabria 1897* (25 Years of the Museum of Applied Knowledge in Moscow). Moscow: Russkaia tipografiia.
Cherkasov, V. (1907) *F. F. Pavlenkov: otryvki iz memuarov* (F. F. Pavlenkov: Excerpts from Memoirs). St. Petersburg: Knigopechatnia Schmid.
Dash, M. (2011) "In Search of Queen Victoria's Voice. The British Monarch Was Present When a Solicitor Demonstrated One of the Earliest Audio Recording Devices. But Did She Really Say 'tomatoes'?", *Smithsonian Magazine*, October 6, online at https://www.smithsonianmag.com/history/in-search-of-queen-victorias-voice-98809025/ (last accessed on 8 January 2021).
Denisov, V. (2016) "O fonograficheskoi zapisi golosa Tchaikovskogo iz kollektsii Juliusa Blocka (On a Phonograph Recording of Tchaikovsky's Voice from Julius Block's Collection)", *Vestnik Udmurstkogo Universiteta* (The Udmurt State University Herald), 24 (4), pp. 135–140.
Du Moncel, Th. (1878) *Le téléphone, le microphone et le phonographe*. Paris: Librarie Hachette.
Du Moncel, Th. (1879) *The Telephone, the Microphone and the Phonograph*, trans. Th. Du Moncel. New York: Harper.
Du Moncel, Th. (1880) *Telefon, mikrofon i fonograf* (The telephon, the microphone and the phonograph), trans.F. Pavlenkov and V. Cherkasov. St. Petersburg: Tipografiia Kotomina.
Eisenberg, E. (2005). *The Recording Angel: Music, Records, and Culture from Aristotle to Zappa*. New Haven: Yale University Press.

Emte, A. (1907) "Vozzvanie k chitateliam (An appeal to readers)", *Novosti grammo-phona* (The Gramophone News) 1, p. 3.

Fishzon, A. (2011) "The Operatics of Everyday life, or, How Authenticity Was Defined in Late Imperial Russia", *Slavic Review* 70(4), pp. 795–818.

Gelatt, R. (1955) *The Fabulous Phonograph. From Tin Foil to High Fidelity.* Philadelphia and New York: Lippincott Company.

Grammofon i fonograf (Gramophone and phonograph), 1 (1902).

Grammofon i fonograf (Gramophone and phonograph), 1 (1904).

Grammofon i fonograf (Gramophone and phonograph), 3 (1904).

Grammofon i fonograf (Gramophone and phonograph), 8 (1904).

Grammofonnaia ghizn' (The gramophone life), 12 (15 February 1912).

Grammofonnoe libretto oper, operetok, romansov, pesen, chorov i kupletov. Izdanie sobstvennosti pervogo v Rossii spezial'nogo sklada usovershenstvovannyh grammo-fonov torgovogo doma optika i mechanika A. Burchard (The Gramophone Libretto of operas, operettas, romances, songs, choruses and satirical songs. The publication of the first Russian special store of improved gramophones owned by the tradehouse of the optician and mechanishian A. Burchard) (1901). St. Petersburg: Burchard publishing house.

Gronow, P. (1981) "The Record Industry Comes to the Orient", *Ethnomusicology* 25 (2), pp. 251–284.

Gronow, P. and Englund, B. (2007) "Inventing Recorded Music: The Recorded Repertoire in Scandinavia 1899–1925", *Popular Music* 26 (2), pp. 281–304.

Grunberg, P., and Ialin, V. (2002) *Istoriia nachala gramzapisi v Rossii. Katalog vokal'nyh zapiseĭ rossiĭskogo otdeleniia kompanii 'Grammofon'* (The History of the beginning of Russian recorded music. The Catalogue of the vocal music recordings of the Gramophone Russian branch office). Moscow: Iazyki slavianskoĭ kul'tury.

Jüttenmann, H. (1979) *Phonographen und Grammophonen.* Braunschweig: Klinkhardt & Biermann.

Katalog izbrannyh p'es dlia grammophona (The Catalogue of selected pieces for the gramophone) (1903). St. Petersburg: Parovaia tipografiia i litografiia M. Rosenoer.

Katz, M. (2011) 'The Amateur in the Age of Mechanical Music' in Pinch, T. and Bijsterveld, K. (eds.) *The Oxford Handbook of Sound Studies.* New York: Oxford University Press, pp. 459–479.

Koenigsberg, A. (1992) 'The Russian Connection: Julius H. Block meets the Czar' *Antique Phonograph Monthly*, 88 (X/4). pp. 3–9.

Kopytova, G. (2009). "The Julius Block Phonographic Collection: The Anthology of the Musical Performance of the End 19th – the Beginnings of 20th Centuries." *Musicus* 3, pp. 63–65.

Noble, Th. T. J. (1913) "Three Years' Recording Trip in Europe and Asia", *Talking Machine World*, 9 (9), pp. 52–53.

Novosti grammofona (The Gramophone news), 1 (1908).

Novosti grammofona (The Gramophone news), 1 (1907).

Ofitsial'nye izvestiia aktsionernogo obtschestva Grammofon (Official news of the Gramophone company), 6 (May 1909).

Polnyi katalog dvustoronnih plastinok brat'ev Pathé (The full catalogue of double-sided discs of Pathé brothers) (1911). Moscow: Tipografiia russkogo tovaritschestva.

Rapgof, I. (1900) *Katalog izbrannyh p'es dlia grammofona, sostavlennyh dlia Torgovo-promyshlennogo agenstva* (The catalogue of selected pieces for the gramophone, composed for the commercial and industrial agency). St. Petersburgs. n.

Roy, E. A. (2016) "'You Ought to See My Phonograph'. The Visual Wonder of Recorded Sound (1877–1900)", in Storey, J. (ed.) *The Making of English Popular Culture*. London: Routledge, pp. 185–196.

Sabaneev, L. (2005) *Vospominanie o Rossii* (Memoirs on Russia), ed. T. Maslovskaia. Moscow: Klassika, p. XXI.

Sousa, J. Ph. (1906) "The Menace of Mechanical Music", *Appleton's*, 8, pp. 278–284.

St. P. H. (1878) "Phonograph", *Niva* (Grainfield), 17, pp. 90–91.

Strötbaum, H. (2010) *The Fred Gaisberg Diaries, Part 1: USA & Europe (1898–1902)*, online at http://www.recordingpioneers.com/docs/GAISBERG_DIARIES_1.pdf (last accessed on 8 January 2021).

Tepliakov, G., and Kudriavtsev P. (1996) *Alexander Grigor'evich Stoletov*. Moscow: Prosveschenie.

Tevosian, A. (2008). "'Moskovskii regent Ivan Iukhov i ego khor' ('The Moscow Church Choir Director Ivan Iukhov and His Choir')", *Vestnik PSTGU, II: Muzykal'noe iskusstvo khristianskogo mira* (PSTGU Bulletin II: The Musical Art of the Christian World), 1 (2), pp. 153–162.

Trigos, L. A. and Ueland, C. (2018). "Creating a National Biographical Series: F. F. Pavlenkov's 'Lives of Remarkable People', 1890–1924", *The Slavonic and East European Review* 96 (1), pp. 41–66.

Tvorchestvo kompozitora P. I. Tchaikovskogo v fonodokumentah RGAFD. K 180-letiu so dnia rozhdeniia (The Composer Tchaikovsky's Music in the Phonographical Documents of the RGAFD. Commemorating the 180-Birth Anniversary). (2020) Moscow: Rossiĭskiĭ gosudarstvennyĭ fond fonodocumentov.

Vaidman, P. (2003). "My uslyshali golos Tchaikovskogo (We Heard the Voice of Tchaikovsky)", in Vaidman, P. and Belonovich, G. (eds.) *P.I. Tchaikovsky. Zabytoe I novoe* (P. I. Tchaikovsky. Forgotten and Something New), vol. 2. Klin: Integraf Servis, pp. 393–7.

8 'Phonographic awareness'

Recorded sound in early twentieth-century Italy between aesthetic questions and economic struggles

Benedetta Zucconi

In the first half of the 1930s, several Italian periodicals began referring to a given 'phonographic awareness' (*coscienza fonografica*). Today's reader would find it rather difficult to understand, based on these accounts, what exactly such sentiment was supposed to be. Nonetheless, whatever such phonographic awareness was, authors seemed to unanimously agree that it was missing in Italy at that time: 'within the Italian public, what we already called "phonographic awareness" is far to be spread enough'[1] complained columnist Alberto Rossi in the magazine *Il dramma* (*The drama*) in 1934 (Rossi 1934, p. 43). That same year, *Il disco* (*The disc*)[2] titled an opening article with this same utterance: here the lack of a phonographic culture was related to the lack of musical culture in general all over the peninsula, in comparison with countries such as the United Kingdom and the United States (*Il disco* 1934, pp. 1–2). Both periodicals had good reasons to criticise the situation with music in Italy at that time, especially with reference to recorded sound, which had neither reached the status of a cultural object nor had encouraged any new cultural or artistic expression; however, as a matter of fact, it was in the 1930s that recorded sound arose as a topic of discussion in several printed media, which even happened to independently share the same jargon, as shown in the aforementioned example. At that time, and due to different factors,[3] phonography experienced a growth of interest among cultural circles, which also led to a negotiation of its epistemology and ultimately of its ontology.

The very fact that recorded sound began to be a recurrent topic in Italian printed media brought about the necessity of defining specific taxonomies and categories; in other words, of creating a common ground that enabled to communicate about this topic. 'New media are media we do not yet know how to talk about', suggests media historian Benjamin Peters (2009, p. 18), thus highlighting the connection between inventions and their epistemological definition within contemporary discourses. Such processes of verbal definition can be considered to be part of the creation itself. In fact, inventions are not punctual events, but rather complex phenomena which

DOI: 10.4324/9781003006497-12

also involve rules, institutions, social practices, texts and, more in general, discourses. As Tom Gunning claims:

> history deals not only with events but, primarily, and some would claim exclusively, with the discourses they generate and which record them. The introduction of new technology in the modern era employs a number of rhetorical tropes and discursive practices that constitute our richest source for excavating what the newness of technology entailed.
>
> (Gunning 2003, p. 39)

Rhetorical tropes and discursive practices are not just tools to describe media *a posteriori*. As Marcia Siefert claimed, 'narratives also define inventions' (Siefert 1995, p. 419), meaning that descriptions of media, of their users and uses always refer to specific contexts, values and ideas, and ultimately can become normative. Such accounts, according to Siefert, can define both social practices related to media and 'new uses and directions for developments' (p. 420). On the one hand, then, technological inventions always trigger the production of written texts of different nature (articles, manuals, illustrations and advertisements); on the other hand, all these written sources foster the establishment of new rules and jargons connected with these new technologies; in other words, they contribute to its social and cultural construction. According to Lisa Gitelman, 'technology, whether inscriptive or not, involves a lot of paper. Machines get some of their meaning from what is written about them in different ways and at specific junctures, in research plans, patent applications, promotional puff, and so on' (Gitelman 1999, p. 6).

Discourses surrounding recorded sound started flourishing worldwide shortly after the invention of the phonograph, and the definition of cultural practices related to the new medium was thus part of this process. All around the Western world several texts about phonography were published, periodical publications in particular, aimed at describing and discussing the technological novelty of recorded sound.[4] As described above in more general terms, the terminological and epistemological empty space opened by recorded sound allowed writers, intellectuals and users to play not just a descriptive but also a prescriptive role in defining the ontological nature of musical reproduction.

In this chapter, I will discuss the emergence of a discourse about phonography in Italy in the interwar period. I will focus on the first half of the 1930s, when two different contexts, namely the environment of music composers and the copyright-related juridical arena, happened to deal with similar issues; both, in fact, tackled very similar questions connected to recorded sound, which nonetheless led to deeply different answers. The questions they asked aimed at defining the exact nature of recorded sound, but were triggered by completely different needs and aims and 'formed a matrix of heterogeneous, changing, and even contradictory messages' (Gitelman, 2003, p. 66). Ultimately, they all contributed to define the 'phonographic awareness' mentioned above, namely a more mature and complex understanding of recorded sound. At first sight, there was no direct relationship between the two fields at that time, and even a certain imbalance can be noticed, since the legal sphere seems to be more informed about the discourses circulating at the time in the music environment than vice versa. However, they both operated in the same cultural and social context, albeit autonomously, and they discussed similar issues and used similar tools to circulate their ideas, mainly the press and especially magazines, a form of thought transmission typical of Italy in the post-war period (Hallamore Caesar et al. 2011).

But the purpose of this contribution is not so much to claim that, as already effectively demonstrated by Trevor Pinch and Wiebe Bijker in a classic essay, 'different social groups have radically different interpretations of one technological artefact' (Pinch and Bijker 1987, p. 41), which involve 'the contents of the artefact itself' (p. 42). In a more culture-oriented, musicological rather than media-focused perspective, I intend to illustrate how a full definition and acceptance of recorded music came in interwar Italy from a rather unexpected milieu, namely the juridical community, which was for several reasons freer from aesthetic constraints and more inclined to deal pragmatically with questions arising from practical issues.[5]

Italy represents an interesting field of investigation in this respect, due to its cultural and social features at that time.[6] One the one hand, recorded sound was far from having reached the status of cultural object in the peninsula, especially within environments connected with musical life; discourses, institutions and initiatives connected to phonography displayed a certain backwardness if compared to similar realities in Europa, where, for instance, sound archives had been established since decades[7] and phonographic periodicals were regularly printed and distributed.[8] On the other hand, and surprisingly enough, interwar Italy reveals a particularly lively picture with regard to the evolution of copyright law and, in particular, the legal protection of the record industry's products. Such a discrepancy in dealing with similar issues from different environments makes the Italian case emblematic and an ideal case study in order to investigate the epistemological construction of sound recording.

Sound recording in theory: musicians and intellectuals in interwar Italy

The low consideration in which recorded sound was held in Italy could be attributed to several factors. Whether the absence of specific publications and of a national sound archive were to be considered both as a cause and as a consequence of the Italian lack of interest towards phonography, a system of music production still linked to nineteenth-century dynamics, relying on theatres, impresarios and music publishers, and the modest size of the Italian music market were determinant obstacles to the emergence of a sound recording culture. In fact, and despite the central role played by Italian opera and Italian performers in the early decades of the recording industry, cylinders and discs circulating in Italy were mostly produced by foreign big majors. The initial enthusiasm shown by the population for the phonograph, witnessed by over 200 'demonstrations' throughout Italy already in 1878–1879 (Vita 2019), did not turn into a solid cultural interest, due to a country still very disunited and almost completely lacking an industrial background capable of supporting a significant record production. The two main centres where record production developed were Naples and Milan. However, Naples concentrated almost exclusively on local music repertoire, with no market outside the city,[9] while Milan became mainly home to foreign companies, which often absorbed the sporadic entrepreneurial attempts to establish a local disc production. This may have contributed to the general perception of phonography as something foreign, considered more as a threat than an economic opportunity.[10]

But even more relevant for the failed development of a phonographic discourse was the cultural hegemony played by Italian neo-idealistic philosophy in the first decades of the twentieth century, and whose leading figure was the philosopher, historian and intellectual Benedetto Croce (1866–1952). Neo-idealism, which had developed and spread from the 1910s onwards, succeeded in permeating every cultural branch and institution in Italy in the first half of the century. Philosopher Norberto Bobbio, in describing what he doesn't hesitate to call 'Croce's dictatorship', points out how 'the intellectual movements of [Croce's] time both irradiated from and converged in Croce's thought' (Bobbio 1969, p. 69). Neo-idealistic philosophy was based on the total supremacy of humanities over technology and scientific thought, producing therefore a strong shift from the previous positivistic culture, which was widespread in Italy until the turn of the century. According to Crocian idealism (so as ethnomusicologist Giovanni Giuriati) 'historical and human "facts" [...] could only be considered in their uniqueness and non-repeatability, thereby denying value to the comparative and generalising procedure' (Giuriati 1995, p. 106). Such a denial of repeatability did not only affect the scientific method and empirical research. Without a doubt, it also constituted an obstacle to the legitimisation of recorded sound – as mass-produced and repeatable object – as part of high culture. Furthermore, neo-idealism also tended to avoid and refuse any technical feature related to art, by virtue of the moment of intuition-creation, an inseparable and crucial combination of artistic expression. According to Benedetto Croce:

> In the process of art production there is no practical or technical element: fantastic spontaneity rules unrivalled, from the beginning to the end of that process; the concept of technique is completely unrelated both to pure aesthetic and to real art criticism.
>
> (Croce 1905, p. 62)

Such a radical position made it nearly inconceivable to even discuss the potential artistic value of the recording, tied as it was to technical and mechanical circumstances. Technology was, for neo-idealistic thinkers, nothing more than a necessary evil that could and had to be overcome by art as such. The less cumbersome technology was, the closer art would be to an ideal of perfection. Therefore, recorded music, although it represented a relevant phenomenon in the middlebrow musical life, struggled to access the arenas of intellectual exchange. In this framework, some of the words written on mechanical reproduction by Crocian intellectual Francesco Flora on the Crocian-oriented music journal *La Rassegna Musicale* (*The Musical Review*) are particularly telling:

> That the machine creates new sounds, new sonic mixes, in this destruction of space which is the most violent task of modern temporal speed, nobody wants to deny it. I say sounds, because I intend to refer to those that do not remain desert noise; but I do not consider them to be in any way a new art form, falling into that easy and candid error for which a certain technical procedure aimed at producing certain acoustic effects, is considered for itself an artistic fact, forgetting that its qualities are purely mechanical.
>
> (Flora 1930, p. 397)

Its qualities could not be artistic owing to the very fact that they were mechanical; this opinion was broadly shared in Italian intellectual circles, and addressed not only phonography, but also other mechanical arts such as cinema. Nevertheless, and similar to what happened for cinema (Pitassio 2014), the 1930s witnessed the first attempts to aesthetically acknowledge phonography within cultural discourses.[11] In order to do that, musicians and critics often embedded the discussion within the most prominent intellectual framework, namely the Crocian neo-idealism. As a matter of fact, these first considerations about phonography were deeply influenced by idealistic issues and aims. More than by purely aesthetic questions, discourses were often triggered by more concrete concerns, such as complaints about (quoting a very well-known line) 'the menace of mechanical music' (Sousa 1906). Hence composer Mario Castelnuovo Tedesco, in an attempt to defend recorded sound against the alarmist idea that new technologies were going to substitute musical instruments, argued that 'the disc is a new form of edition: the "sonic edition"' (Castelnuovo Tedesco 1931, p. 233). Indeed, such a claim did not originate from an aesthetic query; it was the reaction to a concrete concern, namely the alleged threat played by recorded sound towards live music professions (orchestras, music schools, instrument makers and music publishers), which drove to the urge of discussing the role of recorded sound within musical life. Nonetheless, with these words Castelnuovo Tedesco entered the ontological realm: he discussed the nature and essence of sound recording.

Such an attempt wasn't isolated. In fact, in interwar Italy, neo-idealistic instances were connected with other intellectual stimuli from beyond the Alps, such as the discourse – which had already arisen at the end of the nineteenth century – on phonography and authorship, that is, on sound recording as a witness to the author's will as opposed to the interpreter's (Katz 2001), and advocated, among others, also by Stravinsky. Here the typically Crocian idea of the artistic moment perfectly corresponding to the artist's creative process matched with a characteristic trait of the New Objectivity movement (*Neue Sachlichkeit*), namely the refusal of individualistic interpretation – typical of the Romantic aesthetic – in favour of an 'objective' display of the composers' ideas.[12] To assert the existence of a single 'correct' interpretation (the one authorised by the author), or to say that recordings should be a model to be followed, namely 'imitated' by interpreters, meant then to question interpreters' roles. According to intellectual Alfredo Parente:

In a century's time [...] the subjective claims of performers, with their variety of performances and connected contrasts and disagreements, will no longer take place. The Beethovens and Mozarts of the twentieth century, if there ever are or ever will be, will be able to entrust their music, performed or made to perform according to their desire, to the talking machine; and when they are no longer themselves or others who enforce their will, the impressed records will bear witness and the varieties of interpretation will have a point of agreement. [...] If the gramophone allows to listen to music in the most faithful way, as its creator intended it, then it will be easy to admit that the ideal of the interpreter (concerning music not yet recorded on disc), is to get as close as possible to a machine, without adding or leaving anything to the most realistic historical reality of sounds.

(Parente 1934, pp. 248–9)

Similarly, during the First International Music Congress held in 1933 in Florence, composer and ethnologist Luigi Colacicchi emphasised the importance of recorded sound in erasing the interpreter's role: 'Music, which is inferior to other arts because of this necessary intervention by the interpreter, who translates signs into sound, has become completely independent and abstract thanks to the disc' (Colacicchi 1933, p. 78).

From these few accounts, it is clear how the disc rose to the role of keeper of composers' intentions as the authority for an 'objective' performance. As a matter of fact, these first discussions about recorded music eventually elevate it to a higher consideration as a cultural object, dismissing the rather well-spread prejudice of recorded sound as a mere toy or pub entertainment. The legitimation of recorded sound happened through the definition of its nature and function, namely through an epistemological process which brought to a first sketch of its ontological features. It is nevertheless evident how these discourses constrained phonography within already defined categories of thought; the focus is often a different one (the question of interpretation, the role of the author, the situation of musical life), and phonography is taken into consideration only as functional to aims and goals of a specific subject. It should not be forgotten that the authors of these texts as well as the journals where the texts were published had a strongly neo-idealistic imprinting. As a consequence, no consideration was devoted by any of these writers to the (still) cumbersome technical side of recordings. Sound devices and recording processes seemed to be considered here as neutral elements, empty containers of information. Ultimately, this neo-idealistic legitimation implied the refusal of phonography's medial nature as well as of its materiality.

Sound recording in practice: copyright law and industry

But Croce-inspired musicians and intellectuals were not alone in discussing the nature and features of recorded sound in Italy at that time. As a matter of fact, a parallel discourse about phonography can be found in a different cultural arena, far from the official outputs of Italian artistic and musical culture, namely in the discussions about copyright and royalties which stemmed in the same years among jurists and music industry lobbyists.

The urge to define some aspects related to recorded sound originated from the hard times suffered by the phonographic industry in the interwar period, partly due to the 1929 global economic crisis. In addition, the emergence of radio into the mediascape made it necessary to define boundaries and spheres of influence between broadcasting companies and the phonographic industry. In this particular framework, discs' trade contraction occurring in the 1930s persuaded industrials that profits should shift – as Simon Frith pointed out – from record sales to performing rights and royalties (Frith 1988, p. 17). The crisis of the phonographic industry was not confined within Italian borders, but rather experienced by many European countries, and concerns about the radio were common among disc producers and performers all around the world. Quite surprisingly, Italy played a pioneering role in pushing for a new legal safeguard of the phonographic industry in Italy and within the international discussions.

In those years, reflections and debates about copyright spread and evolved in Europe and in many countries around the world. In 1886, the Convention for the Protection of Literary and Artistic Works took place in Bern, Switzerland. On that occasion, several countries (initially including Germany, Belgium, Spain, France, the United Kingdom, Haiti, Liberia, Switzerland, Tunisia and Italy) officially ratified an international settlement in order to protect artistic and intellectual products, and marking thus the official birth of copyright. The agreement signed in Bern (still effective nowadays) was followed by further revisions and lively discussions, joined by an increasing number of countries. On the one hand, it was necessary to define the principles of a newly born idea and, on the other hand, participants

needed to constantly update their decisions in accordance with new technological improvements, media and contexts, which were themselves undergo-
ing rapid evolution and significant changes at that time. The main revisions
took place in Berlin in 1908 and then in Rome in 1928. Issues concerning
recorded sound were extensively discussed for the first time during the Berlin revision, whereas recorded sound found no space in the Bern outcomes
(only nine years after Edison's invention).[13] But it was during the meeting in
Rome that new disputes about 'mechanical music' arose. In the last decades,
recorded sound had become a relevant phenomenon within society, culture
and economy, and required thus more serious consideration. Furthermore,
attendees in Rome had to tackle the newly born phenomenon of broadcasting, which also needed to be defined in its juridical terms, and to be regu-
lated with respect to the phonographic industry.

Consequently, on the occasion of the Rome revision Italy became the
geographical epicentre of copyrights discussions. It is no coincidence that
regarding copyright legislation, Fascism (which had ruled the country since
1922) intended to play a particularly prominent role in the international
arena. The Rome revision, promoted by the regime as an Italian success,
was therefore part of Fascism's hegemonic plan, which intended to showcase fascist economy as a successful alternative to liberalism and socialism
(Fleischer 2015). The copyright law approved in 1925 was also presented
under this light and, although it was in fact no more than a due act, regulating years of discussions and suits, it was appropriated by the regime to
propagandise that idea of progress and modernity it wanted to represent
abroad (Roghi 2007).[14]

However, it is also thanks to the impetus given by the fascist government
that discussions about recorded sound and copyright flourished in Italy in
the 1930s. Such discussions articulated, and can now be traced, within three
main contexts: the outcomes of the Bern Convention and its further revisions, chronicles of the first congress of the phonographic industry (held
in Rome in 1933) and juridical periodicals. In these sources, it is possible
to follow the evolution of a phonographic discourse, starting from empirical observation of everyday life, but evolving into a more complex analysis
of recorded sound nature. In legal discussions, it was largely a matter of
specifying what exactly defined recorded sound and some of its features in
particular.

An intensively debated issue during the Rome revision of the Bern convention in 1928 was the legal protection of performers: attendees discussed
whether it was necessary, and how, to protect performers' rights. It was
the Italian delegation that raised the question whether (and to what extent)
performers should be considered as co-authors of the work performed, and
what kind of contribution they brought as a participant to the creative process. Clearly, the issue was tightly connected with the growth of technical
reproduction: discs and radio had brought music performances into every
home, every public space, and as Monika Dommann observes, 'it was not

composers but performing artists that everyone could hear' (Dommann 2019, p. 107). As a consequence, performers started to stand up to claim their rights as contributors to the production and economic success of discs. As the Rome proceedings report, 'it is indeed indisputable that phonographic records in particular derive their commercial value in large part from the fame of the performer' (Union internationale pour la protection des œuvres littéraires et artistiques, 1929, p. 78). Performers' rights were then considered within the realm of gramophonic reproduction, and from this starting point several questions arose. Jurist Amedeo Giannini summarised them efficaciously some years after the conference in Rome:

> Musicians, comic and tragic actors, and speakers used to conclude their activity by playing, acting, singing, and speaking, without the possibility of further exploitation of their performances. Today, by means of the disc, the most famous performer can be listened at will by disc and radio owners [...]. All these new means represent an additional exploitation of interpreters' activity. Do they have a right of ownership over their performances? If they do, can they be denied the benefit of it, as is done with authors? If they do not have a property right, can one deny that their activity is exploited? And does this exploitation not deserve protection? Does it deserve protection, in what way and by what means can it be protected?
>
> (Giannini 1931, pp. 162–3)

Sound recording not only changed the artistic output into an object (*res*) which could be sold, enjoyed, owned and acquire economic value (Protto 1931), it even put the common understanding of authorship into question. In fact, such a statement overcame the neo-idealistic understanding of the musical experience as a direct communication between authors and audiences, that is, a vision that aimed at neutralizing the role of the interpreter. As the witness of performers' activity, the disc was not a mere intermediary anymore, a neutral passage, but rather a separate element within the process of music consumption.

From this topic a second issue stemmed in Rome 1928: Britain, in refusing to grant rights to performers, proposed to create an independent protection for supports (i.e. the disc as a material object) as 'second-hand work'. These words meant 'not a reproduction or published copy of a work' (Union internationale pour la protection des œuvres littéraires et artistiques 1929, p. 263), but rather a derivative, albeit autonomous, product of the original work. Although the British suggestion was considered by other members as quite contradictory (in fact, record fabricants would have been better acknowledged and protected than performers, and their work considered more valuable), similar issues concerning the epistemology of mechanical reproduction were discussed with reference to radio during the Rome revision: the question was raised as to 'whether broadcasting constituted a public reproduction, a performance or a recitation'

(Union internationale pour la protection des œuvres littéraires et artistiques 1929, p. 76).

To distinguish between reproduction and performance reveals an inclination to consider music performances by mechanical means something more than a mere copy of an abstract original: recordings were now a new product, in which not only the performer, but also technical mediation acquired a characterising role that could even be labelled as creative. It is evident that the discussion on interpreters' rights had cracked the monolithic concept of creation typical of the previous century, also shared by Italian neo-idealists. This is what Giannini stated shortly after the revision:

> It is important to understand the meaning of the word *creation*. The musician is not the only one who creates[...]. Also who reproduces the music creates [...]. Even who sees a sculpture or a painting creates, because he recreates it with his imagination, or he displays it. The creative act will be different, but qualitatively it is always creation.
>
> (Giannini 1931, p. 163)

Also connected to creation, a further point concerning phonography and copyright played a major role in promoting a more complex understanding of recorded sound, namely what kind of protection should be attached to recordings. Amedeo Giannini, who attended both the Bern revision in Rome 1928 as well as the first international congress of the phonographic industry in 1933 (also in Rome), had a leading role in the discussion, which reverberated on juridical periodicals of the time such as the Italian *Il diritto di autore* (author's right) or the German *Archiv für Urheber-, Film- und Theaterrecht* (archive for copyright, film and theatre law) The question arose whether recordings should be protected as an industrial product (i.e. as a material object) or as an artistic output. The issue stemmed from some crucial questions regarding the nature of recorded sound, which apparently occurred now for the first time. During the Congress of the phonographic industry in Rome 1933, Giannini suggested two different legal solutions: the first solution was to consider recordings as an industrial product (i.e. considering sound recording as an *object*) and protect them accordingly; alternatively, they could be acknowledged as a work of intellect, thus following what was decided by the Bern Convention and its subsequent revisions regarding the protection of artworks (Giannini 1934, p. 287). This latter solution was preferable in Giannini's eyes, also in view of future developments of the phonographic industry. It derived from some fundamental questions on the nature of sound recording, which seem to take full shape here for the first time:

> Is it possible to consider the disc as a 'creation'? We have seen what the disc has become: an autonomous work of art, which must be created by an author. All the essential elements for disc production, both technical

and artistic, become elements of a complex work, where they harmoni-
cally blend into one: the disc.

(Giannini 1934, p. 277)

The difference between such a view and contemporary idealistic considerations of Crocian cultural circles towards recorded sound is indeed striking.
The dichotomy between art – intended as a pure intellectual work – and technical objects, excluded from the aesthetical discourse because of their technical
and material elements, was put into question by copyright experts, who acknowledged the epistemological condition of recordings (among others) to be
in rapid evolution. Giannini went further in the aforementioned contribution:

> If one observes carefully the current trend in the field of industrial and
> literary property, one can easily observe, on the one hand, the tendency
> to industrialise certain intellectual works and, on the other hand, the
> tendency to consider certain products, previously considered purely in-
> dustrial, as protected intellectual works. Part of this movement are also
> the problems of the discs that concern us here.

(Giannini 1934, p. 277)

During the legal and industrial meetings of the 1930s, a multifaceted understanding of recorded sound took shape: phonography seemed to be gradually acknowledged as a manifold phenomenon, a complex creation involving
different actors and skills. Moreover, disc production wasn't considered as
a mere mechanical process anymore: to recorded sound and its production
were now ascribed creative aspects, artistic features – and, therefore, a novel
aesthetic value. Alfredo Jannoni-Sebastianini, director of the Bureau for
intellectual property, wrote on the journal *Il diritto di autore*:

> Disc production cannot be considered anymore as a simple material
> work, since its task does not consist in the pure and simple reproduction
> of specific sounds: it is necessary to make a special adaptation in order
> to obtain the desired sound effects in the record, and this adaptation
> work is intellectual work that under a certain point of view can also be
> said to be creative.

(Jannoni-Sebastianini 1935, p. 344)

Jannoni-Sebastianini's view was also shared by the phonographic magazine *Corriere musicale*, which supported and showcased the interests of the
recording industry, and also appears to be the sole link between the musical
and the juridical realms. In mentioning a decision made by German radio
to stop broadcasting records (since radio had been suited by discs producers with respect to the payment of royalties), the Italian periodical wrote:

> It is not enough to simply pay something to the author of the piece or to
> its publisher. It can and should be argued that they should be considered

as sharing the publishing rights, performance rights, etc. all those who in any case have worked on the realization of a record, which is a "work of art", even if not a masterpiece: the phonographic publisher who publishes it, so that it can be purchased in the greatest possible number of copies, by the public of private phono-amateurs; the artist who sang the recorded piece; the conductor who "accompanied" it or who recorded the orchestral performance; the engraver, who takes every care to ensure that "that" record succeeds perfectly, etc. etc. etc.

(Giufer 1935, p. [1])

Thus, the Crocian dichotomy between work of art as output of pure intellect and anything that couldn't aspire to aesthetic reflection due to an overriding technical component appears now to be dismissed. The awareness of being in front of a complex object, such as to be able to aspire – at least in some cases – to the definition of artistic product and therefore not merely industrial, contributed to the idea that recording did not constitute an aesthetically neutral process. The recording process as well as to the listening practice of recorded music instead of live were acknowledged to carry a number of consequences in terms of aesthetic fruition of musical works. The 1933 Congress of phonographic industry in Rome fully displayed this new awareness. It was the Italian delegation to highlight it: starting from the idea of the disc as a blend of different elements, technical as well as artistic, Italians showed how recorded sound had already achieved the status of an artistically distinct element from the musical performance carried on supports:

Phonographic industry claims that the disc combines the contribution of the author, of the musical production (which includes both artistic and technical elements), and the packaging of the disc, which also encompass artistic components. Even more, we claim that what the disc offers to the listener is different from the elements it is made of, so that the disc holds a new artwork of multiple nature, which also recall what happens in the cinematography.

(1° Congresso internazionale dell'industria fonografica 1933, p. 566)

Conclusion

The results of juridical discussions didn't remain isolated. In February 1937, the Italian government passed a law meant to protect the recording industry (Gazzetta Ufficiale 1937, n. 111). But even more importantly, from the 1930s onwards, Italy experienced an unprecedented growth of recording-related discussions. At that time, the first periodicals and columns devoted to recorded sound were established, and a whole session was dedicated to recorded music at the first musical congress in Florence in 1933, involving personalities of international fame such as André Coeuroy and Ludwig Koch.

It is hard to tell whether copyright discussions played a role in this general enhancement of a 'phonographic awareness'. But either way, they constituted a relevant arena where narratives about recorded sound evolved, at least from the end of the 1920s. It has been already observed that with respect to radio, 'the creation of laws and rules concerning the new medium contributed to form the affordances limiting the interpretation and use of the new medium' (Balbi and Natale 2015, p. 31). Indeed, also in the case of phonography, legal discussion fostered a more articulated idea and concept of sound reproduction.

If we go back to Crocian neo-idealistic thought, an unequivocal and organic epistemological definition of recorded sound in interwar Italy appears quite hard to outline, especially since these two cultural arenas remained quite independent from each other. In fact, as I mentioned above, jurists and idealist thinkers hardly crossed each other paths, and continued being separate expressions of Italian cultural and social life. The outbreak of the Second World War shortly afterwards also contributed to annihilate any possible crossover between the two camps, and the world that emerged from the conflict was then profoundly changed and under the influence of very different cultural stimuli. Nonetheless, if we broaden the gaze to cultural history as a whole, as the sum – if not the entanglement – of several autonomous actors, then it is clear that many phenomena and events involving phonography in the 1930s was the result of the increased sensitivity towards phonography, which was also owed in part to these debates. Such a multifaceted reality, composed by contradictory phenomena, stemmed from different needs and premises. Even more importantly, debates on recorded sound in interwar Italy show how the phonographic discourse had a profound national connotation, since it was generated largely by two cultural contexts of which the first – Crocian idealism – was endemic and exclusive to the peninsula, whereas the other – the legal one – was shared by different parts of Europe, and yet particularly advanced in Italy. If, therefore, phonography in Italy between the two wars may appear 'backward' if considered from a merely technical or uncritically transnational perspective, it is, on the contrary, more than other national declinations particularly telling if intended as the output of ideas, laws and regulation stemmed from national needs, fostered by national (sometimes even nationalistic) agendas and inspired by national *Weltanschauungen*: ultimately, as the expression of a national culture.

Notes

1 All translations from Italian, French and German sources have been appointed by the author of this paper.
2 *Il dramma* and *Il disco* were both periodicals of cultural in-depth investigation on specific topics, but not designed for specialists. *Il dramma* was a magazine devoted to dramatic novelties and especially comedies, which was published from 1925 to 1968 (and until 1983 as a periodical of theatre, cinema and modern art), whereas *Il disco* was published by a music shop in Milan from 1933 to 1937. For further information about *Il disco*, see Zucconi (2015); on the central role of periodicals in interwar Italy, see Hallamore Caesar et al. (2011).
3 Beside the growth of recording industry worldwide, other factors (among many) can be considered the birth and spread of Italian broadcasting (1924), the

foundation of the Italian national archive of recorded sound in Rome (*Discoteca di Stato*, 1928) and as we will see in the next pages, the growth of copyright laws and the aesthetic movement of the New Objectivism (*Neue Sachlichkeit*).

4 On the same topic, beside the aforementioned publications, see also, among others, Flichy (1991), Symes (2004), Gitelman (2003, 2006).

5 I have already presented some of these results in Zucconi (2018). With regard to the theoretical part (but with a focus on broadcasting), see also Zucconi (2019).

6 For further information about cultural and social conditions in fascist Italy, see Forgacs (1990) and Forgacs-Gundle (2007).

7 The *Phonogrammarchiv der Österreichischen Akademie der Wissenschaften* (Phonogram Archive of the Austrian Academy of Sciences) was established in Vienna in 1899; in Germany, the Berliner Phonogramm-Archiv dates back to 1900; and the British Institute of Recorded Sound in London in 1905. In 1908, the Sound Archive of the Russian Academy of Sciences was founded, while in France *Les Archives de la parole* (archives of the voice) was [this is supposed to be a plural, right? I'd leave "were"] inaugurated in 1911 as part of the Sorbonne University.

8 Beside many marketing-oriented editorial attempts, *The Gramophone* (founded in 1923) was the first serious magazine devoted to phonography to be regularly published in any language (LeMahieu, 1982).

9 An exception in this sense is the consumption of Neapolitan music, both as sheet music and as gramophone records, by immigrants in the United States, especially in Philadelphia; see Siel Agugliaro's chapter in this book.

10 It is no coincidence that foreign recording companies at that time carried out marketing projects on Italian territory, perhaps to bring the public closer to recorded music through elements that could be recognised as local and familiar. Between 1903 and 1904, for instance, the Italian branch of the Gramophone Company commissioned the most prominent Italian composers, such as Puccini, Leoncavallo, Mascagni, to write songs 'written specifically for the Gramophone' (*scritte espressamente pel Grammofono*) for the Italian market.

11 Several factors contributed to the inclusion of recorded sound within cultural discourses at that time: the parallel development of other mechanical arts such as radio and cinema, which had an overwhelming impact in interwar Italy and fostered a consistent production of printed media; the receptiveness of many musicians towards discourses from beyond the Alps related to the issue of the interpreter, which indirectly affected phonography; and finally – as I will explain later on – the acknowledgement that recorded music could no longer be ignored, as it had become a massive phenomenon in the cultural and artistic fruition of the time.

12 A decade later, Italian composer Gian Francesco Malipiero still claimed that the ideal performer should be 'a more or less perfect transmitting machine, who must renounce to his own personality in order to accomplish the mission he has been given' (Malipiero 1945, p. 108. Original in Italian).

13 During the Berlin revision, the topic was introduced as follows:

> [...] the manufacture of mechanical musical instruments has taken an unexpected development; considerable industries have been formed in various countries; millions of copies of increasingly noble pieces of music have been reproduced. It seemed to the German Administration that it would be most opportune to reconsider the question [...].
>
> (Union international pour la protection des œuvres littéraires et artistiques 1910, pp. 258–9. Original in French)

14 In 1926, the fascist government founded the Institut international pour l'unification du droit privé (International Institute for the Unification of Private Law) under the auspices of the League of Nations (Dommann, 2019, pp. 108–9).

References

[n.a.] (1930) Rapporto della Delegazione italiana. Discorso pronunciato da S.E. Piola Caselli nella seduta del 24 dicembre 1929. *Il diritto di autore*, 1(1), 119–31.

[n.a.] (1933) 1° Congresso internazionale dell'industria fonografica. *Il diritto d'autore. Rivista giuridica trimestrale della Società Italiana degli Autori ed Editori*, 4(4), 561–70.

[n.a.] (1934) Coscienza Fonografica. *Il disco. Bollettino discografico mensile*, 2(6), 1–2.

Balbi, G. and S. Natale (2015) The Double Birth of Wireless: Italian Radio Amateurs and the Interpretative Flexibility of New Media. *Journal of Radio & Audio Media*, 22(1), 26–41.

Bobbio, N. (1995) *Ideological Profile of Twentieth-Century Italy*, translated by L.G. Cochrane, Princeton: Princeton University Press.

Castelnuovo Tedesco, M. (1931). Difesa (ovvero elogio funebre) del pianoforte. *Pegaso*, 3(8), 232–5.

Colacicchi, L. (1935) Il disco e la musica». In: *Atti del 1. Congresso internazionale di musica, Firenze 30 aprile-4 maggio 1933*. Firenze: Le Monnier, pp. 76–83.

Croce, B. (1905) Il padroneggiamento della tecnica. *La Critica. Rivista di Letteratura, Storia e Filosofia diretta da Benedetto Croce*, 3, pp. 160–5.

Dommann, M. (2019) *Authors and Apparatus. A Media History of Copyright*, Ithaca: Cornell University Press.

Fleischer, R. (2015) Protecting the Musicians and/or the Record Industry? On the History of "neighbouring rights" and the Role of Fascist Italy. *Queen Mary Journal of Intellectual Property*, 5(3), pp. 327–43.

Flichy, P. (1991) L'historien et le sociologue face à la technique. Le cas des machines sonores. *Réseaux*, 46–7(1), pp. 47–58.

Flora, F. (1930) I nuovi suoni. *La rassegna musicale*, 3(5), pp. 397–401.

Forgacs, D. (1990) *Italian Culture in the Industrial Era, 1880–1980: Cultural Industries, Politics and the Public*, Manchester and New York: Manchester University Press.

Forgacs, D. and S. Gundle (2007) *Mass Culture and Italian Society from Fascism to the Cold War*, Bloomington/Indianapolis: Indiana University Press.

Frith, S. (1988) The Industrialization of Music. In: S. Frith (ed.), *Music for Pleasure: Essays in the Sociology of Pop*, New York: Routledge, pp. 11–23.

Giannini, A. (1931) Il diritto dell'artista esecutore. *Il diritto di autore*, 2(2), pp. 161–75.

Giannini, A. (1934) Rechtsprobleme der Schallplatte. *Archiv für Urheber-, Film- und Theaterrecht*, 7, pp. 267–88.

Gitelman, L. (1999). *Scripts, Grooves, and Writing Machines. Representing Technology in the Edison Era*, Stanford: Stanford University Press.

Gitelman, L. (2003). How Users Define New Media: A History of the Amusement Phonograph. In: Thornburn, D. and H. Jenkins (eds.) *Rethinking Media Change*. Cambridge: The MIT Press, pp. 61–79.

Gitelman, L. (2006) *Always Already New. Media, History, and the Data of Culture*. Cambridge and London: The MIT Press.

Giufer (1935) La radio tedesca decide di cessare la trasmissione di dischi. *Corriere musicale. Rassegna fonografica*, 3(29), [p. 1].

Giuriati, G. (1995) Country Report: Italian Ethnomusicology. *Yearbook for Traditional Music*, 27, pp. 104–31.

Gunning, T. (2003) Re-Newing Old Technologies: Astonishment, Second Nature, and the Uncanny in Technology from the Previous Turn-of-the-Century.

In Thornburn, D. and H. Jenkins (eds.), *Rethinking Media Change*. Cambridge: The MIT Press, pp. 39–60.

Hallamore Caesar, A., G. Romani and J. Burns, eds. (2011) *The Printed Media in Fin-de-siècle Italy. Publishers, Writers, and Readers*, Italian Perspectives 21, London: Modern Humanities Research Association and Maney Publishing.

Jannoni-Sebastianini, A. (1935) Sulla necessità di riforme nella legislazione riguardante il diritto d'autore. *Il diritto d'autore. Rivista giuridica trimestrale della Società Italiana degli Autori ed Editori*, 6(3–4), pp. 333–47.

Katz, M. (2001) Hindemith, Toch, and *Grammophonmusik. Journal of Musicological Research*, 20(2), pp. 161–80.

LeMahieu, D.L. (1987) *The Gramophone*: Recorded Music and the Cultivated Mind in Britain between the Wars. *Technology and Culture*, 23(3), pp. 372–91.

Malipiero, G. F. (1945) *La pietra del bando*. Venezia: Ateneo.

Parente, A. (1934) Creazione, interpretazione e tecnica musicale. *Pan*, 2(2), pp. 245–52.

Peters, B. (2009) And Lead Us Not Into Thinking the New Is New: A Bibliographic Case for New Media History. *New Media and Society*, 11(1–2), pp. 13–30.

Pinch, T. and W. E. Bijker, (1987) The Social Construction of Facts and Artifacts: Or How the Sociology of Science and the Sociology of Technology Might Benefit Each Other. In: Bijker, W. E., T.P. Hughes, and T.J. Pinch (eds.) *The Social Construction of Technological Systems. New Directions in the Sociology and History of Technology*. Cambridge: The MIT Press, pp. 17–50.

Pitassio, F. (2014) Technophobia and Italian Film Theory in the Interwar Period. In: Van den Oever, A. (ed.) *Technē/Technology. Researching Cinema and Media Technologies – Their Development, Use, and Impact*. Amsterdam: Amsterdam University Press, pp. 185–95.

Protto, E. (1931) Note intorno alla questione dei diritti degli esecutori. *Il diritto di autore*, 2(1), pp. 24–45.

Regio decreto-legge 18 febbraio 1937, n. 595, Norme relative alla protezione dei prodotti dell'industria fonografica. *Gazzetta ufficiale* del 14 maggio 1937, n. 111.

Roghi, V. (2007) Il dibattito sul diritto d'autore e la proprietà intellettuale nell'Italia fascista. *Studi Storici*, 48(1), pp. 203–40.

Rossi, A. (1934) Dischi. *Il dramma*, 11(214), p. 43.

Siefert, M. (1995) Aesthetics, Technology, and the Capitalization of Culture: How the Talking Machine Became a Musical Instrument. *Science in Context*, 8(2), pp. 417–49.

Sousa, J. P. (1906) The Menace of Mechanical Sound. *Appleton's Magazine*, 8, pp. 278–84.

Symes, C. (2004) *Setting the Record Straight. A Material History of Classical Recording*, Middletown: Wesleyan University Press.

Thalheim, R. (1934) Der erste internationale Kongreß der phonographischen Industrie in Rom und die Gründung der internationalen Vereinigung der phonographischen Industrie. *Archiv für Urheber-, Film- und Theaterrecht*, 7(1), pp. 71–5.

Union international pour la protection des œuvres littéraires et artistiques (1910) *Actes de la conférence réunie à Berlin due 14 octobre au 14 novembre 1908. Avec les actes de ratification*. Bern: Bureau de l'Union international pour la protection des œuvres littéraires et artistiques.

Union internationale pour la protection des œuvres littéraires et artistiques (1929) *Actes de la conférence réunie à Rome du 7 mai au 3 juin 1928*. Bern: Bureau de l'Union international pour la protection des œuvres littéraires et artistiques.

Vita, V. (2019) *Musica Solida. Storia dell'industria del vinile in Italia*, Torino: Miraggi Edizioni.

Zucconi, B. (2015) Esordi della riflessione fonografica in Italia: *Il disco. Bollettino discografico mensile* (1933–1937). *Forum Italicum*, special Issue: *Music and Society in Italy*, 49(2), pp. 474–90.

Zucconi, B. (2018) *Coscienza fonografica. La riflessione sul suono registrato nell'Italia del primo Novecento*, Napoli and Salerno: Orthotes.

Zucconi, B. (2019). Pensare la radio. Fratture mediali nel dibattito giuridico italiano degli anni Trenta. *Musica/Realtà*, 40(129), pp. 25–45.

9 The construction of "das Volk" through acoustic knowledge. Recordings of "ethnic German repatriates" from the Institute for Acoustic Research, 1940–1941

Britta Lange

[Translated into English by Reed McConnell*]*[1]

"When it started, I thought about everything that might come. Things were tough. If only the German people would come soon. I longed to see something come of the putsch."[2] Theophile Helme spoke these words on March 18, 1940, in East Low German, a dialect of the so-called Volhynian Germans. She spoke them, most likely without a written template, into a phonograph horn, in a school room where "ethnic German repatriates" had been brought from the Wurzen/Sachsen camp. She spoke them for employees of the Institute for Acoustic Research (*Institut für Lautforschung* [IFL]) of the University of Berlin, which had taken on the task of making language recordings of "German repatriates" during the SS campaign "Home to the Reich." This raises the question of whether and how scientific and political acoustic knowledge were interwoven with one another in the recordings, and to what extent they were part of the linguistic and ethnic construction of a concept of German or Germans. The sound recordings of "ethnic Germans" were meant to serve as evidence for a claim with regard to the representation of the German language and German "national character" *[Tr.: Volkstum]*, a claim that not only cemented the alleged linguistic-cultural unity of the German people, but that could also contribute to the negotiation of political and geographical borders by means of this cementing.

Today there are dozens of records with recordings of "ethnic Germans" in the Acoustic Archive of Humboldt University in Berlin that were reproduced and distributed during the Second World War but evidently not used for research purposes.[3] Thus far, this episode has constituted a gap in the scholarship, both in the university history of Humboldt and institutional history of the Acoustic Archive as well as in the history of linguistics and the history of acoustic knowledge. In the following, I aim, first, to sketch out the origin story and the process of creating the recordings as well as to trace

DOI: 10.4324/9781003006497-13

their support and funding in the political context of the population resettlement that took place under Heinrich Himmler (Leninger, 2006). I classify the academic research in the "ethnic German" camps synchronically in the context of other IFL research conducted in camps during the Second World War as well as diachronically in the tradition of German dialect recordings that began in 1922. In this way, I hope to call forth the specific interweaving of science and politics, acoustic knowledge and knowledge about power, and explicate this using the Volhynian recordings as an example. It is apparent, according to my main thesis, that the recordings of "ethnic Germans" were compatible with the political and propagandistic goals of the Nazi state because they documented the linguistic and cultural status quo of the settlers before the planned colonization of the "Lebensraum in the East."

The use of camps for sound recordings, 1939–42

A mere six weeks after the outbreak of the Second World War, Diedrich Westermann (1875–1956, Professor of African Languages at the University of Berlin beginning in 1925, member of the Acoustic Commission beginning in 1928 and director of the IFL beginning in 1934) sent the Prussian Academy of Sciences (PAW) his first application for financial support for sound recordings of Polish prisoners of war.[4] In the application, he made explicit reference to the fruitful and exemplary collaboration between the PAW and the (at the time) Royal Prussian Phonographic Commission during the First World War, when sound recordings had been made and linguistic research projects conducted on a grand scale in German prisoner of war camps (Lange, 2007). In December 1939, after the Wehrmacht High Command (OKW) had given its approval, Westermann and Max Vasmer (1886–1962, Professor of Slavic Studies at the University of Berlin from 1925 on and member of the Acoustic Commission from 1928 on) were able to make recordings[5] in the Prenzlau prisoner of war camp with a grant of Reichsmark (RM) 1,500[6] from the Academy. Immediately afterward, in January 1940, Westermann requested a grant from the Academy to the amount of RM 10,000 for recordings of "German repatriates" or "ethnic Germans."[7]

Until 1945, "ethnic German" *[Tr.: Volksdeutsche]* was used to refer to people who resided outside the 1937 borders of Germany and outside Austria, especially in Eastern and Southern Europe, and who were of German ethnic origin but did not possess German citizenship. Under Nazism, the right to citizenship—a matter of descent (*ius sanguinis*) as per the German Constitution of 1913—came to be understood to be shaped by racial criteria on the basis of the 1935 Nuremberg Laws. Indeed, Jewish people were foreclosed from Germanness due to their—as the Nazi jargon went—"foreign blood," but "ethnic Germans" could be integrated into the "racial corpus" *[Tr.: Volkskörper]*. The slogan "Home to the Reich," which had been in use since the 1920s, was promoted with increasing frequency among "ethnic Germans" starting in 1938, first in order to reclaim the former emigrants in the establishment of a Greater German Reich and later to resettle them in the regions occupied by the Germans. This policy was concretized with the Secret Protocol of the Molotov-Ribbentrop Pact of 1939; Hitler's speech to the German parliament on October 6, 1939; and the establishment of the Coordination Center for Ethnic Germans *[Tr.: Volksdeutsche Mittelstelle, VoMi]*, an SS organization tasked with the implementation of the campaign (Lumans, 1993). Heinrich Himmler presided over VoMi as the Reich Commissioner for the Consolidation of the German National Character (RKF). From 1939 to 1940, the VoMi resettled around 700,000 "ethnic Germans" living in the East, some of them in the newly or reannexed regions of Reichsgau Wartheland and Reichsgau Danzig-West Prussia (Leninger, 2006). I am unable to speak at length here about the fact that the SS Race and Settlements Main Office soon interposed on the question of the new settlements and began to conduct racial examinations in the resettlement camps, dividing the repatriates into different grades of "racial purity," where only the "racially purest" were actually designated for resettlement, while the others were meant to be kept in the "Altreich" and used as forced labor (Heinemann, 2003). Propaganda advocating for the resettlement of "ethnic Germans" had already been disseminated on a mass scale starting in late October 1939—though it was prudently concealed that the political grounds for the resettlement campaign were first and foremost satisfying Stalin and gaining a work force and soldiers for the German Reich. Alongside official party papers like the *Völkischer Beobachter*, another important part of the propaganda machinery was, of course, newsreels, which raised shots of Heinrich Himmler welcoming "treks" of large families from Ukraine on the bridge from Przemysl to the level of iconic symbols (Fielitz, 2000). The feature film *Heimkehr* (1941) constituted the high point of the propaganda campaign against the alleged oppression of the "ethnic German" minority by the Polish population in the region surrounding Łódź.

In Westermann's aforementioned January 1940 request for RM 10,000 for recordings of "ethnic Germans," he mentioned the practically and temporally constrained opportunity to conduct research in camps, as in the First World War. At the same time, the IFL director gave a political rationale:

> In defense of this significant sum I would like to say the following: at the moment there exists a unique opportunity to make linguistic recordings of German repatriates from the East. We have established a connection with a variety of authorities and are experiencing eager support from all sides. As a result, there are so many speakers available to me that we would be able to record a very high number of the dialects spoken in the East and process them scientifically. The recordings must be made immediately, because people give up their dialect after living in Germany for a long period. The recordings have just as much ethnological worth as they do linguistic worth, because people speak about life in their settlements. The documents created will be of the greatest importance for the future.[8]

Three lines of reasoning stand out. First, Westermann makes recourse to the *salvage paradigm*, the savior logic standard in ethnography since the nineteenth century that justified lavish trips and expensive documentation projects of "primitive" groups with the argument that these groups were threatened by physical extinction, or at the very least that their culture and ways of life were threatened by dilution or disappearance through contact with Western civilization. In 1940, Westermann transferred this argument to the "repatriates," who would be released from their insular state through resettlement and would come into contact with other German idioms, resulting in the disappearance of their own dialects. True to the logic of *salvage anthropology*, the linguistic researchers of the 1940s were just as uninterested as the early ethnographers in preserving the living conditions of the groups they researched, and instead were solely concerned with documenting the current state of things, which was ideally still as uncontaminated as possible by cultural contact. Second, Westermann emphasized the high "linguistic" yield the planned recordings would provide for research, and third their "ethnological worth," which would derive from the content of the recordings. Here he makes reference to a unique property of language, which can be analyzed with regard to its lexical and grammatical characteristics but is also capable of transporting content and narrative (which can, in turn, be received and researched from multiple perspectives—for instance, out of ethnological interest).

From these three arguments, Westermann drew the conclusion that the sound recordings of "ethnic Germans" would "be of the greatest importance for the future." With these words, he likely was referring to the research horizon or the significance of the recordings for linguistic research and their role in the political—and geographical—future: the new settlements of repatriates planned for the annexed regions of Warthegau and Danzig-Prussia. The preservation of language and cultural traditions would play a considerable role in the colonization of the East, the "Lebensraum im Osten" conjured up by the Nazis, even if "German" ways of life were only to be enforced parallel to the violent expulsion of the resident Polish population.

Scientific and political interests

More applications for grants to conduct sound recordings in the camps followed. In the framework of the "ethnic German" project, Westermann successfully secured financing for Bessarabian recordings in camps in Sachsen and the "Sudetengau" (late 1940) as well as for train trips for "ethnic Germans" already situated in the "Altreich" to travel from Bukovina and the Dobrudscha to Berlin to make sound recordings later on. He received additional support from the Academy, the Reich Education Ministry (REM), and the Reich Propaganda Ministry (RPM), enabling the completion of two comprehensive expeditions to German prisoner of war camps in occupied

France where African colonial soldiers had been taken or were meant to be taken.[9] In November 1941, sound recordings were made of Russian, Serbian, and other prisoners of war in the Neubrandenburg camp under the leadership of Max Vasmer.[10] If no external grants were requested in this case, it was likely because it was not exploitable for propaganda purposes, but rather "only" justifiable from a purely scientific standpoint, on the basis of Vasmer's research interests.[11]

Additionally, in 1941, 1942, and 1943, Russian and even more frequently Ukrainian sound recordings were made in the offices of the Lindström Company in Berlin, which as the successor to Odeon Works had been responsible for the technical processing and matrixing of recordings and the pressing of the Institute's LPs since the 1920s. The speakers were likely prisoners of war, forced laborers, or the so-called foreign laborers, who had been taken from their work sites or camps and brought to Berlin and the surrounding areas.[12] Although Westermann submitted an application in 1942 to the REM for recordings with African prisoners of war in Southern Italian camps that was forwarded to the German embassy in Rome,[13] the project was never realized. In addition to the scientific and likely political aims of the camp research, we must not forget that there were practical considerations: the extensive research tasks enabled Westermann to classify certain workers at the IFL as "essential" and thereby prevent them from being conscripted.

The recordings of "ethnic Germans" can be situated both synchronically and diachronically in the context of research conducted in camps, if one recalls their antecedents in the First World War. They differ significantly from the other camp recordings of the Second World War, the prisoner of war recordings, because they took Germans (and not "foreigners") as their object. Politically, the "ethnic German" recordings were good candidates for grants, just like the sound recordings of African prisoners of war, which provided ammunition for the neocolonial aspirations of the German Reich in Africa (aspirations actively championed by Westermann).[14] Because the recordings of "ethnic Germans" documented the status quo of the repatriates before the colonization of the "Lebensraum in the East," they were easily legitimized and made useful, I propose here the political and propagandistic goals of the Nazi state regarding the "politics of national character." They made the "provinces" of the German language as well as the provinces of "Germanness" audible, and as such were part of the complex that built a tradition of German linguistic belonging and "German national character" that in turn was meant to prepare, accompany, and secure the establishment of geographically new yet culturally consistent German colonies in the Polish eastern regions. Thus, the interplay of scientific and political, geographic and cultural interests, concretized in the collection of audio documents, must be taken as a starting point. At the same time, the dialect recordings of the groups formerly designated as "foreign Germans" served to complete the collection of audio samples of German dialects that had been initiated in 1922. In this context, the question "How do the German dialects sound?" seemed to shift toward the question "How do Germans or does Germanness sound?"

The IFL's collecting practice also served to establish the new "ethnic community" under National Socialism in the first place by integrating the "ethnic Germans" (as well as potential regions for annexation). In a way, the collection of dialect samples from repatriates meant to be colonists anticipated the expansion politics of the Reich on the scale of the collection. Thus, the aim was not only the linguistic conservation of German dialects as well as the cultural conservation of morals and habits, but also making all of these politically useful, convertible, and translatable.

The tradition of German dialect recordings beginning in 1922 and their increased politicization beginning in 1934

At first, the completion of sound recordings of "ethnic German" dialects primarily amounted to the continuation of a collecting practice that had been initiated in 1922 by the predecessors of the IFL, the Acoustic Division of the Prussian State Library (LA). The LA had been founded in 1920 on the basis of three gramophone recording collections: Wilhelm Doegen's recordings for modern language instruction, voice portraits of famous personalities recorded from 1909 on (Ludwig Darmstaedter Collection), and the Phonographic Commission's (1915–1918) recordings of prisoners of war. When the Edison cylinders that had been recorded during the First World War under the direction of Carl Stumpf were given to the Phonogram Archive, Doegen was made director of the new LA, and from then on answered to the General Director of the State Library as well as his superiors at the Prussian Ministry of Science, Art, and Culture (Kultusministerium).

On October 7, 1921, Doegen proposed that the LA complete recordings of German dialects and, to this end, collaborate with the German Commission of the PAW, whose member Ferdinand Wrede was, in turn, in charge of the *German Linguistic Atlas* project *[Tr.: Deutscher Sprachatlas]*.[15] The Acoustic Division would take on the organizational and technical management of the recordings, while the "responsibility for expertise" would lie with the German Commission of the Academy, "in conjunction with the central office of the German Linguistic Atlas and German vernacular research in Marburg."[16] As for a concrete course of action, it was decided that the dialect recordings would be best made *in situ*. Unlike in the prisoner of war camps, where researchers had used the parable of the prodigal son[17] as part of their dialect research, in this undertaking, the Wenker Sentences—40 standardized sentences that linguist Georg Wenker had established in the 1870s and 1880s for (initially only written) research on dialects—would be used as a normative text in the tradition of the *German Linguistic Atlas* in Marburg, though free narration, fairy tales, and similar texts would also play a supplementary role. It was also requested that "women be considered for the recordings, as they usually conserve language better, though they also frequently transplant the dialect of their birthplace elsewhere."[18]

In response to this partnership, the Kultusministerium established an Acoustic Commission on November 23, 1921, which was meant to advise the LA with respect to the selection of language experts and the drawing up of written accounts to accompany the sound recordings.[19] They decided to augment the *Linguistic Atlas*, the written and phonetic notation process that had been practiced in Marburg for decades using the Wenker Sentences as a standard text, with an acoustic notation system: sound recordings from the LA.[20] It was meant to be extended throughout Germany; on a concrete level, it was about "getting the systematic recording of the German dialects in the provinces underway."[21] With the expansion of the collection's scope from foreign languages to German dialects, the LA managed to develop a feature unique in Berlin that served not least to delimit it from the Berlin Phonogram Archive, which focused on non-European music. In contrast, the *Linguistic Atlas* in Marburg augmented its written methods of inquiry with sound recordings from the LA.[22]

Although the members of the Acoustic Commission repeatedly expressed concerns about the scientific validity of the strictly constructed Wenker Sentences, they remained the obligatory standard text for the sound recordings of the LA until 1927. A 1938 list of "recordings in the German language" available on LPs in the IFL shows that next to the voices of famous personalities and "declamation records" featuring German poetry and canonical texts, hundreds of recordings of German dialects had been completed since 1922.[23] In 1927, the LA began to publish books and LPs of selected recordings of the "German vernaculars," including "Mecklenburgisch" (No. 21), "Low German" (No. 38), "Upper German (Meran)" (No. 39), and "Pfälzisch City Dialect in Pirmasens" (No. 40) in *Sound Library: Phonetic Records and Transcriptions*, the series of monographs it had edited since 1926. If we also take the large collection of "Swiss Vernaculars" into account, the overall range shows that the passion for collecting German dialects already extended beyond the contemporaneous German borders.

A *Selbstgleichschaltung [Tr.: Nazi speak for an internal, voluntary process of bringing an institution in line with National Socialism]* of the LA's spread of activities that followed in mid-1933 was meant to further strengthen the archive's emphasis on the production and publication of German dialect recordings. After disciplinary proceedings were brought against Doegen, the director of the LA, for abuses of the budget, the Acoustic Division was rebranded as the "Acoustic Archive" in October 1931 and put under the direct jurisdiction of the Kultusministerium as well as annexed to the University of Berlin with regard to administration.[24] Doegen's administrative leave in May 1933 and his ultimate dismissal in September 1933 under the Law for the Restoration of the Professional Civil Service were preceded by an abundance of complaints about his scientific incompetence. In a statement ordered by the ministry, Arthur Hübner (Professor of German philology at the University of Berlin beginning in 1927, succeeding Gustav Roethe, the student of Scherer's who had died in 1926; member of the Royal PAW beginning in 1932) attested that the Acoustic Division, regarded from a German Studies standpoint, was not living up to its purpose, and pleaded for the "*systematic* increase of German vernacular recordings." Doegen lacked "the scientific disposition for the tasks of the Acoustic Division. To him, the department is more like some type of museum."[25]

Westermann, who had already taken over provisional leadership of the Acoustic Archive in May 1933, sent a letter to the Kultusministerium in December of the same year in which he suggested reconfiguring the Acoustic Division into an "Institute for Acoustic Research." In the letter, he argued that technical recording devices were of such outstanding quality at the moment that not only phonetic research, meaning "investigations into stress, accent, intonation, and phrasing," could be conducted with them, but also "actual investigations into sound," which had "increased their scientific usefulness extraordinarily."[26] The main scientific tasks of the phonetic institute would consist in the continuation of scientific speech recordings, the issuing of phonetic instruction, and research into phonetics.[27] With regard to the main point of the scientific speech recordings, Westermann made a [clear] distinction:

> Special emphasis should be put on German vernaculars and, to this end, the joint venture that has already been initiated between the German Linguistic Atlas (Marburg) and the Swiss Group for Dialect Research should be structured even more tightly. In the recordings made in German-language regions, we should make use of old cultural content, but also content of a musical sort, as long as there are possibilities to do this without coercion. The institute must contribute to the research and preservation of German vernaculars and German national character in a way that is commensurate with their uniqueness, which consists of recording living voices and ensuring that they are heard.[28]

The "living voices" that told of "uniqueness" thus themselves appeared as a characteristic of "German national character." Westermann realized the duties of a museum in the concept of "preservation," but in contrast with Doegen, he coupled this with the task of "research" and in this way legitimated the scientific-universal character of the institute that was to be founded. The fact that in the process, a parallel was made between the content of "German vernaculars" and "German national character" echoes the formulation that Westermann used in 1940 in his application for the "ethnic German" recordings: stories and songs were research material not only from a linguistic perspective, but also from an ethnographic perspective, for the "uniqueness" of "national character" could be reported about in the "uniqueness" of language. The fact that the research into and preservation of the "German national character" corresponded with the National

Socialist playbook for propaganda and politics—significantly more than the execution of, say, English or French recordings—is obvious. With his application, Westermann did his part in the *Selbstgleichschaltung* of universities and cultural institutions; as to whether this was done more out of personal conviction or more on the basis of strategic and opportunistic motives with an eye to founding an institute, more cannot be said here. In any case, the application was successful: with a letter from the Ministry for Education and Culture dated February 14, 1934, the Acoustic Division of the LA was officially reorganized and renamed as the "Institute for Acoustic Research at the University of Berlin" (IFL).[29]

The restructuring further strengthened the collection of German vernaculars started in 1922. A collection of "folk songs of the German districts" was begun contemporaneously, for which Fritz Bose (1906–1975; music ethnologist and employee at the IFL), a man who dealt increasingly with "musical racial science" in his research for his habilitation, was responsible starting in 1935 (Bose, 1943–44). In his 1934 activity report for the "musical division with the special tasks of folk song research and musical racial science," Bose indicated that he had recorded Lorrainese folk singers during a second expedition into the Saar Basin, who had presented "the oldest German folk songs in the living tradition": "In this way, these records also constitute evidence for the centuries-long connection between the Lorrainese and German national character and German culture."[30] In the fact that the Lorrainese would sing old German folk songs, Bose saw proof of "connection"—and the step to the argument of linguistic and cultural or ethnic belonging of Alsace-Lorraine (which had been ceded to France after the First World War) to the German Reich was not far off. Evident in Bose's activities is the fact that he was focusing entirely on so-called Germans abroad; he was planning a lecture on the "Folk Songs of Germans Abroad" for February 1935,[31] and in the catalog of the Institute's "song LPs" that he published in 1936, he differentiated the "German Reich" from the "Folk Songs of Germans Abroad" and filed not only the Lorrainese recordings in the last category, but also the recordings of the Volga Germans from the First World War. He stated that the "borders of the German national character" would extend east, south, and west over the "borders of the German Reich," although the songs of the German colonists would often exhibit "a much older musical and poetic character" than the folk songs of the "homeland" (Bose, 1936, p. 28 f.).

If Bose was committed to making recordings of Germans abroad, in doing so he was also explicitly strengthening political goals, as is evident from an additional episode. In June 1938, he requested that the University curator place him on administrative leave for a three-month recording expedition to South Tyrol, as the Reichsführer-SS, in his capacity as the "Reich Representative for the Reintegration of the 'Ethnic Germans' in South Tyrol," had appointed him to the staff.[32] On this trip—the beginning of which was delayed until mid-1940—Bose also worked together with the music scholar

Alfred Quellmalz from the SS-Ahnenerbe *[Tr.: a Nazi think tank run by Heinrich Himmler]*.[33]

The sound recordings of Germans abroad who, as was mentioned earlier, were classified more and more frequently as "ethnic Germans" starting in the mid-1930s thus constituted a logical continuation and expansion of the conservation programs of German vernaculars, which were broadened to include the recording of folk songs understood to be genuine expressions of "ethnicity." The LA's and later the IFL's project was conducted in the tradition of encyclopedic linguistic research projects like the late nineteenth-century *Linguistic Survey of India* by George Abraham Grierson (http://dsal. uchicago.edu/books/lsi/).[34] While the *Survey* had never had purely scientific goals in the colonial British context, as it also focused on documenting and profiling British rule in a colonized and dominated India, the IFL's 1934 research program proved to be even broader in that it extended linguistic borders further than existing state borders. Language was also power, and linguistic and "ethnic" belonging could be used to legitimize the resettlement of people and the expansion of borders and regions. Accordingly, the documentation of German vernaculars and folk songs of Germans abroad or "ethnic Germans" had a potential that could be activated for political projects. In the meantime, an almost exactly contemporaneous project of the *German Linguistic Atlas* in Marburg did not overstep national boundaries: as a gift for the birthday of Adolf Hitler in 1937, the researchers in Marburg issued a *Lautdenkmal reichsdeutscher Mundarten zur Zeit Adolf Hitlers* (Acoustic Monument of Reich-German Vernaculars in the Time of Adolf Hitler). It consisted of a collection of 300 shellac LPs with recordings of vernacular speakers from every region of the territory of the German Reich (Näser, 2001; Wilking, 2003; Purschke, 2012). It was only *after* the Anschluss of Austria that in 1938 70 more LPs with Austrian dialects were recorded, while nothing is known about over 20 planned "Sudeten German" recordings (Purschke, 2012, p. 84).[35]

However, the following episode from the history of the IFL shows that the scientific results of the dialect research could also be used *against* the researchers politically. In 1937, the slavicist Reinhold Olesch (1910–90), himself born in Upper Silesia with Silesian Polish as his mother tongue, published some sound recordings made in 1933 under the direction of Vasmer in the monograph series *Arbeiten aus dem Institut für Lautforschung an der Universität Berlin* (Works from the Institute for Acoustic Research at the University of Berlin) (Olesch, 1937). After earning his doctorate in 1935 with a dissertation supervised by Vasmer on the Polish vernaculars of Upper Silesia, he was regarded as a linguistic expert on the region. Olesch was soon forced to give up his job as a language assistant at the University of Greifswald, which he had assumed in 1937, because it was charged that his dissertation reinforced Poland's claim to Upper Silesia. This exact argument was also raised against Olesch's publication of the sound recordings. An unsigned letter to the REM explained that with the *publication* (rather than the mere collection) of the sound recordings, Olesch had erroneously shown that in Upper Silesia, the population primarily spoke good Polish. In doing so, he provided evidence to Polish linguistic researchers (namely the Krakow Professor Kazimierz Nitsch of the Polish Academy of Sciences) and to "the Poles" in general that supported their regional claim to Upper Silesia.[36] An additional expert opinion confirmed the evaluation of Olesch's work as "propaganda" that in turn dealt a serious blow "to German propaganda in Upper Silesia":

> Whoever deals with the linguistic situation in a border region must be clear about the fact that he cannot work scientifically without stirring up political matters in the strongest way, especially when a neighboring people is making political demands on the basis of language. For this reason alone, the attitude of "I am working scientifically with no regard to political questions" is either a form of naïveté that should no longer exist, or hypocrisy.[37]

Thus, with regard to their publication, scientific results had to be adjusted to please the authorities and brought in line with the playbook for propaganda; in general, scientific work, geopolitical insofar as it dealt with border questions, was also to be understood as political work. The task of linguistics and research into national character could hardly have been more clearly articulated; it was only supposed to produce politically desirable results. Here, the intermingling and interpenetration of scholarship and politics emerges in the domain of language, which on the basis of its architecture implies forms of linguistic belonging, but on the level of semantics—in its stories—also captures elements of "national character" like morals and habits.

In February 1938, the Reich Ministry of Public Enlightenment and Propaganda consequently submitted an official request to the Reich Literature Chamber that Olesch's publication be added "to the list of detrimental and undesirable literature," as it offered "scientific material for Polish propaganda,"[38] not without first seeking the consent of the "Reich and Prussian Minister for Science, Education, and Culture" with reference to the "danger of the applied research methods for the politics of German national character."[39] It is significant that a letter received from "Folklorist" Heinrich Harmjanz (tenured professor of *Volkskunde [Tr.: antiquated* term with nationalist undertones for what is now called European ethnology], Folk Research, German Border Culture, and the Culture of Germans Abroad in Königsberg beginning in 1937; tenured professor in Frankfurt am Main beginning in 1938; National Socialist Party and SS member beginning in 1930) shifted the blame to Olesch's doctoral advisor Vasmer. Vasmer, born in St. Petersburg, was—according to Harmjanz in his letter to the Ministry of Education—a Russian, "politically insensitive and perhaps not harmless."[40] Councilor Dr. Karl Albert Coulon consequently endorsed banning Olesch's dissertation from public bookstores, but also insisted: "Westermann is entirely innocent, he was right in having relied on Vasmer!"[41]

Whether or not Westermann ever learned of the official intent to make Vasmer responsible and ban Olesch's dissertation is still an open question. It is clear however that linguistic research was used as a political argument and instrument. Viewed before the negative foil of the case of Olesch, it seems plausible that Westermann's research on "ethnic Germans" was also understood to be politically useful, and that the truth of his nebulous statements about the great significance of the recordings "for the future"[42] appeared to be self-evident. In the public meeting of the Academy on January 23, 1941, he stressed: "The return home of the ethnic Germans to the Reich offers a unique opportunity to record the distinct cultural heritage of these members of our ethnic community and in this way make this available to scientific research."[43] Linguistic research was justified on the basis of the argument of "ethnicity," and at the same time it awoke the impression that it was "cementing" "the German ethnicity" by documenting stories from the lives of settlers.

The camp recordings of Volhynian Germans

Before the background sketched out here, Westermann's 1940 project recording "ethnic German" repatriates makes sense. Germany's own "ethnicity," its own "ethnic community," came into play as the object of the recordings, stretching beyond the borders of the "Old Reich." Now regarded as sites of knowledge about Germany's own "ethnic community," camps became more appealing as possible sites for the recordings; camps at the time and earlier had been serving to gauge "foreign bodies" scientifically and via gramophone.

As early as January 1940, Westermann who had made contact with the VoMi reported that the IFL was making "phonographic recordings of languages and vernaculars for scientific purposes" with a special interest in "Vohynian repatriates," and requested that access be secured to the corresponding camps.[44] In the Humboldt University Archive, there is also a large selection of letters concerning later "expeditions" addressed to the VoMi, which ran the repatriate camps, as well to individual camp leaders, all seeking to provide members of the Institute with information about the occupants of the camps and the possibility of entrance.[45] On February 19, 1940, official letters were issued for the recordings of Volhynians and Galicians that confirm that the employee Ursula Feyer and the technician Fritz Kapsch were charged with the execution of the recordings and were authorized to travel to "Lodsch."[46] In Polish Łódź, where the "Litzmannstadt Field Office" answering directly to the VoMi resided, there were large assembly camps where repatriates were received. But the IFL gave up the plan to travel to Łódź only a few days later, and instead visited repatriate and transit camps in Sachsen and in Reichsgau Sudetenland in March 1940.[47]

Recordings were made in Pirna (Sonnenstein Camp and Schandau Camp), in Ústí nad Labem/Aussig (Aussig, Leitmeritz, and Komotau Camps), and in Oschatz (Wurzen and Oschatz Camps).[48] According to Westermann's letter to the Academy in July 1940—which in part borrowed passages word-for-word from his January 1940 application—the results were developing exactly as promised:

> The ethnic German camps in Sachsen and in the Sudetengau offered the unique opportunity to make language recordings of the German repatriates from East Galicia and Vohynia. The recordings needed to be made immediately, because after long stretches of living in Germany, people give up their home dialects. In total, sixty-five recordings were made, and thirty-five are being prepared. These recordings are not only of great linguistic worth, but also just as great ethnological worth, as the speakers spoke about life, mores, and customs, as well as historical events in their settlements. In this way, documents were created that are of great significance for the national character of Germans abroad.[49]

Palatine, Egerlandish, Bohemian Forest, and Transpomeranian dialects were recorded in the context of this project.[50] IFL staff made a second trip to the camps in December 1941, once again with financial support from the PAW and the REM, to record dialects and songs of the so-called Bessarabian Germans (Schulze, 2014). Once again the VoMi took charge of making the necessary contacts, and recordings were made in Dresden (Pirna Camp and the Technical College), in Nuremberg (Hotel "Red Rooster"), in Teplice/Teplitz-Schönau (a camp), and in January 1941 in Česká Kamenice/Böhmisch-Kamnitz (Camp) in the "Sudetenland."[51] Westermann subsequently reported in a public lecture before the Academy on January 23, 1941:

> With the exception of the Pfalzian settlement, we dealt overwhelmingly with Swabian and Low German dialects this time. Additionally, especially interesting mixed dialects were gathered along with these, in which High German and Low German elements stood alongside one another with differing relative strengths, and were blended with one another accordingly. Seeing as it will be possible, with help of the kinship research authorities, to name the origin place of the bulk of the Bessarabian settler families, these linguistic recordings provide material for the detailed study of language mixing and interpenetration.[52]

And finally, as I have already mentioned, Westermann applied for grants to bring repatriates from camps in the Dobrudscha and the Bukovina to Berlin by train, so that they could be recorded in the offices of the Lindström Company in 1941.[53] All in all, the "return home of the ethnic Germans to the Reich [offered] a unique opportunity to record the distinct cultural heritage of these members of our ethnic community and in this way make this available to scientific research."[54] The language recordings, which in contrast with conventional linguistic research captured "living sound," thus served to produce difference (in language, among the dialects) and unity (in the figure of German "national character" and German "ethnic community") at the same time.

From the correspondence, reports, and bills preserved in the archive of the HU and that of the Academy, it emerges that the "ethnic Germans," as part of Germany's own "racial corpus," were treated with significantly more respect than the Polish, Russian, or French prisoners of war. This is relatively clear from the accounts for the grants, which show that it was not only external scientists who were paid for a certain "linguistic task,"[55] but that individual "ethnic German" persons also received a "language fee," usually to the amount of RM 10.[56] In contrast with the prisoners of war, the "ethnic German" speakers, or at least those from the Oschatz Camp, were also handed their own recordings on LPs.[57]

Yet another difference is conspicuous: while the African colonial soldiers mostly read prescribed texts into the gramophone, as had been done during the First World War, it is notable that for the recordings of Russian prisoners of war, many told the requested fairy tales on the basis of a few notes or predetermined oral agreements, but were free in word choice. The shift to free (instead of controlled) discourse was ordered by the Acoustic Commission primarily for the German dialect recordings, and had already been in practice since the 1920s and 1930s, which constituted a substantial innovation in the recording procedures of 1900 through 1921 from a history of science perspective.

For the sound recordings of prisoners of war speaking foreign languages in camps during the First World War, a protocol in the sense of a program or a set of commands had been produced that tended toward a preemptive record, a transcript.[58] Thus, the Phonographic Commission had made it its task "to systematically record the languages, music, and sounds of all ethnic strains present in the prisoner of war camps on the basis of methodical principles and in connection with their corresponding texts" (Doegen, 1925, p. 10), and thus to document the different languages and dialects sonically, phonetically, and in written form. Viewed from a history of science standpoint, with the completion of this documentation project, the commission fell in with Wilhelm von Humboldt's integrative conception of linguistics and the ensuing virulent discourse about "living language" (Kaplan, 2013), which could now be acoustically captured in all of its vitality with new technical recording and storage possibilities. The procedure was established at the end of 1915:

> Exact records with details that will be significant for later scientific analysis are produced for every recording. The person making the records [Wilhelm Doegen, B.L.], who as a rule is present at the gramophone recording sessions, is endeavoring to prepare for the expeditions and produce the recordings and records uniformly.[59]

The prisoner had to verbalize the transcript of a text into the gramophone horn, i.e. recite it from memory, read it out loud, or repeat it after the prompter, while the supervising scientist continuously took note of deviations.

The "ethnic German" recordings marked the first time in the history of the IFL that a free discourse format was combined with the recounting of contemporary history, of current political events. Accordingly, Westermann reported to the Academy that in making the "ethnic German" recordings, "the greatest worth was placed on freely spoken texts," where it was the goal "to obtain a substantial text that characterized country and people," i.e. to produce ethnological documents.[60] Although "lovely recordings about work and customs" had been successfully produced in the case of the recordings of Galicians and Vohynians, "the recently defeated Polish terror" had been "at the center of interest" in these recordings and "its reflections" could be "found in almost every text."[61] The phrase "Polish terror" invoked not only the (alleged) harassment of the German settlers and their children between the two World Wars (thence Westermann's comment about the Volhynian settlements in Poland suffering the loss of "their ethnic unity"),[62] but also and especially the attacks by the Polish population on the German minority immediately after the German Reich's assault on Poland in September 1939.

A good example might be offered by the recording of the Vohynian German woman cited at the beginning of this article, Theophile Helme from "Deutsch-Antonowka," who spoke into the gramophone in a classroom on March 18, 1940 (Fig. 1). She was born in 1884 and lived in Luck/Luzk (today northwestern Ukraine) as household help. When the recording was made, she was located in the Wurzen Camp in Oschatz/Saxony. Her dialect was entitled "East Low German from Volhynia"; her LP, with the call number LA 1637, "experiences from the World War and from the Most Recent War," meaning from the First and Second World Wars. There is no historical transcription accompanying her recording in the Acoustic Archive. I have translated her words, which are reproduced here in excerpts, by ear from East Low German into High German, from German into German, as yet incomplete and subject to correction:

> I've had a difficult life. You should have seen me eight years ago. I earned, earned, had work to do, finished everything, held everything together. I had to give up everything I earned.
>
> Then the war started. We know the Jews are in the city now. We always shouted: Hitlerish, Hitlerish, Hitlerish. But I didn't encounter anyone. I did everything, I completed everything. When it started, I thought about everything that might come. Things were tough. If only the German people would come soon. I longed to see something come of the Putsch. I looked for such a long time. I went to the cattle. I lay down between the cattle. I lay on the ground with the cattle. There were cannons all around. The entire night I prayed to God that I would see a troop of Germans.

Then they fell upon me, the Pollacks. Asked me what I was doing here. I say, I live here with the goats. Well what am I? I say that I'm a Pahlish [Pole?]. I hid that I was a German [in the original: "en dütsch Mensch," B.L.]. I was beaten the entire night, until I thought that I wouldn't survive the next day. And I came through it.

[…]

But at midday I heard that the Germans were departing. The Germans really should have hit them on the head. But the Germans had gone. Then the Poles all went to church. After church they lay down in the bushes with clubs. I saw none of the Germans. Then they continued on with the cattle, always behind. They always lagged behind. Always lagging. Then they closed in on the *Volk*.

I saw no Germans. Until Rangengau. There I asked for a piece of bread in the church. We worked there in the church. We lived that way for three months. That's how we pushed through. That's how we came to Łódź. We pushed through with the cattle until we got here.

[…]

What has become of my youth?[63]

Predetermined word-for-word texts were relinquished in the "ethnic German" recordings made during the Second World War, and shorthand *a priori* protocols were, at the very least, not preserved. As for agreements as to what should appear in the sound recordings, the vocabulary used was that from the speaker's "preparation." This was roughly what the IFL communicated to the VoMi on May 7, 1941: "We are currently contemplating whether or not to record the ethnic Germans from the Buchenland [Bukovina, B.L.] and the Dobruja. We have visited the camps that we are considering and have chosen and prepared suitable persons for the recordings."[64] Word-for-word transcriptions are only available for a few of the recordings, and were clearly drawn up retrospectively while listening to the LPs—this is indicated by several crossings-out. The handwritten transcriptions (with one exception) translated the texts into High German, which likewise indicated that these were not produced prior to the recordings and then read aloud. Typewritten transcriptions could have accompanied texts that were reproduced for educational purposes.

This altered recording procedure reflects a general alteration in the history of German dialect recordings and testifies to a historical shift in the context of both the history of science and the history of knowledge. As regards the history of knowledge, there was a change in what was considered interesting in a dialect recording: it was no longer only meant to provide information about the sound of phonemes and word choice, but now, attention was also given to diction, progression, spontaneous word choice, intonation, and storytelling structure as well as further characteristics of oral discourse. Scientific acoustic knowledge—as an epistemological method meant to produce knowledge by analyzing acoustic modes of expression—was supplemented by a form of political acoustic knowledge in which a scientific innovation is visible. Attention was now paid to the contents and political messages of the narratives: What could be established about hearsay through acoustic knowledge? What did the "ethnic Germans" have to report about their lives, their oppression? Scientific acoustic knowledge was in this way bound up with political acoustic knowledge. The first question directed at the sound recordings was how the "ethnic Germans" sounded as part of Germany's own "racial corpus," in order to incorporate or expand by means of them as well as to expand the German linguistic borders; the second question was what politically relevant or instrumentalizable statements the "ethnic Germans" made about their lives, say as part of the conflict with the Polish majority called the "Polish terror." Thus it was a matter of constructing a political form of acoustic knowledge that at the same time both depicted and constructed the German people, in which power and science were intertwined through the concept of "das Volk."

Synthesis

Archival documents indicate that the LPs of "ethnic Germans" were matrixed and pressed soon after they were recorded.[65] The IFL made them available to educational establishments. In September 1942, it responded to an order from the Schleiz State Image Archive, with an advertisement for more available LPs:

I would also like to direct your attention to our recordings of ethnic German repatriates. These constitute speech samples of both cultural-historical and ethnological value, of Pfälzisch from Galicia, Volhynia, Bessarabia, from Bukovina, and from Dobruja. East Low German from Volhynia, Bessarabia, and Dobruja. Böhmerwäldisch and Egerländisch from Galicia and Bukovina. Zipser German from Bukovina.[66]

A complete index of the recordings was said to be under way.[67]

Finally, letters from 1943 indicate the use of the recorded material by political officials. In May, the SS Leadership Office Dept. VI (Ideological Training and Troop Entertainment) ordered sound recordings "for educational purposes" for interpreter apprenticeships.[68] In July 1943, the institute urgently requested paper from the Dean of the Philosophical Division, explaining that the LPs would not only be in demand in business circles, but "also on a large scale, eliciting interest from a great many members of the military administration and from the Reich Ministry for the Occupied Eastern Territories." The "importance of the LPs to the war effort" seems to be implied by the fact that many collections were "repeatedly provided with financial support from the Reich Minister for Education and Science, the Propaganda Ministry, and the Reich Führer SS as Reich Commissioner for the Strengthening of the German National Character."[69]

With the recordings of "ethnic Germans," the IFL expanded a spectrum of German dialect recordings that had encompassed idioms of so-called

Germans abroad as early as before the outbreak of the Second World War. The speakers of those dialects, who became political symbols as a result of the enormous resettlement campaign "Home to the Reich," initiated by Heinrich Himmler, gave the university institute the opportunity not only to attract additional funding but also to simultaneously depict its scientific work as "essential to the war effort." The former LA had been pursuing the question "How do the German dialects sound?" since 1922 by making sound recordings of dialect speakers in cooperation with the German Commission of the PAW and the *German Linguistic Atlas* in Marburg. Now this question expanded to include extremely political elements, insofar as the "ethnic belonging" that Himmler was constantly testifying to seemed verifiable and incorporable by means of linguistic belonging and being part of a "German national character": "How do the Germans sound, how does the German national character sound?" and "What were, what are the Germans like, and how should they be?" The demonstration of both linguistic and cultural belonging can be attributed to the free-discourse "ethnic German" sound recordings. Thus, by making recourse to the concept of "national character," the language question also became a question of essence, with a tendency toward ahistorical or eternal being: "Who are the Germans?" Moreover, the Volhynian and Galician recordings were predestined for use in direct political propaganda due to the aforementioned reports of the "Polish terror," for they articulated another facet, a political facet, of the questions concerning language and ethnicity: "How do the Germans suffer?" In this way, they were well suited to fuel patterns of reaction that amounted to revenge, retribution, displacement, and expansion.

Acoustic knowledge based in phonetics and German philology thus proved itself to be knowledge about and for power, not only because the production of the LPs was an immediate effect of geopolitical power relations, expansion strategies, and ideological content, but also because the LPs served to train linguistic and cultural experts—in the interpreter schools of the SS, for instance—and in this way provided knowledge about and for domination.

Notes

1 This chapter was originally published in German under the title "Die Konstruktion des Volks über Hör-Wissen. Tonaufnahmen des Instituts für Lautforschung von ,volksdeutschen Umsiedlern' aus den Jahren 1940/1941," in Daniel Morat's edited book *Wissensgeschichte des Hörens in der Moderne* (2017), Berlin and Boston: De Gruyter.

2 Acoustic Archive of Humboldt University in Berlin (LAHUB), LA 1637-1, Theophile Helme, recorded on March 18, 1940; Sound recording in East Low German, without transcription, transcribed by ear into High German by Britte Lange. A special thanks to the following individuals for supporting my research: Sarah Grossert, Jochen Hennig, Constantin Hühn, Klaas Ehlers, Gerhard Sieberz.

3 https://www.lautarchiv.hu-berlin.de/bestaende-und-katalog/bestaende/ (February 22, 2017). The metadata for the recordings can be found at www.sammlungen.hu-berlin.de (February 22, 2017).

4 Letter from Westermann to the PAW dated September 14, 1939; Archive of the Berlin-Brandenburg Academy of Sciences (ABBAW): Files of the PAW 1812–1945, German Commission, Sign. PAW II-VIII-44.

5 Cf. the sound recordings in LAHUB, LA 1559—LA 1579, December 4–6, 1939.

6 Cf. the correspondence in ABBAW, PAW (1812–1945), II-VIII-44.

7 Letter from Westermann to the PAW dated January 20, 1940; ABBAW, PAW (1812–1945), II-VIII-44.

8 Letter from Westermann to the PAW dated January 20, 1940; ABBAW, PAW (1815–1945), II-VIII-44. The Academy allocated RM 3,000 for this project and requested the remaining RM 7,000 from the REM. As early as January 26, 1940, two recordings had already been made in the Berlin sound recording offices of the Lindström Company in the "East Low German of Taurien" as well as two in the "Swabian of Bessarabia" (LA 1580–1583).

9 Cf. the files in the archive of Humboldt University of Berlin (AHUB) on the IFL as well as the secondary literature of Stoecker (2008, pp. 138–43).

10 Cf. the sound recordings in LAHUB, LA 1893—LA 1955 (recording time period: November 6–9, 1941).

11 Cf. the volume *Das Lager als Sprachlabor* by Marie-Luise Bott, Britta Lange, and Roland Meyer (Stuttgart 2021).

12 Cf. the recording journal of the Acoustic Archive. In a letter from the IFL to the Berlin editor of the prisoner of war newspaper *Nowa Doba* dated April 21, 1941, the Institute sent the approval of the OKW for scientific voice recordings in prisoner of war camps and requested permission to record Ukranian prisoners of war; AHUB, IFL, folder 12. The holdings of the IFL in the AHUB are not chronological, systematic, or alphabetically ordered.

13 Letter from Westermann to the REM dated September 19, 1942; Bundesarchiv Berlin-Lichterfelde (BArch), holding R 4901, file 1477, sheet 40 ff.

14 Westermann became involved with the newly established Department of the Study of Foreign Countries of the University of Berlin in early 1940. Additionally, together with anthropologist and "race hygiene" activist Eugen Fischer as well as Egyptologist Hermann Grapow, he planned to organize a commission for the research of "White Africa" during the militarily successful campaigns of the German Africa Corps; cf. Klein, 1985, p. 89. As the assessment office of the National Socialist Teachers' League for Educational Literature attested on February 21, 1938, "politically there was nothing detrimental known" about Westermann; cf. BArch, R 9361-VI/3411 (Berlin Document Center).

15 The following were named here as participants: Doegen, Wrede, linguist and Indo-Germanist Wilhelm Schulze, Germanist and later rector of the University of Berlin Gustav Roethe, and Africanist Martin Heepe from Westermann's Seminar for Oriental Languages.

16 Ibid., p. 4.

17 On the introduction of the parable of the prodigal son into dialect research, cf. Albrecht (2014).

18 Minutes from the meeting of the future Acoustic Commission on July 10, 1921, p. 2f; AHUB, IFL, folder 9.

19 Cf. yearly report 1921/1922 dated January 1, 1923; AHUB, IFL, folder 9. Cf. ibid. additionally the minutes of the first meeting of the Acoustic Commission on April 7, 1922, in which the outcomes of the meeting on October 7, 1921, were confirmed. In addition to Fritz Milkau (General Director of the Staatsbibliothek), members of the Acoustic Commission were Humboldt professors Alois Brandl (English Language and Literature), Heinrich Lüders (Oriental Seminar), and Wilhelm Schulze (the Academy), who had already been members of the Phonographic Commission, in addition to Prof. Roethe, who like Schulze was a member of the German Commission of the Academy of Sciences. In addition

to the members of the Acoustic Commission (other than Roethe, who excused himself), Doegen and Martin Heepe also took part in the first meeting in 1922.

20 For more on the *Linguistic Atlas* project at the University of Marburg, see the German Linguistic Atlas Research Center on the university website http://www.uni-marburg.de/fb09/dsa (February 22, 2017). Members of the *Linguistic Atlas* project worked in prisoner of war camps during the First World War, where they took down Wenker Sentences but made no sound recordings. Cf. the as of yet unpublished essays by Prof. Jürg Fleischer, Marburg.

21 Yearly report 1921/1922 dated January 1, 1923, as well as the minutes of the first meeting of the Sound Commission on April 7, 1922, here p. 2; both AHUB, IFL, folder 9.

22 This raises the question: to what extent do the gramophone recordings in Marburg change the premises of the research? What status, what significance did they have there, and what status did freely formulated texts have? Marburg first began making its own sound recordings in the 1930s. At present, the sound recordings of the Acoustic Archive at Humboldt and the Marburg collection are being synchronized.

23 Cf. *Schallplatten des Instituts für Lautforschung der Universität Berlin. Aufnahmen in deutscher Sprache*, assembled by Ursula Feyer, Berlin 1938. According to Dieter Mehnert, in 1996 the archive possessed all in all 710 records with recordings of so-called German vernaculars (Mehnert, 1996, pp. 38f); the "ethnic German" recordings may also be considered part of the 1938 holdings.

24 Cf. Stoecker, *Afrikawissenschaften von 1919 bis 1945*, p. 132 f.

25 Letter from Professor Hübner to the Prussian Ministry for Education and Culture dated February 2, 1933; BArch, R 4901, file 1475, sheets 194–5, emphasis in original.

26 Letter from Westermann to the Minister for Science, Art, and Ethnic Education, FAO Administrative Director Büschel, arrived on December 15, 1933: "Reconfiguration of the sound department into an Institute for Sound Research"; AHUB, UK 903, sheets 27–31, here sheet 28.

27 Cf. ibid., sheets 29–31.

28 Ibid., sheet 29.

29 Letter from the Prussian Minister for Science, Art, and Ethnic Education (Bernhard Rust), signed Haupt, dated February 14, 1934, and sent to the administrative director of the University of Berlin; AHUB, Holdings of the University Curator (UK) 903, Institute for Sound Research, sheet 34. However, this did not initially change the delivery of the budget.

30 Report on the activities of the IFL at the University of Berlin in 1934; BArch, R 4901, file 1476, sheets 3–12, here sheet 9.

31 Ibid., sheet 11.

32 Letter from Bose to the University Curator dated June 13, 1940; BArch, R 4901, file 1477, sheet 27.

33 Cf. University of Regensburg (Regensburg Folk Music Portal), "Folk Music (Songs and Dances) from South Tyrol (1940–1942)," online at http://www.uni-regensburg.de/bibliothek/projekte/rvp/suedtirol/index.html (February 22, 2017).

34 Incidentally, this project began with the aim of also making gramophone recordings for the *Survey* as a response to the Prussian Phonographic Commission in 1922.

35 In a letter dated August 18, 1937, Wilhelm Doegen pointed out the LPs to Adolf Hitler personally in reaction to the public handoff of the *Sound Monument*, and above all pointed out photographs of the Phonographic Commission from the First World War; cf. Doegen's letter to the Führer and Reich Chancellor dated August 18, 1937; Berlin State Museums, Prussian Cultural Heritage Foundation,

Phonogram Archive of the Ethnological Museum (PHEMB), holdings of the Five Continents Museum, files concerning the Phonogram Archive in Museum Building Dahlem, Volume 1.

36 Manuscript to WR 708/38, transcript of the enclosed assessment. WR 443/38, Breslau, August 8, 1938; BArch, R 4901, file 1476, sheet 184.

37 "Olesch," WR 708/38, transcript of the enclosed assessment. WR 443/38; BArch, R 4901, file 1476, sheet 185.

38 Application from the RPM to the Reich Literature Chamber in Berlin-Charlottenburg dated February 24, 1938; BArch, R 4901, file 1476, sheet 188.

39 Petition from Senior Councilor Johannes Schlecht (Reich Ministry for Public Enlightenment and Propaganda, Dept. Literature) to Herr Reich and Prussian Minister for Science, Education, and Ethnic Education in Berlin dated January 3, 1938; BArch, R 4901, file 1476, sheet 186. At the inquiry of the Nazi Reich leadership in July 1939, it became evident that no concrete steps had been taken; in January 1940, it was finally clear that nothing could be done due to the war. Cf. BArch, R 4901, file 1477, sheets 18–22.

40 Transcript of a letter from Harmjanz to the undersecretary Dr. Kummer dated January 26, 1938 (General Department for the library system in REM); BArch, R 4901, file 1476, sheet 187.

41 Transcript of a letter from Councilor Dr. Coulon to Kummer after Kummer's delivery (*nach Vorlage durch Kummer*) on January 28, 1938; BArch R 4901, file 1476, sheet 188.

42 Letter from Westermann to the PAW dated January 20, 1940; ABBAW, PAW (1812–1945), II-VIII-44.

43 Diedrich Westermann, "Bericht über Sprachaufnahmen in volksdeutschen Lagern," in *Jahrbuch der Preußischen Akademie der Wissenschaften* for 1941, Berlin 1942, pp. 166–70, here p. 166 (report on the occasion of the "Public Celebratory Meeting for the Observance of Friedrich Day and the Day of the Founding of the Reich on Thursday, January 23, 1941").

44 Letter from the IFL to the VoMi, Berlin W., Tiergartenstr. 18a, dated January 9, 1940; AHUB, IFL, folder 12.

45 Cf. AHUB, IFL, especially folder 12.

46 Cf. two carbon copies from February 19, 1940, signed Westermann; AHUB, IFL, folder 16.

47 Cf. Letter from Westermann to Prof. Frings dated January 1, 1922; AHUB, IFL, folder 16.

48 LAHUB, Recordings LA 1584—LA1641.

49 Diedrich Westermann, "Bericht über die Sprachaufnahmen an deutschen Umsiedlern aus Ostgebieten" to the Academy, dated July 12, 1940; ABBAW, PAW (1812–1945), II-VIII-44.

50 Cf. ibid.

51 LAHUB, recordings LA 1652—LA 1700.

52 Lecture of Westermann's before the Academy on January 23, 1941, typescript, AHUB, IFL, Nr. 12; Orthography and grammar follow, as with all other sources, the original.

53 LAHUB, sound recordings LA 1711–LA 1731, LA 1734–LA 1735, LA 1737–LA 1741 (April–July 1941).

54 Cf. Westermann, "Bericht über Sprachaufnahmen" in Akademie-Jahrbuch 1941, p. 166.

55 Dr. H. Braun from Leipzig thus received a retainer of RM 150; cf. "Abrechnung über 10.579,75 RM, die das Institut für Lautforschung an der Universität Berlin für Bereisung der volksdeutschen Lager im Gau Sachsen und im Sudetengau zwecks Schallplattenaufnahmen von der Preußischen Akademie

der Wissenschaften erhalten hat," July 13, 1940; ABBAW, PAW (1812–1945), II-VIII-44.

56 Cf. ibid. The persons named are here also matched with recording call numbers: H. Claassen RM 10 for LA 1580/1581, F. Woloschyn RM 10 for LA 1643 etc.: ABBAW, PAW (1812–1945), II-VIII-44.

57 Cf. Letter from Ursula Feyer to Westermann dated June 3, 1940; AHUB. IFL, folder 16. On May 5, 1941, in a letter to the employees in the Böhmisch-Kamnitz Camp, Ursula Feyer added: "I would like to request that you hand out the recordings to the speakers. This was promised to them for their time doing the recordings"; AHUB, IFL, file 12.

58 On the differentiation between a verbal record and result record, progression record and memory record as well as retrospective and programmatic records (cf. Niehaus and Schmidt-Hannissa, 2005).

59 Letter from Carl Stumpf, chairman of the Phonographic Commission, to the Minister of Culture, dated January 20, 1916; AHUB, IFL, folder 12, 1935–44.

60 Westermann, "Bericht über Sprachaufnahmen" in Akademie-Jahrbuch 1941, p. 170.

61 Ibid.

62 Ibid., p. 168.

63 LAHUB, LA 1637-1, Theophile Helme, recorded on March 18, 1940. Transcription into High German: Britta Lange.

64 Letter from the IFL to the VoMi dated May 7, 1941; AHUB, IFL, folder 12, 1935–44.

65 In February 1941, Lindström delivered 40 LPs to the IFL for recordings from the Bessarabian expedition "for free," 15 more for money; cf. bill issued by the Carl Lindström company to the IFL dated February 8, 1941; ABBAW, PAW (1812–1945), II-VIII-44.

66 The IFL's response to the Schleiz State Image Archive dated September 29, 1942; AHUB, IFL, folder 14.

67 Cf. ibid.

68 Letter from the Interpreter Apprenticeship and Ersatz Division of the Waffen-SS in Oranienburg to the IFL, dated September 2, 1943; AHUB, IFL, folder 14.

69 Letter from the Interpreter Apprenticeship and Ersatz Division of the Waffen-SS in Oranienburg to the IFL, dated September 2, 1943; AHUB, IFL, folder 14.

References

Albrecht, B. (2014) *Von Verlorenen Söhnen und wiedergefundenen Sprachen. Die Parabel des verlorenen Sohnes als Standardtext in der Sprachwissenschaft an Beispielen von Lautaufnahmen aus Kriegsgefangenenlagern des Deutschen Reiches im 1. Weltkrieg*, Master's Thesis. Humboldt-Universität zu Berlin.

Bose, F. (1936) *Lieder der Völker. Die Musikplatten des Instituts für Lautforschung an der Universität Berlin. Katalog und Einführung*. Berlin, Humboldt-Universität zu Berlin.

Bose, F. (1943–44) Klangstile als Rassenmerkmale. *Zeitschrift für Rassenkunde* (14), pp. 78–79 and 208–224.

Doegen, W. (1925) Introduction. In: Doegen, W. (ed.) *Unter fremden Völkern. Eine neue Völkerkunde*. Berlin, O. Stollberg, pp. 9–16.

Fielitz, W. (2000) *Das Stereotyp des wolhyniendeutschen Umsiedlers. Popularisierungen zwischen Sprachinselforschung und nationalsozialistischer Propaganda*. Marburg, Elwert.

Heinemann, I. (2003) *Rasse, Siedlung, deutsches Blut. Das Rasse- und Siedlungshauptamt und die rassenpolitische Neuordnung Europas*, Second Edition. Göttingen, Wallstein Verlag.

Kaplan, J. (2013) 'Voices of the People:' Linguistic Research among Germany's Prisoners of War during World War I. *Journal of the History of the Behavioral Sciences* (49:3), pp. 281–305.

Klein, H. (ed.) (1985) *Humboldt-Universität zu Berlin, Überblick 1810–1985*. Berlin, Humboldt-Universität zu Berlin.

Lange, B. (2007) Ein Archiv von Stimmen. Kriegsgefangene unter ethnographischer Beobachtung. In: Wegmann, N., Maye, H. and Reiber, C. (eds.) *Original/Ton. Zur Mediengeschichte des O-Tons*. Konstanz, UVK, pp. 317–341.

Leninger, M. (2006) *Nationalsozialistische "Volkstumarbeit" und Umsiedlungspolitik 1933–1945. Von der Minderheitenbetreuung zur Siedlerauslese*. Berlin, Frank & Timme.

Lumans, V. O. (1993) *Himmler's Auxiliaries: The Volksdeutsche Mittelstelle and the German National Minorities of Europe, 1933–1945*. Chapel Hill/London, University of North Carolina Press.

Mehnert, D. (1996) Historische Schallaufnahmen—Das Lautarchiv an der Humboldt Universität zu Berlin. In: Mehnert, D. (ed.) *Elektronische Sprachsignalverarbeitung. Tagungsband der siebenten Konferenz, Berlin, 25.–27. November 1996*. Berlin, Humboldt-Universität zu Berlin, pp. 28–45.

Näser, W. (2001) Das Lautdenkmal reichsdeutscher Mundarten' als Forschungsinstrument, online at: http://staff.uni-marburg.de/~naeser/ld00.htm (last accessed: Feb 22 2017).

Niehaus, M. and Schmidt-Hannisa, H.-W. (2005) Textsorte Protokoll. Ein Aufriß. In: Niehaus, M. and Schmidt-Hannisa, H.-W. (eds) *Das Protokoll. Kulturelle Funktionen einer Textsorte*, Frankfurt am Main, Peter Lang, pp. 7–23.

Olesch, R. (1937) *Die slavischen Dialekte Oberschlesiens* (= Arbeiten aus dem Institut für Lautforschung an der Universität Berlin 3). Berlin, Humboldt-Universität zu Berlin.

Purschke, C. (2012) 'Wenn jüm von Diekbou hört und leest...' Itzehoe im 'Lautdenkmal reichsdeutscher Mundarten zur Zeit Adolf Hitlers,' *Niederdeutsches Wort* (52), pp. 70–110.

Schulze, T. (2014) Weihnachten in Krasna. Aufnahmen der Bessarabien-Deutschen Anisia Ziebart. In: Riva, N. (ed.) *Klangbotschaften aus der Vergangenheit. Forschungen zu Aufnahmen aus dem Berliner Lautarchiv*. Aachen, Shaker, pp. 71–95.

Stoecker, H. (2008) *Afrikawissenschaften von 1919 bis 1945. Zur Geschichte und Topographie eines wissenschaftlichen Netzwerks*. Stuttgart, Pallas Athene.

Wilking, S. (2003) *Der Deutsche Sprachatlas im Nationalsozialismus*. Hildesheim/Zürich/New York, Georg Olms.

Part IV

The social geographies of record-shopping

10 The aesthetic of arrest

The Victor Talking Machine Company's Ready Made Windows program, 1909–1913

J. Martin Vest

In 1906, an earthquake and subsequent firestorm ravaged the City of San Francisco. Among the thousands of San Franciscans who took refuge in the forests and hills outside the city was one Ellis Hansen, window dresser for Sherman, Clay and Company, a local retailer of phonographs[1] and pianos. As he later recalled, Hansen only recently received word that one of his window displays had won a $10 prize in a competition held by one of the company's vendors, the Victor Talking Machine Company (VTMC) of Camden, New Jersey. His winning display (Figure 10.1)[2] had been rather idiosyncratic. It featured only one phonograph surrounded by portraits of Victor recording artists and Victor phonograph records, all mounted on white easels— a swarm of white circles and ovals suspended in space. It had contrasted sharply with other winning windows, many of which had featured earthy springtime scenes complete with bunnies, chicks and fake moss, or phonograph-accompanied mannequins lolling in canoes (Victor Talking Machine Company [VTMC], 1906a, pp. 3, 9). As Hansen tossed and turned with a hollow belly beneath the California stars, he might very well have clutched his recent victory like a talisman against his miseries, because on the second night of his wilderness sojourn, the prize-winning window appeared in his dreams. As he later explained (VTMC, 1911, p. 8), Hansen dreamt that night that his creation could somehow be reproduced over and over and shipped to every Victor dealer in the country. At some point (presumably after Hansen had found himself suitable indoor lodgings) he wrote a letter to Victor suggesting a program of centralized window-dressing production.

On its face, the proposal was a promising one. Like its major competitors, Columbia and Edison's National Phonograph Company, Victor presided over a quickly growing network of local dealers who worked out of dedicated phonograph shops as well as hardware, dry goods or department stores. Whether working in phonograph dealerships or these other more general commercial establishments, however, phonograph salespersons (a vocation only around a decade old in 1906) were usually rank amateurs in the art of window decoration and their efforts in this direction often left much to be desired. A program for the centralized production of Victor Phonograph window displays could ameliorate the problem.

DOI: 10.4324/9781003006497-15

Management, however, initially declined Hansen's offer, preferring instead to continue encouraging dealers' window-trimming efforts in the pages of the company organ, the *Voice of the Victor*, and hoping that this relatively cheap solution would suffice to inspire their dealers to excellence in the craft. But within a few years it had become clear to Victor that dealers were not rising to the exacting standards set by the company in its own advertising. In 1909, the management relented. Victor reversed its original decision on the matter and offered Hansen a position as head of the company's new Ready Made Window Department. Hansen built a mock-up store window at Victor's factory in Camden, New Jersey, and used it to design a series of window displays. He wrote detailed instructions explaining the assembly of each window, photographed it and—with the help of his new Ready Made Window department—began producing the various components of each design in volume. Victor produced a small catalog of the first displays and offered them at cost. With the demand for such a service not yet established and with the Ready Made Department still in a fledgling state, Victor tentatively sent catalogues to a few large retailers to test the waters. To Hansen's and Victor's great satisfaction, the trade responded positively. Orders quickly outstripped the production capacity of Hansen's department, and by the end of the year he supervised the labor of over 30 employees (VTMC, 1911, p. 8; Bird, 1913, pp. 57–71).

This essay examines the Ready Made Windows Program that ran at the VTMC beginning in early 1909, paying particular attention to Hansen's first seven designs for the firm. Ellis Hansen's stature within the pre-war profession of window dressing makes his work a particularly fruitful site for historical investigation. He was a recognized master of the art of window dressing, taking gold in a 1909 window-dressing competition held by the trade journal *Merchants Record and Show Window* (VTMC, 1910b, p. 5). In that sense, he was atypical. But his designs for the VTMC enjoyed an influence far exceeding the work of almost any other window dresser of his day. Over the course of four years, window displays made to his exacting standards were installed in thousands upon thousands of commercial windows across the country. Today Hansen is little known even among historians of advertising and consumer culture. But by virtue of the documented "throw" of his work, his designs offer an unparalleled glimpse into the aims of commercial window display as practiced in the years just before the First World War.

I argue that in his work for Victor, Hansen developed a design vocabulary best described as an "aesthetic of arrest." On the streets of the early twentieth-century American city, pedestrians were enmeshed in a structure of *mobile* distraction, compelled along by their workaday business, by the enticements of a million sights and even by the current of the sidewalk's traffic.[3] The successful commercial window had first to stop the potential customer in her tracks and focus her attention on the offered wares before any sale could be made. To that end, Hansen utilized symmetry and repetition to capitalize on the mechanics of the wandering eye. Most importantly, he pursued a parsimonious approach to window dressing, employing empty space to disrupt the visually saturated modern streetscape and attract and hold attention.[4]

Hansen also hit on a technique to make passersby stop and "listen" to his displays. The windows, of course, were silent. But by strategically deploying Victor phonographs themselves, he was able to produce currents of *implied* sound that projected through the glass of the Victor dealership, encouraging prospective purchasers to stop and "listen." Synesthesia, then, was a crucial element in the aesthetic of arrest as deployed by Hansen. This was no accident. It was exceedingly difficult to "play" phonographic music for the would-be purchaser on the street. In some cases, dealers installed phonographs in vestibules or on sidewalks, but this was often impractical. On noisy streets, the machine might be drowned out. On quieter thoroughfares, dealers' attempts to broadcast their sonic wares often met with the hostility of quiet-craving neighbors. The peculiar task set before Hansen, then, was to sell sound through the eye.

In my focus on the aesthetic of arrest, I depart from several masterful treatments of the early twentieth-century show window which have focused on these displays' reliance on an ethos of mobility. According to these treatments, show windows transported passersby to imagined, fantastic spaces that whetted the consumeristic appetite and acculturated them to the technologically mediated forms of physical and psychic mobility characteristic of late modernity (Friedberg, 2000, pp. 58, 80; Leach, 2001, pp. 39–70; Lasc, 2018, pp. 24–45)[5] As the work of Ellis Hansen attests, however, the show window's role as a facilitator of fantasy, longing and mobility did not exhaust its intended effects. It was also necessary that prospective customers be prevented from walking past the shop. Selling phonographs was as much an exercise in understanding and controlling the movement of human bodies and their relationships to economic behaviors as it was stirring the imagination and creating fantasy worlds.

It is also worthwhile dilating on the concept of "centralization" as it appears in this chapter. In bringing phases of production and distribution into his employer's purview that had once lain in the hands of dispersed actors, Ellis participated in a process that had gone on since the birth of modern capitalism and which had proceeded with particular celerity beginning in the late nineteenth century (Chandler, 1977; Lamoreaux, 1988; Trachtenberg, 2007; Wiebe, 2007; Appleby, 2011). But while centralization was going on in every facet of the American economy (and beyond), Victor's centralized production of window displays shared key elements with it and its competitors project of centralized production of sound. Hansen and his employers hoped to replace the diverse *sights* of dealer's homemade window displays with the company's own mass-produced designs. Similarly, the mass production of phonographs and records facilitated the replacement of diverse sounds and sounding practices by those "manufactured" by a handful of well-capitalized firms. This was especially true in the case of the VTMC whose phonographs famously dispensed with the recording option that had been a standard feature of all sound reproduction equipment before 1900. Centralization of the production of sights and sounds, in turn, facilitated control over practices of looking and listening. As we shall see, Victor's efficacy in shaping both looking and listening practices (and its ability to combine appeals to both senses strategically) gave it an enormous advantage in its mission to sell phonographs and records to the world-at-large.

A few words are in order regarding methodology. In focusing on the entangled nature of the senses in early twentieth-century phonograph displays, I shed light on some of the complex and multifaceted processes by which the consumption of recorded sound was constructed. By forcing him to combine modes of sensory address, Hansen's work on the Ready Made Windows gave him a disproportionate influence on the repertoires of human/phonograph interaction taking shape in the early twentieth century. As I will discuss, in his project of arresting passersby and luring them in to "listen" to his windows, Hansen drew on and reinforced Victor corporate iconography that positioned the phonograph and its sounds as ersatz human subjects. In so doing, he positioned his window displays as powerful lessons on the ontology of recorded sound, but he also contributed significantly to the construction of the modern listener.

In order to make sense of Hansen's designs, I have read them in parallel with contemporary window-dressing manuals, sources replete with pointers for the aspiring display man or woman (though usually a man). As these sources make clear, professional window dressing certainly aimed at the creation of fantastic other worlds in the minds of onlookers. Before any such protracted reverie could take place, however, it was necessary that the prospective purchaser, amidst the roiling river of humanity on the urban sidewalk, be stopped in her tracks; that her curious eye be forced to cease its wandering; and that her mind be stilled. The subject must be arrested.

Figure 10.1 Ellis Hansen's winning display in the Victor Talking Machine Company of Camden window-dressing competition, 1906.

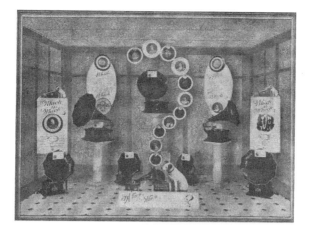

Figure 10.2 Ellis Hansen's "Which is Which Display" for Victor.

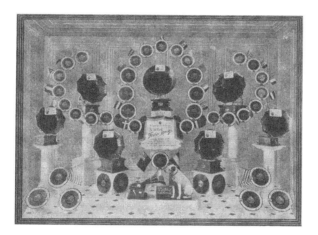

Figure 10.3 Ellis Hansen's "All Nations Display" for Victor.

The Victor Talking Machine Company and mass advertising

When Victor inaugurated its Ready Made Windows program in 1909, the company was less than a decade old. In 1895, gramophone inventor Emile Berliner established the Berliner Gramophone Company to market his creation in the United States; but in 1900, he sold most of his interest in the company to an ambitious and talented mechanic named Eldridge Reeves Johnson. The following year Johnson incorporated his operation as the VTMC. With breathtaking speed, Victor grew into one of the largest and most profitable companies in the world, conquering the market for sound reproduction technology and forcing competitors to move away from the existing wax cylinder recording formats in favor of Victor's own increasingly popular flat disc format (Wile 1996, pp. 139–70; Fabrizio and Paul, 1997, pp. 42 and 73–8).[6]

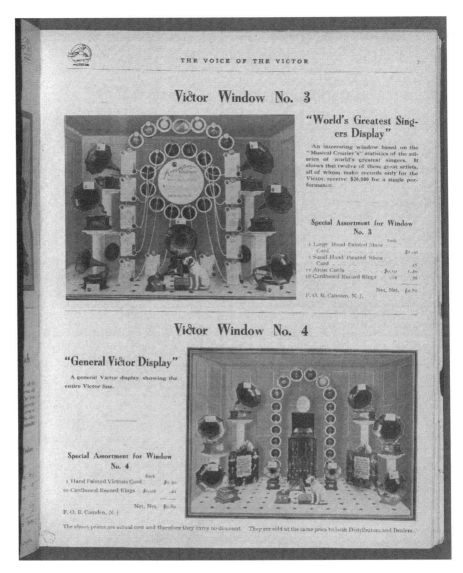

Figure 10.4 Ellis Hansen's "World's Greatest Singers Display" for Victor.

Victor's conquest of the market, however, owed as much to its enthusiastic embrace of advertising as to any inherent superiority of its technology. When Johnson incorporated the VTMC in 1901, advertising was an ascendant and self-confident industry with enormous potential, its champions proclaimed, to improve business and society.[7] Johnson agreed and almost from its very beginnings, Victor poured capital into sophisticated print advertisements in

Figure 10.5 Ellis Hansen's "Special Thanksgiving Window" for Victor.

national magazines and local newspapers as well as into outdoor advertising in major markets. Between 1901 and 1929, the company dedicated an average of 8.24 percent of its annual budget to advertising, and by 1923 it was the largest advertiser in the United States (Suisman, 2012, p. 114).[8]

Victor viewed this massive investment as one-half of a bargain struck with their local dealers, who, in turn, owed it to the company and to themselves to do their own grassroots advertising (VTMC, 1916, p. 211). To that end, Victor produced mountains of standardized promotional material which dealers need merely order through the *Voice of the Victor* and then spread through their community. Pre-made newspaper advertisement "electrotypes" (VTMC, 1912c, p. 13); street car placards (VTMC, 1906b, p. 4); lantern slides (VTMC, 1913a, p. 6)—all could be had at cost from company headquarters. The company was particularly eager that the dealership itself be covered in company branding. Victor neon signs (VTMC, 1912c, p. 13); Victor doormats (VTMC, 1912a, p. 9); Victor key chains (VTMC, 1913b, p. 19); scarf pins, watch fobs (VTMC, 1912b, p. 7); and other items were also available through the *Voice of the Victor.*

Victor's decision to mass produce window dressings was one part of this larger project of centralization of company advertising. The commercial show window was itself, however, an institution of relatively recent vintage. In both the United States and Europe, marketing manuals of the early nineteenth century had emphasized personal salesmanship rather than the niceties of display. As the scale of consumer trade expanded in the late nineteenth century, however, it became necessary that the goods should sell themselves (Iarocci, 2013, pp. 1–15). By the 1880s, American department stores had begun to stage elaborate and eye-catching displays for their street-level windows, a trend that spread to smaller retailers in the next decade (Strasser, 1995, pp. 163–202).

With very few exceptions, window dressing persisted into the twentieth century as an artisanal undertaking, with displays produced on-site and one-at-a-time by local professional and amateur craftsmen. Victor's Ready Made Window program, under the supervision of Ellis Hansen, represented one of the very first attempts to rationalize the production and distribution of commercial window displays. The process began when Hansen and his artist assistant designed a prototype display using three basic components. The first was "paraphernalia"—connecting rods, platforms, frames and pedestals that served as a skeleton for the display. A set of paraphernalia had to be purchased by dealers before they could install one of Hansen's creations in their own store, but it could be used with all subsequent Ready Made designs. Second, each window display included a range of painted cardboard and paper elements which were to be mounted on the aforementioned paraphernalia and which provided each window with its distinctive character. Finally, the designs required the use of actual Victor products— talking machines and records—and these were to be taken from the dealer's own stock (VTMC, 1909b, pp. 4–9).

Having assembled these elements into a new window design, Hansen handed the prototype over to a team of artisans who produced hundreds or thousands of identical sets of the design's cardboard and paper elements. The paint shop hand-replicated copies of the artists' painted backgrounds and other elements, while a group of employees was set the task of coloring enlarged photographs for use as cardboard cutouts. In another area, workers designed and cut out stencils and hand-lettered display cards. On emerging from these various subdepartments, the components of the Ready Made Window Displays were taken to the Packing and Shipping Room, where they were boxed and sent out to dealers. Detailed instructions and a photograph of the assembled window were included to facilitate assembly. Local Victor dealers need merely unbox the centrally produced paper and cardboard components, and combine them with paraphernalia, phonographs and records in accordance with the instructions sent along by the company (VTMC, 1909a, p. 4, 1910a, p. 14).[9]

Figure 10.6 Ellis Hansen's "Grand Opera Display" for Victor.

Ready Made Windows

For the window dresser, the distracting environment of the American street was a crucial variable to consider and it was one that Ellis Hansen confronted head-on in his work for the VTMC. By the mid-nineteenth century, the urban streetscape on both sides of the Atlantic had become a "dense and visually competitive matrix," to employ Jeffrey Cohen's formulation (2013, p. 20). Deep buildings with narrow street frontage crowded the sidewalk, vying for the attention of passersby with piles of commodities and signs announcing the sale of hats, hammers, patent medicines and every other imaginable salable good or service. By the dawn of the twentieth century, this visual anarchy had been alleviated in some areas as department stores bought up entire city blocks. Such a department store swept away dozens or even hundreds of smaller concerns along with their profuse signage, and replaced them with a single edifice with a centrally planned bank of street-facing window displays. Whatever relief department stores achieved for the weary modern eye, however, was undermined by new visual distractions, including electric lights, larger crowds and the increasingly ubiquitous automobile (Cohen, 2013, pp. 19–36).

One of the most important innovations in early twentieth-century window advertising was a new, more parsimonious aesthetic. For decades, common sense had dictated that commercial windows be crowded with piles of goods, occupying most, if not all, of the visible space. These "stocky windows," so went the logic, should serve as an index to the entire store, advertising everything that might be had within (Marriott, 1889, p. 5) By 1900, however, an ascendant cohort of professional window dressers was nearly unanimous in its disapproval of the stocky window. Rather, they argued, the display window should incorporate ample negative space allowing the design to breathe (Marriott, 1889, p. 15; and Mason, 1908, p. 10; Tracy, 1909, p. 13).

This new parsimonious aesthetic was reflected in Hansen's work for Victor. In contrast to the stocky window's ponderous massing of goods, the Ready Made Windows were characterized by ample negative space, and a certain airiness effected by suspended and elevated display elements. In Window No. 2 the "Which is Which Display," for example (Figure 10.2), the window is given over to seven tabletop phonograph models, each accompanied by a show card daring passersby to find a difference between the live performances of artists like Enrico Caruso and their Victor recordings. Three of the phonographs are mounted on tall, columnar pedestals emphasizing the empty space beneath them, while at the center of the display, a thin question mark built out of alternating Victor records and circular portraits of recording stars rises from the floor like a fakir's snake. It wends its way through the bank of phonographs, and stretches toward the ceiling before terminating over the display's central phonograph. At the base of the display sits a show card ("Which is Which?") and a cutout of Victor's omnipresent dog-and-phonograph trademark (VT MC, 1909b, pp. 4–9).

Some of the other Ready Made designs appeared much busier. But while these windows were still substantially less noisy than their stocky counterparts, Hansen employed techniques to lighten their visual load. In Victor Window No. 6, the "All Nations Display" (Figure 10.3) for example, all seven phonographs rest atop columnar pedestals. A long, thin string of haloed phonograph records winds across the display forming two "arms" on either side with an ovular arch at their center. Six phonograph records, mounted on short white stands, sit at the front of the display, hovering in space. The yawning mouths of the phonographs' amplifying horns, together with the swirl of suspended records, presents to the viewer a field of floating black circles, surrounded and dominated by a sea of white and light gray (VTMC, 1909b, pp. 4–9).

The role of parsimony in early twentieth-century window advertising sat at the nexus of several historical trajectories, including a general shift in middle-class taste (Laird, 1998, p. 261). While fashion was a powerful force in shaping the new aesthetic, window dressers adopted parsimony for another reason: in most experts' opinion, overloaded windows made it impossible to focus attention on any particular article and thus to consummate a sale. As author G.L. Timmins expressed it, "the crowded window dressing in which no particular article stands out prominently is far less effective as a means of arresting attention" (Timmins, 1924, p. 29). Overstuffed windows also failed to arrest attention because they recapitulated the visual logic of the modern streetscape. The overcrowded display window, according to George H. Downing, "bewilders the public" (Downing, 1900, p. 12), while J.H. Wilson Marriott believed overcrowded windows appeared "confused" (Marriott, 1889, p. 8). The *Voice of the Victor* itself informed readers that customers respond positively to austerely trimmed windows because they "are not confused by a multitude of articles" (VTMC, 1909a, p. 2). Overfilled windows bewildered. They evinced confusion. And in that, they merged seamlessly with the distracting visual chaos of the street, failing to make an impression.

Simplicity in design helped Ready Made Window displays to spatially disrupt the existing visual field. But it also contributed to the project of *temporally* disrupting the streetscape. As Warren Woodward and George Fredericks pointed out in their handbook for window dressers, windows dressed sparsely attract much more attention when they are changed, for the simple reason that the contrast is likely to be more dramatic than when an overstuffed display is replaced with another overstuffed display (Woodward and Fredericks, 1921, p. 130). This was particularly important because the creation of novelty through regular changes of window display was one of the most often recommended tactics of the trade literature (*A guide to window-dressing* 1883, p. 12; Marriott, 1889, p. 16; Mason, 1908, pp. 7–8). For its part, the Victor Company recommended dealers change out displays every week, adding that "the more elaborate and prominent a display is, the quicker it becomes boresome" (VTMC, 1907, p. 9). The Ready Made Window program helped facilitate this battle for the pedestrian's attention by supplying cheap, easily installed windows at regular intervals. By July 1910, Victor was encouraging dealers to put in a standing order for the Ready Made Windows, to be delivered at their shop at the rate of one per month (*Voice of the Victor*, 1910b, p. 5).

One of the simplest techniques Hansen employed to create arresting windows within the strictures of modernist austerity was to effect particular visual interest at the center of his displays. This focus on the center was common among professional window trimmers of the era like Charles Tracy, who noted that the human eye gathers data from a small conical section of its surroundings, but that even within this cone, the space directly before the eye was the area of most focus and attention. For that reason, it was necessary that the design be heaviest at the center "where the eye of the observer rests first and most frequently." Tracy cautioned that a display designed without regard to these and other visual laws invariably "fails in its most important mission, i.e., to arrest the attention of the casual and indifferent passerby" (Tracy, 1909, pp. 12 and 15–16).

Hansen concurred. In Victor Window No. 6, the "All Nations Display," for example, a large show card reading "Victor Foreign Records" presents a substantial field of white directly in the middle of the display drawing the eye to the heart of the window. Similarly, a large show card, this one ringed with a halo of mounted phonograph records, drags the eye to the center of Victor Window No. 3, the "World's Greatest Singers Display" (Figure 10.4). Window No. 7, the "Special Thanksgiving Window" (Figure 10.5), however, was the most center-heavy of Hansen's first batch of Ready Made Windows. It featured a large white show card encircled by 14 phonograph records, each with its own outward-pointing, pennant-shaped show card. The unit is imposing, dominating the display with its size alone, but is also lent added attractive power by its dramatic radial symmetry. The 14 pennants arrest the eye and direct it inward toward their imaginary intersection point at the center of the display. Like the sun, which it was intended to invoke, the module draws into its orbit the elements around it and, by design, those who stop to gawk (VTMC, 1909b, pp. 4–9).

Next to symmetry, radial and otherwise, the most striking visual trick employed in the Ready Made designs is that of repetition—the use of iterated and identical units in massings that may or may not be symmetrical. All seven of Hansen's first designs feature long, arching rows of nearly identical circles in the form of phonograph records, artist portraits or—in Window No. 7—chrysanthemum blooms mounted on black discs (VTMC, 1909b, pp. 4–9). As anthropologist Alfred Gell argues, complex geometric patterns such as those of Celtic knotwork tend to bind the eye, drawing the observer into their involutions and repetitions. As we have seen, turn-of-the-century window dressers had rejected such visual complexity because it failed to captivate in the context of the modern street. But simple patterns, such as those that feature a single repeated motif, according to Gell, produce a slightly different effect in viewers—motion. As the eye follows an iterated motif from left to right (or right to left), it perceives a single entity moving through space (Gell, 1998, pp. 73–95). On the busy urban street, then, Hansen's rows of mounted circles could have squared the circle. To the distracted passerby, they presented a sparse, static and purposeful arrangement of shapes in space that would have quickly drawn attention. Once that attention had been arrested, however, these patterns offered an easily comprehended simulation of motion, inviting the viewer to follow the contours of the pattern with his eyes and to indulge the kinesthetic pleasure of imaginary movement, holding him or her in place.

The black-and-white photograph documenting Victor's Ready Made Window displays make difficult a definitive assessment of the role of color in their design. It does not appear however that Hansen utilized a variety of colors in his early designs. Window-dressing handbooks of the era almost invariably contained notes on the effective deployment of color (Bond, 1905, p. 5; Tracy, 1909, pp. 23–8; International Correspondence Schools, 1921, pp. 229–33; Woodward and Fredericks, 1921, pp. 50–80; Picken, 1927, pp. 176–83), and as George Cole informed readers of his window-dressing manual, "color is by far the most effective means for attractive [sic] the eye, and a window dressed in colors secures the attention of the passer inevitably…" (Cole, 1892, p. 474). In this case, Hansen's tack reveals the multiple motivations and strictures that lay back of his work for the Victor Company. While the aesthetic of arrest might dictate a lively chromatic vocabulary, the advertiser of Victor phonographs (unlike that of groceries or textiles) was wed to a narrow range of black and brown wares. In this context, bright colors might distract from the consumables in question.

Not surprisingly, phonographs themselves feature prominently in Hansen's window designs. The ultimate aim of the Ready Made Window displays was, of course, to sell phonograph and phonograph accessories, and this project would have been poorly served by windows that failed to arouse desire for the articles in question. But here the possibilities for interpretation are not entirely exhausted by commercial common sense. In Hansen's window displays, phonographs often faced directly outward toward the sidewalk, their exposed amplifying horns bathing passersby in a stream of implied sound (see especially Window Display No. 1, the "Grand Opera Display" [Figure 10.6], and Window No. 6, the "All Nations Display" [Figure 10.3]) (VTMC, 1909b, pp. 4–9). In *Reading Images: The Grammar of Visual Design*, Gunther Kress and Theo van Leeuwen identify as "demands" those images in which the viewing subject is met with the direct gaze or gesture of a represented subject. The image may look at us with a smile, a seductive pout or a disdainful glare. It may point at us, beckon us to approach or warn us to keep away. "In each case," argue Kress and Leeuwen, "the image wants something from the viewers —wants them to do something …or to form a pseudo-social bond of a particular kind with the represented participant" (Kress and Leeuwen, 2010, pp. 116–24).[10]

Hansen's phonographs, in facing the street, made their own demands on passersby. Should an observer doubt that the outward-facing horns made "demands" or wonder what they were, they need look no further than the base of the display where the window dresser always rested a cardboard cut-out of Victor's trademark fox terrier, listening to a phonograph. The image had originated when English artist Francis Barraud observed his recently deceased brother's fox terrier, Nipper, listening quizzically to a phonograph. The dog, he concluded, believed the voice spilling from the phonograph's horn to be that of his dead master. Barraud worked the pathetic vignette up into an impressive oil painting entitled "His Master's Voice," which, in 1899, he sold to Victor's European affiliate, the Gramophone Company. Both companies eventually adopted the image as their trademark (Sterne, 2003, pp. 301–3).

Victor's corporate mythos and iconography, then, positioned the phonograph within a specific framework of social relations in which the technology served as an ersatz human agent, *able* to make demands on the observer every bit as insistent as those of Uncle Sam or a beautiful cigarette-smoking model. Further, "implied sound" allowed Hansen's designs to interpellate passersby as listeners to a degree that would have been impossible with *real* sound. As several scholars have pointed out (Bijsterveld, 2008; Thompson, 2008), the early twentieth-century street was not only visually oversaturated, but was characterized by such a din of voices, whistles, car horns and construction noises as the world had never before heard. A sidewalk in the business district of most American towns and cities was a poor sonic environment in which to put the talking machine through its paces to best advantage. Embedded in Hansen's austere and visually arresting displays, however, the phonograph's yawning black horn could reach the subject's ears by way of her eyes, forcing her to stop in her tracks, train her wandering eyes on the horn and "listen." Having arrested the subject, the window could commence the work of selling.

Conclusion

Hansen's career with the VTMC was relatively short-lived. In the summer of 1913, he announced his departure from the company and spent the next few months traveling abroad ("Notes among the ad folks," July 12, 1913, p. 23). On returning to the United States, he went to work as a window dresser for the Wurlitzer Company of Chicago, manufacturer of organs, before taking his window-dressing expertise to Victor's competitor, the Edison Phonograph Company. In 1919, he moved once more, this time the Carl Netschert Estate (later, Company) of Chicago, a manufacturer and importer of artificial flowers and other "high class decorations" ("New directions," 1919, p. 48; "Change in historic flower house," 1920, p. 64).

Hansen's work with the VTMC, however, left enduring marks on the culture of recorded sound in the United States by contributing to a reconceptualization of the listening subject. For decades after Edison's invention of the phonograph in 1877, Americans had conceptualized the device in a variety of ways, chief among them being the "talking machine." In this understanding, sound reproduction technology did not mediate the actual voices of recorded subjects so much as it "wrote" sonic messages down and read them aloud at a later date in its *own* voice. In this understanding, the phonograph appeared to be a kind of automaton, one of the many clunky mechanical contrivances that had aped human behaviors (including speech) for centuries. For most late nineteenth-century listening subjects, then, the personalized and emotionally charged rapport twentieth-century Americans came to establish with recorded voices would have been inconceivable (Wood, 2002; Kang, 2011; Riskin, 2016; Vest, 2018, pp. 22–77).

Through the iconography of Nipper and the "demands" placed on passersby by outward turned phonograph horns, however, the Ready Made Windows modeled a new kind of relationship between human beings and recorded sound. Listening subjects were encouraged to believe like Nipper that their consumption of mechanically reproduced sounds placed them in communion with temporally and geographically distant (or even deceased) human subjects. They were encouraged to identify with semi-mythical recording "stars" like Enrico Caruso or Nellie Melba, to imagine themselves in intimate relationships with them and to follow their real-life exploits in the tabloids. In the twentieth century, the capacity of recorded sounds to cement such profoundly personal relationships with listening subjects imparted to the technology an outsized role in shaping American society, from its role in crystallizing ethnic and subcultural identities to its central place in the political transformations of the 1960s.[11]

Of course, the Ready Made Windows were not solely responsible for these transformations in listening. Print ads as well as concurrent transformations in the physical infrastructure of sound reproduction made it easier for the American public to think of the phonograph as a conduit for distant human personalities (Vest, 2018). But there were properties of the store window which made it a particularly powerful agent of acculturation. According to window dresser W.R. Morehouse, "other forms of advertising permit of more general and wider circulation of the goods, or idea to be 'put over,' but because of this very fact, are more general and scattered in their effect and are apt to be slower and less direct in results" (Morehouse, 1919, p. 5). For Morehouse, the store window's concreteness—its existence at a specific time and place—allowed it to hail subjects in ways more direct and forceful than the era's quickly expanding torrent of print advertisements.

The aesthetic of arrest also continued to be an important element of commercial window display. Indeed, some window dressers pursued it with increasing rigor in the years leading up to the First World War. In 1914, window dresser Francisco Laurent Godinez published the results of an experiment he had recently conducted to determine the attracting power of various window displays. "Inspectors," armed with mechanical counting devices, tallied the number of passersby as well as the number who stopped to observe each window. After three evenings, the "attraction factor" of each window was tabulated by dividing the number of arrests by the total number of passersby (Godinez, 1914, pp. 47–8).

As Godinez's experiment makes clear, the aesthetic of arrest represented more than an intervention in commercial display. By attending with increasing intensity to the deportment of the body, window trimmers took part in an early twentieth century turn toward the analysis and systematization of human behavior (Taylor, 1911; Watson, 1913; Rabinbach, 1992, pp. 238–70). Foucault and others have thoroughly documented how being *looked at* (whether by others or by one's own disciplining introspective glare) has played a central role in the maintenance of social order since the early modern period (Flynn, 2008; Foucault, 2009). As the example of early twentieth-century window dressing suggests, however, subjects have also been compelled to employ their own eyes and ears for the benefit of existing social relations, and the project of selling phonographs (or any other good) has forced corporations and their employees to seek control over the sensing habits of prospective consumers. It is an arrangement familiar to all in the early twenty-first century. At certain times, but in no uncertain terms, we have all been directed to stop. Look. And listen.

Notes

1 In keeping with early twentieth-century American usage, "phonograph" (rather than "gramophone") is employed throughout this essay as a generic term for sound reproduction technologies.

2 Additional images can be found at www.jmartinvest.com/arrest.

3 On late nineteenth- and early twentieth-century transformations in visuality, see Crary, 1990, 1999; Jay, 1994; Cook, 2001; Benjamin, 2002, 2004; Baudelaire, 2004; Simmel, 2004.

4 In theorizing an aesthetic of "arrest," I also draw on anthropologist Alfred Gell's concept of captivation; see Gell (1998). The language of "arrest" was often employed by the very professionals who designed and fabricated window displays and who taught others the craft. In 1909, for example, Charles Tracy informed readers of his *The Art of Decorating Show Windows and Interiors* that a properly centered window exhibit would "arrest the gaze of the passer-by" (Tracy, 1909, p. 12).

5 Though outside the focus of this chapter, another tendency in this literature is the role of class or professional interest in the content of window displays; see, for example, Lomax (2006) and Walden (1989).

6 For the history of the VTMC, see Barnum, 1994; Welch et al., 1995.

7 On the history of advertising, see Marchand, 1985; Lears, 1994; Strasser, 1995; Ohmann, 1996; Fox, 1997; Laird, 1998; McGovern, 2006.

8 For a survey of advertising and other promotional efforts by the phonograph industry, see Schwartzman, 1993; Edge and Petts, 1997; Weber and Skelton, 1997.

9 For the history of manufacturing in the United States, see Smith, 1977; Hounshell, 1997; Scranton, 1997.

10 See also Mitchell (2005, pp. 28–56).

11 There is a voluminous literature on the social, political and cultural effects of recorded sound in twentieth-century America; see, for example, Altschuler (2005), Kenney (1999), Garrett (2008), and Douglas (1995).

References

Altschuler, G. C. (2005) *All shook up: How rock 'n' roll changed America.* New York: Oxford University Press.

Appleby, J. O. (2011) *The relentless revolution: A history of capitalism.* New York: W.W. Norton & Co.

Barnum, F.O. (1994) *His master's voice in America: Ninety years of communications pioneering and progress.* Camden: General Electric.

Baudelaire, C. (2004) The painter of modern life. In: Schwartz, V.R. and Przyblyski, J.M.) (eds.) *The nineteenth-century visual culture reader.* New York: Routledge, pp. 37–42.

Benjamin, W. (2002) *The arcades project.* Cambridge: Belknap Press of Harvard University Press.

Benjamin, W. (2004) The work of art in the age of mechanical reproductioni. In: Schwartz, V.R. and Przyblyski, J.M. (eds.)) *The nineteenth-century visual culture reader.* New York: Routledge, pp. 63–70.

Bijsterveld, K. (2008) *Mechanical sound: Technology, culture, and public problems of noise in the twentieth century.* Cambridge: The MIT Press.

Bird, T.A. (1913) *Show window display and specialty advertising.* Chicago: Chicago University of Commerce.

Bond, W.H. (1905) *Window trimming for the men's wear trade.* New York: Merchants Text Book Co.

Chandler, A. D. (1977) *The visible hand: The managerial revolution in American business.* Cambridge: Belknap Press of Harvard University Press.

"Change in historic flower house" (1920) *Merchants record and show window,* October, 64.

Cohen, J.A. (2013) Corridors of consumption: mid-nineteenth century commercial space and the reinvention of downtown. In: Iarocci, L. (.ed.) *Visual merchandising: The image of selling.* Burlington: Ashgate, pp. 19–36.

Cole, G.S. (1892) *A complete dictionary of dry goods and history of silk, cotton, linen, wool and other fibrous substances.* Chicago: Conkey Company.

Cook, J.W. (2001) *The arts of deception: Playing with fraud in the age of Barnum.* Cambridge: Harvard University Press.

Crary, J. (1990) *Techniques of the observer: On vision and modernity in the nineteenth century.* Cambridge: MIT Press.

Crary, J. (1999) *Suspensions of perception: Attention, spectacle, and modern culture.* Cambridge; MIT Press.

Douglas, S. J. (1995) *Where the girls are: Growing up female with the mass media.* New York: Three Rivers Press.

Downing, G.H. (1900) *Art applied to window display.* Aylesbury: Granville Works.

Edge, R. and Petts, L. (1997) "The collectors guide to "His Master's Voice" Nipper souvenirs. London: EMI.

Fabrizio, T.C., Paul, G.F. (1997) *The talking machine: An illustrated compendium, 1877–1929.* Atglen, PA: Schiffer Publishing.

Flynn, T.R. (2008) Foucault and the eclipse of vision. In: Levin, D.M. (ed.) *Modernity and the hegemony of vision.* Berkeley: University of California Press, pp. 273–86.

Foucault, M. (2009) Panopticism. In: Schwartz, V.R. and Przyblyski, J.M. (eds.) *The nineteenth-century visual culture reader.* New York: Routledge, pp. 73–9.

Fox, S. (1997) *The mirror makers: A history of American advertising and its creators.* Champaign: University of Illinois Press.

Friedberg, A. (2000) *Window shopping: Cinema and the postmodern.* Berkeley: University of California Press.

Garrett, C. H. (2008) *Struggling to define a nation: American music and the twentieth century.* Berkeley: University of California Press.

Gell, A. (1998) *Art and agency: An anthropological theory.* Oxford: Clarendon Press.

Godinez, F.L. (1914) *Display window lighting and the city beautiful; facts, and new ideas for progressive merchants.* New York: The William. T. Comstock Company.

A guide to window-dressing (1883) London: Warehousemen and Drapers' Trade Journal.

Hounshell, D.A. (1997) *From the American system to mass production, 1800–1932: The development of manufacturing technology in the United States.* Baltimore: Johns Hopkins University Press.

Iarocci, L. (2013) The image of visual merchandising. In: Iarocci, L.) (eds.) *Visual merchandising: The image of selling.* Burlington: Ashgate, pp. 1–15.

International Correspondence Schools. (1921) *The window trimmer's handbook: A reference book dealing with the display of merchandise of all kinds in show windows, show cases, and store interiors.* Philadelphia: John C. Winston Co.

Jay, M. (1994) *Downcast eyes: The denigration of vision in twentieth-century French thought.* Berkeley: University of California Press.

Kang, Minsoo. (2011) *Sublime dreams of living machines: The automaton in the European imagination.* Cambridge: Harvard University Press.

Kenney, W. H. (1999) *Recorded music in American life: The phonograph and popular memory, 1890–1945.* New York: Oxford University Press.

Kress, G.R. and Leeuwen, T. van (2010) *Reading images: The grammar of visual design.* 2nd edn. London: Routledge.

Laird, P.W. (1998) *Advertising progress: American business and the rise of consumer marketing.* Baltimore: The Johns Hopkins University Press.

Lamoreaux, N. R. (1988) *The great merger movement in American business, 1895–1904.* Cambridge: Cambridge University Press.

Lasc, A.I. (2018) The traveling sidewalk: The mobile architecture of American shop windows at the turn of the twentieth century. *Journal of design history,* 31(1), 24–45.

Leach, W. (2001) *Land of desire: Merchants, power, and the rise of a new American culture.* New York: Vintage Books.

Lears, T.J.J. (1994) *Fables of abundance: A cultural history of advertising in America.* New York: Basic Books.

Lomax, S. (2006) The View from the shop: Window display, the shopper and the formulation of theory. In: Benson, J. and Ugolini, L. (eds.)) *Cultures of selling: Perspectives on consumption and society since 1700.* Aldershot, England: Ashgate Publishing, pp. 265–92.

Marchand, R. (1985) *Advertising the American dream: Making way for modernity 1920–1940.* Berkeley: University of California Press.

Marriott, J.H.W. (1889) *Nearly three hundred ways to dress show windows.* Baltimore: Show Window Publishing Company.

Mason, H.B. (1908) *Window displays for druggists.* Detroit: E. G. Swift.

Mitchell, W. J. T. (2005) *What do pictures want? The lives and loves of images.* Chicago: University of Chicago Press.

McGovern, C. (2006) *Sold American: Consumption and citizenship, 1890–1945.* Chapel Hill: University of North Carolina Press.

Morehouse, W.R. (1919) *Bank window advertising.* New York: The Bankers Publishing Company.

New directions (1919) *Merchants record and show window,* May, p. 48.

Notes among the ad folks (1913) *Fourth estate,* July, 23.

Ohmann, R.M. (1996) *Selling culture: Magazines, markets, and class at the turn of the century.* New York: Verso.

Picken, J.H. (1927) *Principles of window display.* Chicago: A.W. Shaw Co.

Rabinbach, A. (1992) *The human motor: Energy, fatigue, and the origins of modernity.* Berkeley: University of California Press.

Riskin, J. (2016) *Restless clock: A history of the centuries long argument over what makes living things tick.* Chicago: The University of Chicago Press.

Schwartzman, A. (1993) *Phono-graphics: The visual paraphernalia of the talking machine.* San Francisco: Chronicle Books.

Scranton, (1997) *Endless novelty: Specialty production and American industrialization, 1865–1925.* Princeton: Princeton University Press.

Simmel, G. (2004) The metropolis and mental life. In: Schwartz, V.R. and Przybylski, J.M. (eds.) *The Nineteenth-Century Visual Culture Reader.* New York: Routledge, pp. 51–5.

Smith, M.R. (1977) *Harpers Ferry armory and the new technology: The challenge of change.* Ithaca: Cornell University Press.

Sterne, J. (2003) *The audible past. Cultural origins of sound reproduction.* Durham: Duke University Press.

Strasser, S. (1995) *Satisfaction guaranteed: The making of the American mass market.* Washington: Smithsonian Institution Press.

Suisman, D. (2012) *Selling sounds: The commercial revolution in American music.* Cambridge: Harvard University Press.

Taylor, F.W. (1911) *The principles of scientific management.* New York: Harper.

Thompson, E.A. (2008) *The soundscape of modernity: Architectural acoustics and the culture of listening in America 1900–1933.* Cambridge: MIT Press.

Timmins, G.L. (1924) *Window dressing; the principles of "display."* London: Sir Isaac Pitman & Sons, Ltd.

Trachtenberg, A. (2007) *The incorporation of America: Culture and society in the gilded age.* New York: Hill and Wang.

Tracy, C.A. (1909) *The art of decorating show windows and interiors: A complete manual of window trimming.* 4th edn. Chicago: The Merchants Record Company

Vest, J.M. (2018) *Vox machinae: Phonographs and the birth of sonic modernity, 1870–1930* [Doctoral dissertation, University of Michigan]. Deep Blue Database.

Victor Talking Machine Company. (1906a) *Voice of the Victor,* May.

Victor Talking Machine Company. (1906b) *Voice of the Victor,* July.

Victor Talking Machine Company. (1907) *Voice of the Victor,* July.

Victor Talking Machine Company. (1909a) *Voice of the Victor,* March.

Victor Talking Machine Company. (1909b) *Voice of the Victor,* September.

Victor Talking Machine Company. (1910a) *Voice of the Victor,* January–February.

Victor Talking Machine Company. (1910b) *Voice of the Victor,* May–June.

Victor Talking Machine Company. (1911) *Voice of the Victor,* December.

Victor Talking Machine Company. (1912a) *Voice of the Victor,* April.

Victor Talking Machine Company. (1912b) *Voice of the Victor,* June.

Victor Talking Machine Company. (1912c) *Voice of the Victor*, May.

Victor Talking Machine Company. (1913a) *Voice of the Victor*, May.

Victor Talking Machine Company. (1913b) *Voice of the Victor*, November.

Victor Talking Machine Company. (1916) *Voice of the Victor*, November.

Walden, K. (1989) Speaking modern: Language, culture, and hegemony in grocery window displays, 1887–1920. *Canadian Historical Review*, 70(3), 285–310.

Watson, J.B. (1994) Psychology as the behaviorist views it. *Psychological Review*, 20(2), 158–77.

Weber, J.N. and Skelton, E. (1997) *The talking machine: The advertising history of the Berliner gramophone and Victor talking machine.* Midland, ON: Adio, Inc.

Welch, W.L., Burt, L.B.S. and Read, O. (1995) *From tinfoil to stereo: The acoustic years of the recording industry, 1877–1929.* Gainesville: University Press of Florida.

Wiebe, R. H. (2007) *The search for order: 1877–1920.* New York: Hill and Wang.

Wile, R. (1996) The Gramophone becomes a success in America. *Association for Recorded Sound Collections*, 27(2), 139–70.

Wood, G. (2002) *Edison's Eve: A magical history of the quest for mechanical life.* New York, A.A. Knopf.

Woodward, W.O. and Fredericks, G.A. (1921) *Selling service with the goods; an analysis and synthesis on the planning, designing, construction and installation of window displays.* New York: James A. McCann Co.

11 The phonograph and transnational identity

Selling music records in Philadelphia's Little Italy, 1900s–1920s

Siel Agugliaro

Business and communication historians have sometimes defined the 25 years between the outbreak of World War I and the beginning of World War II a period of "de-globalization" caused by the gradual abandonment of the gold standard and the economic closure of the nations involved in the two conflicts (Verde, 2017, pp. 6–7; Mishra, 2019, pp. 13–14). To an extent, changes in the global flow of capital have repercussions on the way cultural products, music included, circulate across different nations. Indeed, as scholars of ethnic records have observed (Spottswood, 1990; Kenney, 1999; Swiatlowski, 2018), the emergence in the United States of a domestic market for locally composed, performed, and recorded music in different foreign languages was largely a consequence of the closure of international borders following the beginning of the first world conflict. Physically isolated from their respective motherlands, immigrant communities used the phonograph and recorded music both to negotiate their cultural connections with their countries of origin and to define their own place in American culture and society.

Anthropologist Arjun Appadurai has discussed the impact of mass media in processes of identity formation and retention within transnational communities. "For migrants," he wrote, "both the politics of adaptation to new environments and the stimulus to move and return are deeply affected by a mass-mediated imaginary that frequently transcends national space" (Appadurai, 1996, p. 6). In this chapter, I build on Appadurai's argument to consider how the Italian community of Philadelphia adopted the phonograph as a tool for the definition of a transnational identity. In particular, I focus on record dealers of Italian descent active in the city between the late 1900s and the late 1920s. As I will show, Italian record dealers took part both in the highly centralized distribution network of American recording companies and in the local and transatlantic circuits of Neapolitan songs and other repertoires in dialect from Italy.[1] Because of this, I argue that they found themselves uniquely positioned to circulate and in some cases to produce the musical records—the vessels of the "imaginary" described by Appadurai—that they and their clientele used to craft or maintain their

DOI: 10.4324/9781003006497-16

own identities as Italians, American citizens, and members of specific local or regional communities.

The case of Italian record dealers in the United States is especially worthy of examination because of the unique implications that the commercialization of home phonographs had for Italian immigrants and their descendants in the first decades of the century. As one of the largest immigrant groups in the country, Italians regularly experienced racial discrimination and even physical violence in both urban and rural settings across the United States (LaGumina, 1973; Luconi, 2009). The crucial role that the recording industry assigned to Italian opera in the process of cultural legitimization of the phonograph (Kenney, 1999, pp. 44–64; Leppert 2015, pp. 97–164) invested this musical machine with new meanings in the eyes of Italian immigrants and their descendants, who used opera to prove their cultural respectability (and, as a consequence, their social desirability) to the *Americani* (Ceriani, 2013; Luconi, 2016).

At the same time, recorded music allowed Italian immigrants to maintain cultural affiliations with their regions of origin in the motherland. As several scholars have shown (Frasca, 2005, 2014; Pesce, 2008, 2016; Fugazzotto, 2010, 2015, 2016), records and sheet music produced in specific regions of Italy, and particularly in the Naples area, widely circulated in Italian communities in the United States. After the beginning of World War I slowed down the import of records from overseas, Italian amateur and professional artists living in the United States began to record for both independent labels operating in the Italian communities and the so-called "ethnic" catalogs of the large American recording companies specifically catering to an Italian clientele.

Finally, for many residents of Italian descent, the phonograph itself, as a product of American industry, was a symbol of their newly achieved social status in American society. According to contemporary observers in Italian communities across the country (Schiavo, 1928, p. 44; Mangione, 1998, p. 212), phonographs and player pianos as well as home furniture and other goods that used to be out of the financial reach of formerly impoverished newcomers were examples of those "coatings of American life" (Strafile, 1910, p. 17) that made the United States appealing to many Italians willing to emigrate.

In this chapter, I examine the case of Italian record dealers in Philadelphia to show how the phonograph enabled these overlapping processes of identity construction. Two factors contributed to choosing Philadelphia as the focus of this chapter. First, in 1910 Philadelphia was home to the second largest Italian community in the country after New York (Villari, 1912, p. 213). Philadelphia residents of Italian descent grew from 117 in 1850 to about 136,000 in 1920, which amounted to more than 7% of the total city population in that year (Juliani, 1998, p. 145; Luconi, 2001, p. 23). Second, Philadelphia held a central position in the history of recorded music in the United States at least since the spring of 1888, when Emile Berliner presented his new musical machine, the gramophone, at the city's Franklin Institute (Wile, 1926, p. 45). In October 1895, backed by Philadelphia investors, Berliner transferred to the city the manufacturing and recording activities of his newly founded Gramophone Company (Aldridge n. d., p. 10), and the following spring he opened the company's first retail store—one of the oldest in the nation—in the city's business district (*Philadelphia Inquirer*, 22 March 1896). Philadelphia was also located in the immediate proximity of the Victor Talking Machine Company, the phonograph and record manufacturer that was mostly responsible for the revitalization of Italian opera in the United States at the beginning of the twentieth century. Built in 1902 in Camden, New Jersey (a medium-sized town located on the side of the Delaware River opposite Philadelphia), and continuously expanded in the following years, Victor's industrial complex was one of the world's largest record manufacturing centers and it had a strong impact on Philadelphia's musical life. Not only did the company directly participate in educational and cultural assimilation activities organized by the city's public schools and other cultural organizations in the 1910s and the 1920s (Agugliaro, 2021), but famous Victor artists also regularly frequented Philadelphia theaters, restaurants, and Italian-owned music stores (Carlevale, 1954, p. 365; Saltzmann, 1966; Hardy, 1984).

Based on a wide array of primary sources, including archival materials, genealogical records, city directories, contemporary Italian-language press, trade journals, and interviews with descendants of Italian storeowners, this chapter enriches the existing literature on ethnic music businesses in the early twentieth-century United States (Greene, 1992, pp. 47–69; Koegel, 2017) by providing the first detailed map of record-related stores active in any immigrant community in those years. In particular, the location of the majority of Italian immigrants and their descendants in a relatively small area in the southern portion of the city allowed me to uncover, to a large extent, the commercial network of which record dealers of Italian descent, their clientele, and other businesses in the neighborhood were part.

Italian record store owners in Philadelphia: business models and background

In the 1870s, a massive wave of immigrants from Italy began to hit the United States. Immigrants from pre-unification Italy were in large part clerics, political exiles, merchants, and artists from northern Italy, many of whom had received a solid education in their motherland (Russo, 2017). More recent immigrants, however, were mostly illiterate and unskilled laborers from rural areas in Abruzzo, Campania, Basilicata, Calabria, Sicily, and other southern Italian regions, who were forced to emigrate due to the lack of farmland and professional opportunities following the unification of the country (Tirabassi, 2017). Between 1870 and 1920, more than four million Italians reached the United States, soon establishing communities in large urban centers such as New York, Philadelphia, Boston, Chicago, New Orleans, and San Francisco (Villari, 1912, p. 213; Livi Bacci, 1961, p. 3). The industrial growth experienced by Philadelphia after the Civil War made the city especially attractive to Italian immigrants, who could find employment in railroad companies as well as in the textile and clothing industry (Luconi, 2001, pp. 20–1). Most of these newcomers settled in a relatively narrow area in South Philadelphia that had been inhabited by earlier generations of Italian immigrants at least since the 1840s. Toward the end of the century, however, new Italian communities also emerged in the northern and western portions of the city (Juliani, 1981, 1998; Luconi, 2001, p. 18).

Although a limited number of entrepreneurs and professionals were active in every large Italian community, the majority of Italian immigrants living in American cities were unskilled workers who found employment as street peddlers, garbage collectors, and construction and factory workers. According to Luigi Villari, who served as the Italian vice-consul in New Orleans, Philadelphia, and Boston between 1906 and 1910, most Italian immigrants were temporary residents who hoped to relocate back to their homeland once they saved enough to support themselves and their families (Villari, 1912, pp. 215–16).[2] Although Villari praised the spirit of initiative of these immigrants, he lamented that their subordinate position offended the "national self-respect" of Italians, and only exacerbated the racial differences perceived between the darker-skinned Italians and the white US middle and upper classes.

Since linguistic, racial, and cultural barriers limited Italian immigrants' opportunities for social mobility outside their communities, it is no surprise that many of those who decided to permanently settle in the United States attempted to improve their social condition by opening small businesses catering to their compatriots (Villari, 1908, pp. 28–9). Italian small entrepreneurs in Philadelphia were typically active in several lines of business at the same time, and in most cases their stores offered different goods and services (*La colonia italiana di Filadelfia*, 1906; Frangini, 1907; Villari, 1912, pp. 217–18). This particular business format was congenial to phonograph and record manufacturers, who especially in the early 1900s strove to involve small dealers in the creation of a national distribution network. To become a phonograph dealer, all that it took was a small amount of financial resources to invest in the new business line and some retail space to put phonographs and records on display. Recording labels would provide window displays, catalogs, and other promotional materials to help new retailers thrive (Suisman, 2009, pp. 180–91).[3]

Between the late 1900s and the mid-1920s, more than 20 record dealers of Italian descent operated in Philadelphia (Table 11.1), mostly in the historic Italian neighborhood in the south of the city (Maps 11.1–11.2). Like their non-Italian colleagues operating elsewhere in Philadelphia and in other cities in the United States and Europe (Chew, 1967, p. 29; Greene, 1992, pp. 47–69), Italian store owners who had long been offering other services

Table 11.1 Key to Maps 11.1 and 11.2[a]

Name	Dates	Birthplace	Address	Number(s) on Maps 11.1 and 11.2
Eugenio Apice	1886–1972	Naples (Campania)	a) 1124 Passyunk Ave. (1919–1922)	1a
			b) 1327 S. 8th St. (1920–1924)	1b
Giuseppe Capici	1880–1959	Mazzarino (Sicily)	1328 S. 7th St.	2
Francesco (Frank) Cirelli	1873–1939	Altavilla Irpina (Campania)	a) 1227 Germantown Ave. (from 1919)	3a
			b) Colonial Trust Building (distribution) (1237 Market Street) (1920–1922)	3b
			c) 806 N. 15th St. (from 1924)	3c
Frank Conicelli	1891–1963	Lama dei Peligni (Abruzzo)	1140 Tree St.	4
Leopoldo De Benedictis	1863–	probably Casoli (Abruzzo)	5723 Vine St.	5
Giuseppe (Joseph) De Ritis	1891–	Atessa (Abruzzo)	a) 924 S. 8th St. (1917–1924)	6a
			b) 920 S. 8th St. (from 1924)	7a
Pietro Di Marzio	1881–	"Castelnuovo"	a) 920 S. 8th St. (1917–1922)	7a
			b) 1009 S. 8th St. (from 1922)	7b
Giovanni (John) DiStefano	1890–1954	Acquafondata (Lazio)	a) 11th and Carpenter Streets (ca. 1917–ca. 1921)	8a
			b) 1503 S. 13th St. (ca. 1921–1926)	8b
			c) 1303 Dickinson St. (1926–1933)	8c
Harry Fedullo	1888–1964	Casal Velino (Campania)	a) 128 S. 9th St. (1906–1913)	9a
			a) 214/221 S. 9th St. (1914–1916)	9b
			b) 804 Walnut St. (1916–1924)	9c
			c) 1539 S. Broad St. (1924–1935)	9d
Luigi Giuliano	unknown	unknown	404 N. 64th St. (active in 1921)	10
Gennaro Granese	circa 1872–1929	possibly Naples (Campania)	a) 1124 Passyunk Ave. (1919–1925);	1a
			b) 1168 Passyunk Ave. (1925–1926)	11

Name	Dates	Place of origin	Address(es)	No.
Frank Iannarella	circa 1867–1939	unknown	a) 786 S. 7th St. (1906-1907) b) 703 Christian St. (1907-btw. 1930 and 1935)	12a 12b
Antonio Lupinacci	1872–1938	Acri (Calabria)	a) 732 S. 7th St. (1911–1916) b) 718 S. 7th St. (1916–1930) c) 751 S. 8th St. (1930–1932)	13a 13b 13c
Frank Maganuco	1893–1972	Terranova"	1707 S. 9th St.	14
Luigi and Massimo Melchiorri	Luigi: 1882– Massimo: 1879–1948	Ascoli Piceno (Marche)	a) 4932–40 Lancaster Ave. (1906–1920) b) 4862 and 4926 Lancaster Ave. (1921–1923) c) 180 S. 8th St. (1923–1924) d) 1242 N. 52nd St. (1924–btw.1930/35)	15a 15b 15c 15d
Giuseppe Molino and Vincent Farina	G. Molino: 1877– V. Farina: 1882–1961	G. Molino: possibly Carlentini (Sicily) V. Farina: Philadelphia	a) 1216 Annin St. (1913–1917) b) 1231 Federal St. (1917–1925)	16a 16b
Jerry (Jeremiah) Pataterno	unknown	unknown	740 S.8th St.	17
Rodia family	Stanislaus Rodia: 1853–1922 Giuseppe Rodia: 1883–1951	possibly Serino (Campania)	1541 8th St.	18
Joseph (Giuseppe) Russo	1887–1938	Caivano (Campania)	930 S. 8th St. (1919–1922) 880 S. 8th St. (1922–1931)	19a 19b
Frank (Francesco) Silvagni	1874 (or 1875–1954	Balvano (Basilicata)	744 Christian St.	20
Harry (Enrico) Stolfo	1871–	Avigliano (Basilicata)	612 S. 9th St.	21

a   For a complete list of the sources on which I have based this table and the biographical information on Italian record dealers included in this chapter, see Agugliaro 2021, appendix C.

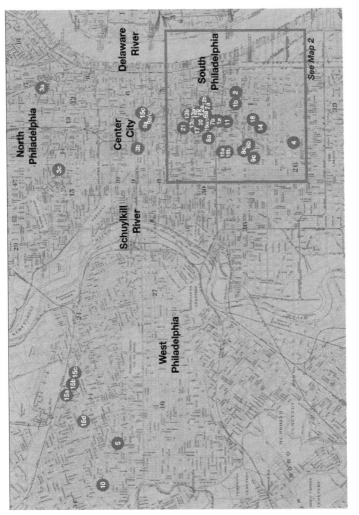

Map 11.1 Location of Italian-owned record stores in Philadelphia, 1906–1924. Plan, Map of Philadelphia, Camden, and vicinity, compiled from City Plans and personal surveys, published by Elvino V. Smith. C.E., 1039 Walnut St., Philadelphia, PA, 1921. Digital image courtesy of Philadelphia Streets Department Historical Collection/philageohistory.org.

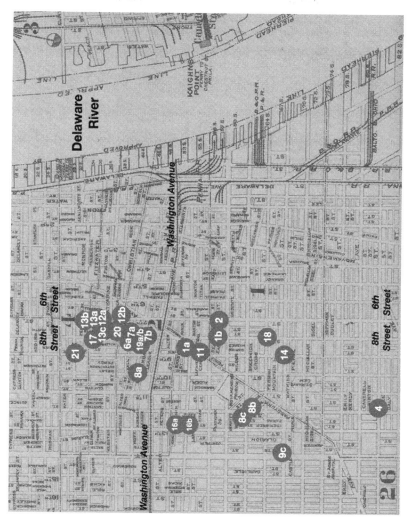

Map 11.2 Location of Italian-owned record stores in South Philadelphia, 1906–1924.

and products could rarely afford to completely shift their lines of business, and in most cases simply freed up some space in their stores to add phonographs and records to their merchandise.[4] For example, Henry Stolfo, a former stove vendor and the founder of the Italian Phonograph Company in 1906—possibly the oldest Italian-owned record store in Philadelphia—was listed as a bicycle retailer in the city directory for 1919–1920. Melchiorri Bros., a grocery store that had been open in West Philadelphia since 1906, became a Columbia retailer in the mid-1910s, carrying phonographs along with "jewelry, watches, weapons, tools, hardware, clothes, shoes, [...] harmonicas, [and] special fountain pens" (*Philadelphia Inquirer*, 29 November 1915; *Il momento*, 10 March 1917). Cabinetmakers and store fixture vendors Joseph Molino and James Farina introduced phonographs around 1919, no doubt benefiting from the contemporary marketing of phonographs as elegant pieces of furniture. Frank Iannarella's store was primarily known as an ice cream parlor, and so was probably also the shop of Giuseppe Russo, whose name appears in Columbia advertisements from the early 1920s. The store of the Rodia family also operated as a barber and candy shop during the same years. The highly diversified supply of these and other stores makes it challenging to locate all the Italian phonograph retailers active in these years. In fact, while a substantial number of Italian record dealers could be identified, others were probably active but were not listed as such in city directories.[5]

Censuses, immigration records, and city directories provide useful information on the cultural and social background of Italian record storeowners. With the sole exception of the Philadelphia-born carpenter and phonograph dealer Vincent Farina, all the Italian record storeowners active in the city were first-generation immigrants from southern Italy. Born between the late 1860s and the early 1890s, these record dealers settled in the United States during their childhood or in early adulthood. While it is possible that some of these store owners attended American schools, if only for a few years, most of them received their education in Italy. Little is known about their financial situations at the time of arrival. Business ownership alone is not proof of initial wealth, especially considering that none of the record retailers, according to available evidence, opened their stores in the years immediately following their arrival in the United States. This does not necessarily mean, however, that all storeowners had working-class origins. For example, Eugenio Apice, a piano varnisher and phonograph dealer on 8th and Earp Streets, attended a costly military school in his native Naples before reuniting with his mother in Philadelphia in 1902 (Jim Apice, youngest son of Eugene Apice, personal communication, 23 May 2019).

Common patterns in the life stories of Italian record retailers active in Philadelphia shed light on the social implications of music store ownership. Many record dealers had previously found employment as barbers, ice cream makers, or bootblacks, all professions that offered almost immediate earning opportunities to foreign unskilled laborers, as they did not require extensive training, large initial investments, or even the mastering of the English language (Quinzio, 2009, pp. 103–8; Mills, 2013, pp. 109–14). It is thus possible that some Italian immigrants, after having saved enough money from working in one (or more) of these trades, decided to open their own barber shop or ice cream parlor, where they would later begin to sell records, phonographs, piano rolls, and other musical merchandise. Interestingly, many Italian record dealers had been previously interested in the arts or were musicians or artists themselves. For example, barber Giuseppe Rodia was also a well-known bandleader who had regularly been performing with his orchestra in local amusement parks before he started to sell records in his family barber and candy shop. Gennaro Granese and Giuseppe Russo frequently performed as actors in Neapolitan comedies for the Italian community. Iannarella opened his ice cream parlor, grocery, and cigar shop around 1905, but he was also apparently active as a musician in the same years in which he began to promote himself as a record dealer. In all these cases, music records offered an opportunity to make professional connections in the music industry while also providing a steady source of income, which in turn could be used to financially support artistic interests or careers.

Especially in the early years of the recording industry, phonograph manufacturing also became an appealing business opportunity in the eyes of some members of the local Italian community. The case of talking machine maker Frank (Francesco) Cirelli is exemplary. A bricklayer from Campania, Cirelli entered the barbering trade shortly after his arrival in Philadelphia in 1890, and by 1901 he had been successful enough to run several barbershops in the city in partnership with his two younger brothers (Frangini, 1907, 72–4). Although no previous musical connection surfaces in earlier city directories and other primary sources, in 1915 Cirelli founded a phonograph company named Cirelligraph in the Fishtown area. According to a 1917 advertisement, the company was specialized in hornless phonographs similar to the Victor Victrolas that sold for prices ranging from $50 to $1,500 (Hoffmann, 2005, p. 383).

The phonograph and identity construction in Philadelphia's Little Italy

The dual position that Italian record stores occupied in the Italian community and outside of it, as part of a larger network circulating records and musical machines, offers insight into the processes of identity construction performed by Philadelphia Italian record dealers and their customers. As demonstrated by contemporary advertisements in the Italian-language press and interviews with descendants of local dealers, Italian-owned record stores in Philadelphia mostly specialized in Italian opera and so-called "ethnic" musical repertoire, including patriotic songs in Italian and recorded comic scenes and songs in regional dialect.

Although late nineteenth-century Italian-language papers regularly covered live performances of Italian opera in Philadelphia and other cities, the popularity of this repertoire among Italians and Italian Americans increased markedly with the new century as a result of the cultural prestige that Victor and other companies had assigned to Italian opera repertoire and singers. From the early 1900s, trade publications and performance reviews in English and Italian regularly commented on Italians listening to opera recordings or attending live performances of Enrico Caruso, Luisa Tetrazzini, Titta Ruffo, and other famous Italian recording stars.[6] In the years in which most immigrants spoke their local dialect rather than Italian and tended to identify themselves along regional lines, Italian opera offered Italians and Italian Americans a common source of national pride (Luconi, 2001, pp. 17–37; Luconi, 2016).

But while the phonograph allowed Italian listeners to engage in this nation-based process of identity construction, it also encouraged the circulation of repertoires in dialects that reinforced or redefined cultural ties with specific regions in Italy. The most common of these repertoires were songs and theatrical sketches in Sicilian and especially Neapolitan dialects, which could be either imported from overseas or—as it would more commonly happen after the beginning of World War I—directly recorded or produced in the United States by both major recording companies and small independent labels operating within the Italian communities. As I will show in the next section, not only could these repertoires work as markers of regional culture, but they often became symbols of Italian identity at large depending on who composed and performed them.

The role of Italian record dealers as promoters of both opera and regional music repertoires made them especially visible within the community. Italian-language newspapers encouraged their readers to purchase records at Italian stores and praised local Italian phonograph makers such as Cirelli whenever their technological developments helped improving the reputation of the Italians. In turn, many Philadelphia record dealers of Italian descent showed their commitment to the community by enrolling in mutual aid organizations such as the Order Sons of Italy and selling tickets for theater shows in Italian American theaters and for Italian opera performances elsewhere in the city.

At the same time, because record dealers of Italian descent were affiliated with large American phonograph and record manufacturers, their stores were often featured in the Columbia, Victor, and Edison advertisements that frequently appeared in the Philadelphia mainstream press. As a consequence, some of their stores were well known outside the community. After World War I, for example, customers from all over the city would regularly visit John DiStefano's Victor record store in South Philadelphia to take advantage of the store's large stock of opera records (Hardy, 1984). A charismatic figure with numerous connections in the music industry, DiStefano was in good terms with the Victor management and with its president Eldridge Johnson, who even attended with his staff the inauguration of DiStefano's new store in 1926. Victor associates and famous artists like

Zenatello, Titta Ruffo, Tito Schipa, and many others were frequent visitors of the store. In the early 1930s, a drop in sales led DiStefano to buy an alcohol license and convert his record shop into a café, with the help of his wife, Rose (Rosa) Zamichieli, who would work as the restaurant's cook for many years (Hardy, 1984; Sandra and Rick DiStefano, personal communication, 9 May 2019). Still open to this day and owned by members of the DiStefano family, the Victor Café is advertised as a "music lover's rendezvous" where customers can enjoy their meals and listen to famous arias and ensembles—performed live by classically trained singer-waiters—while being surrounded by operatic memorabilia.

Local and transnational networks: The case of Neapolitan record dealers

A quick glance at the distribution of Italian record dealers in Philadelphia reveals they were highly concentrated in the Italian neighborhood in the south of the city. In the year 1920, for example, there were at least seven record retailers located within just a few blocks between 6th and 8th Streets and north of Washington Avenue, and a few more shops were located not too far away to the south.[7] How could the local Italian community support such a high number of music businesses? An initial answer to this question comes from the particular business model adopted by record retailers, most of whom—as noted above—sold phonographs and records along with a variety of nonmusical items and services. More importantly, however, Italian record retailers were not necessarily in competition with each other; rather, they often created networks of mutual support, often on the basis of common regional origins.

A particularly interesting case is that of Neapolitan dealers, who developed a transatlantic network of collaborators to take advantage of the popularity that Neapolitan songs enjoyed in major Italian communities. An urban genre that emerged in the first half of the nineteenth century, Neapolitan song was heavily influenced by the melodic and harmonic style of contemporary Italian opera, and frequently repackaged in new arrangements preexisting folk songs, opera buffa arias, and other musical materials circulating in Naples and the area surrounding the city (Stazio, 1991; Di Mauro, 2013). In the second half of the century, thanks to the promotional efforts of music publishers in Naples and other Italian cities, Neapolitan songs became appealing to both Neapolitan working-class audiences and middle and upper classes in Naples and other major cities in Italy, Europe, and North America. Songs like "Fenesta ca lucive," "Te voglio bene assaje" (1835), "Santa Lucia" (1848), and later "Funiculì Funiculà" (1880) and "O sole mio" (1898) were popularized in the United States by sheet music and street musicians, and were thus well known to middle-class, non-Italian audiences.

At the turn of the century, however, the growing popularity of Neapolitan comedies in the US Italian communities (Aleandri, 2006, p. 175; Haller, 2006, p. 21; Frasca, 2014) created a new demand for Neapolitan songs among working-class Italian immigrants, regardless of their specific region of origin (Frasca, 2005, p. 149). As Anita Pesce (2016, p. 57) has recently observed, this situation generated two distinct markets. On the one hand, there was an "international," middle-class-oriented market dominated by larger recording companies and promoting a relatively small number of Neapolitan (or Neapolitan-inspired) hits performed by opera singers like Caruso and other famous artists. On the other hand, an "ethnic" market, partially overlapping with the ethnic Italian catalogs of large US recording labels, circulated a repertoire of dialect songs and scenes that would hardly appeal to those living outside the Italian community.

Beginning in the early 1910s and continuing until the Great Depression, Italian record dealers became involved in both markets by selling the records of large US labels such as Columbia, OKeh, Victor, Brunswick, and others, and manufacturing or importing from Italy records and piano rolls of Neapolitan songs and other repertoires in dialect. Two of the largest importers of records from Naples, Ernesto Rossi and Antonio De Martino, were active in New York. Both of them funded their own recording labels to commercialize records produced in Italy or recorded by local artists in New York. By regularly corresponding with the Esposito family, the owners of the Neapolitan label Phonotype, Rossi and De Martino were always up-to-date on the latest popular songs (Frasca, 2005, pp. 148–9; Pesce, 2008, pp. 119–21). De Martino's record and book company also developed a network of distributors in other American cities, including Detroit and San Francisco (Greene, 1992, pp. 66–7).

Although it was not possible to find connections between Philadelphia record dealers and recording companies in Italy, Italian store owners operating in South Philadelphia were part of artistic networks similar to those developed by their colleagues in New York. For example, many local dealers gravitated around the theatrical venues active in the Italian neighborhood, and it is probably not a coincidence that the highest concentration of Italian record retailers can be observed in the area surrounding Verdi Hall, Philadelphia's most important Italian American theater. The most theatrically engaged Italian record dealer was Neapolitan Gennaro Granese, who also worked as an actor and managed two movie theaters in South Philadelphia's Italian neighborhood.

Granese's shows also saw the participation of other Italian record dealers. In 1921, Granese, Frank Silvagni, Giuseppe Russo, and Russo's wife Anna Borrelli appeared in a performance of the play "Fra Ciavolino," based upon a recent, well-covered trial involving a Neapolitan priest who had been found guilty of murder (*La libera parola*, 26 June 1921). In 1922, Granese and Russo were part of the same cast in a production of the Neapolitan *scenetta* (comic play) "Giustizia divina," staged at the Casino Theatre (*La libera parola*, 20 May 1922). During the same evening, Sicilian comic actor Giuseppe De Rosalia performed some of his popular Nofrio *macchiette*, while musician Ralph Borrelli (Russo's brother-in-law) directed the orchestra. Another record dealer, Neapolitan Eugenio Apice, also belonged

Figure 11.1 Eugenio Apice in his record store, early 1920s. Photo courtesy of Jim Apice (Eugenio Apice's youngest son).

to a theatrical family: his mother Modestina Napoletano was an amateur actress who sometimes performed in local theaters (Gloria Smith, personal communication, 21 May 2019).

These theatrical connections sometimes translated into commercial partnerships between record dealers and their artistic collaborators. In the late 1910s, Granese owned a music shop in partnership with Apice, who a few years later would open his own phonograph and piano roll store on 8th and Earp Streets (Figure 11.1). In 1926, mandolinist Frank Trombetta became Granese's new partner at his store, while just a few blocks away Ralph Borrelli had been running his own music shop since 1920.[8]

Italian record dealers also sold records, scores, and music rolls of music composed by artists in their community. A particularly interesting case is that of *E. Caruso è Mmuorto* ("E[nrico] Caruso is Dead"), a song in Neapolitan dialect published in Philadelphia in the months immediately following the death of the celebrated opera singer. The music to the song was composed by John Agovino, a musician and woodworker from the Salerno area who owned a small music-publishing house a few blocks away from Apice's store. The song has survived in a *copiella*, a single-page print format commonly used by music publishers in Naples for promotional purposes. In the *copiella*, the lyrics were printed on the front of a single sheet of paper, also including a portrait of the singer (Figure 11.2). The mandolin accompaniment to the song was given on the back of the page (Figure 11.3). The *copiella*, to be sold at the modest price of 10¢, was intended as a promotional vessel for the complete vocal score and the record and the piano roll versions of the song. The score was sold by Agovino, while the record and the piano rolls were commercialized by Eugenio Apice, who was one of the two authors of the lyrics. As indicated by a caption at the bottom of the front page, Apice's store shipped orders to Philadelphia and other cities. While the complete score, the record, and the piano roll of the song haven't apparently survived, the *copiella* sheds light on the network of music

Figure 11.2 E. Caruso è Mmuorto (music by John Agovino, lyrics by Eugenio Apice and Colaianni [Philadelphia: John Agovino, 1921]), front. I am grateful to Jim Apice for providing me a reproduction of this document.

dealers, publishers, and artists that contributed to the promotion of this and other Neapolitan songs in Philadelphia.

Another episode further illustrates the significance of the association between opera singers and Neapolitan repertoire. In January 1922, Gennaro Granese organized a banquet in honor of Beniamino Gigli in his Passyunk Avenue home. Gigli, then in his early 30s, had recently become the main resident tenor of the Metropolitan Opera House, and was seen by many as the only possible heir to Caruso. In front of a small audience, Gigli sang the Neapolitan hits "Tu ca nun chiagne" and "Torna a Surriento," respectively accompanied at the piano by Ernesto De Curtis, the author of the two songs, and by Ralph Borrelli. Not only does the attendance of a rising star of opera and a celebrated songwriter prove the prominent position that Granese had achieved in his community, but it also illustrates the importance that Italian opera singers and Neapolitan song artists placed in the cultivation of personal connections with Italian American dealers to promote themselves and their music.

Figure 11.3 E. Caruso è Mmuorto (music by John Agovino, lyrics by Eugenio Apice and Colaianni [Philadelphia: John Agovino, 1921]), back.

Conclusion

The legacy of Italian record stores in Philadelphia in the 1930s further nuances the processes of cultural exchange and identity-building I have outlined above. While the beginning of de-globalization processes caused by the outbreak of World War I contributed to the growth of a US-based record market catering to ethnic communities, another global event, the Great Depression, was responsible for a sharp drop in record sales in the early 1930s. Shrinking profits led important recording companies such as Brunswick, Columbia, Edison, and Victor to either cease their production or merge with other labels (Sutton 2008, pp. 303–05). Local dealers also suffered. In Philadelphia, many record stores, including several owned by Italian dealers, were forced out of business in these years.

The economic crisis also struck the fatal blow to recording companies' interest in ethnic repertoires. The Americanization programs of the 1920s, coupled with the drastic limitation to immigration caused by the Immigration Act of 1921 and the Johnson-Reed Act of 1924, exacerbated the cultural separation between first-generation immigrants who clung on to their respective regional traditions and their US-born children who spoke English and became increasingly intolerant to the mores of their older relatives. When the record market recovered in the mid-1930s, the cultural assimilation of second-generation Italian Americans and the growing competition with the radio made it extremely hard for the surviving stores and independent labels to keep selling regional music (Gronow, 1982, p. 8; Pesce, 2016, p. 69). At the beginning of World War II, as a new generation of American artists of Italian descent, including Louis Prima, Dean Martin, and Frank Sinatra, was gaining mainstream attention, Italian American interest in musical repertoire in dialect had mostly faded away (Frasca, 2014, p. 182).

In her recent examination of Chinatown opera theater in North America during the 1920s, Nancy Yunhwa Rao has discussed how the existence of a performing circuit involving several cities across the continent, and the personal investment of local entrepreneurs of Chinese descent in the circulation of performers and theatrical practices, contributed to the definition of a transnational opera culture common to many important Chinese communities in America (Rao, 2017, p. 15). In this chapter, I have shown how the phonograph and recorded music similarly operated in the same years at the center of a transnational culture shared among Italians in Philadelphia and in other American cities and involving forms of "translation, hybridity, transformation, and resistance" analogous to the ones described by Rao (2017, p. 34). By selling and listening to Italian opera records, Italians in Philadelphia and in other cities confirmed the idea of Italian national culture promoted by the recording industry and employed by the Italian-language papers to uplift Italians in the eyes of the American middle class. At the same time, records of regional music imported from Italy or produced in the United States by independent Italian labels and large recording companies helped Italians immigrants to express their cultural roots or redefine their Italian identity by embracing songs from different Italian regions. Finally, dealing in phonographs and records allowed Italian storeowners to partake in a commercial network that mostly relied on the products and services of non-Italian manufacturers and distributors, while giving their compatriots access to what they perceived as American technological modernity. If, as Myria Georgiou has argued (2006, p. 45), individual identities can only be sustained "as more people than one share symbols and codes," then the phonograph enabled the creation of a transnational space in which record dealers and their clientele in the Italian neighborhood of Philadelphia could nourish their cultural ties with an increasingly imagined Italy as they and their descendants adapted to life in their adoptive country.

Notes

1 For the purpose of this chapter, the expression "Italian record dealers" is to be intended as a synonym of record dealers of Italian descent unless otherwise specified.
2 Indeed, according to available statistical data, about 1.5 million Italians went back to their home country between 1900 and 1915, and more than 60% of the

Italian immigrants residing in the United States returned to their motherland in the 1910s; see Livi Bacci, 1961, p. 35; and Cinel, 1991, pp. 105–6.

3 On ready-made window displays, see also J. Martin Vest's contribution to the present volume.

4 For similar examples of merchandise diversification of record stores in contemporary Portugal, see the chapter by João Silva included in this volume.

5 Similar considerations apply to the record dealers active in the rest of the city, which makes it almost impossible to determine their exact number in the years under consideration in this chapter. However, based on local Victor, Columbia, and Edison advertisements from the late 1900s and early 1920s listing affiliated record retailers in the city, it may be argued that Italian-owned record stores represented between 5% and 10% of the total number of record shops operating in Philadelphia in those years.

6 In an upcoming article, I will examine in further detail the marketing of home phonograph on the part of the US recording industry in connection with the growing prestige assigned to Italian opera within Italian immigrant communities in the first decades of the twentieth century.

7 Such a concentration of record retailers was far from uncommon also outside the main immigrant neighborhoods. As observed by David Suisman (2009, pp. 75–9) and by Thomas Henry in his contribution to this volume, record stores tended to cluster around the main business districts of large American and European cities—that is, the neighborhoods most frequented by urban, middle- and upper-class shoppers—in the first decades of the century.

8 I was not able to find any documentary evidence supporting Borrelli's possible activity as a record dealer. For this reason, his name is not included in Table 11.1.

References

Agugliaro, S. (2021) *Imagining Italy, Surviving America: Opera, Italian Immigrants, and Identity in Philadelphia*, Doctoral dissertation, University of Pennsylvania.

Aldridge, B.L. (n. d.) *A Confidential History of Victor Talking Machine Company*, unpublished typescript, RCA Victor Camden/Frederick O. Barnum III Collection (Accession 2069), Hagley Museum and Library.

Aleandri, E. (2006) *The Italian-American Immigrant Theatre of New York City, 1746–1899*. Lewiston: Edwin Mellen Press.

Appadurai, A. (1996) *Modernity at Large: Cultural Dimensions of Globalization*. Minneapolis: University of Minnesota Press.

Carlevale, J.W. (1954) *Americans of Italian Descent in Philadelphia and Vicinity*. Philadelphia: George S. Ferguson Co. Publishers.

Ceriani, D. (2013) 'Opera as Social Agent: Fostering Italian Identity at the Metropolitan Opera House During the Early Years of Giulio Gatti-Casazza's Management', in M. Waligórska (ed.), *Music, Longing and Belonging: Articulations of the Self and the Other in the Musical Realm*. Newcastle-upon-Tyne: Cambridge Scholars, pp. 114–34.

Chew, V.K. (1967) *Talking Machines 1877–1914: Some Aspects of the Early History of the Gramophone*. London: Her Majesty's Stationery Office.

Cinel, D. (1991) *The National Integration of Italian Return Migration, 1870–1929*. Cambridge: Cambridge University Press.

Di Mauro, R. (2013) 'I Passatempi musicali di Guglielmo Cotttrau: matrici colte e popolari di un repertorio urbano', in P. Scialò and F. Seller (eds.), *Passatempi musicali. Guillaume Cottrau e la canzone napoletana di primo '800*. Naples: Guida, pp. 119–70.

Frangini, A. (1907) *Italiani in Filadelfia. Strenna Nazionale. Cenni biografici.* Philadelphia: L'opinione.

Frasca, S. (2005) 'La coscienza sull'altra sponda del 'lago italiano': colloqui con alcuni testimoni della canzone napoletana', *Meridione* 5(2), pp. 145–64.

———— (2014) *Italian Birds of Passage: The Diaspora of Neapolitan Musicians in New York.* New York: Palgrave Macmillan.

Fugazzotto, G. (2010) *Sta terra nun fa pi mia. I dischi a 78 giri e la vita in America degli emigranti italiani del primo Novecento.* Udine: Nota.

———— (2015). *Ethnic Italian records. Analisi, conservazione, e restauro del repertorio dell'emigrazione italo-americana su dischi a 78 giri.* Cargeghe: Editoriale Documenta.

———— (2016). 'The Folk Within: On Some Neapolitan Productions in Early Twentieth-Century American Records', in Goffredo Plastino and Joseph Sciorra (eds.), *Neapolitan Postcards: The Canzone Napoletana as a Transnational Subject.* Lanham: Rowman & Littlefield, pp. 73–80.

Georgiou, M. (2006) *Diaspora, Identity, and the Media: Diasporic Transnationalism and Mediated Spatialities.* Cresskill: Hampton Press.

Greene, V. (1992) *A Passion for Polka: Old-Time Ethnic Music in America.* Berkeley: University of California Press.

Gronow, P. (1982) 'Ethnic Recordings: An Introduction', in *Ethnic Recordings in America: A Neglected Heritage.* Library of Congress, Washington: American Folklife Center.

Haller, H.W. (2006) *Tra Napoli e New York. Le macchiette italo-americane di Eduardo Migliaccio.* Rome: Bulzoni.

Hardy, C. (1984) *Interview with Armand DiStefano*, 30 January, I Remember When: Times Gone But Not Forgotten Oral History Project, Louie B. Nunn Center for Oral History, University of Kentucky.

Hoffmann, F. (ed.) (2005) *Encyclopedia of Recorded Sound*, second edition, vol. 1. New York: Routledge.

Juliani, R.N. (1981) 'The Italian Community of Philadelphia', in R.F. Harney and V. Scarpaci (eds.), *Little Italies in North America.* Toronto: The Multicultural History Society of Ontario, pp. 85–104.

———— (1998) *Building Little Italy: Philadelphia's Italians Before Mass Migration.* University Park, PA: Pennsylvania State University Press.

Kenney, W.H. (1999) *Recorded Music in American Life: The Phonograph and Popular Memory, 1890–1945.* New York and Oxford: Oxford University Press.

Koegel, J. (2017) 'Mexican Musical Theater and Movie Palaces in Downtown Los Angeles Before 1950', in J. Kun, *The Tide Was Always High: The Music of Latin America in Los Angeles.* Berkeley: University of California Press.

La colonia italiana di Filadelfia all'esposizione di Milano (1906) L'opinione, Philadelphia.

LaGumina, S.J. (ed.) (1973) *Wop! A Documentary History of Anti-Italian Discrimination in the United States.* San Francisco: Straight Arrow Books.

Leppert, R. (2015) *Aesthetic Technologies of Modernity, Subjectivity, and Nature.* Berkeley: University of California Press.

Livi Bacci, M. (1961) *L'immigrazione e l'assimilazione degli italiani negli Stati Uniti secondo le statistiche demografiche americane.* Milan: A. Giuffré.

Luconi, S. (2001) *From* Paesani *to White Ethnics: The Italian Experience in Philadelphia.* Albany: New York State University Press.

———— (2009) 'Tampa's 1910 Lynching: The Italian-American Perspective and its Implications', *The Florida Historical Quarterly*, 88(1), pp. 30–53.

———— (2016) 'Opera as a Nationalistic Weapon: The Erection of the Monument of Giuseppe Verdi in New York City', *Italian Americana* 34(1), pp. 37–61.

Mangione, Jerre. (1998). *Monte Allegro: A Memoir of Italian-American Life*, with a foreword by Eugene Paul Nassar and an introduction by Dorothy Canfield. Syracuse: Syracuse University Press.

Mills, Q.T. (2013) *Cutting Along the Color Line: Black Barbers and Barber Shops in America*. Philadelphia: University of Pennsylvania Press.

Mishra, S. (2019) 'Transnational Media: Key Concepts and Theories', in S. Mishra and R. Kern-Stone (eds.), *Transnational Media: Concepts and Cases*. Hoboken: Wiley Blackwell, pp. 13–25.

Pesce, A. (2008) 'La canzone napoletana e il disco a 78 giri', in Enrico Careri and Pasquale Scialò (eds.) *Studi sulla canzone napoletana classica*. Lucca: Libreria Musicale Italiana.

———— (2016) 'The Neapolitan Sound Goes Around: Mechanical Music Instruments, Talking Machines, and Neapolitan Song, 1850–1925', in Goffredo Plastino and Joseph Sciorra (eds.), *Neapolitan Postcards: The Canzone Napoletana as a Transnational Subject*. Lanham: Rowman & Littlefield, pp. 45–72.

Quinzio, J. (2009) *Of Sugar and Snow: A History of Ice Cream Making*. Berkeley: University of California Press.

Rao, N.Y. (2017) *Chinatown Opera Theater in North America*. Urbana: University of Illinois Press.

Russo, J.P. (2017) 'When They Were Few: Italians in America, 1800–1850', in W.J. Connell and S.G. Pugliese, *The Routledge History of Italian Americans*. New York: Routledge, pp. 54–68.

Saltzmann, L. (1966) 'The Victor Café', *Opera News*, 16 February.

Schiavo, G.E. (1928) *The Italians in Chicago: A Study in Americanization*. Chicago: Italian American Publishing Co.

Spottswood, R.K. (1990) *Ethnic Music on Records: A Discography of Ethnic Recordings Produced in the United States, 1893 to 1942*, vol. 1. Urbana and Chicago: University of Illinois Press.

Stazio, M. (1991) *Osolemio. La canzone napoletana – 1880/1914*. Rome: Bulzoni.

Strafile, A. (1910) *'Memorandum' coloniale ossia sintesi storica di osservazioni e fatti che diano un'idea generale della vita coloniale degli italiani nel nord America con monografia illustrativa della colonia di Philadelphia*. Philadelphia: Mastro Paolo.

Suisman, D. (2009) *Selling Sounds: The Commercial Revolution in American Music*. Cambridge, MA: Harvard University Press.

Sutton, A. (2008) *Recording the 'Twenties: The Evolution of American Recording Industry, 1920–29*. Denver: Mainspring Press.

Swiatlowski, M. (2018) *The Sound of Ethnic America: Prewar 'Foreign-Language' Recordings & the Sonics of U.S. Citizenship*, Doctoral dissertation, University of North Carolina at Chapel Hill.

Tirabassi, M. (2017) 'Why Italians Left Italy: The Physics and Politics of Migration, 1870–1920', in W.J. Connell and S.G. Pugliese (eds.), *The Routledge History of Italian Americans*. New York, Routledge, pp. 117–31.

Verde, A. (2017) *Is Globalisation Doomed? The Economical and Political Threats to the Future of Globalisation*. London: Palgrave Macmillan.

Villari, L. (1908) 'L'emigrazione italiana nel distretto consolare di Filadelfia', *Bollettino dell'emigrazione* 16, pp. 26–50.

———— (1912) *Gli Stati Uniti d'America e l'emigrazione italiana*. Milan: Fratelli Treves.

Wile, F.W. (1926) *Emile Berliner: Maker of the Microphone*. Indianapolis: The Bobbs-Merrill Company.

12 From the Grands Boulevards to Montparnasse

An essay on the geohistory of the phonograph and sound recording business in Paris (1878–1940)

Thomas Henry

The passerby following in the footsteps of Walter Benjamin through the Parisian covered arcades might be familiar with the Passage Verdeau, which connects the rue Grange-Batelière to the rue du Faubourg Montmartre, in the heart of the 9th arrondissement. Once through its imposing portal, a look at the wood paneling surrounding the first store window on the left reveals an old sign written in white letters on a black background: Maison Gaillard. This name is not unknown to those interested in the history of sound recording in France. It takes back to the early days of the phonographic trade in Paris. From its opening in 1900 to its definitive closure in the 1980s, this shop saw several generations of phonograph buyers, music lovers and record collectors pass through its doors. Its location a few dozen meters from the *Grands Boulevards* is not without significance. It lay at the heart of the neighborhood that gave birth to the French phonographic industry at the *Belle Époque*.[1] Within a one-kilometer radius were dozens of small phonograph manufacturers, labels, cylinder and record retailers or major companies' listening rooms. So were numerous theaters, concert halls and music publishers.

Much has already been written about the pioneer manufacturers and the first brands that contributed to the spread of the phonograph in France,[2] but the role played by dealers and retailers in this history is rarely discussed. However, the way talking machines, cylinders and discs have been sold over time tells us a lot about the status of these objects. This lack of literature on the topic is due to the scarcity of sources and archives documenting their activities. Yet, these mostly forgotten businesses have left some traces that testify to their past: these include illustrated record sleeves and cylinder boxes, stickers, stamps, catalogues, postcards, promotional material and advertising in newspapers. Most of this evidence belongs to the category of ephemera that are not systematically collected by archives and libraries. Therefore, gathering these visual artifacts was the first step of the research presented here and gave birth to an online mapping project called

DOI: 10.4324/9781003006497-17

Disquaires de Paris.[3] Visualizing businesses' locations on a map allowed us to get a sense of which areas shops clustered in and which others were left empty in different time periods. Over time, the research project moved away from simply mapping record shops to opening up an archival investigation aimed at documenting the history of these establishments. This revealed strong connections between their location and the cultural and commercial history of the phonograph in Paris. This chapter will first introduce the methodology followed in this research and the various sources that were used to carry it out. It will then adopt a both chronological and geographical approach to highlight the successive steps in the development of the phonograph and sound recording trade in Paris. The status of the individuals involved in this trade will also be examined, with the aim to analyze the genesis and the development of the "disquaire" profession in the late 1920s.

Methodology and sources

As mentioned before, the first step in this research project consisted of gathering evidence and visual artifacts on Paris phonograph and recorded music shops. In addition to the material found over a decade of personal collecting, a call for contributions was launched in the community of private collectors. This proved to be successful and around 40 individuals provided copies of documents related to these shops. The large collection of the Paris Phono Museum[4] as well as the Phonobase[5] and Phonorama[6] websites turned out to be extremely useful, too. Drawing from that material, a first list of businesses was developed and then completed through systematic research in three major sources: the business directories available at the City of Paris Archive, the digitized newspapers available in Gallica[7] and the various music, phonograph, record and radio magazines in the collections of the Bibliothèque nationale de France (National Library of France). This groundwork allowed me to identify around 1,000 businesses in Paris that once sold phonographs and recorded music before World War II and determine their approximate opening and closing dates. The accuracy of these data had to be fine-tuned as the sources used were often incomplete or not always up-to-date. Furthermore, a significant share of these businesses never specialized in recorded music sales and some existed long before the birth of the recording industry, like the music publishers and the instrument manufacturers. To be able to precisely date the beginning of phonograph, cylinder and record sales, I had to research every single business directory in the archives of the Tribunal de commerce de Paris (Paris Commercial Court). More focused research in the press also provided useful insights for this work, such as the mention of a shop launch or a bankruptcy.

The question that then arose was how to visualize and share the spatial–temporal data and the visual artifacts that were collected. The solution was provided by the web developer and graphic designer Stéphane Cure,[8] who used the open-source softwares OpenStreetMap and Mapbox to create a custom-made interactive map featuring a timeline. The result was a website called Disquaires de Paris that was launched on April 2015.[9] It is still updated on a regular basis with newly discovered information and visual artifacts. The archival research that followed took place at the Seydoux-Pathé Foundation in Paris and in the archives of the Audiovisual department of the National Library of France and the Musée de l'Homme.[10] The archives of the Tribunal de Commerce de Paris (Paris Commercial Court) also provided precise data on the identity of the shops' owners. This paved the way for genealogical research that allowed me to identify and contact some of their descendants. In most cases, this didn't yield any results. The few exceptions gave access to some unexplored archives that were extensively used in this article.

The cradle of the phonograph trade in Paris

This chapter doesn't aim at retracing the early days of the phonograph in France. It might be useful, however, to provide some key milestones. Almost 20 years after the pioneer work of Parisian inventor Edouard-Léon Scott de Martinville, the first demonstration of an Edison's tinfoil phonograph in Paris took place on March 11, 1878, at the Academy of Science. This was followed by a second demonstration in front of journalists held on April 22, 1878, in a theater called Salle des Capucines. Given the enthusiasm for this new invention, several scientific instruments manufacturers soon after started building their own version of the machine: Edmé Hardy, who built the first phonograph made in France, D. Vital, Urbain Marie Fondain and Eugène Ducretet (Chamoux, 2015, pp. 171–2). This first wave of inventions was followed by a decade of silence that ended with the presentation of the Edison Class M wax cylinder phonograph during the Exposition Universelle in 1889. The first French manufacturer of phonographs and recorded cylinders in 1893 was the clockmaker Henri Lioret (Anton, 2006).

In 1894, two brothers named Michel and Eugène Werner became the first importers and distributors of the Edison phonograph in France. Their shop was located at 85, rue de Richelieu, close to the Opéra Garnier, the Opéra Comique and the numerous theaters of the Grands Boulevards neighborhood. This was soon followed by the opening of another shop by the Compagnie américaine du phonographe Edison in the same neighborhood at 30, rue Bergère. The earliest mention of the Werner brothers' activities dates back to a March 1894 advertisement (*Le Journal*, March 15, 1894):

> New attraction! The real Edison phonograph can be rented for events and meetings. Orchestra, song, spoken word. For the rent or sale of the machines, contact: M. Werner, 85 rue de Richelieu, Paris.

A second ad published a few weeks later gave the following information: "Blank cylinders allowing buyer to record himself. The phonograph can bring up to 80 to 100 francs per day when used for public listening" (*Le Radical*, May 19, 1894). This shows that the first category targeted by the Werner brothers were the fairground artists using the phonograph for public demonstrations. The latter belonged to the early adopters of the new invention in France, indeed. In August 1894, a certain Charles Pathé had the idea to start a phonograph business after attending such a demonstration at a fair held in Vincennes, near Paris (Salmon, 2014, pp. 29–30). He subsequently bought a phonograph and organized his first recital at a fair in Monthéty, a village in the East of Paris. At the end of 1894, he started selling phonographs in his own house located on the Cours de Vincennes, in the 12th arrondissement, before opening a shop in early 1896. In September 1896, he finally partnered with his brother Émile to create the Pathé Frères company, which headquarter and shop were established at 98, rue de Richelieu. That was exactly 71 meters from the Werner brother's shop, their main competitors at that time, and a few hundred meters from the Compagnie américaine du phonographe Edison. These three locations can be considered as the cradle of the phonographic trade in Paris.

The conquest of the boulevards

The years 1897 and 1898 marked a turning point in the strategy developed by phonographic companies in Paris. In late 1897, the Compagnie américaine du phonographe Edison and the Columbia Phonograph Company both opened their own shop in the center of the city and chose the very same location: the Boulevard des Italiens,[11] a wide commercial artery that also served as a popular walking area at the "Belle Époque". Very little is known about this short-lived Edison shop which quickly moved to another location. However, the Columbia shop is better documented thanks to several advertisements. It was actually more than a regular shop and can be considered as the first example of the large listening rooms that flourished in Paris in the following years. It was meant to serve both as a promotion and selling point, where passersby could stop and enjoy a listening experience on one of Columbia's "Graphophone" cylinder machines. Its more general purpose was introducing this new attraction to a larger audience.[12]

Figure 12.1 The Columbia listening room in 1903.
Source: Gallica/BnF.

Columbia was soon followed by Pathé, which inaugurated its "Salon du Phonographe" in October 1898 at number 26 of the same boulevard. The genesis and the concept of this new location are well documented in the Pathé's board of directors meeting minutes (Salmon, 2014, pp. 69–70). The idea of its creators was to offer customers free access to a 3,000 cylinder on-demand repertoire in a comfortable and luxurious environment. The first set-up included 12 listening units equipped with earphones but quickly raised to 30 in the next months. Following Columbia and Pathé's examples, the Gramophone Company opened its Maison du Gramophone at number 28 of the Boulevard des Italiens in 1901 and a subsidiary under the name Paris-Phono at number 6 in 1903. These two locations were widely advertised following a large press campaign to promote the Gramophone Company's recordings by celebrities such as Enrico Caruso, Sarah Bernhardt, Emma Calvé, Francesco Tamagno, Nellie Melba and Edvard Grieg. Their listening rooms were presented as the only places where one could have the chance to hear such famous voices.[13] In 1906, Odeon opened its Fonotipia[14] Odeon Palace at number 32 of the Boulevard des Italiens, followed by the Association Phonique des Grands Artistes at number 11. At that time, only a few dozen meters separated the listening rooms of all major phonographic companies in Paris. Alongside those, phonograph shelves were developed by the end of the nineteenth century in most major department stores of Paris. The most significant ones were the Grands Magasins du Louvre and the Grands Magasins Dufayel,[15] which also produced and sold their own cylinders. They were quickly joined by Le Bon Marché and La Samaritaine. The third main actor of Paris phonographic trade at the time was La Bonne Presse, a catholic publishing house which was manufacturing and selling its own phonographs and cylinders. A decade after the birth of the phonographic trade around the rue de Richelieu in the mid-1890s, the phonograph was now firmly established on the Parisian boulevards.

Expanding the frontiers of the phonograph

At that time, Pathé initiated a new commercial strategy in Paris and started developing a network of "depots" for its products throughout the city, in addition to its own sale points. To achieve that, Pathé built alliances with several retailers, some of which were already involved in the music business as phonograph or instrument sellers. This system is mentioned in the meeting minutes of Pathé's board of directors in 1904:

> Our new depots in Paris are going very well. The goods they contain are our property, an inspector is visiting every 8 days to calculate the amount of sold products. This district sale system benefits from the removal of retail sale at the headquarter, that now mainly focuses on wholesale.[16]

The list of these depots can be found in some Pathé commercials from the mid-1900s and in the company's annual inventories available at the Seydoux-Pathé Foundation. They are first mentioned in the 1901 inventory. Starting 1904, these depots were assigned a letter to identify them, from A to G.[17] Their location showed the willingness to expand the geographic presence of Pathé outside the Grands boulevards neighborhood: Biaggi (depot C) in the Northern rue Lepic, Pensuet (depot F) in the South-Western rue de Passy and Le Révérend (depot G) in the Eastern rue du Faubourg du Temple. However, none of these shops were located on the left bank of the Seine River, which remained an intellectual center at that time, with a lower density of businesses compared to the right bank. Some rare photographs held in private collections provide interesting information about them. The similarity between two 1905 pictures showing the store fronts of the depot D (Maison Charlus at 39, avenue de Wagram) and the depot G (Maison Le Révérend at 51, rue du Faubourg du Temple) is striking.[18] Same sign ("Nouveaux phonographes Pathé") completed with the name and the letter of the depot, same products and similar display in the store window. This suggests that Pathé tried to set up a common commercial strategy for these shops. The last mention of these depots can be found in the 1910 inventory.

The first independent shops

In the mid-1900s, the phonographic trade in Paris was dominated by the main recording companies and their listening rooms, the big department stores and the distribution network specifically developed by Pathé. However, the years between 1898 and 1900 witnessed the appearance of what can be considered as the first independent shops in Paris: La Fauvette and Guille-Gaillard. The first one opened in 1898 at 5, Boulevard Poissonnière, in the heart of the Grands Boulevards neighborhood. Its founder was Lucien Vivès, a former opera singer who played a central role in the development of copyrights in the French phonographic industry in the mid-1900s (Chamoux, 2015, pp. 149–65). Vivès sold his own phonographs and cylinders manufactured under the name La Fauvette[19] as well as products from several other brands. The shop's storefront can be seen on a postcard probably dating from the mid-1900s. Various brands' names were written on the window: Gramophone, Zon-o-phone, Odeon and Fonotipia. The Guille-Gaillard shop mentioned in my introduction was the second emblematic independent business of the early phonographic era in Paris. It opened in 1900 and was located at the entrance of the Passage Verdeau. From 1906 to 1913, it also took on the shop once occupied by the Pathé depot at Avenue Wagram using the name "A l'Etoile Phono". The custom-made illustrated sleeves it used in the mid-1900s mentioned several brands, such as Gramophone, Odeon, Fonotipia, Zonophone and Pathé, showing that Guille-Gaillard was not affiliated to a specific one.

Figure 12.2 Mid-1900s illustrated record sleeve for "A l'Etoile Phono", a subsidiary
      of the Guille-Gaillard shop.
Source: author's personal collection.

   In addition to the above-mentioned places, a myriad other businesses
were involved in the phonographic trade before 1914 in Paris. Close to La
Fauvette was the store run by two brothers named Charles and Jacques
Ullmann, who were the official distributors of the Zon-o-phone, Odeon,
Fonotipia, Phrynis and Jumbo records. Smaller companies were using their
headquarters as listening rooms and selling points. Such was the case, for
instance, of Aérophone, Dutreih, Aspir, Phono, Eden, Idéal, La Semeuse,
Ultima or Pantophone. Moreover, unspecialized businesses were also selling phonographs, cylinders and records: music instrument sellers, music
publishers and mechanics. Overall, I have been able to identify 100 shops
involved in this business on the eve of World War I. The large majority of
them were located in the Grands Boulevards neighborhood.

The postwar years

World War I put an end to the growth of the phonographic industry in
France. The phonograph and record production was dramatically reduced
during the conflict while the Pathé factory in Chatou was requisitioned to
take part in the war effort. A significant number of shops had to close during
this period as many of their owners were sent to the frontline. The postwar
years were marked by a gradual recovery until a technical revolution completely changed the face of this industry: the advent of electrical recording
in the mid-1920s (Gelatt, 1977, pp. 219–44). The new technology based on

the use of microphones in the studio led to major improvements in sound recording and playback quality compared to the preceding acoustic era. The new context had several major consequences, starting with the emergence of a new way of listening to music and the development of a larger audience for recorded music, including communities that had sometimes been reluctant to adopt the phonograph: musicologists and music critics. Records went from being a technical curiosity to a "noble" object while raising interest among painters[20] and writers.[21] The period from the mid-1920s to the early 1930s saw the birth of professional record criticism[22] in France as well as the creation of the first amateur record clubs (Maisonneuve, 2009, pp. 220–6). That was also the time when the first modern independent record shops appeared. This subsequently gave birth to a new word in French, "disquaire", meaning both "record store" and "record seller". This neologism will be used in this chapter rather than its English equivalent.[23]

On the word "disquaire"

The oldest use of the word "disquaire" dates back to an article published on September 3, 1932, in the weekly magazine *Ric et Rac*. In a piece titled "L'embarras de l'amateur de disques" ("The embarrassment of the record enthusiast"), the music and record critic Dominique Sordet[24] discussed the various sources of information that could help buyers decide which version of a recording was worth buying. While mentioning the advices that record sellers should be able to give, Sordet made an analogy with the "libraire" (bookseller in French) and used the word "disquaire":

> A "disquaire" worthy of the name knows, for each piece, which are the good and the bad recordings, just like an experienced bookseller can guide customers through the authors, works and editions.

In the following weeks, he used this neologism several times in his record columns published in the nationalist and far-right newspapers *Candide* and *L'Action Française*. On October 7, 1932, Sordet drew an opposition between the traditional "marchand de disque" (record seller) and the "disquaire", who is aware of music, knows how to guide customers and can serve as an ambassador of "phonographic art" (*L'Action française*, October 7, 1932). By the end of 1932, the new word had slowly spread in the press and was used by several other critics. In an article published in December 1932, it found its first incarnation in the person of Jacques Lévi-Alvarès, the founder of the boulevard Raspail shop La Boîte à Musique (*La Semaine à Paris*, December 16, 1932). Two years later, its appearance in *Le Mercure de France*, one of the most important French literary magazines, can be seen as a sort of consecration (*Mercure de France*, October 1934). At the end of the 1930s, "disquaire" was commonly used by most record critics.

Jacques Lévi-Alvarès and La Boîte à Musique

As mentioned before, the founder of La Boîte à Musique, Jacques Lévi-Alvarès, seems to have been the very first record seller designated as a "disquaire" in France. The opening of his shop in 1928 inaugurated a period of effervescence and innovation in the record trade in Paris, giving birth to the modern "disquaire". This phenomenon was not only concomitant with the change of status of the record as a cultural object, it also contributed to it. The case of Lévi-Alvarès is somewhat unique in that besides being a merchant, he also theorized his own activities and wrote about them in various publications. It may be useful to examine the story and the role of his shop here.

In 1926, Lévi-Alvarès opened an art gallery and a bookstore at 133, boulevard Raspail, in the heart of the Montparnasse neighborhood. The gallery's guestbook[25] shows that it was frequented by some major artists, such as the painters Henri Matisse and Tsuhugaru Foujita. In June 1928, Lévi-Alvarès turned his gallery into a record shop called La Boîte à Musique. Besides the usual daytime schedules, it was open from 9 to 11 in the evening to attract the night visitors of numerous nearby cafés. This opening was widely advertised in several newspapers and magazines. The shop was presented as a specialist of "phonographic art" offering a "large choice of selected records and machines" (*La Semaine à Paris*, June 15, 1928). Using the expression "phonographic art" was significant at a time when listening to records was becoming a "serious" activity known in French as "discophilie".[26] This new hobby required a specific equipment and a know-how to handle it: choosing the best edition of a work, choosing the right machine and the proper needle to play a record, choosing the best system to store a collection. In the late 1928 and 1929 advertisements, Lévi-Alvarès was presented as a "qualified and trustworthy guide in the choice of recordings" (*La Semaine à Paris*, October 5, 1928) and a "competent musician" (*Candide*, October 17, 1929). In February 1932, he wrote a piece entitled "Le rôle primordial du vendeur de disques" ("The crucial role of the record seller")[27] in *Le Figaro illustré*. This text can be seen as a manifesto for the profession he was creating:

> The record is not a common merchandise, which price varies according to its label... It's a piece of art that can create emotions and joy. It's a social agent with a strong educational power thanks to its potential for repetition. (...) The retailer has a double mission: reflecting the public taste for the producers; guiding and advising the public, lost in the chaos of the production. In order to fulfill this mission, it must be very well documented on music and able to appreciate not only the musical value of a work, but also the quality or the style of an interpretation, as well as the technical quality of a recording.

Figure 12.3 The storefront of La Boîte à Musique in 1929.
Source: BnF.

Another specificity of La Boîte à Musique was its positioning as a cultural actor as much as a shop. In October 1929, it started organizing free "record concerts" held every Sunday afternoon. During the same period, Lévi-Alvarès briefly hosted a radio show on the Paris local Radio Vitus. From October to December 1930, La Boîte à Musique's "record concerts" took place on a biweekly basis at the Studio des Ursulines art house cinema. Starting early 1931, they were held in the shop on a daily basis from 5 to 6 pm. In April 1931, Lévi-Alvarès inaugurated a series of concerts following the history of music, using records for an educational purpose. According to their programs, these events were not limited to Western classical music and also included jazz and folk music from other regions. In November 1932, they were turned into a weekly program called *An hour with...*, focusing on a specific composer every week. From 1935 onwards, these listening sessions took place in a venue called Revue Musicale located on the nearby boulevard Montparnasse. They seem to have lasted until the late 1930s. The cultural program developed by La Boîte à Musique also included several exhibitions, conferences, meetings with musicians or book signing sessions.

As mentioned earlier, Jacques Lévi-Alvarès widely promoted the activities of La Boîte à Musique in the press. Besides regular mentions in newspapers and magazines, La Boîte à Musique is one of the only record shops promoted in *Le Guide du concert* and *La Semaine musicale*, two weekly publications listing all concerts taking place in Paris. In March 1935, the very first issue of the *Jazz Hot* magazine featured a full-page advertisement for La Boîte à Musique, which was also one of its official distributors. This showed Lévi-Alvarès' willingness to target the most specialized music communities. In addition, he set up a series of technical and marketing innovations inside his shop. In 1930, he was one of the first sellers in Paris to open a shelf for second-hand records and launched a record exchange service at the same time. The same year, he built a booth to let customers record their voice.

The activities of Jacques Lévi-Alvarès as a "disquaire" led to a new development in 1934 and the creation of an independent record label called "B.A.M.".[28] Thanks to his influence in the recording industry, Lévi-Alvarès had already made some commercial recordings, such as a collection of works by Philipp Heinrich Erlebach performed by the baryton singer Yvon Le Marc'Hadour and accompanied by the La Musique Intime Orchestra. This was released in June 1934 on the Columbia label. The same artists can be heard on the first two releases of the B.A.M. label. In autumn 1934, they recorded works by Schumann and Erlebach that were released in December of the same year. These records came with a booklet introducing the composer and his works. Their label featured the recording dates, thereby responding to a long-standing request of several record critics and collectors. After a one-year break, B.A.M. came up with two early music records released in February 1936. After only 18 months of activity, the young label received the early music award of the Prix Candide in May 1936. It carried on publishing early music and chamber music until the outbreak of World War II. It also explored other repertoires, as evidenced by the release of a six-disc set of the Spanish flamenco guitarist Ramón Montoya in November 1936.

Musically trained seller, cultural actor, record critic, communication and marketing specialist, radio host, label founder: the career of Jacques Lévi-Alvares and the numerous innovations that he developed contributed to the emergence of a new profession that had little in common with the activities of the first individuals involved in the early days of the phonograph and sound recording trade. It is no coincidence that La Boîte à Musique was located in the heart of Montparnasse, the center of the art and literary scene of Paris at that time. This connection with the neighborhood and its artistic life was underlined by the French surrealist poet and occasional record critic Robert Desnos in a piece published in 1929 (*Le Merle*, May 24, 1929):

> La Boîte à Musique achieved the union of arts rather than their confusion. Indeed, its dynamic director added it to an art gallery that already included a bookshop: writing, painting and music found themselves combined and in order to illustrate this line, the contemporary art gallery is currently exhibiting paintings on music, while the alternate sounds of jazz and opera are coming from the basement. (...) Montparnasse's jostle of ideas, customs and races needed the bright and open shop of the boulevard Raspail.

Maurice Dalloz, from Montparnasse to the radio

The other central individual involved in the rise of the "disquaire" profession was Maurice Dalloz (1890–1968).[29] In the 1930s, his career echoed that of Jacques Lévi-Alvarès in several respects, starting with the geographic proximity of their shops. It also illustrated the porosity between record

Figure 12.4 The listening salon and record storage unit of Maurice Dalloz's shop.
Source: Archives of the Dalloz family.

trade, record criticism, phonographic edition and radio in the 1930s in France. A native of the Eastern Jura region, Dalloz first ran a family wood business that went bankrupt in 1928. According to a résumé found among his papers, Dalloz received a musical education but really discovered music thanks to the phonograph. In 1930, he moved to Paris and opened a record shop located at 106, Boulevard Montparnasse, between Le Dôme and La Coupole cafés, in the same neighborhood as La Boîte à Musique. The few existing photographs of the shop show an art deco storefront, a luxurious main room full of various gramophone models, a large record storage unit and a cosy listening salon.

Besides his commercial activities, Dalloz also published record reviews in several newspapers and magazines throughout the 1930's. Another common point with Lévi-Alvarès was the role Dalloz played in the creation of an independent phonographic editor. A few weeks before Lévi-Alvarès launched the "B.A.M." label, Dalloz partnered with the German musicologist Curt Sachs and the French publisher Bernard Steele, the co-creators of L'Anthologie Sonore, a label focusing on early music. Dalloz became the sole distributor of the new brand and took an active part in its development.

Despite Dalloz's reputation and multiple activities, his shop went bankrupt in 1936. A letter to Columbia's director Jean Bérard mentioned the project of a commercial partnership with Jacques Lévi-Alvarès to save Dalloz's business. For unknown reasons, this never materialized.[30] However, the story of the shop didn't finish with this commercial failure. Following the bankruptcy, Dalloz received several support letters from regular customers regretting the disappearance of a meeting point for music lovers and record collectors. One of them launched the idea of creating a club that would serve as an extension of the disappeared Dalloz's shop.[31] Based on the letters he subsequently received, the idea seemed to have raised great interest. This finally gave birth to an association called "Les Discophiles"[32] that was officially created in November 1936.[33] Its first president was the folklorist and journalist Roger Dévigne, head of Paris Musée de la Parole et du Geste (Museum of speech and Gesture) who became the first director of the Phonothèque nationale (National Phonotheque) in 1938 (Cordereix, 2005). Detailed accounts of this association's activities can be found in the *Disques* magazine: meetings, conferences and listening sessions were organized on a regular basis until the outbreak of World War II. Members of Les Discophiles included the most important French record critics, collectors and dealers of the time.[34] In the late 1930s, Maurice Dalloz was appointed the head of the "Discothèque" at the Radiodiffusion, a position that he kept until his retirement in the 1950s.

The rise of the Champs-Elysées

Montparnasse saw the birth of the modern "disquaire" starting in the late 1920s. In its wake, another neighborhood appeared on the phonographic map of Paris at the same period: the Champs-Elysées. Within a few years, the iconic Parisian avenue and its nearby streets moved from being a "phonographic desert" to a place with one of the highest density of record shops in town. This started in 1926 with the opening of Sensation Phono at the instigation of Philippe Parès, an operetta composer who had served as the artistic director of the French branch of Columbia since 1924 (Nels 1989). It was located at rue Pierre-Charon, a street perpendicular to the Champs-Elysées. Whereas it was never presented as an official Columbia retailer, this shop probably had a commercial partnership with this brand.[35] Thanks to its prestigious location, Sensation Phono was used by Columbia to host some promotional events.[36] Sensation Phono went bankrupt in 1929, but was immediately revived in the nearby avenue Kléber as La Plaque Tournante (Nels 1989).

Another emblematic record shop of the Champs-Elysées neighborhood was Sinfonia, which opened in 1928 inside a luxurious shopping arcade called Les Portiques.[37] One of its sellers, a jazz specialist named Henri Gédovius, co-founded The Music-Shop in 1934 at the rue de Ponthieu, another perpendicular street to the Champs-Elysées. This store turned out to be one of the very first in Paris focusing on a specific music style: jazz. In addition to its commercial activities, the Music Shop had its own weekly radio show on the Paris-based Radio-L.L. Starting July 1935, *Une soirée à Harlem (A night in Harlem)*[38] was hosted by Gédovius (Ledos and Mansion 2003), who offered a 30-minute selection of hot jazz records every Wednesday night at 10.30 pm. The show was taken over after Radio L.L. became Radio Cité in September 1935. In November 1936, The Music-Shop moved to the nearby rue Pierre-Charon in a new location, whose ceiling representing jazz musicians was painted by an artist named Florent Margaritis.[39] Gédovius left The Music Shop around 1937 but kept his show on Radio Cité. It lasted until May 1940 and even resumed after the war on the newly created

Radiodiffusion française. Gédovius pursued a career as a radio producer until his retirement.

The Music Shop's main competitor in the neighborhood was Broadway, a record store that opened in the mid-1930s inside the Elysées-Gaumont arcade. It also focused on jazz and was one of the few record stores to advertise in the first issues of the *Jazz-Hot* magazine alongside La Boîte à Musique and The Music Shop. Broadway's advertising arguments provide interesting insights on the mid-1930s jazz record market in France. Emphasis was put on the capacity to import rare records "from New York, London and Berlin" that could not be found in other shops. In a full-page ad published in 1936, Broadway claimed that it was the only shop in Paris able to offer "newly released English and American records at the same time as London and New-York".

Following the appearance of the Champs-Elysées on the record map of Paris, the nearby Salle Pleyel and the Salle Gaveau, two of the main classical music venues in town, both opened their own phonograph and record shop in the late 1920s.[40] This illustrates the change of status of recorded music at that time and its appropriation by the classical music community, once again showing that recorded music was increasingly being regarded as a serious matter.

Foreign and regional record sellers

Beside the main shops that have been previously mentioned in this article, a myriad of smaller and often short-lived businesses existed in Paris. Among them is a category that has barely been studied: shops selling regional and foreign records to the various diasporas living in the city. The earliest one that I have been able to identify was owned by a Polish Jew named Ivan Samet, who launched a postcard business in 1904 at rue des Petites-Ecuries, in the 10th arrondissement. He started selling phonographs in 1906 and finally created his own record label in 1908. Disques Ivan Samet specialized in Hebrew and Yiddish records; but their activity only lasted a few years, and Samet eventually moved on to the bookshop business. In the same vein, the Speiser's bookshop at rue des Rosiers in the heart of the Pletzl[41] started selling Jewish records as early as 1925. In 1929, a shop called La Tour de Babel was opened at rue Saint-Martin by a merchant named Joseph de Padova. According to the rare traces it left in the press, this short-lived store (1929–1932) was selling Odeon records in Hebrew, Yiddish, Judeo-Spanish and other foreign languages (*L'Univers israélite*, May 30, 1930).

Home to several immigrant communities since the early twentieth century, the Belleville neighborhood in Eastern Paris saw the development in the interwar period of two Armenian-run record businesses. In 1928, a merchant named Haroutun Artinian started selling Armenian, Turkish and Greek records in his family's shop located at the small rue Lesage in the 20th arrondissement. It was soon followed in 1930 by a similar business run by Lev Nichanian that opened just a few dozen meters further in the rue Piat. Artinian's shop lasted until the early 1960s. Its activities are known, thanks to the catalogues it published in the 1930s to promote the records it was selling.[42]

As far as I have been able to find out, the foreign community record market in Paris was limited to the above-mentioned stores before World War II. The local North African, Western African and Southeast Asian records trade only started in the late 1940s and early 1950s.[43] However, a few generalist shops were already selling what were called "exotic" or "ethnic" records as early as the late 1920s, such as La Boîte à Musique and Maurice Dalloz. Starting 1932, the ethnomusicologist André Schaeffner started building up a collection of folk music records from around the world for the Paris Ethnographic museum and its successor, the Musée de l'Homme. Its official supplier was the Schneider music shop located close to the museum. This overview would not be complete without mentioning the French regional record market. Auvergne folk music was recorded as early as the early twentieth century, and these records were probably quite easy to find in Paris. In 1926, a musician named Martin Cayla[44] launched Le Soleil, a label exclusively dedicated to the folk music from Auvergne. His shop was located at 26, rue des Taillandiers, in a part of the 11th arrondissement where many Auvergnats had settled during the nineteenth century. That was close to the rue de Lappe, a street where some of the most famous *bals musette* in Paris were taking place. Cayla was also selling music instruments and music scores. In 1938, he moved to a new location at rue du Faubourg Saint-Martin.

Conclusion

From the birth of the French recording industry in the late 1870s to the outbreak of World War II, several hundred shops were involved in the phonograph and sound recording trade in Paris. During this period, the way talking machines, cylinders and records were marketed and sold changed dramatically. So did the status of the individuals behind this business. Their contribution to the dissemination of the phonograph in France deserves a specific study that should be carried on. Our research focused on the first decades of this industry, which corresponds to the cylinder and 78 rpm record era. Its timescope could be expanded to a more recent period and include the second half of the twentieth century, allowing us to pursue the history of the "disquaire" profession. With Paris being the capital of France and one of the main cultural centers in Europe, it quickly developed a phonographic industry and trade, which justified the focus on this city. However, the geographic scope of this research could be broadened to other French and European cities. This would let us highlight the logic behind the dissemination of the phonograph across the territory as well as the local, regional and national strategies developed by recording companies.

In this perspective, digital mapping could be especially useful, not only as a visualization tool, but also to develop a comparative approach and identify potential similarities or differences in the historical and geographical spread of the phonograph in these cities.

Notes

1 The period of French history covering the last decades of the nineteenth century until the outbreak of the First World War.
2 See Chamoux (2015), Anton (2006), Salmon (2014) and Maisonneuve (2009).
3 "Disquaire" means both "record store" and "record seller". The origins and usage of this word will be further discussed in this chapter.
4 http://phonomuseum.fr/.
5 https://www.phonobase.org/.
6 https://www.phonorama.fr/.
7 The digital library of the Bibliothèque nationale de France: www.gallica.bnf.fr.
8 http://www.douny.fr/.
9 http://www.disquairesdeparis.fr/index_en.html.
10 I would like to thank Stéphanie Salmon, Pascal Cordereix, Lionel Michaux, Aude Da Cruz-Lima and Joséphine Simmonot for their assistance at these institutions.
11 Number 15 for Edison and 34 for Columbia.
12 The audience of the phonograph in France is discussed in the third chapter of Henri Chamoux's doctoral dissertation.
13 *Le Journal* dated January 27, 1904, reports a visit of French President Emile Loubet to "Paris-Phono" to discover its "sensational gramophones" and "listen to great artists like Tamagno, Caruso, Mme Calvé and Sarah Bernhardt".
14 The German Odeon and the Italian Fonotipia labels were two brands belonging to the Berlin-based Carl Lindström AG consortium.
15 The Dufayel store, which opened in 1856 on the Northern boulevard Barbès, featured a showroom for new inventions, a luxurious theater and an orchestra.
16 Pathé Board of directors dated November 9, 1904.
17 Here is their complete list: O'Brien (A): 34, boulevard de Strasbourg; Billaut (B): 31, rue de Maubeuge; Biaggi (C): 24, rue Lepic; Charlus (D): 39, avenue de Wagram; Doublet (E): 4, rue de Rivoli; Pensuet (F): 42, rue de Passy; and Le Révérend (G): 51, rue du faubourg du Temple.
18 From the collections of Jalal Aro and Julien Anton.
19 See Hurm (1944, p. 38), for a discussion of *La Fauvette*'s recording studio and audition room.
20 See the series "Les peintres et le phonographe" ("Painters and the phonograph") published in the magazine *L'Art vivant* in 1928.
21 Among the record critics of the late 1920s are several celebrities from the literary world, such as Robert Desnos, Paul Morand and Pierre Mac Orlan.
22 The musicologist Emile Vuillermoz is considered as the pioneer of record criticism in France. His texts were published in several major newspapers such as *Le Temps* and *Excelsior*. In 1927, Vuillermoz created *L'Edition musicale vivante*, a magazine dedicated to recorded music.
23 As explained further, this word appeared in the 1930's and is still commonly used in French nowadays. For convenience, it was used to name our website, even though the map includes stores that preexist its appearance.
24 Dominique Sordet (1889–1946) was one of the most influential music and record critics of the interwar period in France. He was also a highly controversial

person, whose reviews were published in several nationalist or far-right newspapers such as *L'Action française* and *Candide*. He also introduced the Prix Candide (also known as Grand Prix du disque) in 1931, the most important award in the French phonographic industry. Sordet was an active collaborator during the Nazi Occupation of France. More details on Sordet's role in the French interwar record industry can be found in Coppola (1943), pp. 70–1.

25 I am thankful to Claude Lévi-Alvarès, the grandson of Jacques Lévi-Alvarès, who kindly let me access this document.

26 The digitized press available in Gallica shows that the expression "phonographic art" started being commonly used by record critics in 1928, especially by Henry-Jacques in *L'Ere nouvelle*; 1928 also saw the launch of a magazine called *Arts Phoniques*.

27 I thank Claude Fihman, who pointed me to this article.

28 The initials of *Boîte à Musique*.

29 I am thankful to his son Jean-Claude Dalloz (1927–2018) who let me explore Maurice Dalloz's papers.

30 Letters sent by Dalloz in the late 1930s to his friend Roger Dévigne, the director of the Phonothèque nationale, suggest that his relations with Lévi-Alvarès were strained.

31 Letter of Pierre Drach to Maurice Dalloz, February 24, 1936.

32 Not to be confused with the classical music record label Les Discophiles français created in 1942.

33 On record clubs, see also Eva Moreda Rodríguez's chapter in this book.

34 Alongside Dalloz and Lévi-Alvarès, a third "disquaire", music editor and instrument seller from Montparnasse named Eugène Ploix took an active part in the association's activities. His shop was located at 48, rue Saint-Placide.

35 This is suggested by the presence of the Columbia logo on its sign, as seen on a promotional postcard edited in the late 1920s.

36 Similar partnerships were developed by Columbia with Opéra Corner, a record shop opened in 1926 next to the Opéra de Paris, and the Innovation department store on the Champs-Elysées.

37 Sinfonia moved to number 68 of the Champs-Elysées in 1933 and was renamed Lido Musique in 1969. It closed in 1988.

38 This title was probably inspired by a show called *Une soirée à Montmartre* that was hosted on the same radio.

39 I am thankful to his son Alain Gédovius, who sent me a copy of a promotional postcard showing this painting. In the same vein, Anne Legrand mentions a record shop called Disques-Occasion whose decoration was made by the jazz producer and illustrator Charles Delaunay (Legrand, 2009).

40 Pleyel-Phono opened in 1929 in the venue and was quickly renamed Nové-Phono. In 1930, the already existing Disco shop, located in front of the Salle Gaveau, moved to the ground floor of the concert hall. Both closed in the mid-1930s.

41 Paris historic Jewish neighborhood in the Marais district.

42 These catalogues were part of a collection that belonged to the Paris Musée de l'Homme sound archive. It is now managed by the Center for Research in Ethnomusicology at Nanterre University.

43 It is worth mentioning the Phono hall shop in the Barbès neighborhood that was founded in 1928 by the Sauviat family. It started selling North African records in the late 1940s. Southeast Asian records were on sale in the Vietnamese Lê-Loi bookshop that opened on the rue de la Huchette in 1952.

44 A native from the Cantal department, Martin Cayla was a *cabrette* player, the traditional bagpipe from Auvergne. His label and shop played a major role in the development of Auvergne music in Paris. See Cayla, 2013.

References

Anton, J. (2006) *Henri Lioret: un horloger pionnier du phonographe*. Paris: CIRES.

Chamoux, H. (2015) *La diffusion de l'enregistrement sonore en France à la Belle Époque (1893–1914): artistes, industriels et auditeurs du cylindre et du disque*. Doctoral dissertation, Paris 1 University.

Cayla, M. (2013) *Les mémoires de Martin Cayla*. Paris: L'Harmattan.

Coppola, P. (1943) *Dix-sept ans de musique à Paris*. Lausanne: F. Rouge.

Cordereix, P. (2005) Les fonds sonores du département de l'Audiovisuel de la Bibliothèque nationale de France. *Le Temps des medias*, 5, pp. 253–64.

Gelatt, R. (1977) *The Fabulous Phonograph (1877–1977)*. New York: MacMillan.

Hurm, H. (1944) *La passionnante histoire du phonographe*. Paris: Les publications techniques, 1944.

Ledos, J.-J. and Mansion L. (2003) Le jazz et la radio, une union durable. *Cahiers d'histoire de la Radiodiffusion*, 75, pp. 14–95.

Legrand, A. (2009) *Charles Delaunay et le jazz en France dans les années 30 et 40*. Paris: Editions du Layeur.

Maisonneuve, S. (2009) *L'invention du disque, 1877–1949: genèse de l'usage des médias musicaux contemporains*. Paris: EAC.

Nels, J. (1989) *Fragments détachés de l'oubli*. Paris: Ramsay.

Salmon, S. (2014) *Pathé : A la conquête du cinéma, 1896–1929*. Paris: Tallandier.

Sources

City of Paris Archive

Business and industry directories (2Mi3), Commercial register's files (D34U3), Commercial register (D33U3).

Jérôme Seydoux-Pathé foundation

Board of directors meeting minutes (1897–1921), annual inventories (1897–1925).

National library of France

Archives of the Audiovisual department, digitized press available on Gallica.

Center for research in ethnomusicology

Administrative and scientific archives of the Musée de l'Homme.

Private archives

Billon, Dalloz, Gévodius, Horvilleur, Lévi-Alvarès, Mathieu, Ploix and Presberg families.

Conclusion

Eva Moreda Rodríguez

In one way or another, maps and topography are at the very foundation of several of the chapters that make up this book (Henry, Vest, Agugliaro, Moreda Rodríguez, Silva). Rather than a conventional map or atlas, however, this book might be more productively understood as a pictorial map which successively zooms into selected territories and presents those to the reader in a three-dimensional fashion. What matters the most here is not to forensically represent the totality of the world, but rather to capture and make sense of some of the detail and complexity of selected territories. When considered together, the 12 chapters in the book do not add up to a narrative of inevitability and technological Darwinism, where superior devices, practices and institutions systematically and implacably replaced others, and where developments were imposed from the top down, with multinational companies dictating musical tastes, listening practices and understandings of recorded sound and music. It is true that the chapters, if read chronologically, might indeed point at a greater uniformization emerging towards the end of the period covered here, replacing the more widespread experimental streak we find in earlier periods. However, the story is anything but linear or simplistic: concomitances sometimes emerge unexpectedly in divergent contexts, while at the same time culturally or geographically close areas might diverge enormously in terms of their engagement with recording technologies, and successive moves towards transnational uniformization were often subsequently countered or complemented by effervescent localized developments.

In the introduction, we singled out several threads that might be productively followed in order to navigate the early history of recording technologies as represented in this book, moving between decades and between localities. Let us reinstate some of these threads. First, the most obvious one is possibly to let place and space guide our journey in an almost meta-discursive way: the successive chapters of the book do not simply allow us to figuratively move from some parts of the world to others, but also to transit between different understandings of space. A number of the chapters discuss how phonograph, gramophones and records were embedded in existing patterns of mobility, or prompted such mobility themselves:

DOI: 10.4324/9781003006497-18

across continents (Agugliaro, Ospina Romero, Lange), between countries (Silva), within countries (Reese, Zybina, Steen), within cities (Reese, Henry, Moreda Rodríguez). The book therefore outlines the echoing notions developed in the field of mobile music studies (Gopinath and Stanyek, 2014a, b), how recording technologies were shaped by and, in turn, contributed to shape notions of mobility; however, it also analyses how they found themselves, giving rise to a range of new spaces that some of the chapters describe in almost topographical detail, such as the record shop (Moreda Rodríguez, Agugliaro, Henry, Vest, Silva) and the recording studio (Steen, Ospina Romero, Agugliaro). These new topographies appear as counterpoints to domestic spaces, whose transformation under the new phonographic regime has already been explored in some detail by existing bibliography (Barnett, 2006; Silva, 2012–13; Pontara and Volgsten, 2017). These domestic spaces also make occasional appearances in the book; often, they do so in the context of larger practices or discourses which sought to normalize or regimentalize exactly how listening should be approached in domestic spaces (Moreda Rodríguez, Volgsten).

Second, an alternative reading of this book is as one which takes its inspiration from traditional social histories of early recording technologies in giving some visibility to the myriads of individuals, who all contributed to shape recording culture as we more or less know it today, pioneering and fulfilling a range of thus-far non-existing roles and professions: the phonograph demonstrator (Reese, Silva, Zybina), the record seller (Henry, Agugliaro, Silva), the record critic (Volgsten, Moreda Rodríguez, Zucconi), the scout (Ospina Romero, Steen) and even the window dresser specializing in record shops (Vest). The book, however, also challenges the linearity that is often characteristic of social history in highlighting the capriciousness of this explosion in the range of career paths emerging around the phonograph and gramophone, which invites an alternative approach, from a different perspective, to the processes of marketization and commercialization of recording technologies that have dominated much of the bibliography by focusing on the birth and development of recording companies (Gronow and Saunio, 1998; Martland, 2013; Barnett, 2020). Some of the chapters, however, point to practices that happened at the margins of commercialization and even resisted it (Lange, Moreda Rodríguez, Zybina, Zucconi).

A third productive path into the book has to do with the gradual, non-linear transformation of recorded sound into recorded music or into specific recorded repertoires that flourished under the new phonographic regime. Indeed, while the present collection does not situate itself squarely within the realm of musicology, it provides in some respects an alternate history "from the outside" to key musicological texts that have occupied themselves with the effects of the advent of recording technologies on performance and discourses about listening (Leech-Wilkinson, 2009; Ashby, 2010; Katz, 2010). Chapters in our book reveal how the beginnings of recording technologies often speak of a fascination with recorded sound that was not necessarily musical (Reese, Lange). As the recording industry developed to focus almost exclusively on music, chapters also explore how specific repertoires shaped industry practices and understandings of recorded music (Silva, Volgsten, Agugliaro, Ospina Romero): it is certainly not the case that recording technologies limited themselves to capture repertoires that were already there; instead, they often contributed to decisively shaping said repertoires.

Our pictorial map, however, has left out some areas of the world and some paths that could have been productively used to navigate the early history of recording technologies. This was not by design; it rather has to do with the particularities of the book format (to put it simply, it would not have been possible to cover all countries in the world, let alone all regions or cities), and also with the serendipity that is inherent in the development of a project of these characteristics, where particular synergies might emerge between chapters independent of editorial intent to the detriment of others. Here, we highlight four of these areas and path as invitations for future research that further complicates rather than simplifies the early history of recording technologies.

The first of these areas concerns empire and colonialism. It is true that three of the chapters can be defined as having these concepts at their core (Ospina Romero, Reese, Lange), and that imperial formations provide a powerful backdrop to others (Henry, Silva). However, we feel there is still room for others to consider how empire and colonialism shaped and in turn contributed to shape recording technologies and practices – following also on the footsteps of existing scholarship which puts empire and colonialism at the center of their enquiries about discourses on recorded sound or the development of the early recording industry (Picker, 2003; Denning, 2015; Williams, 2019). We hope that the example provided by this book encourages others to conduct comparative research encompassing a range of imperial contexts (British, French, Spanish, Portuguese, German, Dutch) as well as considering side by side the multifaceted ways in which recording technologies interfaced with the footprint of empire – from the materiality and practicalities of the manufacturing and circulation of commodities around the world following imperial trade routes, to the development and dissemination of discourses about sound and sound technologies embedded in colonial understandings.

The second area we hope to encourage more research in the future concerns gender. Some of the chapters illustrate, albeit in a tangential way, the role that certain pioneering women had in shaping the early years of recording technologies – as performers, as record critics of record listeners (Silva, Volgsten, Steen, Moreda Rodríguez). These scattered mentions can be read in the context of existing bibliography that has explored notions of gender, domesticity and recording technologies, predominantly in the US context (Kenney, 2004; Bowers, 2007). The contributions of women to the early history of phonography, however, deserve considerably more attention, and we hope the approach we present here – encompassing the full spectrum from the materiality of record manufacturing and circulation to the abstraction of discourses as ideas – might be useful in researching these too; for example, the distribution of labor in some of the early factories was made on the basis of gender. At the same time, we are aware that many parts of the recording world remained predominantly male-dominated, and we hope to see in the future discussions of how notions of masculinity were constructed and negotiated in the studio, the record shop or the record club.

Third, we also hope that this book contributes to stimulating scholarship on local developments and practices in places where this research is scarce or does not yet exist as well as to encouraging researchers all over the world to share their findings with the international community. When organizing the symposium this book originated from ("Early Sound Recording Technologies: Transnational Practices, History and Heritage", held at the University of Glasgow in June 2018) and deciding who we should invite to speak on the day, we found that several inequalities existed: while a few national contexts were quite extensively studied and well-represented in the literature (namely the United Kingdom, France, Germany and the United States), elsewhere things were more scattered and problematic. We found that in some regional and national contexts, a community of early recordings researchers did exist, but their findings were not easily disseminated across national boundaries. Reasons for that typically included language, with the international research community increasingly adopting English as a *lingua franca* to the exclusion of everything else and translations being nearly an impossibility, and a lack of access to the circles of international academic publishing. In other contexts, research was much more limited or almost non-existent due to the lack of accessibility of archival materials, which might have been destroyed or lost for various reasons. In those cases where research did exist, it often tended to focus on a limited number of urban centers rather than on the whole country more generally, and a tendency also existed to focus on the development of the recording industry per se rather than on the broader range of recording practices that make up the bulk of this book; this is understandable, given that record companies have typically left catalogues, business accounts and recordings themselves, whereas listeners or earlier demonstrators might have left little trace of their practices and activities. However, and even though we are well aware of the language barriers that still exist within the research community, we hope that the very different approaches represented in this book might provide inspiration and examples to others. We look forward, too, to seeing approaches that this book has not been able to anticipate and that might emerge from close study of local contexts.

The fourth area we would like to call attention to concerns the potential that multimediality and collaboration between different communities of stakeholders holds for the future of the scholarship of the early history of recording technologies. This book is indeed interdisciplinary in nature, featuring contributions from scholars who would variously define themselves as musicologists, popular music scholars, cultural historians (or simply historians) and scholars of material culture. A commonality between all contributions, however, is that they all take a rather conventional approach to the genres and discursive modes of scholarship, due predominantly to the constraints and requirements of the academic book format. However, knowledge about early recording technologies can be acquired and disseminated in less conventional ways too. One of our articles (Henry) opens up a productive avenue of enquiry by exploring the potential that digital mapping and the digital humanities hold in challenging linear narratives and putting the spatial of the forefront. Of course, numerous projects focused on the digitization and dissemination of early recordings that can be roughly classified as Digital Humanities already exist – such as the University of California, Santa Barbara Cylinder Audio Archive – and it is in fact fair to say that this book would probably not have existed, or would look very different, without these efforts that make primary sources considerably more accessible than they were a mere ten years ago. We hope that the future sees more projects of this sort as well as more considerate conversations and collaborations between archivists/curators, scholars and collectors and their different "ways of knowing" about and engaging with early recordings. We anticipate that creative practitioners who have made use of early recordings to explore issues of memory, nostalgia, identity and others – such as sound artists Marie Guérin, Diana Salazar and Aleks Kolkowski – will have a prominent place in these conversations too.

References

Ashby, A. (2010) *Absolute Music, Mechanical Reproduction*. Berkeley, Los Angeles and London: University of California Press.

Barnett, K. S. (2006) Furniture Music: The Phonograph ad Furniture, 1900–1930. *Journal of Popular Music Studies*, 18(3), 301–324.

Barnett, K.S. (2020) *Record Cultures. The Transformation of the U.S. Recording Industry*. Ann Arbor: The University of Michigan Press.

Bowers, N. (2007) *Creating a Home Culture for the Phonograph: Women and the Rise of Sound Recordings in the United States, 1877–1913*. PhD dissertation, University of Pittsburgh

Denning, M. (2015) *Noise Uprising. The Audiopolitics of a World Musical Revolution*. London: Verso Books.

Gopinath, S. and J. Stanyek, eds. (2014a) *The Oxford Handbook of Mobile Music Studies*, vol. 1. New York: Oxford University Press.

Gopinath, S. and J. Stanyek, eds. (2014b) *The Oxford Handbook of Mobile Music Studies*, vol. 2. New York: Oxford University Press.

Gronow, P. and I. Saunio (1998) *An International History of the Recording Industry*. London and New York: Cassell.

Katz, M. (2010) *Capturing Sound: How Technology Has Changed Music*. Berkeley, Los Angeles and London: University of California Press.

Kenney, W. H. (2004) *Recorded Music in American Life: The Phonograph and Popular Memory, 1890–1945*. New York and Oxford: Oxford University Press.

Leech-Wilkinson, D. (2009) *The Changing Sound of Music: Approaches to Studying Recorded Musical Performance*. London: CHARM.

Martland, P. (2013) *Recording History: The British Record Industry, 1888–1931*. Lanham, Toronto and Plymouth: Scarecrow Press.

Picker, J. M. (2003) *Victorian Soundscapes*. New York: Oxford University Press.

Pontara, T. and U. Volgsten (2017) Domestic Space, Music Technology and the Emergence of Solitary Listening: Tracing the Roots of Solipsistic Sound Culture in the Digital Age. *Svensk tidskrift för musikforskning*, 99(1), 105–123.

Silva, J. (2012–13) Mechanical Instruments and Phonography: The Recording Angel of historiography. *Radical Musicology*, 6, available at http://www.radical-musicology.org.uk/2012/DaSilva.htm

Williams, G., ed. (2019) *Hearing the Crimean War. Wartime Sound and the Unmaking of Sense*. New York: Oxford University Press.

Index

Note: Page numbers followed by "n" denote endnotes.

Printed in Great Britain
by Amazon

50532305R00159